Catherine Spellman

Conversations and Allusions

Enric Miralles

Contents

Forward, Enric Miralles

Sir Peter Cook

It was great to be around Enric. As the interval since his untimely death seems to increase exponentially, the unusual combination of brilliance and agreeableness refuses to fade...and was virtually unique. Manifest through endless territories: of which, here are a few.

As a Manipulator of Three-Dimensional Form

Possessing a rare ability to see the components of an architectural idea somehow out there in space and almost "daring" them to knit, clash, or slither past each other. He did this, of course, without a computer, invoking (I guess), the kind of predictive imagination that comes from observing things and stuff—built examples or natural phenomena—but with the ability to mentally analyze or restructure it.

As his output progressed, he clearly became more and more relaxed in this process, and this may explain the formal audacity of his later work.

As a "Social Animal"

Characteristic of a few of the really greats: as his reputation grew it seemed easy for him to retain the characteristics of a normal, reasonable bloke. Typically, under some trees in Frankfurt with students, colleagues, some beer and some meat, he quite openly admitted to anyone who was in hearing that the flies swarmed around him was because he sweat so badly.

Sitting in another Frankfurt restaurant, he and Cedric Price immediately ordered a refill plate of food as soon as they saw the dainty but tiny "nouvelle cuisine" portions heading their way.

He didn't seem to mind who he was in conversation with and would swap anecdotes with anybody. He was a natural (which is anything but being a naïf), which is very rare amongst younger clever architects—who often like to distance themselves from the hoi-polloi in case they get disregarded—or something.

As a Teacher

Very clear and, in the end, insistent, but not by nagging or pontificating but almost (as in a military action), leading from the front. Of course, it was the combination of talent and example that meant that every student admired him, but this was harnessed to his very normalness as a person. With, the clarity of his reasoning—which didn't need to express itself as mere instruction.

He was also clear in his admiration of the Heroes: Aalto, Le Corbusier, Kahn (as I remember). He was someone who enjoyed reviews, without being a "clever-clever" tricky critic. He was capable of a special feat: having arrived onto a jury straight off a plane he could get into the conversation within half a sentence—such was his involvement.

As an "Architectural Animal"

There were two men, Enric and the late Ron Herron, who shared an almost defunct brand of connoisseurship (which hopefully will revive—if only...). This involved reading and noting—almost like a collector of stamps or moths (or as Adrian Forty once accused me of being, "an architectural train-spotter"). Now they are gone, I have almost nobody with whom one can have those nerdy or arcane runs of enthusiastic chatter over a very minor Swedish architect—active, say, between 1923 and 1931, who wasn't a household name but was influenced by, say, this Hungarian dude who taught him in Berlin in 1918...Then: "Hey weren't they looking at so-and-so?"

You only have to look on the bookshelves in his house in Barcelona to realize the extent of his appetite. Architecture—again as stuff, things, examples, tricks of the trade. And what a wonderful trickster he was with all these bits.

As a "Young" Architect

Well, sadly, he never became really "old," but his architecture hardly stood still. And here I break ranks with several of my colleagues who seem to prefer the early "post–Piñón-Viaplana" Miralles work: undertaken with Carme Pinós. Somehow they prefer the gravitas of that period. An observation of the relative hardness of Pinós' later work reinforces my view that parallels Enric with Frank Gehry in one special respect. When Berta Aguilera walked into Frank's life, his professionalism stayed but the manner of his buildings exploded and, though there was a brilliance to Enric's pre-Benedetta Tagliabue output, his work similarly became naughtier and fruitier after her appearance. Her enthusiasm (and mean architectural intelligence) surely contributed to the exoticness of his Barcelona Olympics work and such strange pieces as the rehabilitation of the Utrecht Town Hall.

As a Phenomenon

Lucky enough to be his host in London after taking over the Bartlett, I could watch the effect that his presence had as a visiting guru, competition judge, and examiner. The greatest of several lectures there featured the Alicante project: first were fragments, shapes, shadows, then little bits of drawings. Then some armatures. Slowly some larger pieces. All accompanied by that special rapid-fire Miralles-English, which demanded some tuning of the ear: but flowed, attacked and enthused all at once. Only towards the very end of a nearly two-hour performance did the whole of the building seem to emerge: in one of the most brilliant exposées I have ever witnessed.

And armature is a key word (despite it being the one most used around that time at the Bartlett). For, like James Stirling's sketching or Thom Mayne at his best, this ability to swing in space is so rare, so precious, and so enjoyable and came, miraculously, from this unpretentious but deeply intelligent friend.

Introduction, Common Threads

Catherine Spellman

1. Diagonal Mar Park, Barcelona.

Enric Miralles (1955–2000) remains one of the most prominent architects of his generation. The significance of his architectural design lies in his seamless integration of site and building and his use of space to serve the everyday conditions of life. His highly personal architectural language reflects on the similarly independent work of great modern architects Antoni Gaudí, Josep Maria Jujol, Le Corbusier, and Louis Kahn. Practicing for less than 25 years, Miralles designed over 110 projects—many of which are now built, including the Scottish Parliament Buildings, Santa Catarina Market, Vigo University, Diagonal del Mar Park, Alicante Gymnastic Center, and Igualada Cemetery. With an expressive use of structure, thoughtful incorporation of mostly local building practices, and a plethora of imaginative ideas derived from everyday and exceptional sources, Miralles' projects inspire a sense of wonder. Rafeal Moneo insightfully wrote, "Enric was convinced his vision of architecture could help to build a freer, more beautiful world,"[1] and I believe it is this conviction brings such a sense of joy and astonishment to Miralles' work.

The idea for this book originated in a conversation with Miralles. Our intention was to initiate a series of essays relevant to the ideas supporting the work. At the time, his distinctive work was widely published; however, little was known about the methods Miralles used. We planned to invite a number of contributors (many of whom are included in this collection) to discuss and then write essays about ideas and methods behind the work with an audience of students in mind. The intention was not to explain—Miralles never spoke didactically about the work—but to explore and develop the ideas, finding new ways to make them a material reality. I remember Enric explaining to a group of students trying to comprehend the work: "Everything needed to understand the work is in this studio. Consider the material and you will find your way." Miralles was magnanimous with students. He maintained an open door policy to the studio and thousands of curious students and groups filtered through. Miralles wanted his collection of material and work to inspire and encourage others to contribute to the discipline he practiced with enormous creativity.

As time would have it, Miralles left us too soon. Fifteen years passed with a blink of the eye, over this time I often spoke about the project with my friend Karl Unglaub, who also studied with Miralles at the Städelschule für Bildende Kunst, followed myself as Miralles' teaching assistant, and later joined Miralles

Tagliabue Architects. In 2014, an opportunity to move forward aligned with support from Director Craig Barton of The Design School at Arizona State University (ASU) to sponsor a symposium and lecture series around the project "Conversations and Allusions on Miralles." This was followed with encouragement and support of Benedetta Tagliabue and the Fundació Enric Miralles, Ramon Prats at ACTAR Publications, and Michael Groves and Andy Byrnes at The Construction Zone Ltd. Participants in the symposium and lecture series at ASU include Manuel Bailo Esteve, Peter Buchanan, Elena Cánovas, Teresa Galí-Izard, Carles Muro, Eva Prats, Benedetta Tagliabue, and Elías Torres, as well as the numerous students and faculty of the architecture and landscape architecture programs at ASU.[2] Essay contributions include works from Peter Cook, Jaun José Lahuerta, John Meunier, Maurici Pla Serra, Josep Quetglas, Elena Rocchi, Catherine Spellman, Ana Valderrama, and Claudio Vekstein.

The book title *Conversations and Allusions on Miralles* connects to Miralles' PhD dissertation, "Things Seen Left and Right (Without Glasses)," which he gave to me as a way to outline essay topics and participants. Our intent was for each essay to be a conversation around a topic influencing Miralles' work. When talking with students, Miralles often referred to his projects as conversations, implying the Latin meaning of conversation—"act of living together, having dealings with others." Miralles was expert at conversing in a positive, productive, and creative manner. Allusions suggest one of the most captivating aspects of Miralles' work, his mastery with indirect references, many of which are barely revealed to his clients and users, and others I am fairly certain he kept completely to himself, leaving the rest of us to imagine just what he was actually thinking.[3] Here in these essays, contributors are creating their own allusions from their personal experiences with Miralles and his body of work.

The book contributors were, in some way, directly involved with Miralles. They are his former classmates, teachers, colleagues, friends, students, and family. For me, the essays here parallel the building process once described by Miralles: "Construction introduces an uncanny dimension into this process: One gets the impression the forms emerge for the first time, far removed from any repetition."[4] In this book the "uncanny dimension" results from the personal and creative approach each contributor offers on the subject they identify with Miralles. These essays are completely original works while simultaneously creating a familiarity with Miralles' work. It should be noted, the essays are mostly from contributors who are involved in making, and therefore, the perspective of these essays is one of process, interest in making, interpretation of ideas, and the translation of ideas into things—issues of primary interest to Miralles.

A wide variety of subjects inspired by Miralles are discussed in this collection: geometry, proportion, scale, drawing, method, boundary, site, constraints, co-incident, crafted plans, ephemeral qualities, analogy, perspective, collections, and paradox. Additionally, many of the essays illustrate how the author has incorporated and developed the subject in his/her own work. Essays are loosely grouped in four sections around common threads: place, iteration, method, and experience. Simultaneously, each essay could easily fit into more than one grouping and discuss a variety of design ideas Miralles used in his work.

Place

Place is one of those moments when thought is woven with reality...In this sense, the drawing, even the paper itself, is place for an instant...The rules let us advance also appear in it. Blank paper never exists. It is only an invisible backing...if we accept the rules of the page, it is to forget it. Shifts and turns make the paper lose its sheet nature. It is a working structure. Its rules are those of economics and commodity.[5]

_Enric Miralles

What makes a place? This is a quintessential question in architecture, without a specific answer. Above, Miralles suggests, "Place is one of those moments when thought is woven with reality." Therefore, the thought expressed through a drawing on a sheet of paper makes the paper a place. Miralles held this definition throughout his practice. His projects are filled with thoughts. I once visited Alicante Gymnastic Center with Miralles shortly before it was complete, we spoke about the ideas present in the project—to look across a roof plane aligning with the horizon in the distance, to make the longitudinal dimension as large as possible, to put the visitor between the practice and performance spaces, to give the column the size of an elephant footprint, to accommodate four people and/or four thousand people, to give the visitor the movement of a gymnast, and many more. Miralles spoke about his nonhierarchical approach to ideas when making a place; one idea is equal to another, and it is a question of what you do with it. The contributors in this section discuss ideas combined with the reality of site to make a place.

Contributors to this section include Jaun José Lahuerta, Maurici Pla Serra, Peter Buchanan, and Eva Prats. Lahuerta and Pla Serra studied with Miralles at Escola Técnica Superior d'Arquitectura de Barcelona (ETSAB) and were part of his inner circle of friends. Each has written several critical essays on Miralles' work including "Signs" and "Introduction to Enric Miralles Works and Projects 1975–1995, For Now..." by Lahuerta and "Enric Miralles and Raymond Queneau" by Pla Serra. Buchanan was the first architectural critique to publish the work of Miralles/Pinós. His essay, "Dialogue and Distillation: The Architecture of Enric Miralles and Carme Pinós," introduced them to the international stage in 1990. Prats began working with Miralles/Pinós in 1988 while a student of Miralles' at ETSAB. In 1992, she joined the Städelschule für Bildende Kunst architecture class to complete her final project thesis. Here she formed friendships with Catherine Spellman, Claudio Vekstein, and Karl Unglaub. After completing her thesis, Prats continued in the Miralles studio until 1995.

In his essay transcribed from a lecture to students in Barcelona, "Miralles Pinós, The Anthropomorphic Form," Juan José Lahuerta describes how the first works of Miralles and Pinós seem to be made with their own hands. He explains how their imprint can be perceived in the materiality of the building and goes on to elaborate on their fascination with the physicality of the human body as a tool for making buildings. The essay develops a critical interpretation of the Igualada Cemetery describing the source of what Lahuerta calls the "fetish of brutality" in their work.

In the essay, "Portrait of Miralles with Vanishing Points, Prospect for Youth," Maurici Pla Serra analyzes the early perspective drawings by Miralles. He reveals how Miralles used landscape as an object to develop one of his first architectural innovations. With insightful detail, Pla Serra explains Miralles' early perspectives as composed landscapes with a series of seamlessly integrated solids and voids. The drawn shapes later become places in the developed projects, turning the landscape into a multiplicity of recesses, with precise limits. These shapes appear to be dreams, combining pre-existing and imagined places into a single mixed view. Pla Serra continues to describe the position of the vanishing point in these drawings—used to maximize the solid and void relationship—creating a place where landscape becomes building and building forms the landscape.

The transcribed lecture "Requiem for the Modern Plan" by Peter Buchanan reflects on hand crafting of the plan, a skill he describes as once central to modern architecture and now largely forgotten. As a way of thinking about the specificity of place, Buchanan argues Miralles' buildings are "crafted to become fractured and dynamic places that demand notice and engagement… indeed, it is the moving observer, through perception and experience, who draws the episodic compositions into some choreographed coherence." Buchanan explains that Miralles was constantly redrawing his plans, "letting his almost unconsciously guided fingers find unresolved sticking points and suggest improvements." At the heart of this way of drawing is a deep understanding of how people relate to each other and architecture.

The lecture "Drawing without Erasing" by Eva Prats followed Buchanan's at the spring 2014 symposium and turned out to be an unplanned but amazing pairing. Prats illustrates, through her (and partner Ricardo Flores) thoughtful work, the principles of crafting introduced by Buchanan. Prats began with a description of the hand-drawing period in Miralles' office when each line was a carefully made decision. She explains relationships between thinking and drawing, the importance of time, and the use of precedents in the development work with strong sense of place. She continues to illustrate these points with numerous video shorts and over 300 slides of their work. Here, the transcribed lecture, "Drawing without Erasing," captures the spirit of the lecture.

The discussion following the lectures titled "Conversation Buchanan + Prats + Students" starts with the question, "How can students develop their ability to make plans?" This expands into conversations on design process, rhythms of working, a way of determining the best scale for a space, and how to utilize a precedent. Underlining the responses to student questions is a consistent emphasis on the importance of social engagement and responsibility as an important factor in the making of quality spaces for people to live.

Iteration

The succession of these states of a single painting through the task of repetition... it is not a series, there are no variations. One always resists on the same thing. The same hand movements seem to be produced. The position is fixed. Perhaps only the light changes. The passage of time.... Where what the work offers anew only appears almost at the end. It appears as a possibility, as the unexpected... in the effort to make the face repeat a familiar geometry (Diego), through a precise geometry (James Lord), this aperture mentioned by Alberto appears...this is where a new work begins. A painting is thus essentially like a piece of time. A place in which the intensity of the work is deposited. I have attempted something like Giacometti's working style in these projects. Not in all of them. Perhaps more in those in which the vague approximate drawing is most important.[6]

_*Enric Miralles*

Above, Miralles explains his use of iteration by describing Giacometti's painting of the portrait of James Lord. The "new work begins" by bringing together the "repeated familiar geometry" and the "precise geometry." Miralles' work developed with an iterative process starting with an idea, sketch, and sometimes a piece from an early project or something entirely new. Once the design begins, it is followed with multiple iterations—traced drawing upon traced drawing. The existing idea emerges from a multiplicity of directions for the sake of seeing what could happen—the project develops options. Miralles was an iteration virtuoso. He liked to explore the endless possibilities of a project; for him, iteration became a game, and as with most games, the more you play, the better you become, and the more possibilities you see.

Contributors to this section include Ana Valderrama, John Meunier, Teresa Galí-Izard, and Carles Muro. Valderrama, Dean of the School of Architecture, Planning, and Design of Rosario National University, Argentina, met Miralles when he lectured and conducted a workshop in Rosario. Through her teaching, she is closely aligned with ETSAB and several of the contributors to this book. John Meunier is an architect and professor, he is also the former Dean of the College of Architecture and Environmental Design at ASU. With Meunier's support ASU sponsored an exhibition and lecture by Miralles in 1996. The landscape architect and agronomist Galí-Izard studied at ETSAB a few years behind Miralles and has known him as a colleague and friend. She is a principal with her husband Jordi Nebot in the practice Arquitectura Agronomia and is currently the Chair of Landscape Architecture at the University of Virginia. Muro was a student of Miralles' at ETSAB. He went on to practice with Torres/LaPeña and Alvaro Siza before establishing his own practice. He also taught several seminar courses with Miralles at ETSAB including "Exercises in Style." Muro is currently a visiting professor of architecture at Harvard University.

The essay "Divine Collectors" by Ana Valderrama discusses the action of accumulating and classifying things. She explains collection as a way of relating things to their origin that "is the latent process of archaeology and metaphysical transformation, sometimes also transmutation." She explains how collecting is an iterative process and relates this process to the generation of Miralles' work, which she sees a continuing the collector-artist tradition. The essay examines historical collections such as "cabinets of curiosities" and explains collecting as "essentially a humanistic creative activity."

John Meunier's essay "Intricacy and the Scottish Parliament Building," is a "celebration of *Intricacy* in the built environment, believing that environments possessing this quality will be elevating to the spirits, the mind, and our sensibilities; that when we live amidst such buildings, streets and places, our lives will be enriched instead of, as so often is now the case, being diminished." In the essay Meunier defines *Intricacy*, then continues with a thoughtful analysis of the Scottish Parliament Building according to these terms.

"Connection and Transmission, Reading and Translating the Potential of Site" by Teresa Galí-Izard explains the necessity to "discover the potential of the site" as part of the design process. She explains the context of Catalonia as an area specifically related to Miralles and all Spanish designers of the 20th century. The essay talks about cultures of consumption across generations and the repetitions and iterations of land practices connecting them together. She discusses the transmission of knowledge between generations, which was vital to Miralles' way of approaching a project.

Carles Muro's text, transcribed from the lecture "Exercises in Style," introduces Raymond Queneau's book of the same title. Queneau's book tells a short, anecdotal story in 99 different iterations. The story is transformed, and the reader inspired by a different sense of time and place. The book inspired Muro and Miralles because it reflected their own use of iteration. They used the book to create a seminar where students developed architectural variations on a single theme. In the text, Muro discusses the role of constraints as a method of design. With examples from artists and designers, Muro illustrates how working with constraints can result in multiplicity and highly refined results. Budgets, regulations, or the most severe of technical constraints, Muro argues, are a springboard for real opportunities in design and that architects will achieve greater freedom in design by embracing given constraints.

The separate student conversations with Teresa Galí-Izard and Carles Muro further develop the topics of iteration, constraints, and ways of reading place. Galí-Izard elaborates on the logic of the landscape and the need for the architect to allow logic to guide design. She recommends students create an immediate relationship with the site by thinking of themselves as a natural element. For example, if your design engages the river, then you should think of yourself as the river in all its different states—flowing, dry, flooded, etc. The conversation continues to discuss issues of design sustainability, which Galí-Izard proposes will be achieved with beautiful designs communicating how change can be made. The conversation following Muro's lecture focused on the topic of constraints as a tool in the design process. Muro further explains why constraints do not necessarily make the ideas behind the work, but they help to give form to the ideas by providing the designer with explicit and consistent guidelines in the design process.

Method

What we need to question is bricks, concrete, glass, our table manners, our utensils, our tools, the way we spend our time, our rhythms. To question which seems to have ceased forever to astonish us. We live, true, we breathe, true; we walk, we go downstairs, we sit at a table in order to eat, we lie down on a bed on order to sleep. How? Where? When? Why? Describe your street. Describe another. Compare.[7]
_*Georges Perec,* L'infra Ordinaire

One of Miralles' common references was the author Georges Perec whose writings include experimental word play and methods of classification. The quote above introduces the simple but common questions in developing a method of working: how, where, when, why? In Miralles' work, the specific contextual conditions provided the answers to questions, creating a method of working.

Taken from the Greek definition *meta* (expressing development) and *hodos* (way), it could be said each project reveals a unique method of transcribing specific answers to common questions. Over time and across many projects, methods are repeated, combined, or skipped; the architect instinctively knows a way to develop the project without all the steps. Similar to learning a foreign language, in the beginning it is about methods of translating; later it becomes instinctive. In the text below, Miralles describes perception in design as a method developing over time and with practice.

Once past the effort required to redo the design every time, one ends up knowing the space as well as the objects in your pocket...to know its form and see how its size changes in that place. Pulling a pocket inside out, the objects fall out and we put them back together again...this gesture, this way of seeing. Remains for other designs. Nonetheless, this would be a theatrical representation to represent here, equivalent to that of its construction. Here, in these montages, to insist only in the simultaneity of perception in relation to the design.[8]

_*Enric Miralles*

Several contributors, in reference to Miralles and their own work, address the topic of method including Catherine Spellman, Claudio Vekstein, Elena Cánovas, and Manuel Bailo. All are former students of Miralles: Spellman and Vekstein were members of the first architecture class headed by Enric Miralles at the Städelschule fur Bildende Kunst. Spellman became Miralles' teaching assistant at the Städelschule from 1992–1994; Vekstein with Karl Unglaub collaborated with Miralles on the Frankfurt Rose Museum in 1994. Both Spellman and Vekstein are currently on the faculty of architecture at ASU. Cánovas and Bailo studied with Miralles at ETSAB. Cánovas is currently a visiting professor of architecture at Washington University in St. Louis, and Bailo is professor of urbanism at the University of Virginia. Each essay in this section begins with a subject explored with Miralles and continues to develop the particular subject by examining the work of others and their own work.

Catherine Spellman, in her essay "Walking to Begin," develops a conversation had with Miralles on the question "Where to begin a project?" It is true that every beginning will lead in a different direction. Miralles was adamant that a project could begin anywhere, and the quality of the project was not dependent on where you began but rather "how far you walked from the place you start." The subject of walking is discussed in relationship to the method of designing a project. The essay discusses the work of a number of artists (Muybridge, Giacometti, Miró) and architects (Pikionis, Le Corbusier, Smithsons) that Miralles referred to in his work and teaching. It explains how walking literally and conceptually influences the design process.

Claudio Vekstein's transcribed interview with Enric Miralles, "Mystery and Mastery, Colloquy in a Courtyard," revisits a conversation dating back to 1992 when the Städelschule architecture class traveled with Miralles to India and Bangladesh. There they visited many historically significant works of Indian architecture and the works by Le Corbusier and Louis Kahn in those countries. The conversation captures Miralles' thoughts on the modern works, revealing his astounding ability to read the built and implied connections between various works by the same architect. Unraveling thoughts on his own work relative to the visited projects, the conversation reveals his dazzling curiosity, humor, and generosity towards his students.

When Elena Cánovas was a first-year design student in the class of Enric Miralles, he gave her unforgettable advice: "When you have a problem in your design and are too focused on it, you must get away from it. Go and draw somewhere else. Go to the edges, define the edges, and the solution will come." While explaining the iterative drawing process she learned from Miralles, the essay "Drawing in the Edges" discusses the significance of edge conditions in such projects as Santa Catarina Market and Igualada Cemetery. She describes Miralles acting as a "great whisperer" or someone crossing boundaries in space and time. In terms of physical space, the edge condition of both projects is blurred, and the built site becomes integral with the surrounding context. The essay goes on to explain how "Drawing in the Edges" becomes the axiom for her own creative practice. She closes with projects from her practice with Antonio Sanmartín illustrating how this approach has led to projects integrating landscape and urbanism, public and private, past and future, man-made and natural systems.

The title "From Body to Field" by Manuel Bailo introduces a seminar on proportional systems taught by Miralles at ETSAB in 1992. The lecture about architectural scale and proportional systems starts with a discussion of the "Vitruvian Man" drawing by Leonardo Da Vinci. Bailo explains Da Vinci's use of geometry to draw a relationship between the centers of earth and man. Utilizing a similar geometric drawing method, Bailo studies a series of urban conditions that he describes as fortunate accidents: movement of a shadow, activity of a street cleaner, occupation of a bench, marker in a plaza. In a series of case study drawings, Bailo illustrates how scalar connections, designed to engage the fortunate accidents, provoke human interaction in public space.

The conversation following the Bailo and Cánovas lectures touched on a number of recurring questions relative to developing a design method: How does one start a project? What is the role of the program versus place in design processes? How does time influence projects? How to incorporate both experience and knowledge? While addressing these questions, the conversation also addresses the difference between complicated and complex methods of making—a way design can reveal a depth of understanding and expression—and taking the project beyond simply solving the problem by giving meaning and intention to the solution.

Experience

From this special vantage point, the bridge itself becomes a landscape. The snow here produces a sort of artificial white mountain...Then thin rain...It is also a nice place for ravens...it is a silhouette that penetrates the landscape due to its exceptional location. And through the set of transparencies, it starts to play with the natural profiles of the mountains, with the water in the river...Fish or birds. Bamboo walls are festive elements to mark the passing of the seasons, as if they were the clothing of a living being.[9]
_Enric Miralles

Above, Miralles explains the project as providing an experience with the landscape. It exposes the visitor over a period of time to the natural elements, increasing their understanding of themselves in this place. Experience is created through meaning understood both physically and intellectually. The structure of this meaning is the work of the architect. With experience, the architect creates positive places for people to conduct daily and exceptional activities. This happens with an accommodation of spatial needs and a heightened awareness of the environment surrounding them. Visiting a Miralles project, one experiences a series of mesmerizing dualities: solid and void, inversions of structure and weight, repetitions of light and shadow. This section of essay addresses the complexity of experience (physical, ephemeral, co-incidental, and intellectual) in Miralles' way of working.

Contributions in this section include essays by Elena Rocchi and Josep Quetglas and transcribed lectures by Elías Torres and Benedetta Tagliabue. Rocchi worked with Miralles from 1994 to 2000 and continued working with EMBT until 2010. Quetglas was a professor of Miralles' at ETSAB. Quetglas has previously written several essays on Miralles' work including "Enric Miralles" in *Vers une Architecture,* and "Oeuvres Complétes" and "Don't Be Deluded" in *El Croquis 49/50.* Torres was also a professor of Miralles' at ETSAB and later became a close friend. Benedetta Tagliabue met Miralles while studying in New York; later they married and established Enric Miralles Benedetta Tagliabue Architects (EMBT) in 1995.

The essay "Enric Miralles, Sweep of the Hand" by Josep Quetglas describes the qualities of "ease and flair" that were very much Miralles' personality and way of making architecture, explaining the inevitable relationship between an architect's way of approaching life around him and the reflection of his approach on the work. Miralles spoke about each person's innate approach to design due in part to their personal background. Like the other contributors to this collection, Quetglas shared many experiences with Miralles. His essay is an insightful and beautiful explanation of Miralles the person and the architect.

Elena Rocchi's essay "Paradox of Preference" introduces the subjective nature of the design process, describing architects as people with preferences determined by their personal context. The essay claims that ideas of free will and determinism, although opposite, are essential to design. Free will provides isolation of external circumstances, allowing for complete objectivity in decision making. Determinism calls for responsibility to surrounding situations. These conflicting and paradoxical ideas are constantly encountered in the design process. Introducing a short story often referred to by Miralles in his studio, "Bartleby the Scrivener" by Herman Melville, Rocchi explains how the studio worked with these contradictory and conflicting ideas.

The lecture "Co-Incidental" by Elías Torres describes the overlapping life and career he shared with Miralles. Quoting Picasso—"genius steals and mediocrity copies"—Torres explains how Miralles learned from multiple disciplines and experiences. Talking from the point of view of a friend, Torres recalls the unbounded optimism Miralles used to turn challenging circumstances into positive situations. Comparing the evolution of their parallel work, Torres describes moments of professional overlap. He presents their one collaborative project, the Situationist Exhibition at the Museum of Contemporary Art in Barcelona, emphasizing their common appreciation of history, modern art, and abstraction. Torres concludes his talk with a story of firecrackers set off by two friends in the night.

Introducing the Fundació Enric Miralles in her lecture "Ephemeral Times," Benedetta Tagliabue explains her intention to make the foundation a place for architects and students to explore and produce new knowledge relative to the field. Tagliabue illuminates for the audience the momentary qualities of Miralles' work and life, showing numerous studio explorations, productions, exhibitions, and temporary situations informing the work today. Embedded in this material is Miralles' desire to view a project "from eyes crossed," meaning he wanted to understand the project from multiple points of view. The heartfelt lecture edited for this book offers much insight into the enigmatic quality common to all their projects.

In their conversation with the students, Elías Torres and Benedetta Tagliabue share many humorous stories of their experiences practicing architecture. Discussion relating Miralles' architectural language and way of responding to context—physical, cultural, and historical—underline many of the stories they tell. They discuss engaging the existing physical qualities of a site and emphasize that architects should focus more on the meaning of the social context in their work. Tagliabue comments, "The context was so important to Enric... He was trying to understand how other people are influenced by a building. Like when someone is walking on the opposite sidewalk from a building, you see the shadow of the building, or if you are even farther away, you have a view. So if you design some massive plan, it implies you understand how your own building will be perceived and will influence its surroundings by extension." Torres explains that the relationship between language and context is directly related to understanding yourself as an architect. He notes, "If you know who you are and where you belong then you can go around the world and design a building in every country, but if you don't know who you are then you are lost."

In conclusion, I return to a topic mentioned repeatedly in the lectures and conversations, and one I discussed with Miralles on several occasions: friends in design. Miralles often referred to his favorite sources as "friends" (Le Corbusier, Kahn, etc.). He also used "friends" to refer to anyone a project could involve, implying and insisting that architecture is for people who thrive by formulating strong relationships with other people (past, present, and future). There is no doubt Miralles was an exceptional (some think genius) architect, and beyond this, he was a remarkable friend who greatly enjoyed and accepted the people around him.

Together, the authors and friends of Miralles' included in this collection start a new dialogue about what it is to design meaningful architecture. It is my hope that this book will motivate upcoming generations of architects to experiment, design, and establish friendships with the same open curiosity as Miralles.

Notes

1. "A Intense Life, a Consummate Work," by Rafael Moneo, *El Croquis 100/101*, 2000, 307.
2. ASU students participating in the "Conversations and Allusions, Enric Miralles" seminars contributing to the development of the book include Abeer Alajmi, Jarod Bogenrief, Harrison Davis, Jeffery Gillway, Kenneth Harker, Lauren Lochry, Ernesto Lopez, Oscar Lopez, Caryl Kant, Matthew Krison, Skylar Mappes, Kevin Martinez, Grant McCormick, Marissa Mendoza, Phillip Morgan, Aaron Ostrofsky, Jiyoun Park, Conor Patton, Martin Ramirez, C.J. Rogers, Carrie Samdal, Nicholas Shekerjian, Casey Steill, Lina Taheri, Alexander Tsaparis, Hoatian Xu, Sara Yehia, and Robert Zokaites. ASU faculty participating at round table conversations include Jose Bernardi, John Meunier, Scott Murff, Elena Rocchi, Catherine Spellman, and Claudio Vekstein.
3. For insight into many of Miralles' allusions, read the greatly insightful collection of essays, *Enric Miralles 1972–2000*, edited by Josep M. Rovira, (Barcelona, Spain: Fundacion Caja de Arquitectos, 2011).
4. "En Construccíon/Under Construction 1987/1991," by Enric Miralles in *El Croquis 49/50*, 1992.
5. "Lugar/Place," by Enric Miralles in *El Croquis 30+49/50*, 1994, 28.
6. "A Portrait by Giacometti," by Enric Miralles in *El Croquis 72*, 1992, 128.
7. Georges Perec, *L'infra Ordinaire*, Paris: Seuil, 1989.
8. "Inside of a Pocket," by Enric Miralles in *El Croquis 30+49/50*, 1994, 110.
9. "Meditation Pavilion in Unazuki," by Enric Miralles in *El Croquis 72*, 1992, 72.

Place

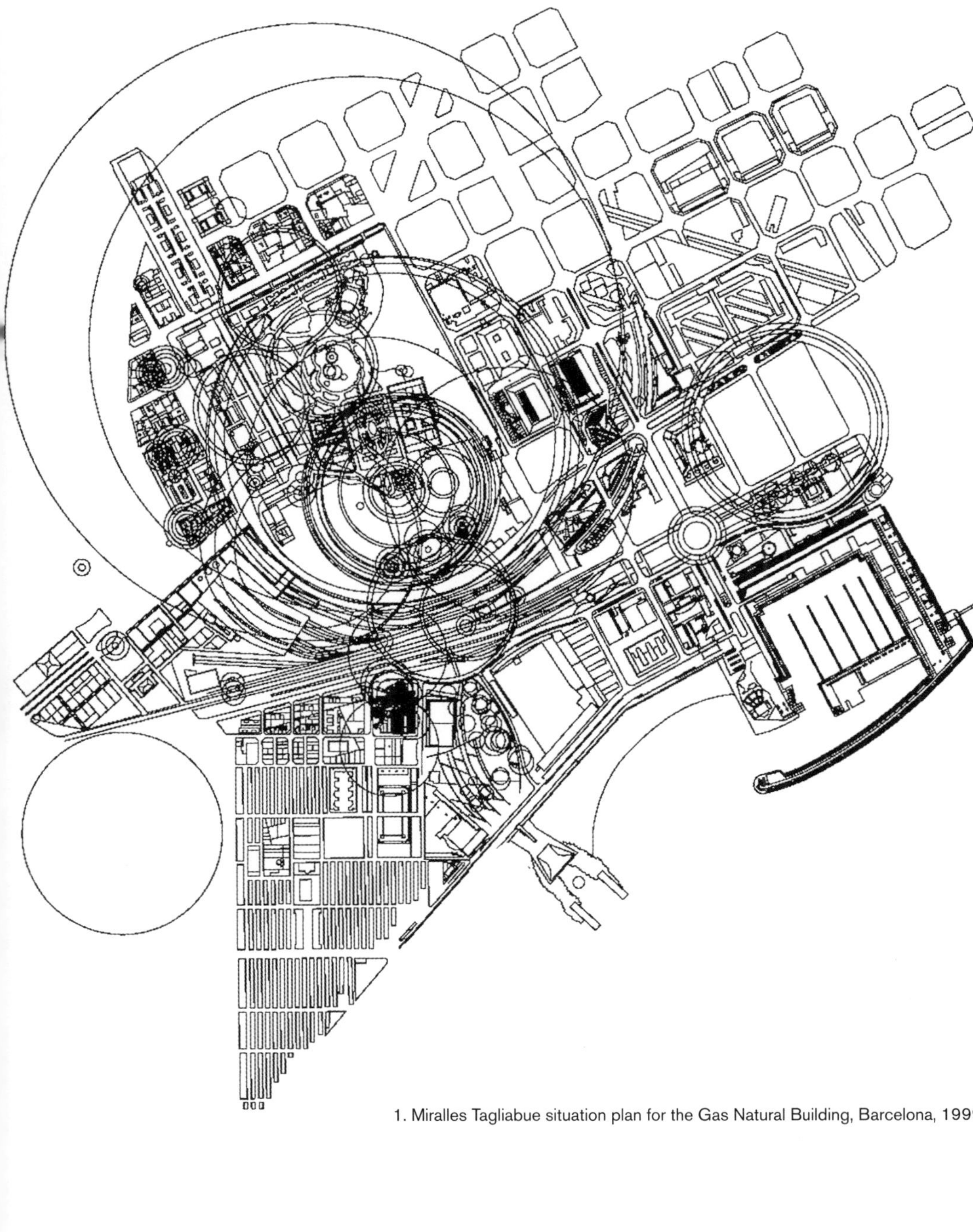

1. Miralles Tagliabue situation plan for the Gas Natural Building, Barcelona, 1999.

2. Miralles Tagliabue situation plan for Diagonal Mar Park, Barcelona, 1997.

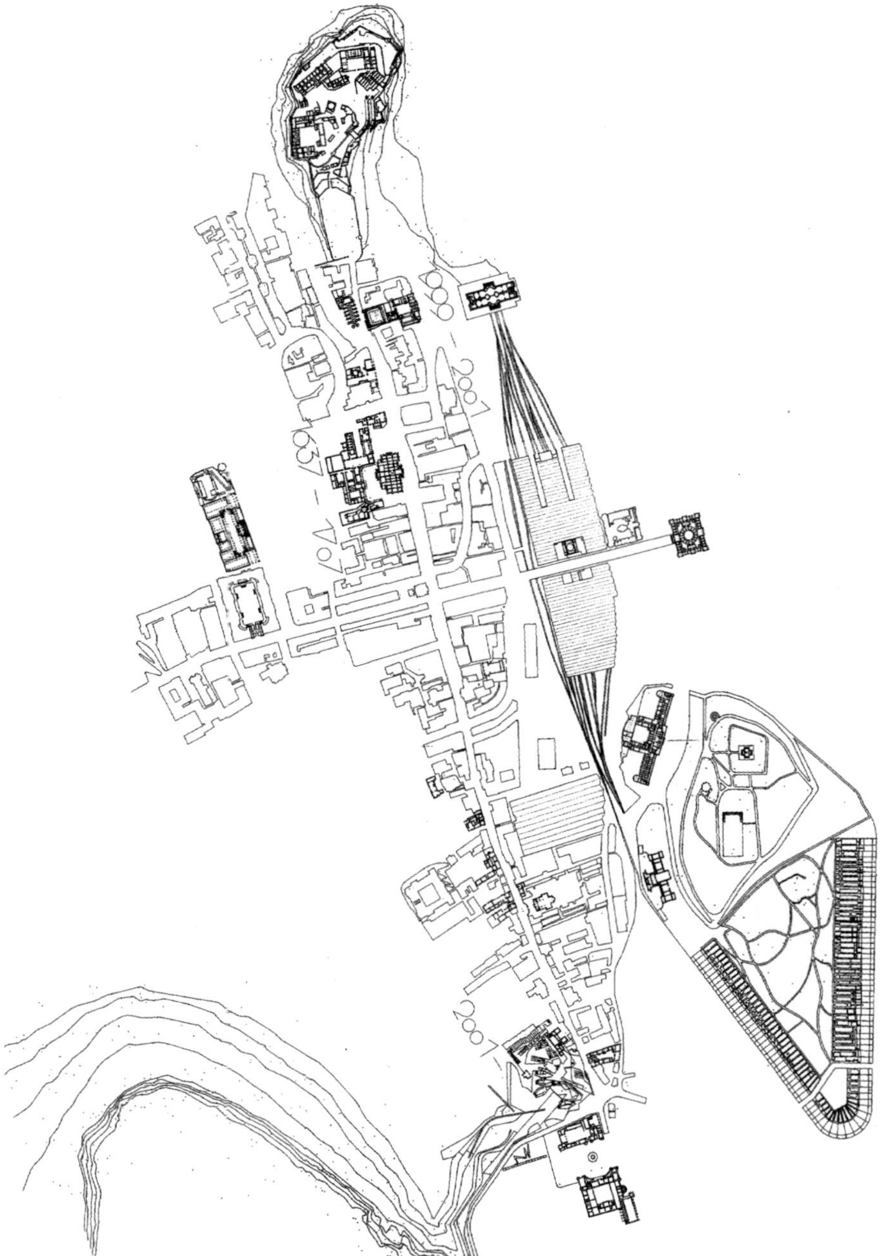

3. Miralles Tagliabue situation plan for the Scottish Parliament Building, Edinburgh, 1998.

4. Miralles Tagliabue situation plan for the Utrecht City Hall, Netherlands, 1997.

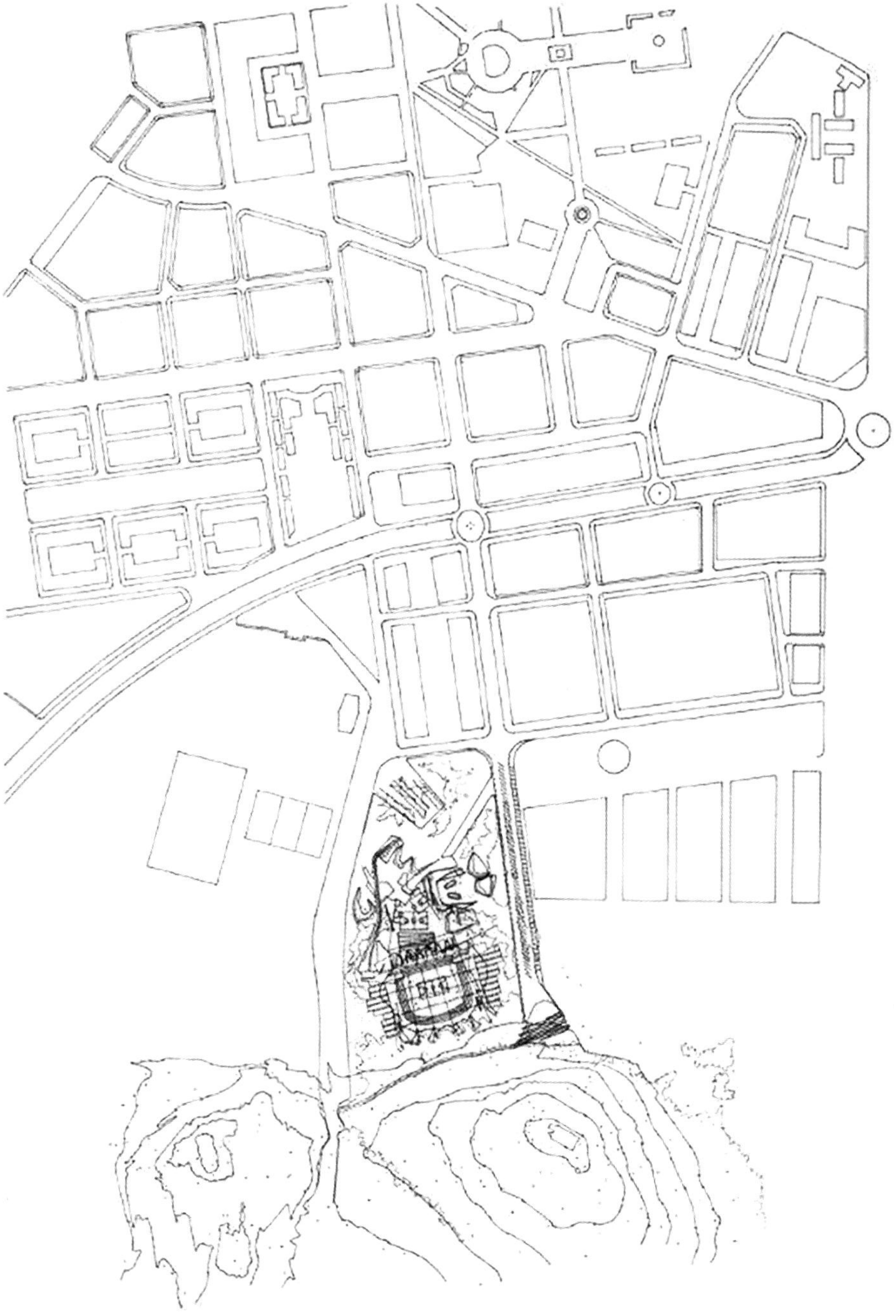

5. Miralles situation plan for the Huesca Sports Stadium, Spain, 1988-94.

6. Miralles situation plan for the Alicante Gymnastic Stadium, Spain, 1989-93.

7. Miralles Tagliabue situation plan for the Isola di San Michele, Venice, Italy, 1999.

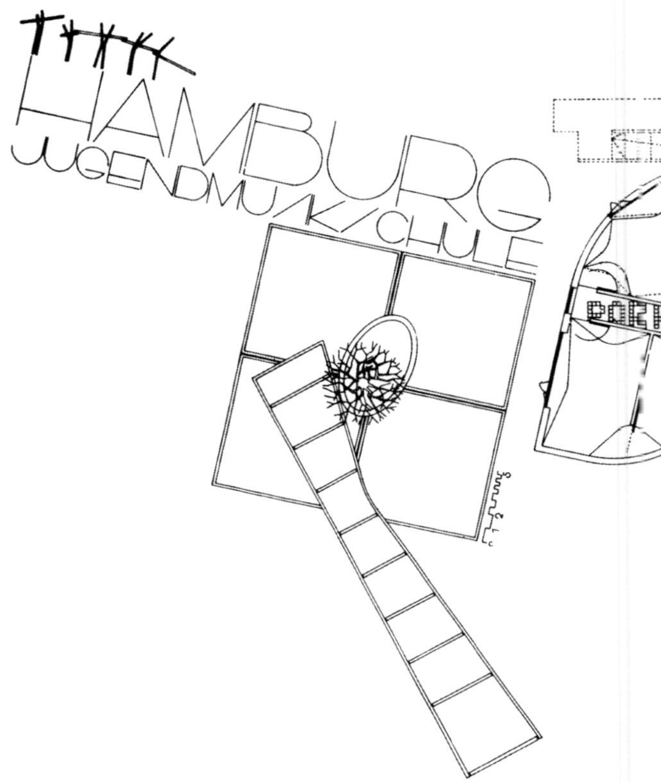
HAMBURG
JUGENDMUSIKSCHULE

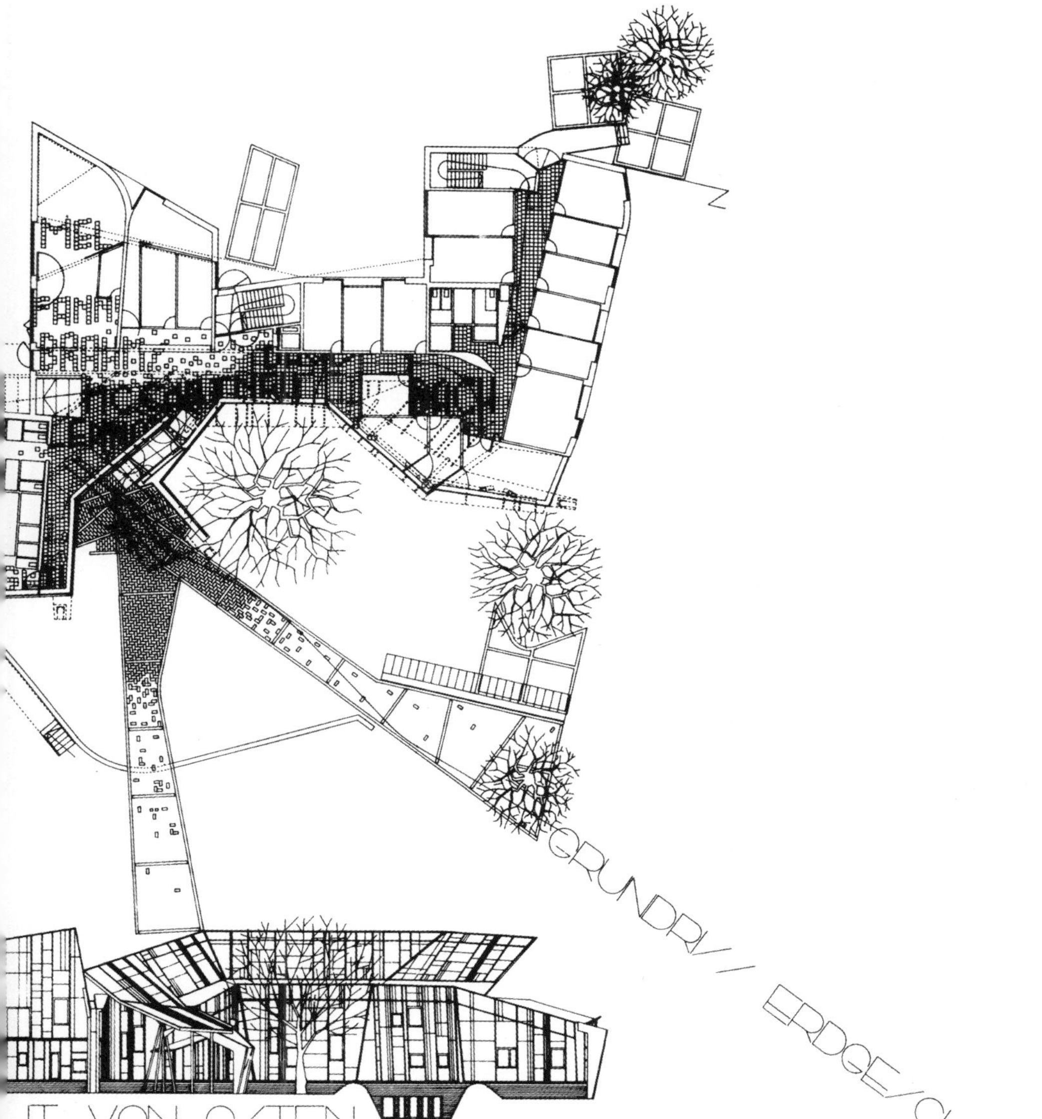

8. Miralles Tagliabue situation plan for the Hamburg Music School, Germany, 1997-98.

Miralles/Pinós: The Anthropomorphic Form*

Juan José Lahuerta

*This text is a direct transcription and translation of a lecture given in Barcelona some time ago.

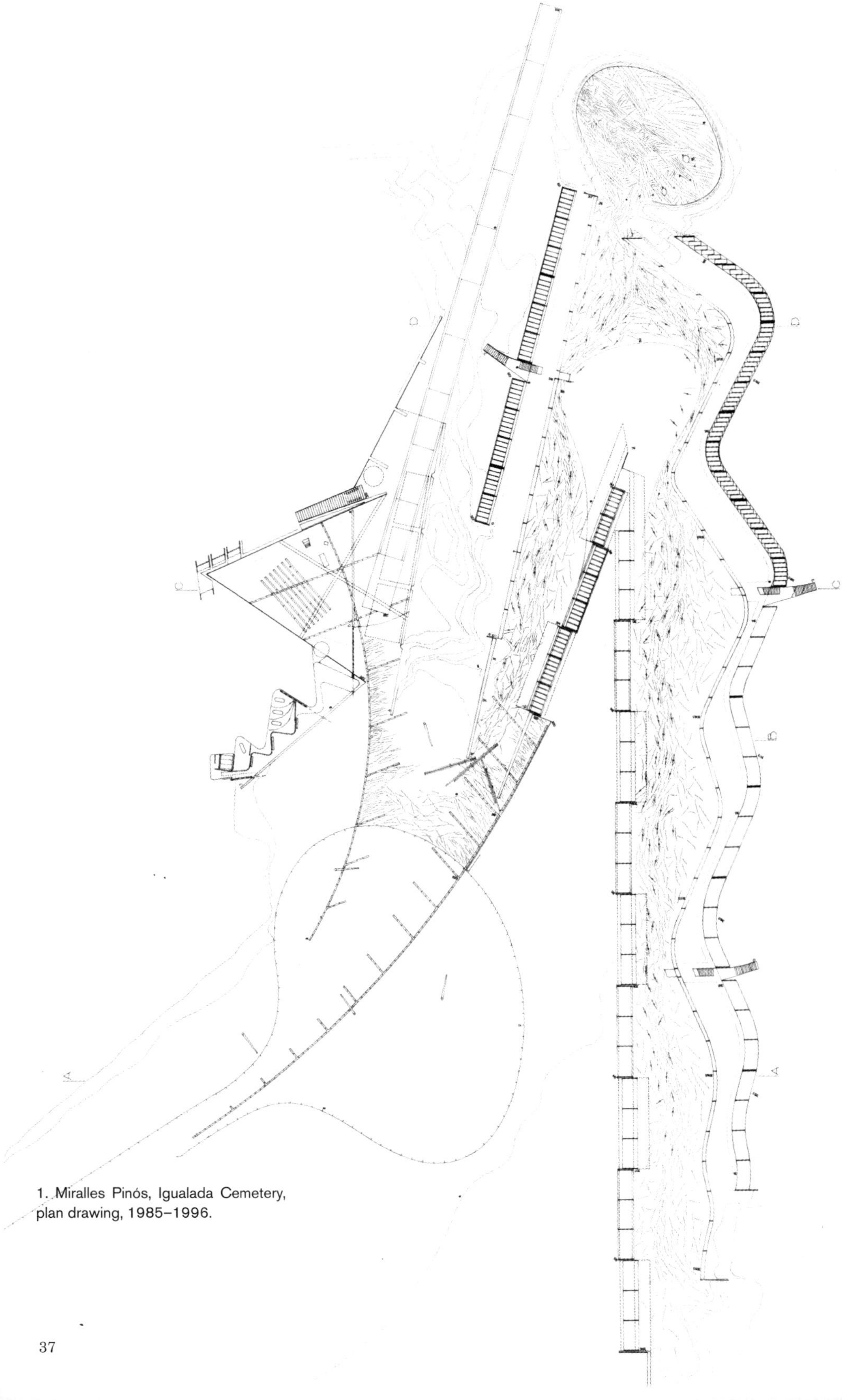

1. Miralles Pinós, Igualada Cemetery, plan drawing, 1985–1996.

In this discourse on the Igualada Cemetery plan (Fig. 1) you will immediately notice that our most essential references and notes are the site and building plans. These plans have a common thread of the presence of anthropomorphic images. These images are something to do with a particular interpretation of architecture, one that is possible and that we should call "paranoiac-critical," because it is about seeing other forms and drawings within specific drawings in order to proceed with critical analysis. This is not an architecture interpreted as architecture in the normal sense of the word, but an architecture interpreted as substrates and layers of images onto which we can project a paranoid vision. It recalls what Salvador Dalí said: A vision that explains to us what we want to see.

When viewing the layers together, what appears in this plan is a human body. It is a fallen human body. Anthropomorphism is a condition of Western architecture or the measure of Man. The images illustrated here are of capitals, and, in particular, a drawing by Francesco di Giorgio Martini (Fig. 2) in which he tries to match—as many architects of the fifteenth and sixteenth century did—the proportions of man with respect to architecture. This is one of the central themes of Vitruvius, newly found by them in those same years. Leading to end all those ideas deduced from chapters on human body as a microcosm (an image of the cosmos and that "anthropomorphic-numeral" relationship between architecture and the human body), they tried to see those proportions of the head in relationship to the cornice or capital proportions. The head as the highest and the cornice and the capital as the top of a body, the human body.

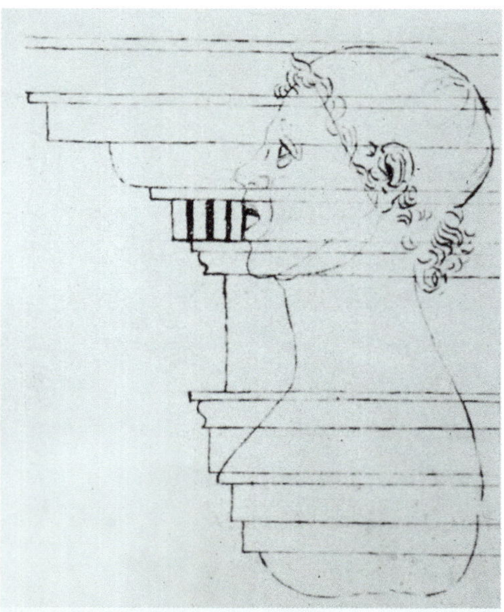

2. Francesco di Giorgio Martini, measure of man in relationship to column capitals, 1439–1501.

The next image is a drawing from a Spanish architecture treaty from the early sixteenth century by Diego de Sagredo (Fig. 3). Here we observe how the head has rotated to the other side. This is a very strange thing that rarely happens. It is turned

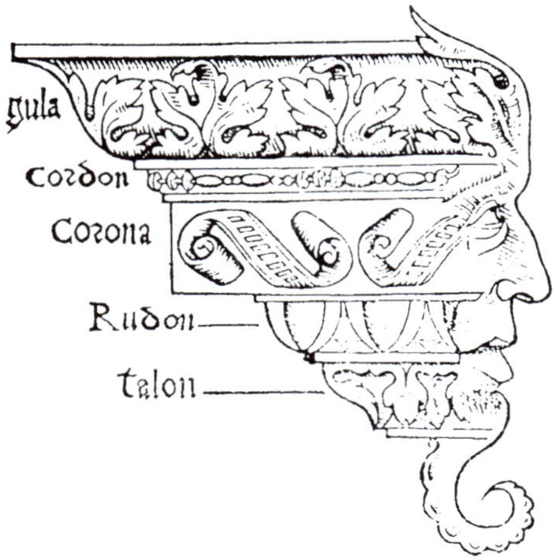

3. Diego de Sagredo, *Medidas del Romano,* 1526.

towards the inside of the molding; it has become almost a mask, and some elements of this section are drawn in relation to that head, not in relation to architecture. As you can see, there is a final molding on the inside which pivots toward no logical place; accordingly, we deduce how the other moldings are arranged to form a knob.

We continue with a drawing by Francesco di Giorgio Martini (Figs. 4, 5) and one by Michelangelo (Fig. 6), who is the one we are really interested in. The measurements relating the parts of the human body have a certain intention in these drawings that we see with the heads, which will be explained later. The drawings, which we have seen by Francesco di Giorgio and this drawing by Sagredo and many others appearing in the *Taccuini* notebooks and in the architecture manuals of the fifteenth and sixteenth century, relate two things: architecture and the human body. These moldings and the head of a man, which in principle are a separate couple, become

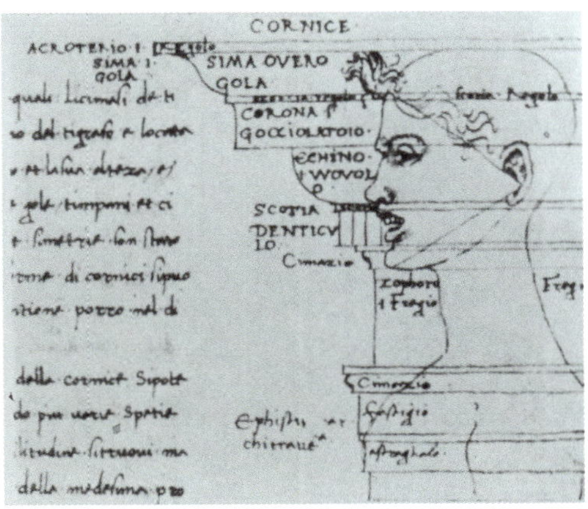

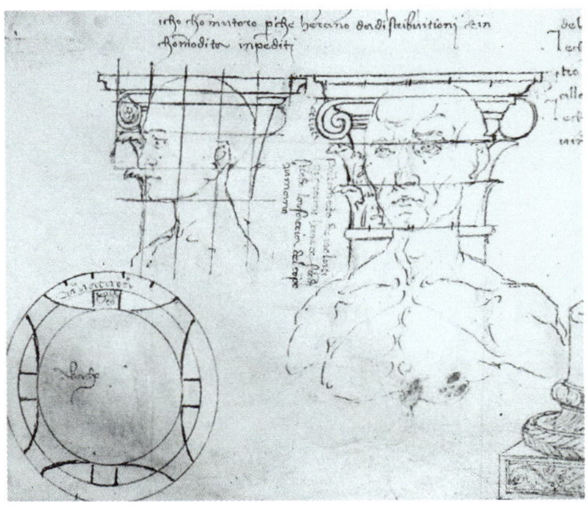

4-5. Francesco di Giorgio, *Trattato di Architettura Civile e Militare*, 1482.

equivalent; the dignity of one is transmitted to the other one and vice versa. On the other hand, in the drawing by Michelangelo, there is a poem on the top and some sort of strange tetra-style formed by the words "heaven" and "earth" repeated twice. Also, there is a fragment of a poem, and below are moldings corresponding to bases of the Sacristia Nuova in the church of San Lorenzo in Florence. He has drawn these toruses and these scotias and has been molding them by hand and with pencil, until he finally discovered through this drawing that a head really arose out of these forms. A head arose that is no longer the beautiful and proportionate head usually drawn by Francesco di Giorgio and that often appears in treaties, but a head with a hooked nose and open screaming mouth. He just had to put a dot on one of the lines of the highest scotia to have a molding profile become a human one, a desperate human profile. The head that ends this construction of the body represents a microcosm and no longer refers to harmonic proportions: this is a head that wants to arise, that wants to get free from inside the stone, from the interior of the moldings, from the ordered stone of architecture. Undoubtedly, this is a paranoid image of Michelangelo. The artist has suddenly discovered a desperate face inside one of his bases, inside the moldings of his architecture—a kind of instinct or paranoid reflection inside the mass, inside the stone.

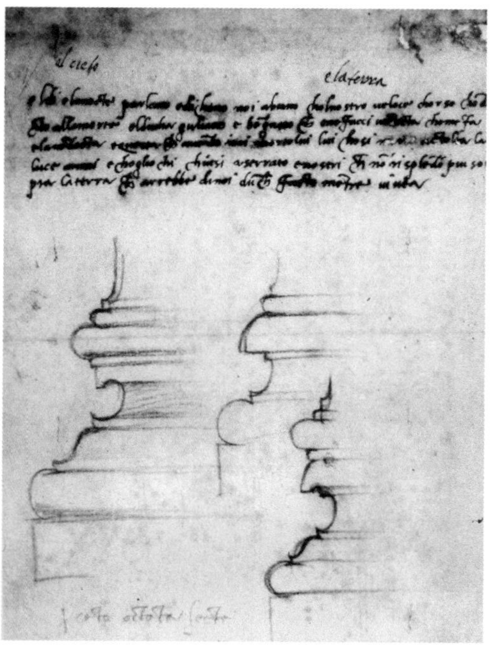

6. Michelangelo, drawings of base profiles, 1523.

This image, compared to the other images of harmony shown in the drawings or engravings of Francesco di Giorgio, is an image that perfectly corresponds to a type of anthropomorphism that has nothing to do with the tradition coming from an interpretation of Vitruvius, one of harmony and correspondence between the cosmos, man, and architecture. Rather this interpretation is a much later vision, one originating from Georges Bataille, and is described in one of the most famous—and to me, one of the most admired—texts on twentieth century architecture. It is a text of eight or ten lines long called "Architecture" published in the *Critical Dictionary of Documents*, in 1929. In the text, Bataille says that architecture is not only the face of power but also that man represents an intermediate point in the evolution from ape to architecture, which has to do with ideas of anthropomorphism precisely because he reversed them completely.

This is, or it could be, how I would interpret the Igualada Cemetery plan (Fig. 1). We have no other choice but to put these plans in relation to the work we already know. It is not just a plan, a cold drawing on a paper, which is what it would be if it had not been built, as happened at first with many of Enric Miralles and Carme Pinós' early projects. This one has been constructed, and therefore, we know that this drawing, those lines that open on that plan, are a crack—a crack on land that has very special conditions, because it is a crack in which human bodies are going to be buried. This becomes an even more special case because one of those bodies buried in that crack is the body of Miralles himself—died just 15 years ago. It's a crack, but look at that kind of oval square in the top: a spermatozoon running to the top of the crack, to the place where the two outer lines—or the two legs—join. The image of an architecture that erodes the land, that digs in the earth, and that has form in movement. This head with that long tail, waving to produce movement, something repeated many times—an architecture that intends to represent the builder of the world. What you see on the other side is one of the illustrations of Bruno Taut's book *The World Builder* (Fig. 7); it is an architecture that is represented as a first moment of Creation, but, with little relation to what is explained by *The Book of Genesis*. It is not God who gets a lump of clay, shapes it, and breathes on it, but the image that occurs inside of a human body in a

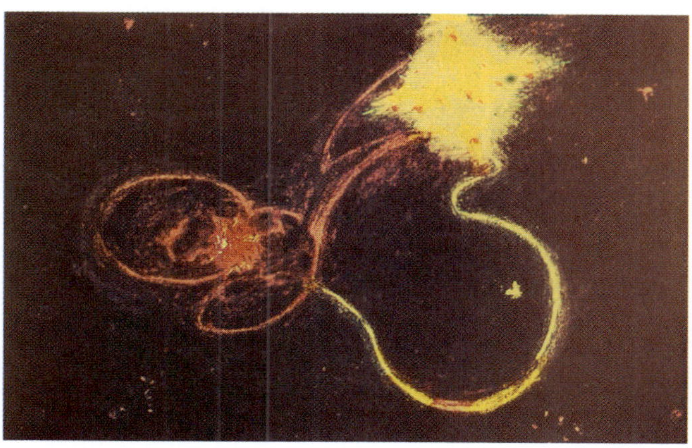

7. Bruno Taut, *The World Builder*, 1920.

womb, the womb of the entire cosmos, which is the place where this kind of anthropomorphism begins.

Bruno Taut's drawing is surrounded on the front and the back by images of cathedrals (Fig. 8). The history of the cathedral and of the empty world is the history of his book, a book of mostly illustrations. It is a cathedral collapsing in space and a cathedral that rebuilds itself from the remains of what has collapsed, but in an empty world, in a world without people. That spermatozoon will find a star. It seems that fertilization occurs, but there is no germination after, but rather, an exploding glass cathedrals world, a world without people. Maybe all these anthropomorphic images in this vision of the creator, as this meeting, as this fertilization in the cosmos, is something that even with images relatively similar to those of Bruno Taut, have also been done from the beginning of the invention of architecture.

8. Bruno Taut, *The World Builder*, 1920.

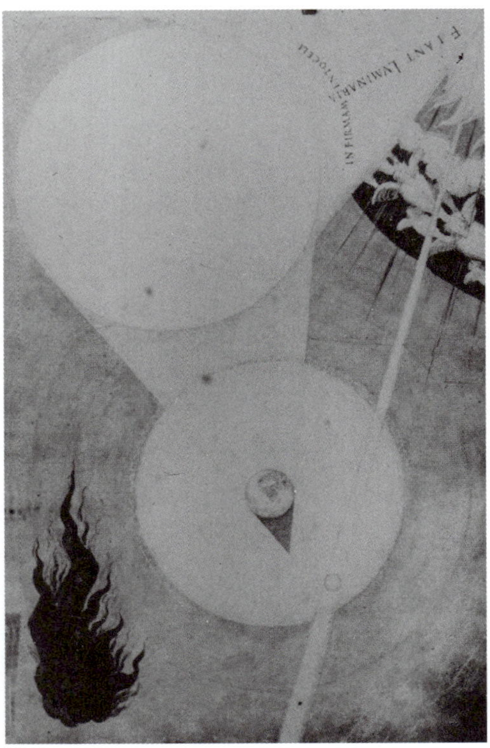

9. Francesco de Hollanda, *De Aetatibus Mundi Imagines*, 1565.

The following image is an engraving by Francisco de Holanda (Fig. 9) representing the fourth day of creation. It is a drawing published in one of his works titled *The Ages of the World in Pictures*; it represents a God painter and master of the world. This is the kind of extreme anthropomorphism of an architecture still not made, but about to be done, in which the architect is already present, and he is God.

The plans from Miralles and Pinós have a lot to do, at least formally, with the next image, which is from a project of Ledoux, "La Maison de Plaisir" (Fig. 10), an image that is formally very similar to the other; however, it has some contours in which the anthropomorphism is reduced to only a part of the human body. This could also be the part we see reflected on the plan of Miralles and Pinós, but which is finally built and displayed in the middle of a panopticon (Fig. 11). The rooms where pleasure is produced by revolving around the halls of this central wing. The same view of the panopticon tells us that this form and that pleasure are a sterile form and pleasure, perhaps the same sterile pleasure the Surrealists liked—at least some of them who liked architecture, such as Salvador Dalí.

We can get closer to the anthropomorphic form of the plan of Miralles and Pinós' cemetery. It is not only a crack, a spermatozoon, fragments of some organs of the human body, but also a human body laying in the ground. There is hair to the left, and it is a body with veins, arteries, and capillaries. You can put this image in relation to the anatomical images depicting the human body as a microcosm. The perfect form is the last form in the academic process of building the human body; the same process used by Gaudí when he began with the skeleton and finished with the clothes (Figs. 12, 13); the process of creating the form that starts with the skeleton and then adds the meat, the skin, and the clothing. It is what Alberti recommended in his *Della Pittura*, and it is what forms the structure of formal education.

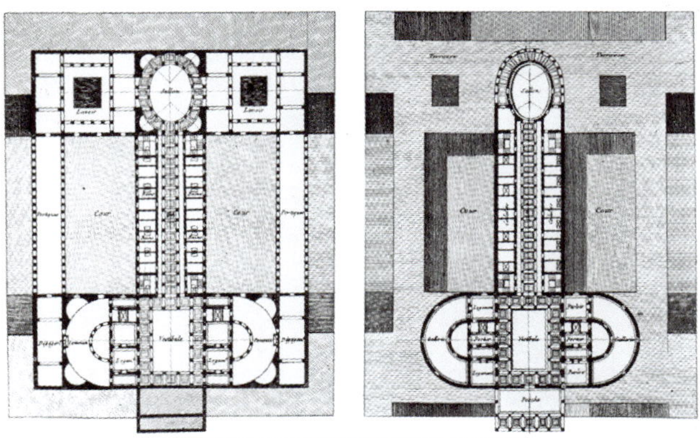

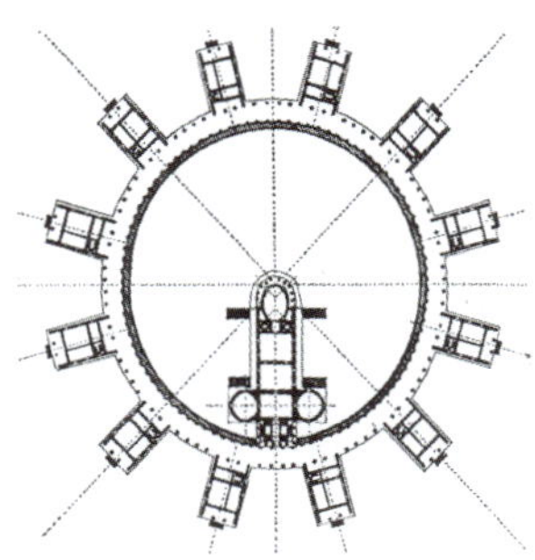

10, 11. Claude-Nicolas Ledoux, Progetto per la Maison du Plaisir, after.1775.

Let's think about when the skin or clothes are not yet placed, or maybe, the other way around, if the process is different: after undressing and taking off the skin, what appears is this body and the postures that represent classical forms of ancient sculpture—postures with which these bodies are represented in the treaties of anatomy of the sixteenth century, where the most famous of all is the one by Andreas Vesalius (Fig. 14). But the clothes are gone, and so the skin, and it starts to produce a form of undressing in a way that suggests terrible things. A strange relationship between these classical forms occurs, between harmonic bodies, whose head determines the canon of measures and proportion. Instead, we have the vision of the skinning that they have suffered. This happens in the next image from the *Treaty of Nicolas Beatrizet* (Fig. 15), where the figure is holding his own skin in his hand. In a way, these images are still of harmonic bodies, of perfect bodies: this one

12. Antoni Gaudí, human skeleton, ca.1900.
13. Antoni Gaudí, human skeleton clothed as angel, ca.1900.

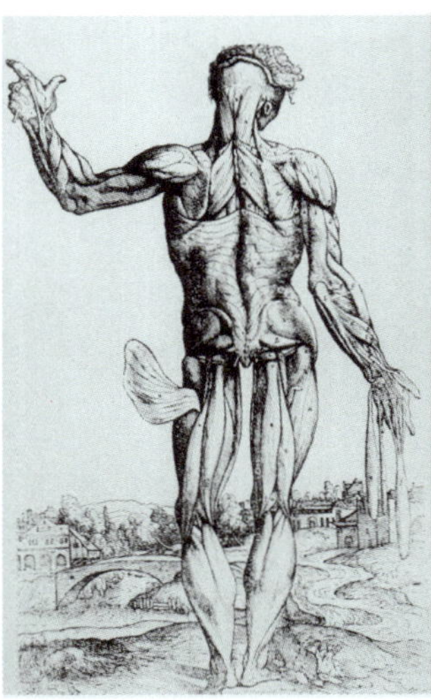

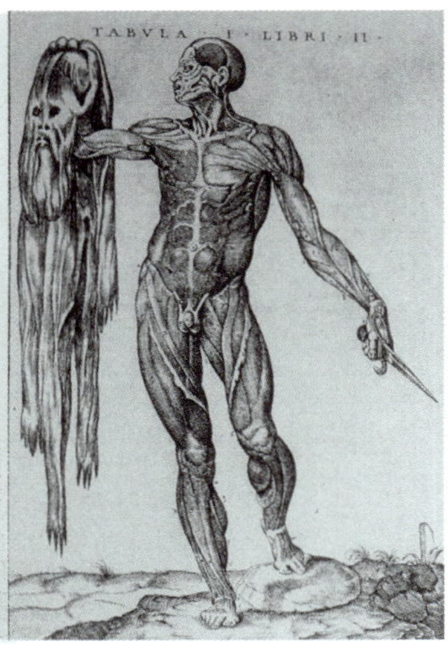

14. Andreas Vasalius, "De Humani Corpis Fabrica," ca.1534.
15. Nicolas Beatrizet, *Juan de Valverde*, "La anatomía del cuerpo humano," 1556.

still keeps his robes, even if oddly turned into his skin. See how the face appears elongated in the soft skin, in a manner that incidentally is quite similar to the way Michelangelo portrayed himself at the *Last Judgment* in the Sistine Chapel.

There is an anthropomorphic architecture that connects the images discussed at the beginning of this essay and relates the human body with the forms of architecture and from interpretations of what they thought Vitruvius wrote in his *Treaty of Architecture*. In some very beautiful drawings by Francesco di Giorgio (Figs. 16-18), bodies appear within columns as images of harmony, in which the actions and relationships of human body measurements are put in relation of the architecture, but also the more superficial and fleeting forms of a body are forms of architecture through its legends. Within the Ionic or Corinthian forms, women appear (Fig. 17); within the Doric forms, or at least what Francesco di Giorgio thought were Doric forms—other then invented different things—what appears are men (Fig. 18). Volutes come into view, and these are interpreted not directly with ideas of proportion and harmony, but they have a disturbing condition, which is in connection with the processes of metamorphosis. The discovery of these bodies within these columns is the discovery of not only what is hidden, as happens to Michelangelo when he is drawing those moldings in the Sacristia Nuova, but rather with the discovery of

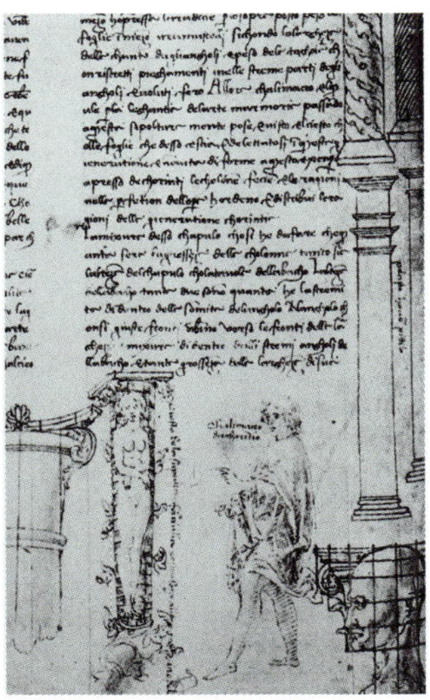

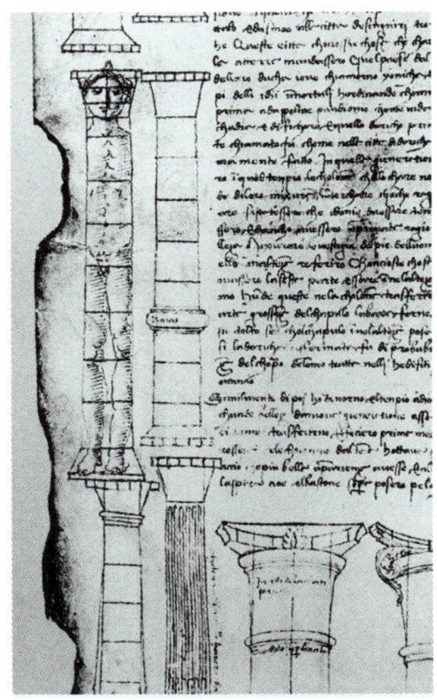

16, 17, 18. Francesco di Giorgio Martini, *Trattati di Architettura,* 1492.

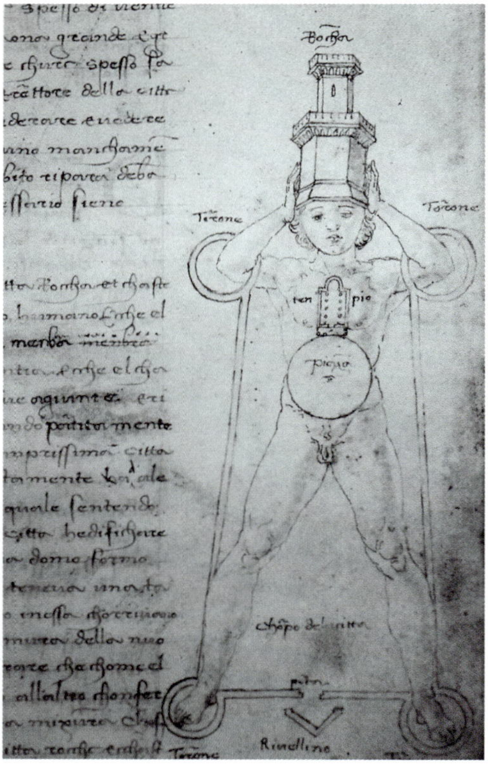

19. Francesco di Giorgio Martini, *Trattati di Architettura*, 1492.

what may happen—a kind of petrification of the imprisoned bodies within these columns that have to do with the processes by which the body is trapped by the stone. Mineralization processes. There are some very beautiful drawings in which the legends of the hairstyles, of women's curls, are put in relationship with the volutes of the Ionic capitals or with a building or an entire city.

The drawings of Francesco di Giorgio, who is not the only one that made these kind of drawings but is certainly the one who made the most beautiful drawings, can transform human bodies—or animals—in whole cities and vast landscapes. It is now no longer a matter of proportion but a symbolic issue: in the city, the head is the king's palace; the belly is the marketplace; the heart is the cathedral; and the elbows, knees, hands, and feet are the towers of the fortification walls. But apart from these symbolic relationships—such ideas of proportion, of assimilation of human body to forms or to legends and meanings of architecture—what appears here are inhabited bodies. See for example, the image of the body converted in a city and the parts of the body as a symbol of the parts of the city (Fig. 19), we could offer a reverse interpretation and think about what it might be to inhabit a body. And then we see what suddenly appears is that emerged face that inhabited the moldings of Michelangelo, a very different image and a real similarity to that other body—the plan of Igualada Cemetery, which will not be inhabited, because it is a cemetery, but which is the reproduction, the multiplication, of this same body.

Returning to an image that is in perfect relation to previous ones and also in relation to the inverted image above, is a picture I wanted to relate as a form of

20. Andre Masson, ca.1955.
21. Andre Masson, "La terre," 1939.

anthropomorphic architecture with the Miralles and Pinós plan. In this plan, we see again a head and a laying body, and we also see a body crossed by the veins, arteries, and capillaries or by the nervous system—a strange nervous system converted into planks scattered everywhere that have something to do, or at least I would think so, with the bodies that inhabit the cemetery. Igualada Cemetery is already an erotic drawing, because we know how to translate its construction into an erotic landscape as did the Surrealists: mountains, caves, waterfalls. Specifically, the erotic landscapes of André Masson (Fig. 20) have some sort of direct relation with the way the Igualada Cemetery is thought about and built—like a crack in the earth that can be experienced—until the end where the oval plaza is, crossing it as we could travel a body. The drawing of André Masson served as a curtain to cover the famous painting by Gustave Courbet, *L'origine du monde,* which shows open legs and female sex. In other drawings, Masson is showing the same idea: landscapes turned into gigantic female bodies and little people who begin to appear (Fig. 21). Little figures who climb mountains or who introduce themselves into the caves and in the forests as if they were characters from the world of Gulliver or, probably even more fun, like in the fantastic voyages in the films, for example, of Richard Fleischer—amazing trips within the body.

Within the Miralles and Pinós Igualada Cemetery, all these things exist, and others too. This is a cemetery in which a route is proposed. What happens is that those who make the tour inside this open body—this open crack in the earth—and

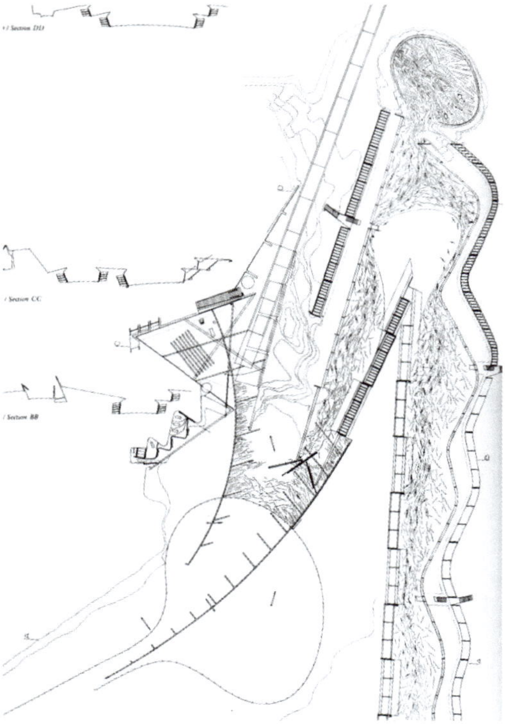

22. Miralles Pinós, Igualada Cemetery, plan drawing, 1985–1996.

those introduced by this slit to get to the end—of this cave or this elliptical room—are the funeral procession (Fig. 22). That is a big difference. We are not those funny little figures who climb mountains. These capillaries we saw above convert the Igualada Cemetery into a body full of hair, or sticks, which is properly what those hairs are, into a kind of hedgehog, which is a fairly common figure in the architecture of Miralles and Pinós. It is a body covered with bristles that are sticks, stiff and short—cut sticks on the floor, as in the floor of a barbershop, which may be the image of a kind of a barrage, of great destruction. That crack is the crack formed by the disaster that has been cutting the hair, and the sticks create a situation of flood in which all things are piled haphazardly. But it is also the form of a body, with his head, the hair, and the legs that open down; it is the form of a fallen body, which has dragged with him many things. It has been an accident. It is not just a geological accident, but a disaster has occurred. It has opened a crack in the earth; the water has passed, and it has brought with it all those sticks. But all these planks are the remains of another accident, not the geological one, but the accident of a body. Imagine someone who has fallen into a ravine—which could be the ravine that was in the place where this cemetery is built—and who has fallen along with everything he had on him. They could be the ropes and the tools, which serve to escalate, which surround him, or which could also be the rules, squares, and the triangles of the architect, which is lying next to and around his body as in a medieval picture in the National Art Museum of

23. National Art Museum of Catalonia.

24. Günther Förg

Catalonia (Fig. 23). Someone who has fallen from the ladder with which he tried to climb the same ravine. Someone who has fallen and is lying at the bottom with the sticks, the ropes, and the irons. Or someone lying under a balcony that he had climbed to kidnap someone or to love someone in secret, but now lies at the bottom, tangled in his rope ladder.

Günther Förg, an artist who Miralles quite liked and about whom we talked sometimes, had portrayed himself like this: as a body fallen to the bottom of a staircase (Fig. 24). But the feeling of this photograph, the way in which the artist lies in the background as an "X" and with the body turned to one side as if struck by some pressure, is obviously the pressure of gravity that has finally stopped at the end of the stairwell. The cropping of this photograph produces precisely the opposite sensation—that Günther Förg has fallen—yes, but, like the other things of the Igualada Cemetery, has fallen to the ceiling, as the suicide minister of *The Golden Age* movie by Luis Buñuel.

Those who fall toward the ceiling seem to finally be released. Bodies that are released because they finally ascend, but they ascend not in soul but in body. These bodies are those that correspond to a cemetery. The cemetery is the fallen body, and the ascended body into the ground. Not a soul that goes to heaven, but the body that finally ascends to the ground.

25. Miralles Pinós, drawing detail Igualada Cemetery, 1987.

26. Charles Lebrun, leonine face, ca.1806.

Let's go, however, to look at the head of that body we are talking about (Fig. 25). Of course, the shape of this head is the oval of a face and, with the lines of the poles or planks that end up in it, this face has much to do with physiognomy. I will not repeat questions that I have already discussed with respect to those heads that appear in the capitals of Francesco di Giorgio Martini. In the end what we'll see on that head is the same that Michelangelo saw, saving all distances. See what it arises. See the oval of a face that can be interpreted from these physiognomic theories.

This is a drawing of Charles Lebrun, who made comparisons between the faces and heads of animals—which represents the strength from the figure of the lion, of a leonine face (Fig. 26). Goya portrayed himself always with a look of lion that had something to do with theories of Lebrun and Lavatier on its own character. We can imagine that what we see in the cemetery's head is a self-portrait of Miralles himself, who also had a leonine head and whose character was, therefore, the fortitude. But in that head there is also hair, shades, a beard, hair, hands, sticks...with weight.

And also all those rectangular boxes, which are tombs and are floating like stars that seem to come from the inside of this head, perhaps, are the stars of the fall; those stars that revolve around their heads when a blow is given. Stars or lighted candles...this on the one hand; furthermore, the boxes, which are tombs. Boxes made with three squares. We find squares very few times in the world of natural things. They are explicitly produced by men, particularly manufactured by the architects, who insisted from the beginning, following some ideas of the *Treaty of Vitruvius*, to introduce men with open arms in a square and a circle. The square is nothing, an abstract figure, something generic that creates an abstract harmony and, consequently, the abstract anatomy of all these bodies under these squares. You can see some of them here: Cesariano, Rusconi, and other treatise writers of the sixteenth century (Figs. 27, 28, 29).

The beautiful body—but sometimes also a furious body—within the circle and the square; some of them, like this one by Francesco di Giorgio (Fig. 30), of course very beautiful, seem a strange Pygmalion, a human body, which in this case, is not a rigid frontal one, but a delicate body, in a fragile position, stretching the hands to gently rub the abstract lines surrounding it. Every time the man stretches his arms, it seems that the square and the invisible circle around it are formed. But the squares of the boxes of Miralles' graves are three, and therefore, they actually form a rectangle. The number three corresponds to the head, the trunk, and the extremities. The rectangle also exists everywhere, man-made, but not in the abstract sense we discuss now. The rectangular form accompanies

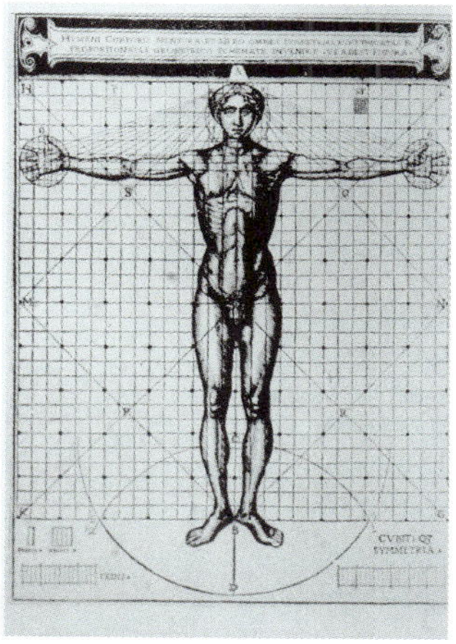

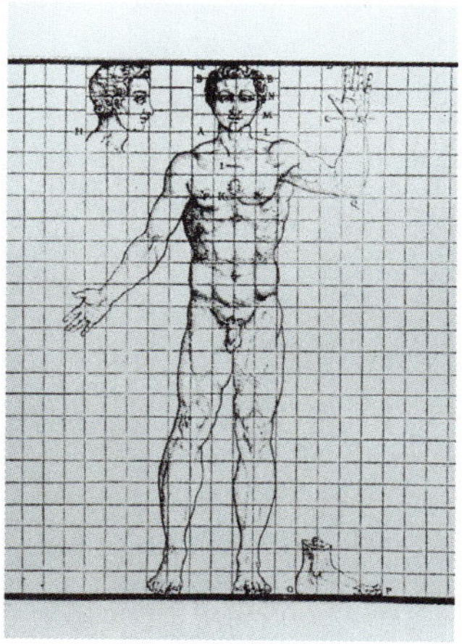

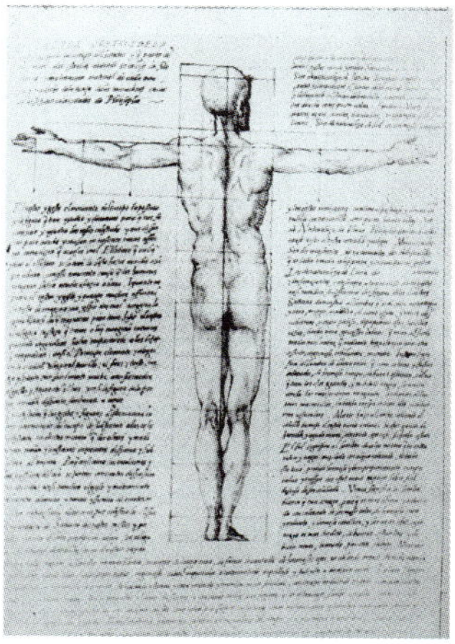

27. Cesariano drawing from *Vitruvius Pollio's De Architectura*, ca.1520.
28. Giovanni Antonio Rusconi, from "Della Architettura," ca.1590.
29. Treatise writer of the sixteenth century.

30. Francesco di Giorgio Martini, *Trattato di Architettura*, ca.1482.

us throughout life: the crib is usually rectangular, the table is rectangular, the window is usually rectangular, the boxes are rectangular, and the coffin in the end, is also rectangular. Surely the rectangle that accompanies us throughout life has the deepest anthropomorphic sense. In the work of Miralles and Pinós, in his head, inside his head, like someone who thinks, all rectangles are tucked, all the boxes, all the coffins. All bodies are in it.

The bodies are themselves released from abstractions. This image is a very impressive drawing of Benito Arias Montano in which the Noah's Ark appears (Fig. 31). The proportion of the Ark is measured with the body of Jesus; Jesus, who is salvation, sets or determines the proportion of Noah's Ark, which is its own image of salvation.

Sometimes in treaties there are gestures, some movement in those bodies trapped inside the square. In the engraving by Rusconi (Fig. 28), a foot and head have turned; they have become independent. Therefore, we can see that head, like a face in profile, as if everything was leaking from his nose. A head bleeding from the nose; and in the back, the stars that I have commented before are shining... these blades, these crosses, which are like seeds blown away. Someone blowing to the other side. Where are all these blades, crosses, stars, or seeds carried by the wind, ending? They go to the chapel. In a detail of the drawing where the chapel appears, it is shown how all those things stop in the great blade or the big final cross, which is the cross that could explain everything (Fig. 32).

Two concrete beams forming a cross support the roof of the chapel of this project, which is the cemetery cross. All the other small crosses that appear spread or are formed by the floor planks will end in this big cross. The cemetery is a journey into the interior of the earth. Funeral processions enter by that route, but first

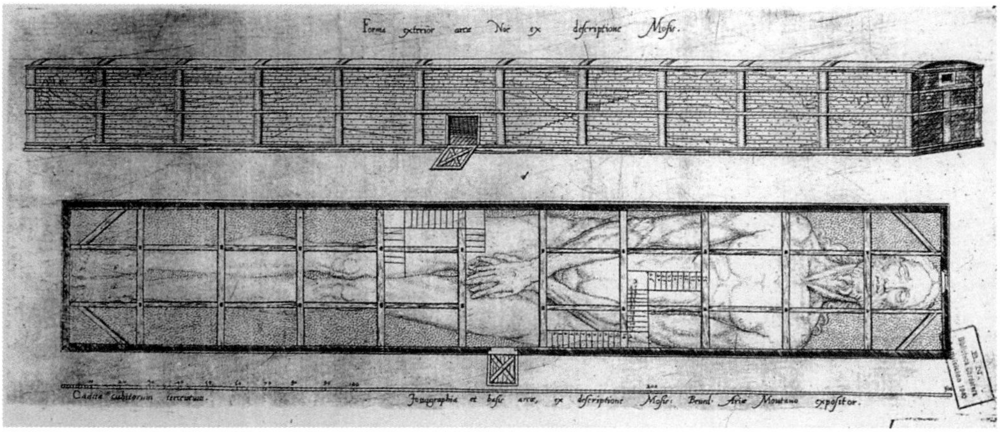

31. Benito Arias Montano, *Antiquitatum Judaicarum Libri IX*, Leiden, 1593.

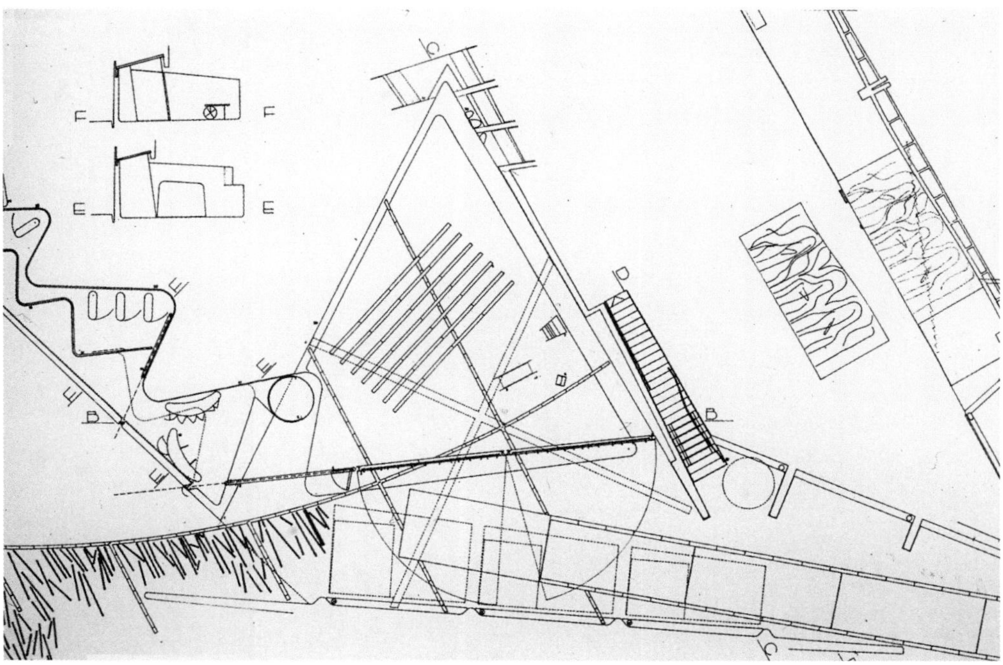

32. Miralles Pinós, Igualada Cemetery, detail drawing of the chapel.

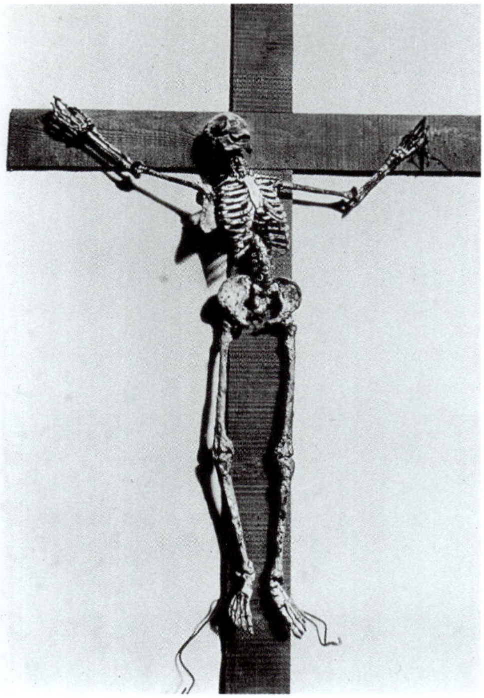

33. Antoni Gaudí, human skeleton on wooden planks, ca.1900.

34. Pablo Picasso, figure drawings, Museu Picasso Barcelona, 1903.

have to go through the cross, by the chapel, and then move inadvertently by many other crosses—crosses made of planks (Fig. 33), like those boards that are certainly mason planks, where Gaudí hung his skeletons. Or crosses that appear in the bottom of a crack, like in this Picasso drawing (Fig. 34) where the cross appears from the inside of open curtains, explaining just what the cross finally means, through all those strange pious depositions, finally converted into loving couples around the cross with the body of Christ—from the anthropomorphism of the cross to the shape of a man with open arms.

I always remember a famous poem by Louis Aragon in which he constantly repeats: "Il n'y a pas d'amour heureux" (There is no happy love). He says at one point that man is a being that sometimes opens his arms, and when he thinks to open them, he discovers that his shadow is shaped like a cross. This shadow is the end of all anthropomorphism. The anthropomorphism of the cemetery is found in the fallen body that contracts the figures of love and sacrifice—the most erotic of all forms, the cross. In the project titles, instead of the correct Catalan word, which is "cementiri," Miralles and Pinós wrote, "ZemenTiri" with "Z" and one capital "T" turned into a cross (Fig. 35). These two signs are the cemetery: a "Z," which is the sign of someone who marks something, an easy form but also the form of a tear on Earth, and the cross, which is the form that, in the end, contains everything.

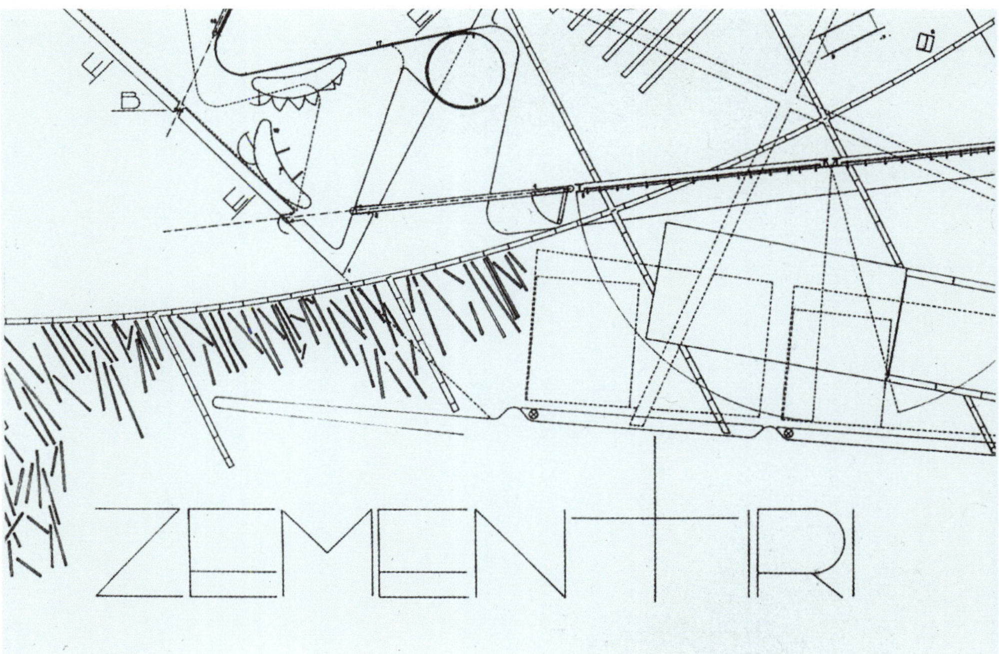

35. Miralles Pinós, Igualada Cemetery, plan detail.

Portrait of Miralles with Vanishing Points: Prospect for Youth

Maurici Pla Serra

1. Competition for the headquarters of the Council of Huesca. Helio Piñón, Albert Viaplana, Enric Miralles (contributor).

Miralles' interest in architecture began with the discovery that solids and voids in perspective can be combined to create a vision of great complexity. Drawings in a chapter titled "Perspectives," in *Obra Completa de Enric Miralles* edited by Benedetta Tagliabue for Electa,[1] show Miralles' first projects independent of employer or academy, which started in 1983—the year he made the first competition with Carme Pinós. In addition, there are drawings in the journal *Jano Arquitectura Numero 48*,[2] which are dedicated to four competitions designed by the Piñón-Viaplana studio, with Miralles credited as a collaborator. Some of the "perspective" drawings come from the graphic presentation of these four competitions, while others correspond to later competitions with the same studio. Also included are the perspectives of the project for Plaça dels Païso Catalans,[3] which concludes the Miralles' collaboration with the Piñón-Viaplana studio. The presence of these drawings in the Electa monograph is sufficient evidence that, effectively, these drawings are the first important graphic works by Miralles. Some of these drawings also appear in his doctoral thesis, "Things Viewed Left and Right (Without Glasses),"[4] presented at the Escola Tècnica Superior d'Arquitectura de Barcelona in 1987. In all, these drawings reach far beyond the ideas of the competition projects than was originally noticed.

Analysis of aspects common to these drawings will be more enlightening than reviewing each drawing separately. However, such an overall analysis will give better results if the drawings are observed chronologically, in order to notice the developmental aspects. Therefore, my first observations will be about the first four competition drawings and then continue with subsequent competitions (Figs. 1–5).

Note that none of the perspectives made for these first four projects represent a building with intrinsic qualities. Rather, we see the desire to compose a landscape built with solids and voids so that the position of the vanishing point tends to move lateral to the perspective. Thus, these solids contribute to the configuration of the void, which is always formed by solid pieces flanking both sides. Also note that the building object of the competition is strongest at one of the flanks, so that the construction of the space is unbalanced by one side. The vanishing point is always at the horizon farthest from the built space, and the perspective usually moves towards an edge to grant reliefs that are different on the two sides that make up the space. In all cases, it is the empty part of the landscape that occupies the center, while one of the flanks corresponding to the position of the building is the object of the competition.

2. Competition for the headquarters in Seville, College of Architects of Western Andalusia, 1975. Helio Piñón, Albert Viaplana, Enric Miralles (contributor).

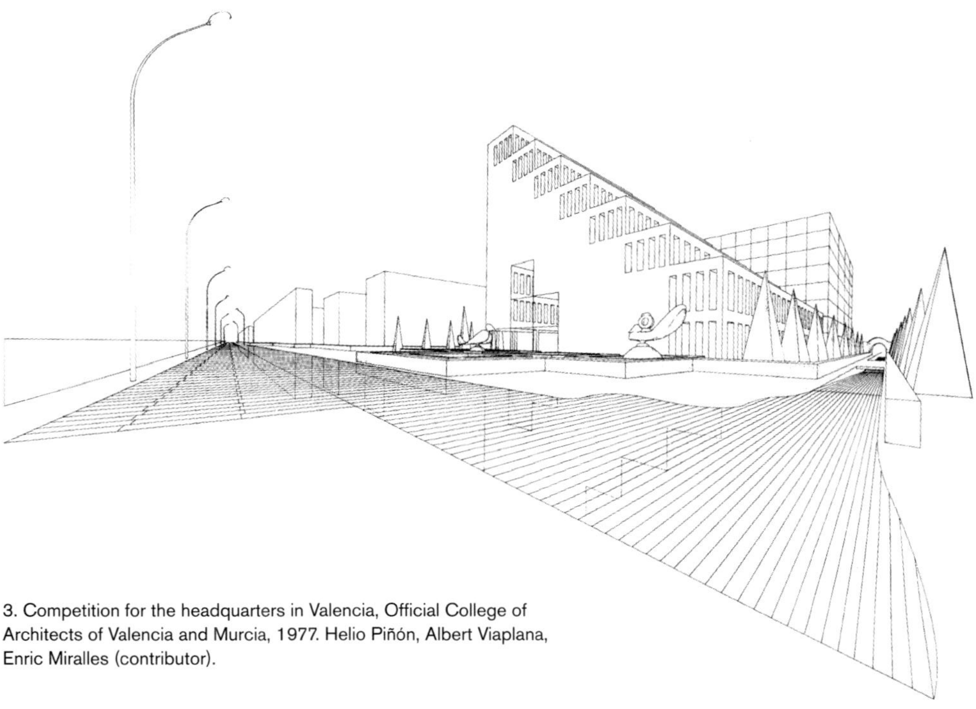

3. Competition for the headquarters in Valencia, Official College of Architects of Valencia and Murcia, 1977. Helio Piñón, Albert Viaplana, Enric Miralles (contributor).

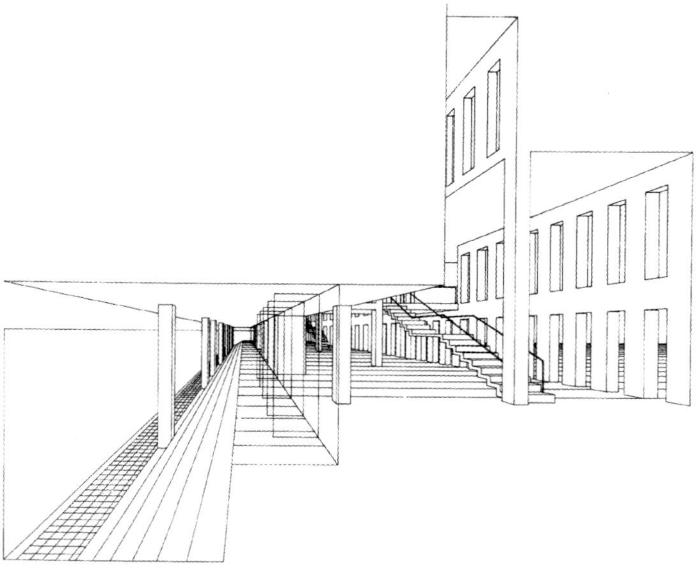

4. Competition drawing, 1976. Helio Piñón, Albert Viaplana, Enric Miralles (contributor).

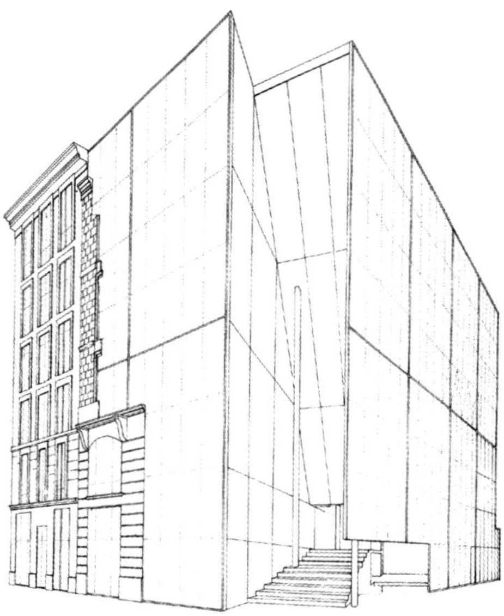

5. Competition for the expansion of the Barcelona headquarters of the College of Architects of Catalonia and the Balearic Islands, 1976. Helio Piñón, Albert Viaplana, Enric Miralles (contributor).

In this first series of drawings, the perspective building is completely closed, that is to say, there is no opening in the periphery of the line drawing. It is likely that this feature was taken from perspectives by Leon Krier for projects of James Stirling;[5] other examples of the same type of closed drawings are difficult to find in the work of earlier architects. This indicates that while the perspectives are about the construction of landscapes, they are also about the construction of objects. With closed lines around the perimeter, the perspective takes on a clear object-drawn dimension, as if it were a model put on a table. The landscape as an object will be one of the main features of architecture that Miralles develops later. If the issue is to represent the void, then in these cases we see the void acquire a solid quality thanks to this trick of drawing. The object makes a void box that can be opened on one side and whose interior can be represented. These perspectives are combinations of solids and voids that together form complex objects so that the empty objects have boundaries made by the solid parts. These solid parts are the buildings of the competition, which become part of the larger entity of the constructed landscape. With these constructions, Miralles' perspective goes far beyond the architectural solution proposed for the competition. The pretext Miralles takes in these drawings is one of the teacher developing the concept of landscape as object—a concept very present in his later work.

In some exceptional cases, the proposed building for the competition is isolated and shown in its pure form as an object.[6] In these cases, the vanishing point is inside of the building, so the point of view is frontal and against the nearest wall surface. Then it appears that the building itself has a slit through which the inner space can be discerned, and the viewing axis is arranged to look as if it penetrates the slit. The vanishing point is located in the heart of the object, and the perspective merely represents the void left by the gap; indeed, this is again an empty object. Buildings are cracked, and the crack penetrates the building, and the drawing represents the making of an empty object. This occurs when the building has these slits. In a very specific case when the slit is isolated in the drawing, it represents the inside of an empty box.

Miralles develops his projects using the materials given to him, and in every case, the projects provide the same opportunities that students are known to find. By constructing closed objects that possess the scale of landscape and defining a very precise scope of intervention by the closed nature of his drawings, Miralles is designing a comprehensive concept for architecture and the city, one of a complex system of solids and voids ordered through the buildings in perspective. The application of this particular procedure can be verified in all his later work; however, the perspectives are no longer as neatly fit into the design process, but his sketches continue to express the character of closed objects made with solids and voids. The competition proposals for the Piñón-Viaplana studio do not consider the potential of certain buildings designed specifically to fill urban voids. Miralles' perspectives construct complex realities from the existing situation and propose that both are wrapped in a unifying magma that reaches the limits of another project that did not exist in the design of the first building. Therefore, Miralles solves the problem of the object, not renounces it, but goes beyond the unique features of the particular building (Figs. 6–8).

The second series of competition projects made by the Piñón-Viaplana studio was published in the magazine *Quaderns d'Arquitectura i Urbanisme 156.* [6] Their projects, designed through 1982, represent new perspectives by Miralles. The most characteristic features of the first series of perspectives remain; however, in this second series, we see a more precise definition of solids and also some visual aids that give the drawing a somewhat impressionistic character. Although these new perspectives can be of rows of trees or long arcaded walks, the vanishing point is still fleeing towards the bottom of the drawing flanked by solids on both sides. The new solids also project more integration into the existing system of solids. The axis of vision can penetrate to the heart of the building through a cut in the section drawn to resemble the interior space as an empty box, that is, as an object represented from the inside. In the park projects, undertaken at this stage, we observe a great capacity to build perspective regardless of all kinds of solids: these cases are given the quality of a pure void, marked by pavement or punctuated by vegetation. The problem of closing the foreground then occurs, since the represented object contains no trace that allows it to be closed. Even though the perspectives are built on an unidentifiable conical base with the vanishing point marking the epicenter of landscape-object to be represented, the perspectives are opened by the foreground or any of the other sides, and new perspectives appear made with pen and freehand.

In *Quaderns 156* [7], there are only four pages summarizing the trajectory of the competition projects. Each project is synthesized in one page with a plan and a perspective. Miralles' perspective is presented as a significant symbolic meaning; the perspective is able to summarize the project without the entire set of

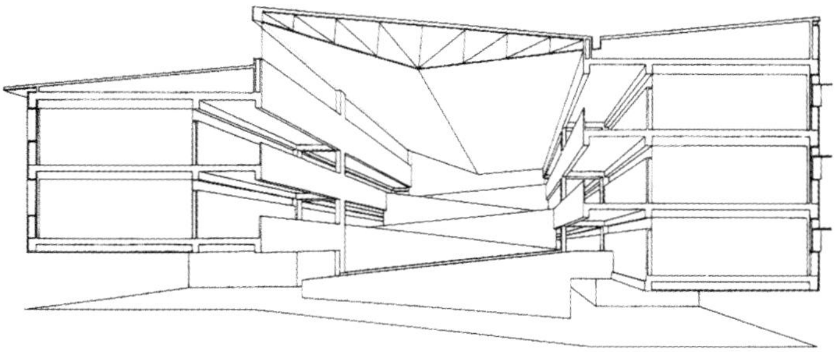

6. National Competition Teaching Institutions, 1978.
Helio Piñón, Albert Viaplana, Enric Miralles (contributor).

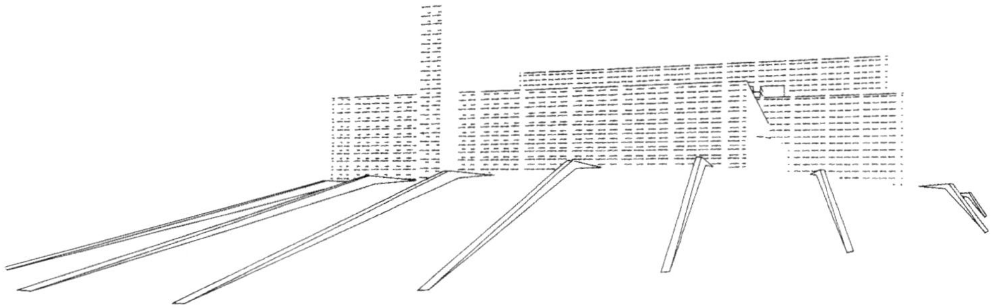

7. Competition for an Islamic Center, Madrid, 1980.
Helio Piñón, Albert Viaplana, Enric Miralles (contributor).

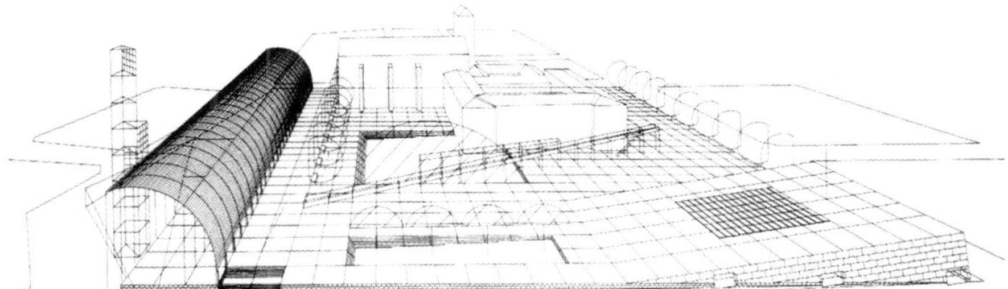

8. Competition for the development of the Polygon San Esteban, Murcia, 1977.
Helio Piñón, Albert Viaplana, Enric Miralles (contributor).

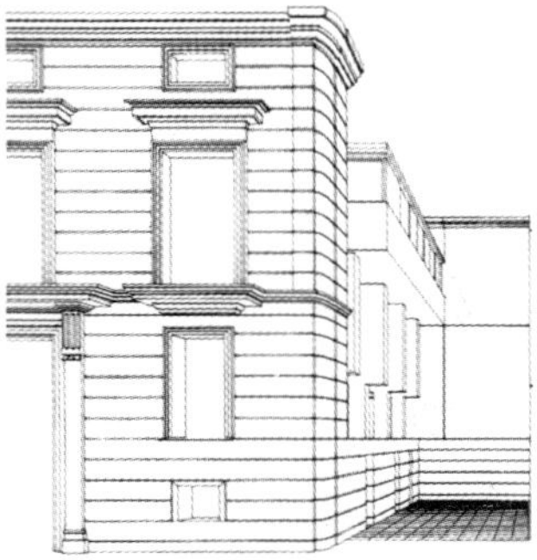

9. Competition for the rehabilitation of the College of Architects of Murcia, 1978. Helio Piñón, Albert Viaplana, Enric Miralles (contributor).

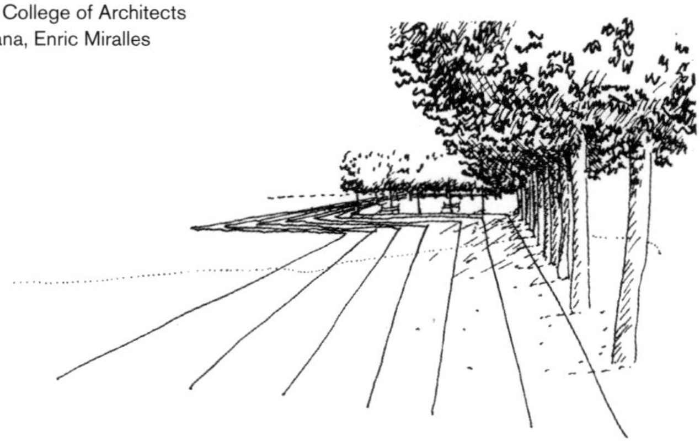

10. Competition for the Parc del Besòs, Sant Adrià de Besòs, Barcelona, 1982. Helio Piñón, Albert Viaplana, Enric Miralles (contributor).

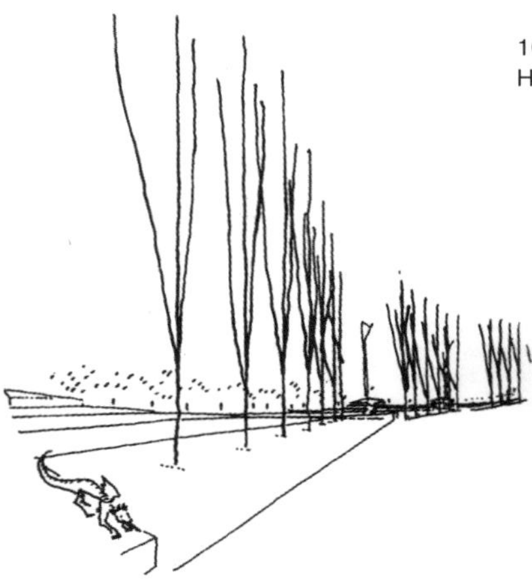

11. Competition for the Plaza de la Constitution, Girona, 1982. Helio Piñón, Albert Viaplana, Enric Miralles (contributor).

representational drawings. In these presentation perspectives, Miralles recovers the symbolic value that the project once had, which in this case is to represent a complex system of solids and voids. The main point is that the eye always slides down the flank of the solids and reveals the structure of the void that is the actual material of the new project. The void is the made object: this is what these extraordinary drawings establish. In some cases in the second series, we realize that even when the existing building is represented with great precision, it is also system of solids and voids. This game allows us to dilute old concepts of architecture, urban space, and all their subsequent distinctions (Figs. 9–11).

The last series of competition projects from the Piñón-Viaplana studio is published in *Quaderns 163* and presents work immediately before the Plaça dels Països Catalans. In this presentation, there appears to be very little perspective drawn according to procedures described above. In this drawing, there are certain innovations—a building is partially shown, so that a closed object is built with only part of the object. Again, the axis of vision slides tangentially along the flank of the object. The building fragment is represented in detail so that the perspective not only describes it as a solid but also as an architecture equipped with a strong character. This also occurs in the Stirling perspectives where parts of the object are isolated and represented as objects in themselves, so that the new object becomes part of the original object that was represented in closed form.

In *Quaderns 163* drawings, we also see a square represented in the distance, so that it shows its character as a closed object placed on top of the table. However, in the set of drawings, we see no significant effect of the ways Miralles built his own perspectives. Rather, things appear that had not been seen before. Some projects are represented by small outlines in pen without constructed perspective lines. It is a quick sketch that maintains the openness of the mark of the perspective and point of view located below the base, thereby restoring the monumental character of the building. The reference here is without a doubt Mendelsohn's imaginary drawings, which are discussed by Manuel Gausa in the same issue of *Quaderns*.[8] Since these sketches have a more pictorial than architectonic character, defining the vanishing point is not necessary. In this way, we can distinguish between a sketch of Viaplana and Miralles—just search and locate the vanishing point. We can also verify if the drawing is closed or not: if it is, then without a doubt it is drawn by Miralles; if it is not, then it would be drawn by Viaplana.

These rapid and ungainly sketches are neither projects nor buildings. It is not possible to identify in them the vanishing point that is hidden behind the building, and therefore, it is impossible to read a structured spatial system. The only hints that can be identified are those of the edges of the building itself, which soar into the sky as if it wants to dissolve the solid in the air. These monumental pieces rise above the viewer emphasizing the stony character of the building, then dissolve in the air. These sketches do not represent buildings or projects, even if they are associated with well-described plans and sections. These sketches represent pure solids that do not belong to any typology or system of relations. They are intended to be dissolved in the air.

In these perspectives, Miralles' capacity to develop the projects from the given materials is no longer seen. The few perspectives made by Miralles describe many details of the intrinsic qualities of the original project (Figs. 12–14).

This process leads to perspectives that are made for the project, Plaça dels Països Catalans, which should be read as pictorial representations made after the project was defined. In those perspectives, Miralles uses a number of indicators such as dotted or dashed lines, which contribute to the creation of a drawing that suggests an external source to which the architect must pay full attention. The project of the square is made of solids and voids that form a closed system, like the whole concept of perspective from Miralles' youth. The plaza is a square, closed around its perimeter, and the perspectives do not make any effort to stay closed. The project identifies completely with perspectives, and vice versa. This happens with very careful views of reality that are predetermined with great precision. Miralles' perspectives do not give any margin that allows the project to go beyond the strict data given for the project. In the Plaça dels Països Catalans, there is a clear identification of the project with the drawings by Miralles. This suggests that the plaza project has some qualities derived from the range of perspectives made earlier by Miralles. The solids, always in the flanks, favor the tangential axis of vision. Solids are in turn the void: that is to say that in the plaza there are no solids. The vanishing points maintain their exact positions, and the lines of the box are closed by the boundary of the pavement; the project itself looks like an earlier perspective by Miralles and is now represented by views endowed with the pictorial qualities of a canvas.

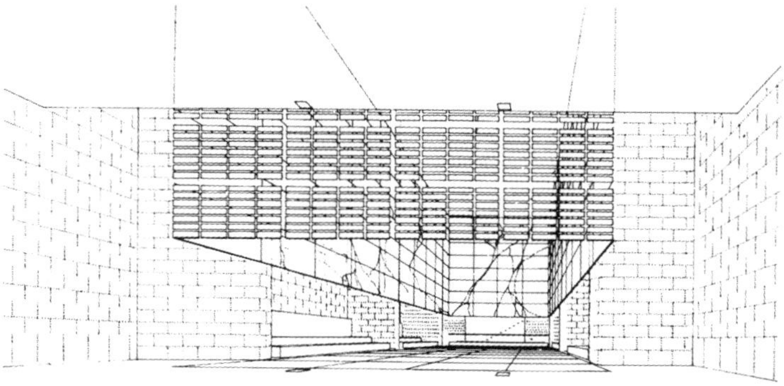

12. Competition for the new headquarters of the Regional Government of La Rioja, Logroño, 1984. Helio Piñón, Albert Viaplana, Enric Miralles (contributor).

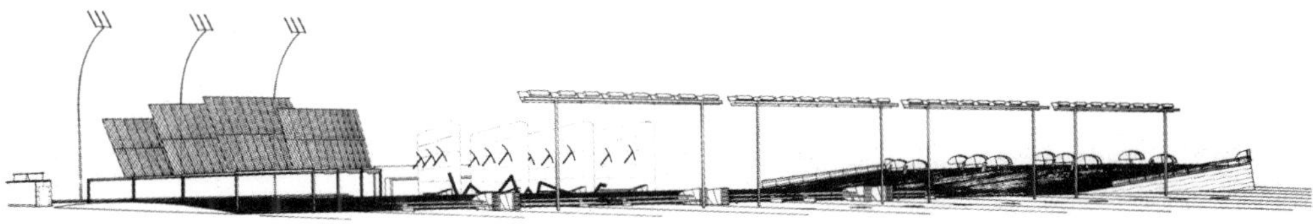

13. Square Project Barangé, Granollers, 1982–1997. The square is represented as an isolated object. Helio Piñón, Albert Viaplana, Enric Miralles (contributor).

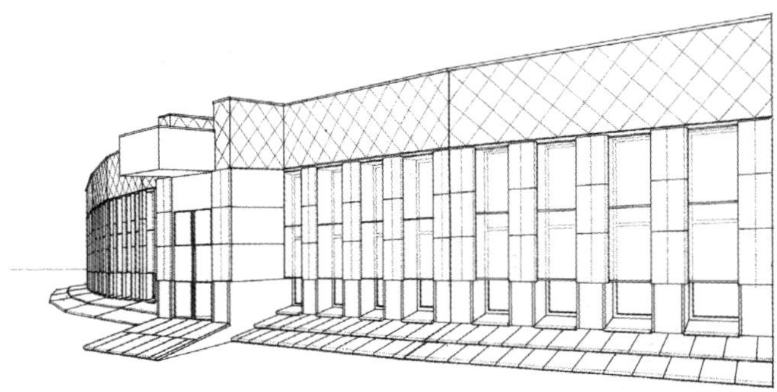

14. Draft Primary Health Care Centre, Sant Hipòlit of Voltregà, Barcelona, 1984–1986. A closed perspective of the building on the right flank of the viewing axis. Helio Piñón, Albert Viaplana, Enric Miralles (contributor).

This investigation can be extended to analyze the first projects undertaken by Enric Miralles and Carme Pinós in 1983.[9] In these early projects, solids that bypass the direction of the view are already common to the definition of the competition building object. This does not renounce the quality of the solid, which is working on a more general system. However, most characteristic of these early projects is that they refer to a previous work developed in plan and section, not just the material given for the competition. The plan and section drawings are precisely the representation in which Miralles and Pinós view the entire project. It is no longer possible to talk about perspectives as other projects. The pictorial representations speak of the thought itself, where the tricks of the drawing remind us of the Plaça dels Països Catalans perspectives. Everything is working to create a frame that resembles the qualities of a canvas rather than the idea of a project.

These are the principle features of the perspectives emerging from the Miralles Pinós studio in 1983 and have nothing to do with the projective quality of the perspectives from Miralles' youth, where the space of the drawing and the arrangement of the solids and voids were the real act of creation. These solids and voids remain in the projects undertaken after 1983, and they will make Miralles the architect who transformed the landscape into a multitude of empty solids and solid voids, endowed with precise boundaries, within which fit the pre-existing situation like dreams, all combined and mixed, forming a single runaway vision (Figs. 15, 16).

Notes

1. Tagliabue, Benedetta (a cura di), *Enric Miralles. Operate e Progetti*, Electa, Milano, 1996, under "Le prospettive," 27–36. Trad. Enric Miralles: cast. Complete work, Electa Spain, Madrid-Milan, 1996.
2. "Piñón Helio/Albert Viaplana: 4 competitions 1974–1977," in *Janus Architecture No.48*, June 1977, 21–48.
3. The drawings for the Plaça dels Països Catalans, Barcelona have been published on numerous occasions. They were published for the first time in *Architectures Bis No. 45*, December 1983, 2–15.
4. Miralles, Enric, "Things Seen and Right to Left (Without Glasses)," 1987. Many of these drawings were also published in the doctoral thesis of Albert Viaplana, "Architecture of Experience," 1980 and later in the monograph *Viaplana/Piñón Work*, Col.legi d'Arquitectes de Catalunya, Barcelona, 1996.
5. The most comprehensive collection of drawings for projects can be found in *James Stirling, Buildings and Projects 1950–1974*. John Jacobus (Introduction), layout by Leon Krier and James Stirling (Barcelona: Gustavo Gili, 1982).
6. *Quaderns d'Architecture and Urbanism n°156*, January-February-March 1983, 10–13.
7. *Quaderns d'Architecture and Urbanism n°163*, October-November-December, 1984, 64–97.
8. GAUSA, Manuel, "La Torre d'Einstein. A inici i end. 1914–1921," in *Quaderns d'Architecture and Urbanism n°163*, October-November-December, 1984, 50–55.
9. Tagliabue, Benedetta (a cura di), *Enric Miralles. Operate e Progetti*, op. cit., 37.

15. Draft Plaça dels Països Catalans, Barcelona, 1981–1983. Closed perspective that includes a portion of the square and some isolated outside elements. Helio Piñón, Albert Viaplana, Enric Miralles (contributor).

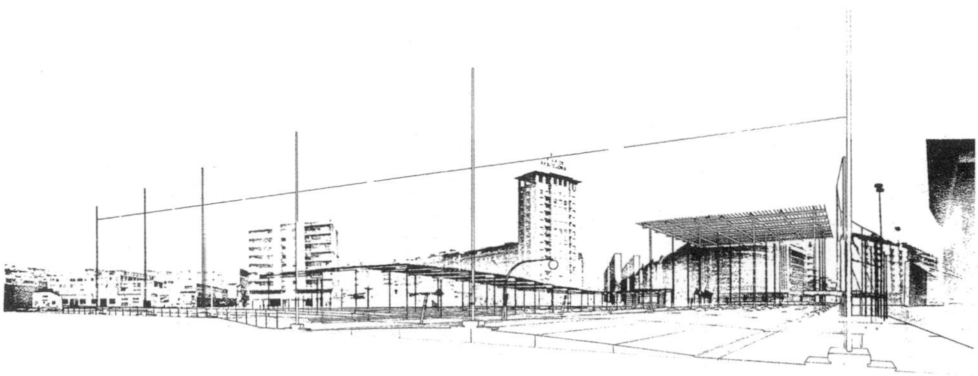

16. Draft Plaça dels Països Catalans, Barcelona, 1981–1983. The whole square, isolated and superimposed on pre-existing background in burnt photograph. Helio Piñón, Albert Viaplana, Enric Miralles (contributor).

Requiem for the Modern Plan

Peter Buchanan

1. Miralles Pinós, plan drawing Archery Pavilion, 1992 Olympics, Barcelona.

TIR AMB ARC.
ENTRENAMENT.
PLANTA ZENITAL.
E. 1/50.

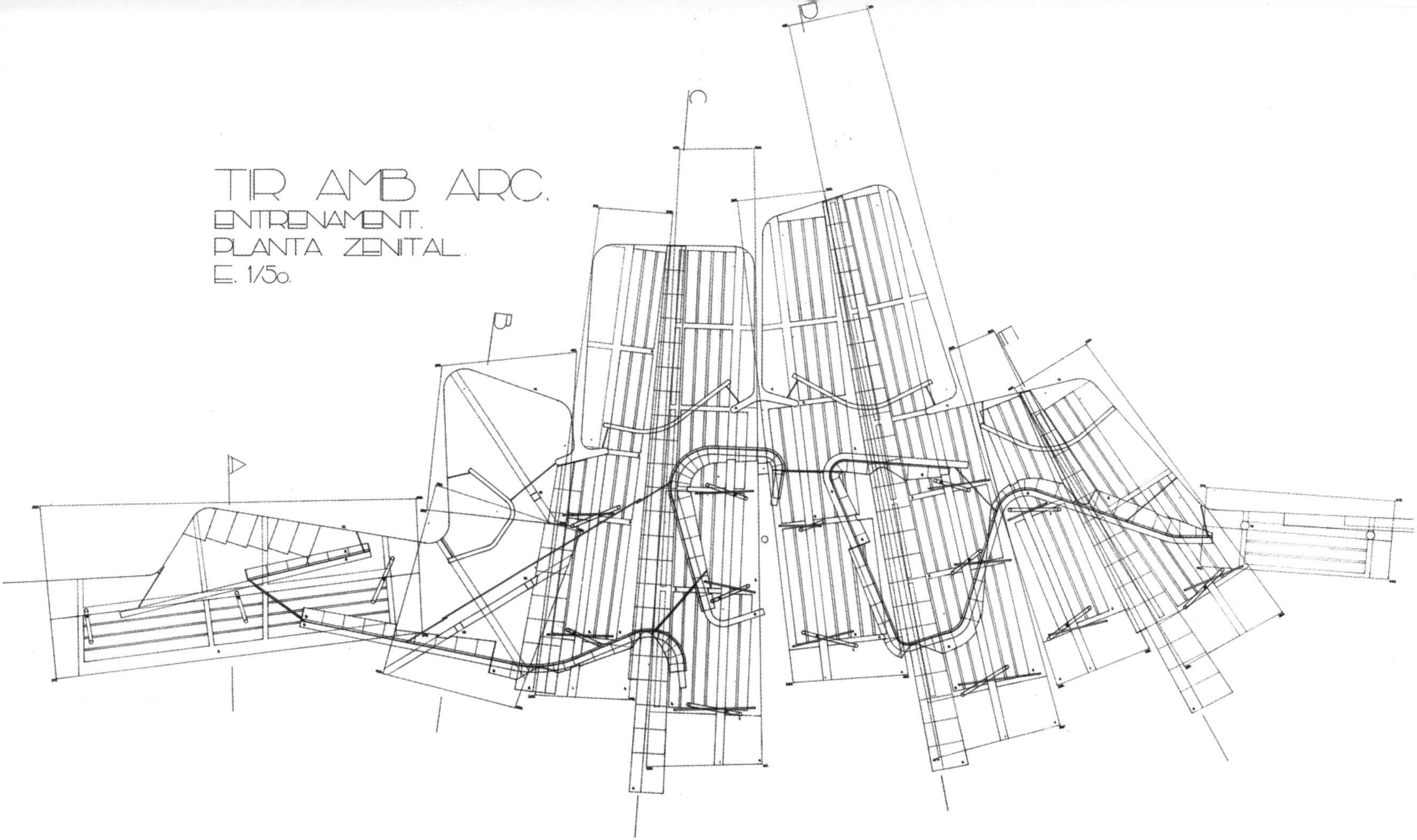

The first person ever to write about Enric Miralles, whose work provokes this rather nostalgic lecture, was me. The nostalgia stems from what I was recalling when preparing it: firstly, Enric, a friend I met thirty years ago, and secondly—because this was for a student audience—those things that had preoccupied me at architectural school—favorite designs that would then influence me when I started building. Now you may ask: "Why should we look at such old stuff?" Well actually, that was the period when crafting "the plan" reached its apogee—the 1950s and '60s—and since then, our attention to the plan and skill at handling it has steadily deteriorated. This started long before the advent of CAD, which certainly contributed to this deterioration, because the good plan is carefully crafted through continuous resketching. You draw, and redraw, and redraw until it has this effortless quality. The big complaint of almost every older architect is that today, young architects move on to the computer too quickly, and so you don't get this crafted quality. There's something magical about drawing on paper, the friction of the pen or pencil moving on it, and of letting your fingers do the thinking. You draw something and think it's pretty good, and then you just keep redrawing and somehow your fingers improve it, in an almost unconscious process. And then your conscious mind kicks in: "Ah yes, that's it, much better." That is something you don't find very often any more. Enric was a compulsive re-drawer, although often the criteria by which he judged one version better than the other was a mystery to everyone but Enric.

Why were we so fascinated with Enric? This was a time when most architecture schools were wrapped up in facile postmodernism, tacking pediments and porticoes onto banal designs or churning out boring Neo-Rationalist restatements of mutely stripped local typology. It was also the heyday of "paper architecture"—all these drawn fantasies—often unbuildable and usually illustrating quite crazy scenarios and theories, all legitimated by relativist postmodern theory in which one concept or scenario was considered as valid as any other.

By contrast, Spanish architecture was a breath of fresh air. It was rooted in construction and the rejuvenation of the rundown public realm, done with "real" materials on frugal budgets—not the realm of fantasy at all. The Spanish were revivifying the modern vocabulary, which elsewhere had been (temporarily) given up on. Spain went in a contrary direction, developing an architectural poetry by stripping down and collaging the vocabulary of modernity. So what might elsewhere have been a semicircle–on a stair landing, say–would instead be a slightly curved slashing arc. It was an expressively suggestive, often gestural, paring down of the modern vocabulary. And while the rest of Europe was building with immense technical expertise to produce high-performance buildings constructed of many different layers (skin, waterproofing, insulation, structure)–as in America too–Spain was building in a still primitive fashion with solid traditional materials: brick and stone, wood and steel, and raw concrete. These buildings are really beautiful, reassuringly solid and tactile, but would not pass any of the codes in the rest of Europe. The dissonance between spare modern forms and traditional construction gave an aesthetic frisson: it was glorious low-tech in the heyday of high-tech.

What I see in Enric is that he took the tired language of modern architecture and fragmented it into figural elements in dynamically disjointed, precariously poised compositions, pushing the language to an extreme that brought it alive again–almost in a desperate last act. These dynamically fragmented compositions arrested your attention and demanded that you–the viewer or user as you move around, with your eyes alone or physically–pull them together and actively unify them into a whole. Although we did not realize it then, in retrospect, Enric was an architect closing an era rather than opening a new one: an architect kicking new life into what was becoming a tired modern architecture. This was clear in his compositional approach generally, including that of the plan, its generator.

The Plan

So I thought it would be apposite to revisit the modern plan, the very heart of modern architecture. Not just modern architecture, but modernity too, which started with the Renaissance, is clearly coming to an end, although it is not absolutely clear what's emerging to replace it. Yet modern architecture leaves a great gift to any future architecture–what should be its lasting legacy–the modern plan and how we understood it.

It may seem rather extreme to title this talk "Requiem for the Modern Plan," because we still design plans. But much of what was important to us when I studied in the 1960s, including how we understood and crafted the plan–which was the central focus of the architect's attention through the 1930s, '40s, '50s, and '60s–is now largely lost. As already mentioned, shaping the plan, then architecture's core craft, is a reiterative process. You sketch something, look at and criticize it, improve it, and keep improving and polishing it until it has a mix of requisite variety and easy flow, an economy and sense of rightness. Eventually you arrive at something that seems effortless but actually does many, many things. That's the art or craft of architecture–to achieve something, through patient honing and synthesis, which in the end just looks inevitable, as if everything just fell into place.

But this appreciation of the plan and its patient crafting has largely disappeared after going downhill from the end of the sixties. So Enric's attempt to reinvigorate modern architecture is, in retrospect, a sunset effect–an evocative expression coined by Marshall McLuhan for the final flare up of a passing trend or era. He describes how at the end of an era you get a caricatured exaggeration of only aspects of that waning epoch–like the sunset marking the fading day. That is what we're seeing at the moment: much contemporary architecture, particularly what gets published, is sunset effects. What you see in the magazines has nothing to do with the future–instead, these projects are saying goodbye to modernity.

In an academic meeting about 15 years ago, I blurted out (without having really considered the matter) that the plan had ceased to be an issue in architecture and its education. To my surprise, the professors all just agreed. Then in a meeting this week with professors from all over the world discussing forming a new architecture school in London, the consensus was, "The plan? Nobody teaches the plan anymore." It's quite a shocking statement.

The modern plan is really about relationships, not just between functions/activities and what is outside (spaces, views, solar orientation), but between the building and we humans. Modern architecture discarded much of the essential repertoire of architecture–the whole symbolic dimension–the rhetorical forms that helped us read and relate to it. The long strip window, for instance, does not reflect the human body the same way the vertical window does. Many people, quite rightly, found modern architecture too abstract, too alienating, which meant that there was this distancing effect. All that was left for architects seeking to reassert some kind of relationship with people was the crafting of the plan.

We now see even this as insufficient and realize that architecture, like us too, needs to reconnect with the world around. Since the advent of cities, and particularly since the Renaissance (and even more so since the Enlightenment and reaching an the current obsession with virtual reality), we have increasingly separated ourselves from each other and from the world. This disconnect has degraded the world and now threatens our continuing comfortable existence. This is why modernity is over—crises of unsustainability and environmental degradation, amongst others, are closing the modern era that is inherently, in many ways and utterly so, unsustainable—which also means architecture must again go through a big shift. How do we get back to a more complete architecture after this age of reductionism and extreme separation?

In partial compensation for this alienation, at least in the interior of buildings, a key discipline in shaping the modern plan was the art of choreography. By that I mean the plan doesn't just bring functions into convenient relationship. It also shapes the way you move between these functions, and so how you experience and engage with the building—both its fabric and its various uses that put on a show or ensures privacy for, as well as what you see and how you are seen. This experiential dimension goes far beyond convenient functioning, although its purpose was to enhance function. The choreography also contributed to the meaning of the uses, denoting which were central and communal spaces and which more removed and private or sacred.

Another thing now forgotten is the concomitant discipline. Even the most fluid of the great modern plans is highly disciplined in its precise responses to accommodating (even encouraging) function, guiding circulation flow, opening up to unfolding views,

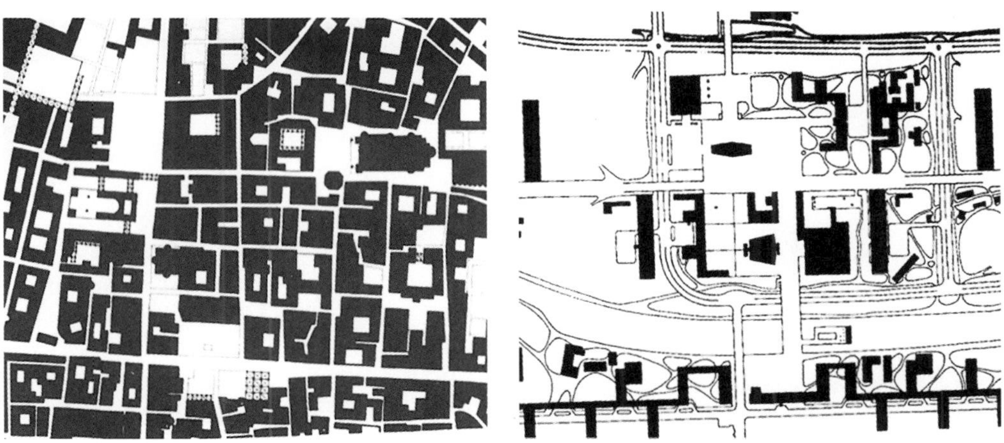

2. Typical Renaissance urban plan and modernist urban plan.

and so on (Figs. 1, 2). To talk about the plan, we also need to talk about structure and section. Structure is important because a free plan could become quite chaotic without the counterbalancing disciplined logic asserted by the structural solution and its organization. This also helps you understand and relate to the building. It is the mediator between you and the building. In Britain, this key collaboration continues today with engineers as design partners with the architect in the leading-edge offices; architects and engineers sit as equals at the table as codesigners. But in other parts of the world and lesser offices, the relationship is sequential rather than simultaneous; the architect draws something, and then the engineer really just really makes it stand up rather than helping shape its essential logic. (Think of the CCTV building in China, or the work of Zaha Hadid and Frank Gehry!)

Historical Perspective

The carefully crafted plan, by which architects once judged another's skill, is now treated by many as a relatively minor aspect of architecture, subordinate to such things as creating exciting forms, displaying technical expertise, and so on. To understand why the plan once assumed such preeminence, and why it has now lost this, we need to adopt the larger temporal perspective of history, a very simplified version of which follows.

3. Traditional community laundry in rural France.

Prior to the era of big cities, our relationship to buildings was very direct. The raw materials they were made of were visibly evident as was the presence of the hand that worked them. You related to such buildings in the most direct and unmediated way; empathetically, you could feel the structures, the loads they carried, and the forces they resisted. This is particularly true inside humble traditional buildings like the beautiful historic communal laundries of rural France (Fig. 3).

As cities grew and culture became more complex, so did the repertoire of ways in which architecture–and its various symbolic devices–

communicated and sought relationships with us. A particularly vivid example is through the recognizable anthropomorphism of church plans based on the crucifix and the human body. The structure/construction of a Gothic cathedral is also immediately legible and together with the light, it evokes a powerfully empathic response, enhanced by the multiple narratives told by iconography, sculpture, and other ornament. These were just some of the many ways that premodern architecture sought a relationship with us, the buildings, and the city around. The buildings, though usually quite simple in plan because of all these elements, acquired a presence and helped them relate to people and to each other. The State Capitol in Sacramento, California (Fig. 4), displays a full rhetorical repertoire of premodern architecture. The building commands space around with rhetorical elements that potently enhance its presence and also helps us relate to and read it. These are design devices modern architecture discarded as meaninglessly obsolete and irrelevant.

4. State capitol in Sacramento, California, 1874.

In some cases, the transition between premodern and modern, and the concomitant abstraction of forms and finishes, can be found in the works of a single architect. Compare Villa Fallet and Villa Savoye, both by the same architect in different phases of his career: Fallet by Charles Eduard Jeanneret, 1906–07, and Savoye by Le Corbusier, 1928–31. Fallet is protomodern Arts and Crafts; Savoye full-blown modern Purism or International Style. Solidly robust and rooted, Fallet has a broad palette of materials communicating decorum and how close you come to its surfaces. The forms and materials also connect the building with the earth, from which the stone base rises, and with the sky to which the roof rises and from which falls the rain it guides down to earth, as well as with the surrounding nature of conifers from which its ornament is derived. Pallidly frail and hovering Savoye, by contrast, has a very limited palette of materials, with the same materials and finishes inside and out.

It hovers above, aloof and disengaged from nature. What caused, or permitted, the transition in architectural vocabulary from premodern to modern? Architectural history lessons may cite the invention of plate glass, concrete, steel . . . but actually it was cheap fossil fuels, particularly oil. The modern building is stupendously wasteful of energy, not least to heat and cool its spaces in their thin enclosures. And at every level, it is made of oil derivatives–from the waterproofing of the flat roofs to all the gaskets and sealants. So another reason why modern architecture is in transition is because the oil era is waning.

5. Charles Eduard Jeanneret, Villa Fallet, 1906–07.

6. Le Corbusier, Villa Savoye, 1928–31.

But the energy profligacy and disengagement with nature are not the only reasons modern architecture is inherently unsustainable. Look again at Villa Fallet and Villa Savoye (Figs. 5, 6). Fallet is a cultural artifact, but Savoye has stripped away all cultural allusions to be a "machine to live in." This is part of a more general devaluing of culture that was intrinsic to the modern mindset. At first, when the clutter of classical motifs and other ornament was swept away, this seemed hugely liberating–free from the accumulated mumbo-jumbo of history. Now we are beginning to see the downsides. Modern architecture produced functional devices, of value only while useful and obsolete thereafter: servants of subservient status to us. A premodern building is completely different, more equal to us in status. As a cultural artifact, of lasting value independent of its use, it is a mediator relating us to the larger world of culture and to history in which it is rooted and to the future which it addresses. Mediating between the inhabitants and that culture, it also connects to them to their ancestors and descendants. The mindset informing premodern architecture is thus the antithesis of the hyperindividualism, sense of separateness, and short-termism underlying modernity.

Achieving sustainability will require the rebirth of culture, one of the most major collective challenges we face, and so also the resurrection of the cultural dimension of architecture as one of the forces regenerating it. We have to reconnect with culture's larger vision of our place in the world, and so of responsibility to and relationship with it, which modern architecture simply couldn't do.

The Quadrants

To get some perspective on all this, we need to adopt a larger framework for thinking, one more inclusive yet also more rigorous than is typical. Fortunately, this is readily available in the form of the All Quadrant, All Level (AQAL) diagram of Integral Theory as developed by Ken Wilber (Fig. 7). This provides a framework or matrix with which to see the relationships between, and synthesize, what are today disparate and unrelated fields of knowledge. Because of its unfamiliar nomenclature, this four-quadrant diagram seems at first to be dauntingly arcane and complex. Yet once understood, the schema is very simple, yet stupendously useful and mind-blowingly rich in the many insights it offers, including into the transitions between and characteristics of different eras.

Two cross-axes define the AQAL quadrants: the upper part of the vertical axis marking the realm of the individual and the lower part that of the collective. The left part of the horizontal axis marks the realm of interiors or the subjective, and the right part that of exteriors or the objective. The Upper Left quadrant (UL) is thus interior-individual, the realm of the subjective, of psychology and intentionality, of experience and unmediated aesthetic response. The Lower Left quadrant (LL) is interior-collective, the intersubjective realm of culture and symbolism, meaning and morals. The Upper Right quadrant (UR) is exterior-individual, the objective realm of observed behavior and of object-hood, whether of biological characteristics or of form, matter, construction, and so on. The Lower Right quadrant (LR) is exterior-collective, the interobjective realm of systems, be they ecological, economic, technical, social, or whatever. The quadrants thus also correspond to the pronouns: I (UL), We (LL), It (UR), and Its (indicating plural, LR).

Bisecting each quadrant is a diagonal line marking the levels of complexity or development within each, which rise with distance from the crossing of the axes. A key insight is that a rise in level in one quadrant is matched by rises in the other quadrants. Modernity lost sight of the fundamental interrelatedness of phenomena in the various quadrants.

Until the Renaissance, all four quadrants were understood as interrelated and equally important. But with the rise of increasingly powerful and useful sciences, only the right quadrants came to be seen as real and important, and so they shaped and dominated our understanding of reality. This explains a lot about why our relationships with all aspects of the world have deteriorated: why we've become more separate from them and each other. An essential aspect of modernity is the pervasive fragmentation into different disciplines and specializations, and the current extreme where each quadrant sees itself as having an exclusive purchase on the truth–what Wilber has aptly called Quadrant Absolutism. A once integrated reality has fragmented to leave us fractious and alienated from a larger, unified reality.

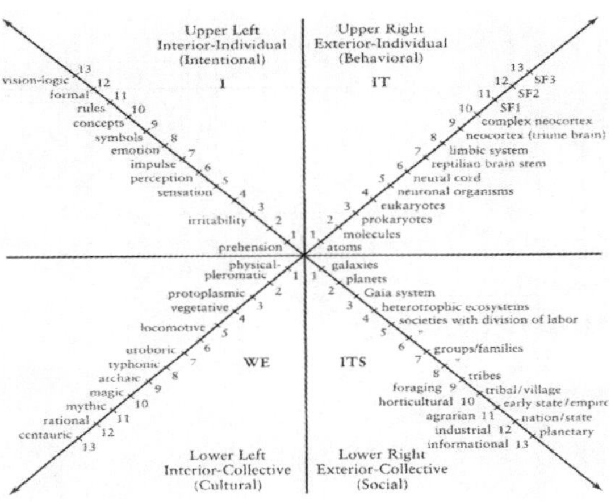

7. Ken Wilber, All Quadrant, All Level (AQAL) diagram of Integral theory in *A Theory of Everything,* 2001.

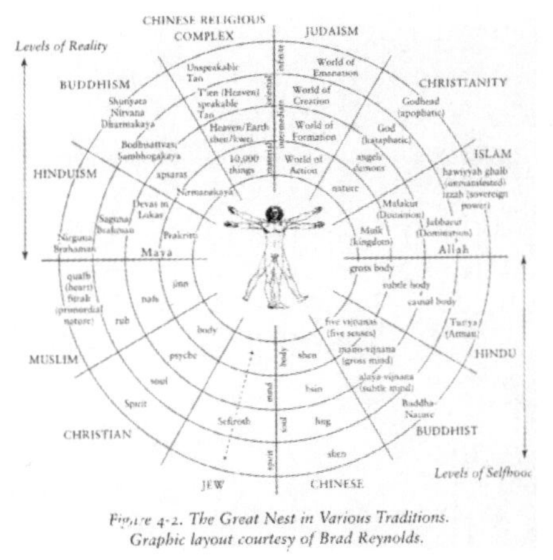

8. Ken Wilber, "The Great Nest in Various Traditions" in *A Theory of Everything,* 2001.

Before modernity, all cultures understood reality as what's called the "Great Nest of Being"–nested levels of reality (Fig. 8). This gave a comforting sense of organic unity, but also limited the power of our thought as we could not explore in-depth matters related to one quadrant only without involving others of the nested layers. For instance, Galileo thought he was exploring matter and physics, but as far as the Church was concerned, he was talking also about theology. So science and modern thinking couldn't develop until we broke from this model. All premodern cultures, without exception, subscribed to this nested view of the world.

The crucial move to modernity was to divide the totality of this organic unity, now encapsulated in the four quadrants, into three different fields: the Beautiful (art/self and consciousness), the Good (morals/culture and world view), and the True (science/behavioral and social systems). This differentiation was initially hugely useful–the essential step to giving modern thinking its power to explore and understand and, eventually seek control over, the world. The problem was that with time, these fields became too independent of each other; so differentiation became disassociation as these fields stopped speaking to, and even became unaware of, each other.

Modern architecture and its notion of function are nearly completely concerned with the right hand quadrants of the True--science and rationality. This assumes that everything is amenable to, and can be fully understood by, detached observation (hence vision becomes the dominant, and distancing, sense), measurement, and reductive analysis. The right hand quadrants privilege objective over subjective, quantitative over qualitative, abstract over experimental, and doing over being. So modernity emphasized standard of living rather than quality of life. There was a concern with aesthetics but a very reduced notion of aesthetics. Pushed to its extreme, we find urban plans like Ludwig Hilberseimer's, the ultimate in modernity's rational reductionist urbanism and architecture, an inhuman vision of the city and buildings shaped around such objective factors as ease of construction and circulation, ideal orientation, sun angles, and so on (Fig. 9).

To achieve a sustainable culture, we have to recover the subjective, inner dimensions of psychology and culture. Until we talk about the environmental crisis in a way that is also about what it means to our lived experience, people will not get excited enough to deal with the environmental issues such as energy conservation. Only once we emphasize such things as an enhanced quality of life and greater meaning invested in our lives and where we live them–all of the left quadrant issues–will we make breakthroughs in the necessary commitment and cooperation.

9. Ludwig Hilberseimer, "Vertical City," 1924.

If we focus on the long-term, including its effects on quality of life, the benefits of green architecture are obvious. Yet sustainable architecture has been slow to take hold. Already in the 1960s, we knew there was a mounting environmental crisis and that profound changes in attitudes and action were required. Already in the previous decade, Buckminster Fuller had said that there's only one legitimate use for fossil fuels, which he described as "a one-time evolutionary gift," and that's to create the means for harvesting what we now call renewables. The central premise underlying science, and so modernity, is that there is an objective reality independent of us. Premodern thinkers would never think that they were isolated from the world–for them, if you did not perform your religious rituals, the sun wouldn't come up tomorrow.

Another central problem with modern architecture is that it does not result in good cities. Instead, the fabric of the city fragmented into isolated buildings, into monofunctional destinations where you acted out limited protocols (worker, shopper, parent, etc.), rather than being known in your totality–as is necessary to gain self-knowledge and maturity. The modern city has been described by sociologists as a machine for not growing up, for evading maturity. Again, another reason the modern era is over is that it is necessary for us now to become adults–to stop being adolescents and start taking responsibility for the world around us, which is difficult in a modern city, yet essential to achieving sustainability.

Underpinning modernity was of course Newtonian science–the notion of a clockwork universe, dead and meaningless. A hundred years ago, the leading edge of science moved away from that vision of the dead and mechanical universe, but architecture is still catching up. Instead, science now sees us as living in a creative quantum universe that is constantly being reborn, which once absorbed cognitively will result in a very different architecture. Walking down a traditional classical street–in Italy, say–late at night when empty, the architecture still conveys the sense that it is full of life. The modern street of stripped and abstract buildings, when no one is there, is just a dead husk. We can't relate to it. It doesn't tell us who we are as human beings. It's a lifeless machine exactly expressive of the Newtonian world view.

Modern architecture is associated with functionalism; in fact, functionalism is a late eighteenth- and nineteenth-century idea (Fig. 10). Modern architecture was in part a reaction to this strict functionalism, which originated particularly in prison and hospital design–hence also the associated notion that architecture can improve

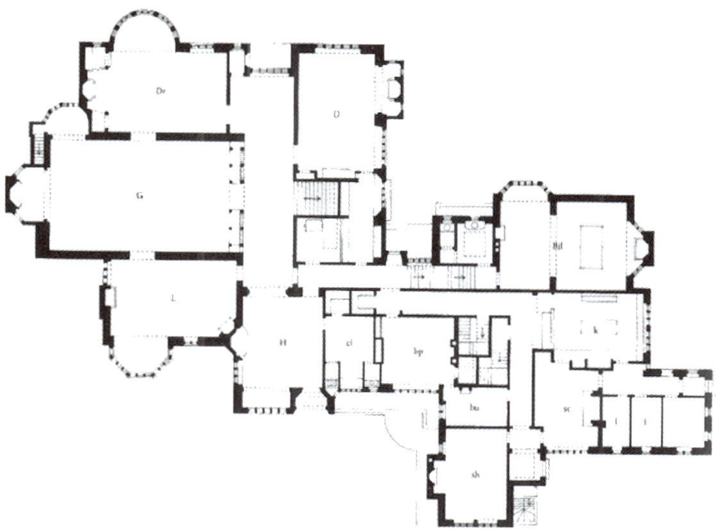

10. Nineteenth-century Functionalist plan, forerunner of the free plan.

and help heal people. In later functionalist plans, as in a nineteenth-century Arts and Crafts, Victorian-era house, each room is shaped around function and thus has an independent identity, the clearly articulated rooms organized along independently expressed circulation passages. Modernity was not as constraining as this, although it retained the notion that how you use a building is a right quadrant concern, and so neglected left quadrant concerns, such as with dwelling and inhabitation. It is like behaviorism in psychology where you understand things by looking at them from the outside. When you deal with inner quadrants, you ask the person what they're experiencing. You are not only concerned with what they're doing; you are also concerned with how they're making meaning and what is going on inside of them. In architecture, early functionalism was a key step towards a reductionist modernity.

Le Corbusier's ingenious plans of 13-square-meters per inhabitant in the book *The Radiant City* influenced me very much in my early years as an architect. In a whole series of plans for different numbers of occupants, those parts of the apartment that are inevitably immovable are static fixes, and the rest of the space is functionally fluid and divided by sliding partitions or furniture. The children's bedrooms are partitioned with sliding doors so the front play/study part can open up to flow into the living and dining area. Corbusier was squeezing the maximum use out of a minimum area. When starting to build houses, the clients you get can't afford much space, so you learn from these kinds of plans how to squeeze maximum functionality into limited space.

Maison Citrohan by Le Courbusier is a mass reproducible machine for living, conceived of as a machine rather than as a cultural artifact. This type of architecture exemplifies the ideals of modern architecture–rationalist: the Citrohan is a pun, of course, on Citroen, the automobile made by the major car manufacturer. This is architecture that combines spatial generosity (the double volume living area) with tight functioning and the potential for mass manufacture (Fig. 11).

We associate postmodernity with the 1980s and 1990s, but actually that was the fourth wave of post- or antimodernity, which still persists. History and theory courses are mostly still postmodern thinking: they're highly relativistic and, for instance, reject science as "just another narrative." The first two waves of anti-or postmodernity were attempts to recover all four quadrants. If modernity is just the two right-hand quadrants, the first anti- or postmodernist movements, Idealism and Romanticism, were attempts to recover the two left quadrants as well. It is no coincidence that the

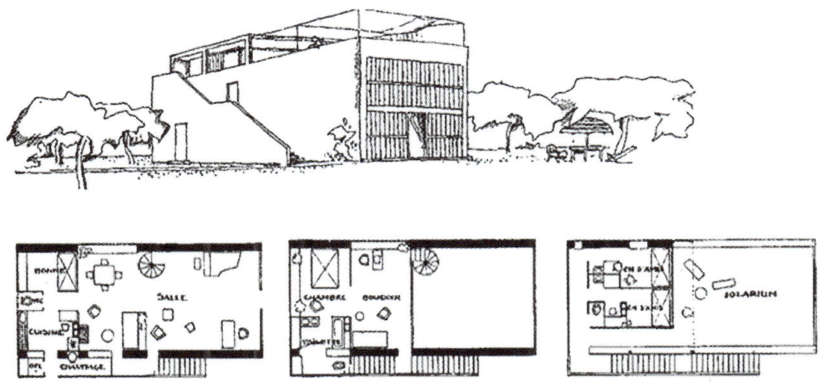

11. Le Corbusier, Mason Citrohan, a mass reproducible machine for living, 1920.

greatest modernist architects came out of Romanticism as much as modernism. Frank Lloyd Wright was a Romantic, rooted in the American Transcendentalists, amongst others things. My professors would say, "Ignore Wright, he's just a Romantic." But for me, that's what's so great about him.

So the third wave of postmodernists was actually the greatest of the modernists: Stravinsky, T.S. Elliot, Frank Lloyd Wright, Le Corbusier, Aalto—all of them antimodernists as much as modernists. That is what gives their work the power that continues to command our attention. All were trying to operate from all four quadrants, in part dismayed by the modernity's rejection of the sacred and the spiritual.

With Frank Lloyd Wright's roots in Romanticism (as were some of Le Corbusier's), he was concerned as much with matters of spirit and place as with the machine and its possibilities. So today he seems as much antimodern as modern. Yet he was concerned with creating homes for a new way of life, particularly apposite to modern America, as in the Usonian house. Consider the First Jacobs House (Fig. 12) where the house and setting interlock in a choreographed contrast of centrifugal flow and centripetal rootedness. Although laid out on a rectilinear grid that disciplines the clearly revealed construction, the choreographed diagonal flow gives a spaciousness while also providing intimate cozy corners. Everything is centered on the hearth, the semisacred focus of house and family, while the light timber construction organized on

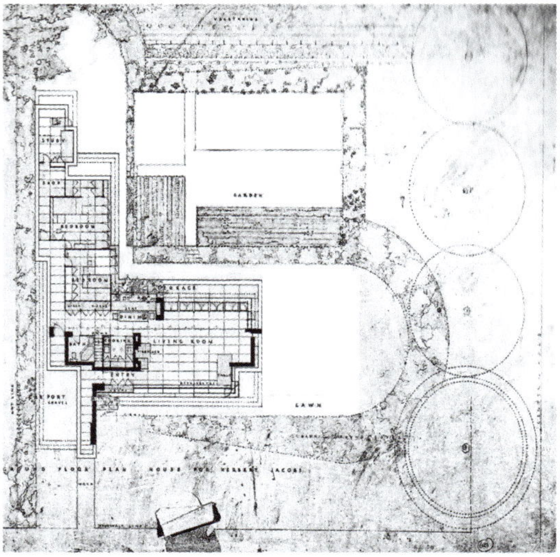

12. Frank Lloyd Wright, plan for the Hershey Jacobs house, 1936.

a strict grid is stabilized structurally and compositionally by heavier brick elements. Within its flowing spaces, clerestories bring light and ventilation into the heart of the home. Anticipating changes yet largely to happen in the American lifestyle, the house is not only designed for servantless living but also for the main rooms to be shared by parents and children, perhaps using different parts of the same rooms that are both comfortable for the solitary reader yet able to easily host large gatherings.

The Ronchamp Chapel by Le Corbusier (Fig. 13), draws on prehistoric precedent such as dolmens and is steeped in astrological and other occult symbolism (Fig. 14). Here one of the greatest modern architects is again revealed as an antimodern because of his concerns with place, the spiritual, eternal values, and so on. It's impossible when you start studying Le Corbusier to think of him as purely modern. He was concerned with and drew upon everything, including local and prehistory, as in the explicit reference to dolmens at Ronchamp and its many occult references, particularly to astrology.

The big problem with today's postmodernity is that it is merely the repressed flip side of modernity–rejecting the notion of objective reality for that of reality as just a conceptual hallucination, an arbitrary construct. Instead of trying to recover a four-quadrant approach, it has flipped from an exclusive emphasis on the right quadrants to the left quadrants only. Not a very powerful mode of thinking, it is the least interesting of the postmodernisms and effecting architectural education. In current studio work, you get asked quite early on in relation to your tentative design, "Where's your concept?" Elevating concept over craft, this is postmodern thinking. But experienced architects know you don't start with an imposed concept; instead, the concept will emerge slowly as you're working on and starting to understand the project. Here, idea emerges from reality, rather than is imposed upon it.

13. Le Corbusier, Ronchamp Chapel, 1954.

14. Ancient dolmen, Neolithic (4000–3000 BCE)

The Plan in Action

Oscar Niemeyer and Alvar Aalto, modernist masters of a period slightly after Wright and Corbusier, provide very precise and beautifully choreographed examples of plans from the 1950s–such as an unbuilt building by Niemeyer and two built works by Aalto. I once wrote about seven different attitudes to functionalism–the first two buildings exemplify two of my categories: emancipatory functionalism and participatory functionalism. The goal of crafting the plan is to do enough to suggest and encourage an activity, but not so much as to over define it. You can do too little, as Mies van der Rohe does for instance, or you can do too much so the plan becomes a constraining straight-jacket, as in houses by Scharoun.

The unbuilt Niemeyer plan is for Yacht Club in Rio de Janeiro (Fig. 15). The main "promenade" is on a slight diagonal from where you enter to look down through a slot to the boat slips. A curved wall projects to take you by the hand, walk you past the bar, where invited to talk with friends at the café tables, and then presents you with a flourish to the main dining/dance room–"ta-da!" As students, this was a favorite because as we were struggling to create such effortless plans, and we knew just how much work went into getting something that seems so easy. All the spaces and relationships are so precisely correct, all under the single sweeping curve of the roof.

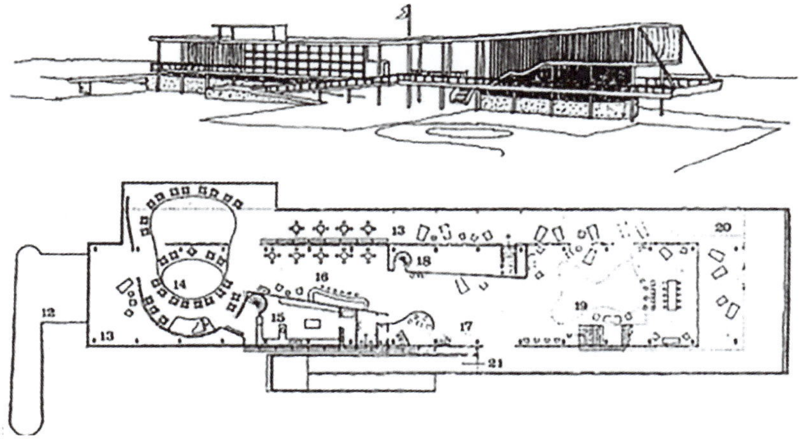

15. Oscar Niemeyer, project for a yacht club Rio de Janiero, 1945.

If the Yacht Club was for a warm climate with the breezes blowing right through it, Aalto's design for the Rovaniemi Library in Finland is for cold winters with light bouncing down from tall clerestories. If the Yacht Club is extrovert, a place for hedonism; the library is introvert, a place of contemplation and study (Fig. 16). With Aalto, you pull open the door; he never had automatically opening doors. For him, it is insulting not to shake hands with, to say hello to, the building. Entering the library, stepping onto its carpet after the clattery tiled floor of the hall, you are suddenly quiet–without consciously noticing why you are hushed. Before you is an asymmetric space, all overlooked from the control desk where the whole space and everything going on can be seen. In each lobe of the library, part of the floor is dropped, creating small, intimate spaces and all this low wall space for shelves. As you walk through the building, it seems as if you, and your movement through space, are shaping the building; at some point you put out your hand and that is where the handrail is–like everything is almost anticipating you or like you're designing the room. Particularly noticeable is how the external wall enclosing the asymmetric lobes of space seem pushed out by the forward pressure of your scanning eyes (like exhaling into a soap bubble), while the indents between these lobes reveal how the hidden structural beams are pulling inwards to shorten the span in a counter movement of inhalation. Moving into the space you almost get the sense that you're breathing it into form and life in an act of intimate reciprocation.

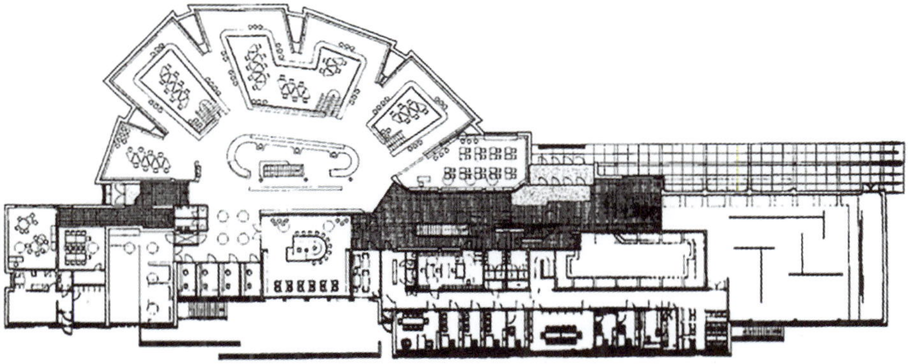

16. Alvar Aalto, plan drawing Rovaniemi Library, 1945.

This intimate engagement with the building, as if you are participating in or recreating the design, is something a number of Scandinavian architects manage to achieve, yet Aalto is probably the master. There is this wonderful relationship between you and the building, which again took constant redrawing to crystallize. If you look at Aalto's sketches, you can see how very lightly and tentatively he draws, because it takes him a long time to where he gets the form and feeling exactly right, so that they will actively engage you. When you go straight into the computer, you can't get this. This is drawing with a soft pencil on paper slowly, over and over again, until you get something that's so perfectly resolved.

Another Aalto project, the Essen Opera House (Germany) (Figs. 17, 18) designed in the 1950s, wasn't built until the 1980s. Typical of Aalto, it consists of fluidly arranged, strangely distorted, plan shapes packed inside the building volume. But when you study these buildings, you realize he's managed to make spaces that feel very big and spacious and flow with an air of inevitably from one to the other along a choreographed architectural promenade, all within a very compact envelope. The spaces forming the entry sequence of the Opera House flow generously forward in what feels inside like an enormous building, yet is relatively modestly scaled in external volume.

On entering the ground floor, to one side are wriggly long counters of the coat check moving you inexorably to stairs ahead climbing into bright light. The counters and the

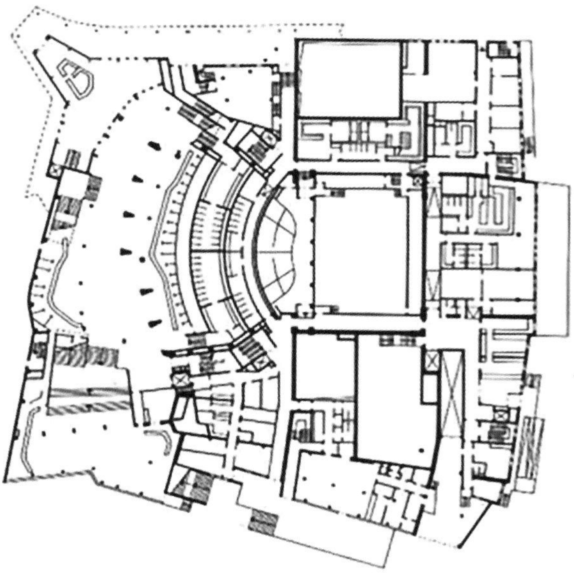

17. Alvar Aalto , Essen Opera House, Germany, 1959–88.

columns, tiled only on the side you flow past, makes you feel as if you are being guided and pushed through this building by the plan. It's quite fantastic, aided also by little details, like handrails with little inflections that talk to your body on many levels. You ascend the stairs to the bright light drawing you on. The design is full of natural metaphors–the fenestration recalling forests, while the stairs are like a broad cascade, or others at the narrow end of the foyer tumble down like a waterfall. In the evening as you come in, the setting sun comes through these tall windows in a jittery rhythm on the west, so evoking the archetypal image of the low sun of dusk flickering through a northern European conifer forest. It's very magical. The building guides you effortlessly upwards to the foyer that tapers as it guides less and less people past the auditorium entrances, from where it guides you to your different seats. The seats, front of house curtains, and side walls with curved wood slats evoking wind-bent trees in a forest, are all in a deep midnight blue, against which the white balconies stand out like moon-lit clouds. When the curtains are raised, as in a ritual process, all attention is on the bright-lit stage as if it were a campfire in a forest glade. This is the climax of a drawn out performance by the entering audience that plays out a timeless ritual procession that enhances the whole operatic event. It's a wonderfully poetic building with this exquisite plan that guides and coaxes you along.

Plans of this sophistication and precision become rare after the 1950s and '60s, killed by a number of things. One was that plans became much more generic and schematic, for logical reasons of economy and flexibility, particularly of short-term partitioning and fit outs. Plans of currently fashionable "Parametricist" designs seem

18. Alvar Aalto , Essen Opera House main lobby, Germany, 1959–88.

to return to the fluidity we have been looking at, but the correlation of form and use is at best very loose and does nothing to contribute relationship and meaning as do these plans. My criticism is not of parametric software, but its idiotic use to arbitrarily sculptural ends. All good architects also now use parametric software but to facilitate high degrees of synthesis (great architecture tends to result from the synthesis of many different forces), which allows you to explore new topologies of form bringing great economies in structure, services cladding surfaces.

A good example is the Kansai Airport by Renzo Piano Building Workshop. Piano's not really a master of the plan, but he often is a master of the section, just as he is of materials and structural elements. What he achieves is an incredible level of synthesis and distillation. With the Kansai Airport, each form and component is the way it is for many reasons. This is another highly crafted building. Drawn and redrawn, it was designed before the availability of today's sophisticated parametric software. And the design team of architects and engineers deliberately did not use even the latest generation of CAD. They actually took a relatively primitive CAD program and developed the design with it, because then they could not gloss over things, and they wanted to be clear about the reasoning behind every decision.

Here, it is the section and exposed structure that exhibits the discipline and distillation I've talked about and also elicits the sort of relationships with us users that I've ascribed to the great modern plans. Immediately on entry, the structure (in the form of a portico made of props sloping up to support the colossal main beams) welcomes you into this very big building–it has a single space more than a mile long. So Piano uses the structure to help you relate to the building and guide you through it. The structure creates an intimate relationship between little you and this vast building as well as revealing at every level how to respond to the building. The structural elements in the building are all identically curved and trimmed from the same jigs, and despite the two directional curves of the outer skin, all 90,000 stainless steel cladding panels are all identical. Each curve is the way it is for a number of reasons. For instance, the asymmetric curve of the roof over the central block actually entrains jets of air blown through the building without ductwork. It is very disciplined in its geometry—the shape is of a decelerating jet of air that also sweeps passengers forward and then down to the boarding wing.

After descending to the shopping level and then down to the boarding wing, as conducted by the main trusses, you then find yourself passed from one structural rib to the next along this one-mile-long room and towards your plane. Every element is shaped for structural efficiency—not to just make shapes. The point here is that there is nothing in this building that's not there for seven or eight reasons. This is architecture as synthesis, not shape making. And it has this quality of utter inevitability that is the hallmark of great design.

The Modern Dream

A certain modernist dream is to create buildings that, like the Kansai Terminal (Figs. 19, 20), approximate both organisms and machines, with an organic integrity and flow combined with a mechanical logic. However, in the near future, being an organism and a machine is not enough; we have to recover the notion of building as cultural artifact, to buildings that we relate to on more levels than just the structure and the plan. This is but a small step towards reconnecting with the world in many ways and on many levels, which is what the quest for sustainability is asking of us—going way beyond saving energy, cutting pollution, etc. Ultimately, sustainability is about stepping into a completely different mindset.

Before agriculture and civilization, the individual was part of the whole. In the tribal world there was little distinction between the self and the world, and the whole world was our home. Starting with agriculture, we started to sense ourselves as separate from the world, and we wrested a home for ourselves within a hostile world. And now, in the postmodern or late-modern view, this tiny reduced self feels lost, isolated, and impotent in this larger world. Rejecting the cultural dimension of architecture contributes immensely to this sense of homelessness, of being lost and

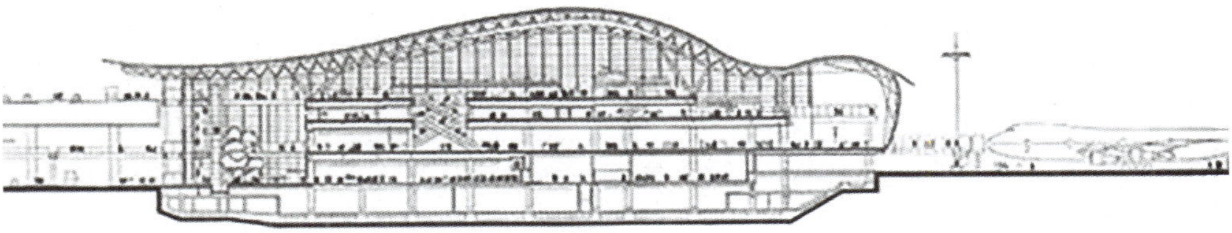

19. Renzo Piano, section Kansai Airport, Osaka, Japan, 1988–94.

20. Renzo Piano, Kansai Airport, Osaka, Japan, 1988–94.

individually powerless, all of which makes us so destructive.

By now, architects have acquired tremendous technical expertise, but we don't really know what to do with it. The reason is that we are in a phase of major cultural change, of nothing less than epochal transition. We've come to the end of modernity, but don't know what's coming next. There are people who have written about what's coming–people like Jean Gebser and Charles Eisenstein, William Irwin Thompson and Ken Wilber–but they have not yet impacted architecture, even though their ideas are incredibly pertinent to architecture. Architects need to reimagine architecture for its cultural impact rather than just for use and function. Only when we and our buildings reconnect with the world in myriad ways, recognizing and making manifest our manifold interdependencies with it, will we start to truly care for and take care of the earth again. But in moving forward to this big, more complete vision of architecture, one of our key skills to recover and incorporate (and though lost, it should be recoverable), is the art of the modern plan and how through its skilled choreography helped us to relate to the building and even to the larger world it is set in.

Drawing without Erasing

Eva Prats

1. Flores Prats studio in Barcelona.

The Line

My partner Ricardo Flores and I have been running our studio in Barcelona for 15 years. It is a small research studio–12 people–and we are growing. We try to keep a constant rhythm of research as part of the continuity of our work. Ricardo and I met in the office of Enric Miralles. I began working there first as a student and then as an architect for nine years. Ricardo came to Barcelona from Buenos Aries to do a master's degree and worked in Miralles' studio for five years. In the studio, we work on hand drawing everyday. We trust that through drawing, we can effectively develop all of our ideas.

When I started in Miralles' office, my first project was a competition for a bridge (Fig. 2). My responsibility was to draw some trees, but the way I had to draw these trees was not direct–I had to use transparent paper on top of the document. Enric instructed me to draw the lines of the trunks for each tree. I was to go with ink and draw each line little by little, and eventually, I had to find a line that linked all the trunks of the trees. I would then have Enric check the drawing to see if it was okay. It was amazing that how something that could be done very immediately would have so much thought into it. There was always a decision to make–I thought some things seemed very small, but they still needed a decision. Then there was a document that was in every project that Enric called the media tool. The tool had two uses: one was to synthesize the project, for example with the bridge it was about how many lines to draw to understand the project; and second, was a test for the eye–people doing this needed to have a good eye.

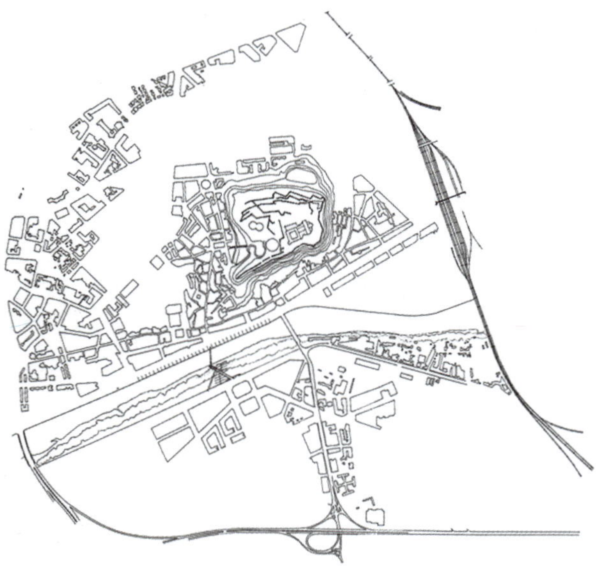

2. Plan drawing for bridge competition, 1986.

It was very intense work that we did to do for the competition. I was 20 years old at the time, and it surprised me how they could mix work and fun. It was nice in the studio, a very quiet place where I could draw. It was the kind of drawing that you would do when you were little, like nine or ten years old. In my first afternoon there, it reminded me of the times I used to draw with my brother after school when I was a child. We would spend hours in the dining room, drawing and drawing.

Of the years that I was in the office, all the work evolved around Enric's drawings, but we couldn't help but to start developing our own ideas. For me the Huesca stadium was an amazing project to work on (Fig. 3). We were trying to connect the stadium with the rest of the city and with the landscape beyond the project. My part was to make this connection. Enric drew the plan of a retaining wall, and I was to develop this drawing into a section. I had to decide how the lines would become a retaining wall and also how two paths were suspended with handrails. The challenge was to interpret and give meaning to all the different lines that he left for me on the table.

The drawings from this time were very analytical, and sometimes it was an effort to make the enclosure of the building complete. In a drawing of a window, for example, there was a geometry that needed to be maintained from section to section. I drew two large sections at the same time so one part of the window would remain constant and the other one would be changing. I remember drawing this section after reading a chapter about water in a book on architectural construction–it explained how water from rain would drop through the building and that the architect had to find a way for the water to go out and down. So through drawing and reading I figured out how to close the building. During this period I worked in the morning at the university and then in the afternoons I was in the studio–working on this window detail.

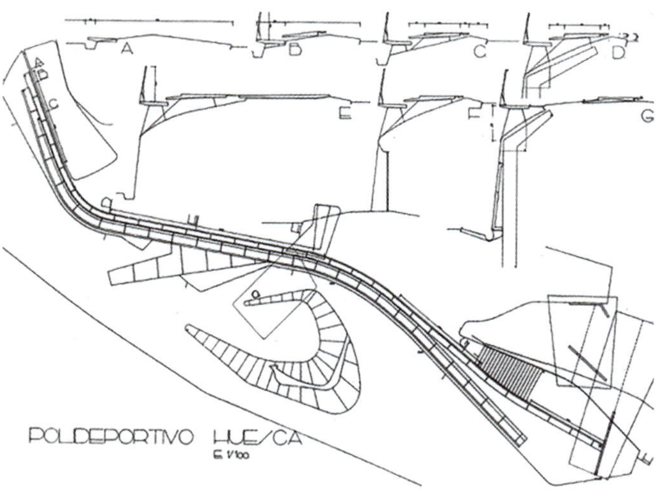

3. Plan and section details for Huesca Stadium.

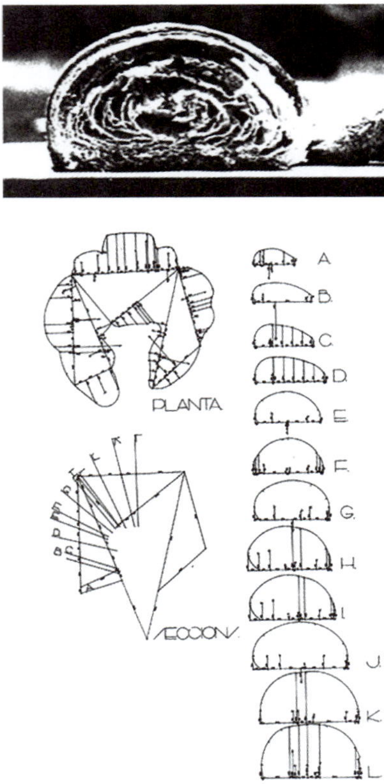

4. Plan and section drawings of a croissant.

One of the nice things about the studio was in the afternoon we would have teatime with cakes. One afternoon I had to draw the plan and section of a staircase for a civic center in Barcelona. Enric came to the table and said, "How are you doing this layout? You could layout anything with this method. You could layout a croissant." This joke about the croissant lasted a long time because he was always asking me, "Have you drawn it yet?" And I would say, "Nah, not yet." And then one day, I finally decided to draw it. (Fig. 4) I went out and bought some croissants. I purposely chose one that had very well defined sections. I started by drawing a horizontal plan, from the oval. I started with the whole croissant and then cut it and made cuts at the beginning of the section; there were three different sections produced. Using the sections of the croissant, along with the plan that I had drawn, we developed a system to develop the staircase.

The Light

My grandfather had a collection of prints by Joan Miró, his favorite was called the *Barcelona Series*. It was his favorite because it displayed humor after the tragedy of the Spanish Civil War. My grandfather had a company that made hats, but he also liked to worked with Miró–I have a photograph of them together in Miró's studio (Figs. 5a, 5b).

Miró did a piece on a Catalan farmer–it is completely distorted and transformed and has this huge head and neck, like the kind of oversized deformation present in Barcelona celebrations with large parades of people wearing big paper maché heads.

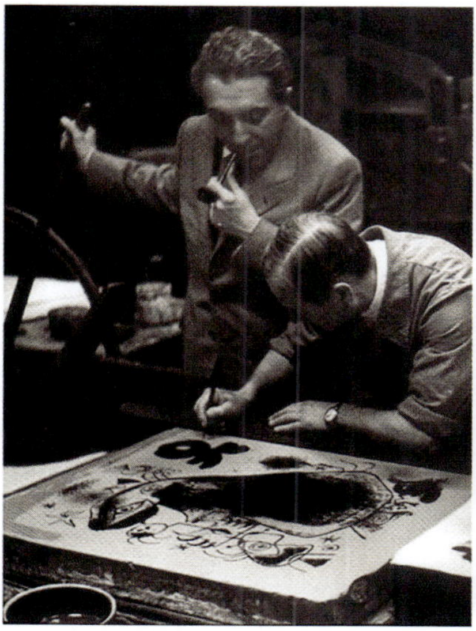

5a. Joan Prats and Joan Miró

5b. Joan Prats' apartment

Miró's piece is very much connected with that deformation. It shows a kind of pain: the mouth and nose are transformed to work together in this terrible image (Fig. 6).

The nose reminds me of Casa Batlló by Gaudí (Fig. 7), which is a transformation of an existing house. It was a two-floor house that Gaudí extended. It is interesting for all the extra work that he did inside the existing building for circulation for the doorman, for people removing the garbage, and for the people who lived there. He made an effort to get light and air into the floors and the basement of the building to enhance life on the inside. The façade was where the existing building was lightly carved; it was transformed to produce undulated shapes and to catch light early in the morning.

Gaudí collaborated with a younger architect, Josep Maria Jujol, who had the patience and artistic ability to place beautiful window panes in many colors for Gaudí. Jujol was also responsible for beautiful bench pieces at Parc Güell. At a point of intensity under the balcony, where the shadow is, there is graffiti that Gaudí made himself. For me, this is a transforming technique to relate one thing to another.

Jujol and Gaudí also worked together on the Montserrat Cathedral. They opened windows into the walls because they wanted more natural light (Fig. 8). Ricardo and

6. Drawing by Joan Miró.

7. Entrance to Casa Batlló by Gaudí.

I went past this wall every time we were on the site for an old flour windmill that we were transforming into a museum–like a huge machine that you could walk into. One day Ricardo said, "What we have been doing with the windmill plan is similar to the window in this cathedral." For the windmill, we were working between the strong light outside and the darkness inside, and we wanted to bring light inside the building so that you could see the walls and existing windows that controlled the natural light. We worked to control the light into the space like the window in the cathedral wall (Figs. 9a, 9b).

The Landscape

Three years ago, Ricardo and I finished a housing project on the outskirts of Barcelona in the old city. It was a master plan organized by Manuel Soto Morales from a competition with five different architects all working on the site. Morales' plan was to organize this edge of the city and stop it from growing. The plan was for eight buildings of 111 apartments each for low-income families of different cultures. The site is located near a park with the city at its back. It is a very aromatic landscape

8. Light opening in Montserrat Cathedral by Jujol and Gaudí.

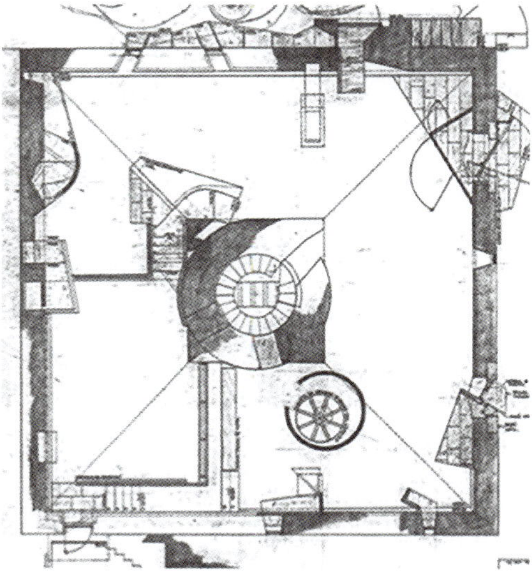

9a. Plan drawing Windmill Museum Mallorca.

9b. Plan and sections drawing Windmill Museum Mallorca.

surrounded by pine trees, and Morales thought it would be good to keep some of the pine trees as a park inside the site. He also did not want to have a building façade toward another façade but towards the landscape. Morales wanted to create a dialogue between the landscape and the plan (Figs. 10, 11, 12).

We started drawing on top of his proposal, thinking about how the people who were going to live there will walk toward their home, leaving the city at their backs, and moving into the open landscape. We thought the project needed an intermediate space like a vestibule.

We were also working on how to place the program. Social housing spaces are very small, 60 square meters or 645 square feet. There were the 111 apartments, a parking place for each resident, some commercial space, a workshop, and green space–a place to fit in the landscape. We made an important decision to have a staircase between every two apartments–important because we wanted each house to have the double situation of street and courtyard–you also have cross ventilation this way and no longer need air-conditioning when there is this kind of ventilation going through the house.

Morales was thinking of different possibilities for the courtyard, that it could be a private space, but in our design, we wanted it to be a more open space. We were

10. Master plan model for social housing in Terrassa, Barcelona by Manuel Soto Morales.

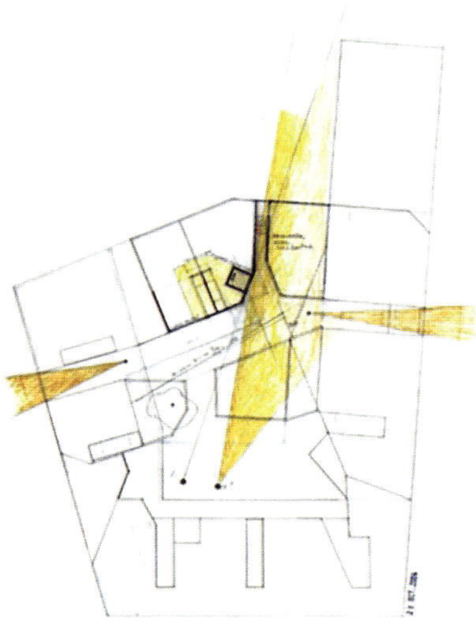

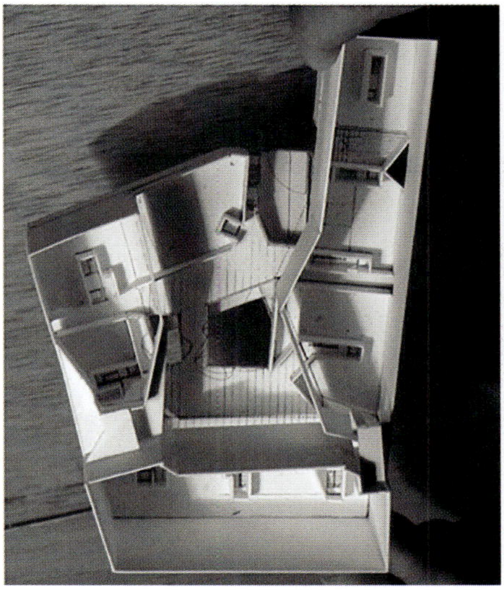

11. Plan and model for social housing in Terrassa, Barcelona.

12. Axonometric drawing for social housing in Terrassa, Barcelona.

more concerned with how to connect the 111 families than just the connecting units. We worked on the courtyard for both the perimeter and inside. Also, in courtyards, you lose the landscape for a while, so we have an area that raises the courtyard from the inside to see outside and place yourself within the landscape.

In our office, we always make drawings before models. There were different possibilities for the courtyard, but how this courtyard would work was really an issue. There is a moment in the courtyard where it opens much more to the landscape. We drew it, and what we really wanted was a set of sequences from the public experience to the private–all these sets of sequences should be very rich.

To test our courtyard we compared our courtyard with a beautiful space, San Felip Neri square in the old town section of Barcelona (Fig. 13)–it is like an open room, and it has only two entrances. During the day, schools use it as a playground, but it is big enough for different groups of people to be there without bothering each other. So we drew it and overlaid our courtyard plan. We also drew a section of the square, so there were two lower arms and a view from the windows to the courtyard, and at every one of the staircases, there would be a general entrance. The different staircases could be hidden so that when you open your door you were not in the middle of the square.

At a certain point in the design of the courtyard it reminded us of the Olympic Theater in Venice, designed by Andrea Palladio. There it is possible for all the actors to appear from different streets and then meet–our courtyard is like that. We wanted neighbors to be able to meet each other in protected space where you can stop and say hello. So we provided benches or points where people can sit. We were also twisting the staircase so after the ground level, the building rises up, and there are areas for terraces that we wanted for each apartment.

After the courtyard we started drawing a individual apartments. We wanted the social part of the house to face the courtyard. The long houses around the courtyard are separated and more regular for the bedrooms. The courtyard would be in contact with the landscape in the front. Many times during the process the plan was not working, and then you have doubts–you want to be sure things are moving the way you want them to appear. Finally, from all this drawing, there was a final plan. In the end, we decided that we would not enclose the bedrooms but would leave the space open. The social areas were quite big. In the smaller unit, the small bedroom was not enclosed.

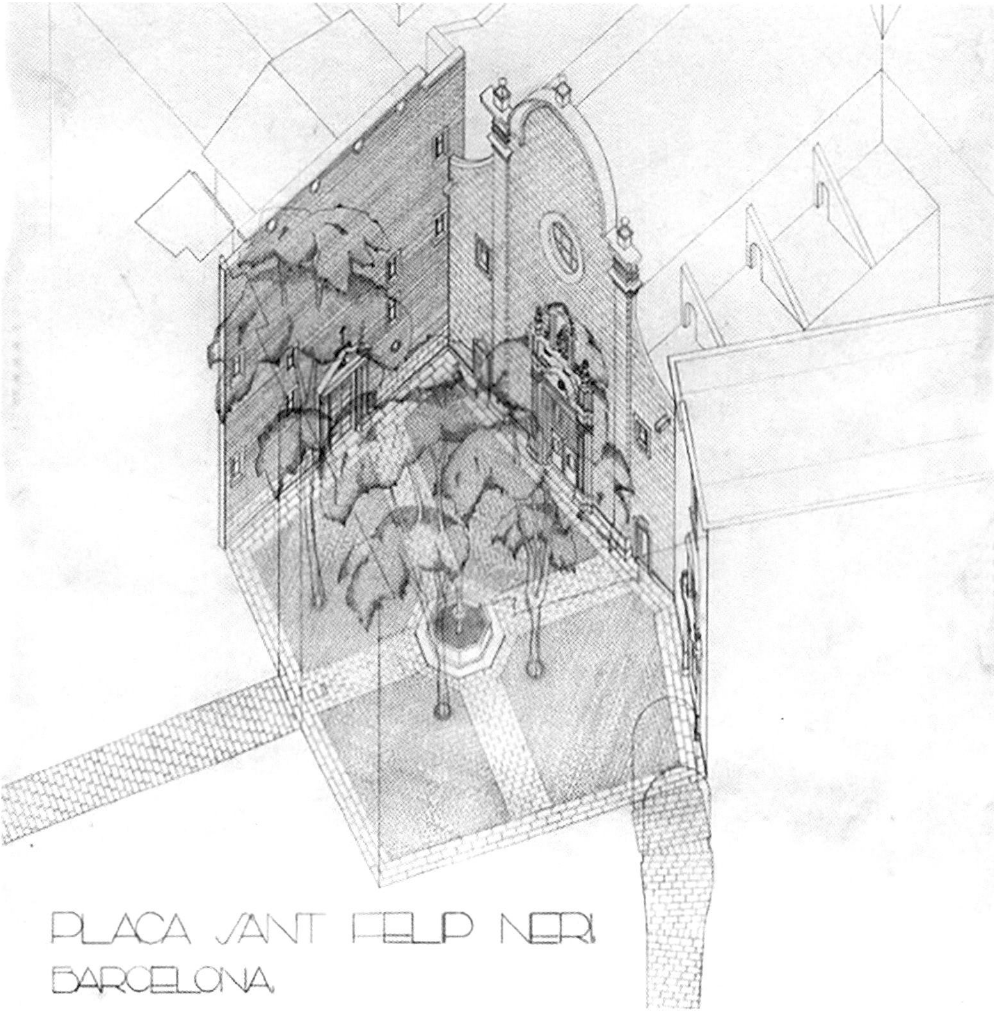

13. Axonometric drawings comparing the courtyard for residential community to the courtyard of San Filipe Neri Square in Barcelona.

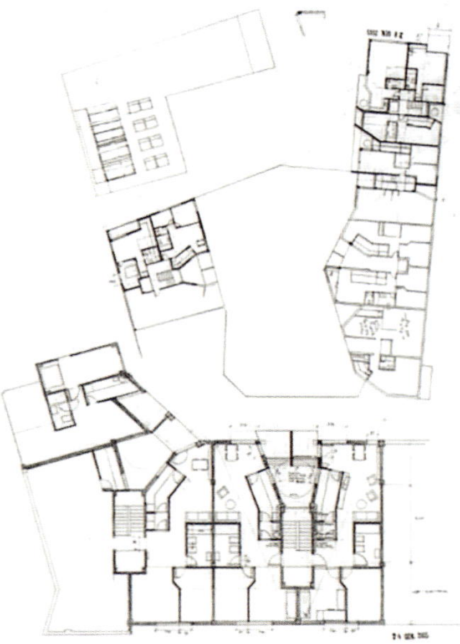

14. Plan and model for social housing in Terrassa, Barcelona.

15. Social Housing in Terrassa, Barcelona.

This may not sound like a problem, but in Spain it was a special thing; however, we thought that the houses were too small to have separate areas. Also, the apartment would have only three doors: the entrance door, the bedroom door, and the bathroom door. Then if the residents wanted to, they could enclose the bedrooms by paying a bit more money, which could be done quickly. So afterwards if a neighbor invited you to his house, you might find that the house is similar to yours, but because of the courtyard or the place within the city block, it would be slightly different.

We finally made a model of one of the smaller units, which could fit into my hand. There is a quiet part of the house, which is on the street, and then the courtyard, which is the social part (Fig. 14). We organized the houses so that everything turns around the kitchen and laundry room and put the electrical appliances together in the middle of the house. The houses have small open-air terraces that are big enough to fit a small table. There is another atmosphere near the square, and in the afternoon, the young children are in the public area. The kids play in the courtyard, which has a great entrance and exit. During the day, the courtyard has different sounds and atmosphere.

When developing the façade we thought it should have some kind of texture that would work with the light. It took a few months until we decided that it would be a wave with shadows (Fig. 15), like the pine trees around it. We knew it would take a long time for businesses and shops to be there, so we thought that at least from the very beginning, the building would identify with its beautiful landscape. We used a molding, which is aluminum on the inside. In the office, we experimented with what you could do with it. Because this was a façade, we started thinking of it in relation to the landscape. The façade walls are structural. After we poured the forms, the concrete was very shiny for a while. At the end of its construction, the concrete façade has all these marks, and with different light, the texture produces a lot of variation.

Conversation

Peter Buchanan
+
Eva Prats
+
Students

Student Peter, how can students develop their ability to make plans?

Peter Buchanan In principle, you learn by watching someone who is very good at it and doing it every day. You need to present your project, and you need to watch someone sketch over it, showing what is really going on. In this way, you get to understand how to draw the plan, how to see the movement, and so on. It takes time and practice.

One problem relative to the plan is how architecture education is fit into university structures. There are more and more PhDs teaching architecture, and people with PhDs generally do not draw plans. Another problem is the recent need for flexibility and a focus on the services. The more budget that goes into the efficiency of the services and the financial return, the less time is spent on developing the plan, not to mention the elevation. If you look at an old building, it has a face, a pattern that relates to the street. Buildings now are faceless and without spirit or life. We have to think about the city full with people; buildings are for people, not just the services and financial return.

Do you think parametric computer design contributes to these problems by oversimplifying and reducing the level of craft?

Peter Buchanan I think there are all sorts of craft. I'm not against parametric software, the best architects use it. They just use it with intelligence. In the Foster office, every project has its own software written by a team of software writers. That's a kind of very interesting discipline. When they have gotten to a certain point, and the project starts to emerge so that somebody can understand it, they start to analyze—what are the rules of the project, what are the rules of construction? When these things are defined, then they will write customized software for the project. That is an example of an intelligent use of software.

Eva Prats The computer is a sophisticated tool, so is the pen. What is important is the thinking of the person who is using the tool. The tool does not think; it is not a person. We are people, and we design for people; it is important not to lose this focus. Projects develop bit by bit, and the most important thing is to have time to insert information into a project. It is a process, and we have to look after this process.

Peter Buchanan I agree that good design emerges slowly. But different architects have completely different approaches to design and for some, thoughts come early in the process. Norman Foster's office is very detached; they look at many alternatives. What are all the ways that we can think of to solve the problem? If there are 10 ways, then they see the strengths and failures of each one, and they take the strongest ones and synthesize those. Alternatively, Renzo Piano tends to get an idea immediately, and then, for him, it's like the metaphor of a river slowly laying down a sand bank; slowly the design emerges. To me, it is a quite interesting design process. Sometimes just as the project is coagulating, Piano will say: "I think enough for today. We will come back to it." And everybody is frustrated, and says, "What are you doing Renzo?" And he says, "If we design too quickly, we will forget something."

Eva, can you speak about your design process? Do you start by solving the problem?

Eva Prats No, we never start with solutions. When the program or client comes into the office, we take in all the information, but we don't have an idea about what is going to happen with it. We go to the site, and there are always many things happening; we observe. Then we will get to work. We will practice architecture. We will begin to draw. For us, it's not about finding solutions. I would be frustrated to start with a particular solution directed toward a certain path. For sure, part of it has to do with culture. To me, Anglo-Saxons like efficiency. I like this too, but it is very different in the Spanish culture that I come from—I enjoy another way. We gather information from many different places, and things begin to appear in a certain way. There is a rhythm to the research for a project, and we follow it.

Can you elaborate on your rhythm of research?

Eva Prats It has to do with our drawing process. In an architectural office, it is difficult to control time. We have learned to ask the client for more time for a project. If a project is going to last 100 years, then one more year at the beginning is nothing. Rushing the design of projects is irresponsible and not at all ecological. The design process needs time. To make significant discoveries in a project, you need time for research, which is another rhythm in the project schedule. You have to follow both, and this can be difficult. It helps to have experience and an office filled with the pieces of things from earlier projects. We develop ideas from one project to the next; it is not repeating—it is about starting.

The rhythm of the office is such that we try to have a workplace that engages and helps us to move ahead with our research. In the studio, you try to be surrounded by things you like, because they affect you. The everyday routine is also incredibly important to the rhythm. It is important to have a nice life, have a good day, and have good place that you like to work in. We take many things from our environment when we design. For example in the housing project that I showed, the size of the terrace is the same as the terrace at our office. It is just big enough to have a table to eat outside. At home, our building is from the 1930s and has a separate entrance for the car and the pedestrian. We really like this, so we brought it to the project. All things that we are enjoying in everyday life, we put in to the building. This is how you draw things you would like to live in.

Peter Buchanan As an architect, you have to become conscious of how to organize your day and your place to be most creative. This is a design problem as much as designing a building.

Eva Prats Yes, everything is a decision. Where to put the title on a drawing is a decision, and you have to make it consciously. The worst thing you can do as a designer is to make automatic decisions.

Are precedents a part of the research?

Eva Prats Yes, absolutely. Often it is about the dimension of spaces—is it too big or too small, or will the natural light reach the lowest level of the staircase? We find similar conditions in places that we know are working, and we check the dimensions. This is a very nice way to work. When you're concerned with something, it probably exists, just look for it.

Peter, you said something: "There is something so wrong with modernity. It's so damn dead." I really like that statement: you were explaining how modernity suppresses culture. Can you expand on this? Is it related to how we think about craft?

Peter Buchanan Culture explains to us who we are and connects us back to our origin. Our culture has newly emergent origins. If you read cosmologists like Brad Stevenmore or ecologists like Thomas Berry, the story of emerging life is a spiritual vision; they have a great mythos of how to rebuild a culture. Modernity has suppressed this. Architecture is behind the wave in terms of rebuilding culture, partly due to French theory in the 1980s, which was a disaster for architecture. Today culture is really emerging in a funny way because of branding. You can see the yearning for a new way for culture in the whole thing of branding objects and making them more than just a tool but part of your identity.

Branding is the subjective and the myth of re-entering objects. Buildings are still crafted, but I mean in terms of the way that they're made and that craftsmanship was at higher levels. In Britain, if you make a public building, the normal brief is a 125-year life minimum and 80 years without maintenance. In London there is building that points to that historic wall and that historic wall is 1,000 years old. So you say, this building was standing like this for 1,000 years! That's becoming more important with sustainability.

Which of the books that you mentioned speak about mythos?

Peter Buchanan Thomas Berry wrote it. He was actually a priest, but he's seen as one of the fathers of ecology. He was also one of the great writers on Buddhism, though he was a Baptist. He also wrote beautiful books about evolution. The other one I mentioned was written by Brian Swimme, who is a mathematician. There are a lot of really interesting people to read. There is an interview with one of the greatest living scientists, James Lovelock, who is now about 95, and from him, we understand types of atmosphere on planets. Thanks to his theorizing and also equipment he designed for NASA, you can measure concentration of gases on Mars and the ozone. But when he was asked how he became so important as a scientist, he said, not from corporations—I work by myself/for myself.

In the twenty-first century, everything is about making connections, putting things together. The other big thing is that twenty-first-century thinking is developmental thinking. It's about crossing through stages. This is a notion of things evolving through stages, bringing ideas of hierarchy. There's a massive conflict in 21st-century thinking and personal relativism, which tends to be a dominant theme. That's why I think nearly all independent people, working outside by themselves, feel that freedom.

When do you think it's time for students to put their designs in the computer?

Peter Buchanan Well, you probably will do better to back and forth it. Your sketching will tell you where you are going. It's like when I'm writing. I just make notes, and I make little bubble diagrams. Then at a certain point, I feel like, well, this is coming alive, and I can start to write. I think sketching can use the same rule. You keep developing, and there is a moment where you know you are getting somewhere. The thing is not to fall in love with what you've done in the computer because it looks smoothly resolved. The thing about the sketch is that you can see what's wrong.

Many of the most talented architects I know don't produce great buildings, because they fall in love at certain points of development of the project and don't move beyond that. Other architects might not be as talented, but the reason they go further is that they say, we're not there yet. I think instinct will impact and will tell you.

Eva Prats I studied with hand drawing, and when I went back to teach, everything was on the computer. For the first year, I accepted the computer, but in the second year, we were talking about the ground level of a housing block. And I was asking, what is this line? And the students were answering: This line? This line is a pavement. There were many lines made by AutoCAD that students did not know what they were. So I said, okay! Let's stop this because we cannot communicate with these drawings. Draw everything by hand, and everything became comprehensible. Every line on the drawing needs to be a thought by you. You have to trust your own thoughts.

Also it is very important to have a drawing with scale, and the problem with the computer is that it doesn't have scale on-screen. The scale moves and changes. And to develop a thought, the scale has to be fixed. If you're thinking of the horizon, you can think of it without drawing it. If you start drawing it, you need to have a drawing with the horizon that helps your mind to move ahead. Not having scale on-screen is a handicap on the computer.

Peter Buchanan One of the things in modernity is each building is a conceived of from scratch. It's not that things are done any quicker than they were historically. In the past, buildings went really quickly, but you were building within a tradition—what somebody else was doing 10 years ago and a part of what you are doing now. In a Georgian house, you had three weeks to build it, and it was probably designed in a day by the architect. We don't do things any quicker than it was historically done. But we started from a tradition and culture of doing things that made for a big head start on the design.

Eva Prats In the past, the university was not needed as much to train architects; you could learn on projects, and there were many building traditions to draw from. We are starting to lose these traditions in Spain. For example, I have contemporaries in landscape architecture that think we have lost a lot of knowledge by not working with the farmers. From one generation to the next, the farmers passed down knowledge about water and the terrain; this knowledge is now getting lost because it does not come into the universities.

Faculty In the first session, Teresa Galí-Izard was talking about how the tradition of landscape architecture really comes from farming. Originally, there was nothing academic in particular about it, but it moved into an academic subject. Now, those two things need to come back together again.

Eva Prats It's a right of everyone to design his or her own life, so it would be good if everyone were culturally richer and traditions were not lost between generations. For us with our creative profession, maybe it's easier to do, but it's something that should be for everyone. For engineers, everyone, should be aware in a rich culture.

Student Peter what do you think about developing an idea in order to present it to the client before you are finished?

Peter Buchanan It is part of our culture to start things from the visual. I'm sure that Palladio showed drawings that were actually not highly developed drawings. But he was confident! He said, well there it is. A Palladio house might be very beautiful, but everything else, like the farm crops, all worked perfectly. They were farmers as well as very good designers. And he just knew. But then it was part of their culture that was evolving far less quickly, and he was building on tradition. It was much easier—much less complicated. The drawings are very simple, by comparison, to what we do today. Also, Palladio was working with craftsman who knew what they were doing. He didn't have to detail the windows because he knew that the craftsmen knew how to put the details in. It was part of an integrated culture in which the craftsmen were part of the same culture as the architect. We live in a different element, which introduces complexities that didn't exist historically.

Once a student enters the profession, is it better to be an excellent hand drafter or an excellent physical model builder? Does one take importance over the other or are they both equally important to the design process?

Eva Prats The important thing is that you know how to think, how to develop things, and how to add information that becomes a design. The axonometric drawing that I showed yesterday of the door of a building, with the tree in the courtyard and the courtyard of the square, was done by a young architect from Australia that we met in a workshop who asked to come to the office. Sometimes it's not even the drawings, but someone who comes suddenly and, "ah ha!," can develop it. It has nothing to do with ability, and a lot of people that come into the office sometimes have never done models or even drawn by hand a lot. We mix all of this. It is good if you produce a drawing that helps with the thinking or the model to help you test ideas. The important thing is that when you work, you know that what you are doing is helping you move ahead and produce documents. So when you go into class, you can discuss it with other students. You can share information.

Peter Buchanan It's where design starts that's not really being talked about, actually, and in modern design, that is looking at the social dynamics. How you learn architecture is watching how people are responding to each other and how the space creates conversation, like how does being in this tall space affect us? How does that effect the conversation? How would the conversation be different if we were sitting in a circle under a low ceiling? That's where design starts. All this technical stuff comes later, but you have to get into social dynamics and understand that. For instance, the Aalto, the Niemeyer, the Le Corbusier plans are brilliant, but they are brilliant because they actually understood the social dynamics first, and then the building arose out of that. They would not have been concerned about the tools, because tools are just tools. They knew what kind of life they wanted to create within the buildings. That's actually what drove their designs. And that, in a large part, is what is missing now. It's that concern of social acts and depth of understanding.

Eva Prats So during university you have to look at what your interest is. What are your responsibilities? And then later you will present this with drawings, AutoCAD, models, whatever. The important thing is that you go out in the street with a certain interest to develop and willingness to improve things.

Peter Buchanan For many people, it's not the tools, but that there's just too much concern about them. They should be secondary. Be respectful of all drawings. What was driving Eva's project was the concept of the lives in these buildings; that's all she was talking about really. Did you notice that all the plans had furniture with food on the table and people in plan? Review those drawings; they're not empty.

Eva Prats And it's much more. It is the thinking, more than the tool. Even in Miralles' career—you can see that he came from hand drawing. In the office, his instructions were, these dashed lines must be super precise, but not by a computer. Then the computer appeared. For the first computer drawings, Enric was like, this is crap—it's terrible! It took a while, years, until the computer drawings were as beautiful as the hand drawings. So the hand drawings should be perfect, but when the machine arrived, it took years to adapt the drawings to what you really like, no? And now we have the 3D printer and how you develop ideas with that. Now, everything is drawn on computer at the office. But it's not about the tool; it's just a tool.

Designing through narrative is helpful. I think we have to orchestrate all our potential mediums. Kind of use them all.

Peter Buchanan A narrative is very important on many levels. It's a very useful tool. For instance, I have a friend who wins lots of architectural competitions. His technique is to create a narrative; he tells a story. He says that it must be so compelling that you don't have to make a drawing; you should be able to tell the story to five draughtsmen, and they would draw exactly the same thing. And if you went to the design jury and just told the story, you would win the competition. And he wins competitions like this. He works on the story, and then the drawing is drawn quickly just to get the idea across.

The other thing is that when you're developing a design—actually this is something that you should really pay attention to—one of the key things is to listen to what you are saying to yourself. Some people draw something, and they say, oh that's crap, and they say, oh gosh, I'm crap. And no wonder they're not very good designers. So you have to pay attention to your internal dialogue. I remember seeing a design by very good architect for a big building, but it just had no life. Talking to him, I realized he hadn't been talking to himself, because you pick up on it. All of that comes through in the building and makes it alive. Now, there are Aalto and Le Corbusier buildings that you can listen to; you can listen to what they're saying to you. It's not kind of mindless. All that narrative gives an intensity to the building. You can design a building that works very well—analyze a plan that's brilliant—but the thing is, if there's no life, then it is because there's no narrative. You know that the architect hasn't been thinking aloud as he's drawing and designing.

And there are different levels of narrative. There's the narrative when you get to the building, and it's telling you a story. Sometimes, it's not necessarily the one that the architect intended. But narrative is a very important design tool. And if you're stuck, and you know that there's something missing, just think of a good story: okay, I go to visit this building, and I'm taking my little nephew along because he will like different things than me. This adds a certain complexity. He may be with granny too and so on. There are things that are exciting them, and you're starting to get really into design ideas.

Faculty I saw you lecture in Peru. There, you also talked about the crafting of the plan. You called it laboring the plan, and you mentioned the relationship between the techniques that we use to make the plan and the necessity of the story telling and the relationship to life. Today we are insisting on the stories and relationship to life and not addressing the need to learn techniques. We are not clear about what techniques we need to teach. They seem to be lost. A composer requires a lot of technique training, right? But we dismiss everything: we say, well, this is a tool, this is a tool, this is a tool—the important thing is the idea, the important is how you carry it, how you work on it. How do you work on it? Do we have techniques? Or are we completely lost in technique?

Peter Buchanan I think you are asking a very important question. And I would say we have lost technique. The first thing you said is what actually are we designing? What is it? What is the generative spirit? What is going on here, and what is this going to do for the city around it? And what is missing in the city around that needs to be here? So initially all of our sketches would not be of buildings, but they would be of social dynamics and relations. For example, here, there would be people meeting like this, so we want the movement to be about so far apart. So, would that spark this to life or would it limit it? And out of slowly looking at and sketching social dynamics, would a building start to emerge. You never see anyone who can do that any more.

Eva Prats I think you are doing that—this comparison of compositions? For me, drawing is the only way because, visiting the buildings, I can recognize if they are well drawn or not. Everything is matching. So you synthesize all the different natures of information—social, weather response, energy—in a drawing.

Peter Buchanan There are some architects who are composer architects, like a composer who has a set of rules in a musical situation. When you look at Frank Lloyd Wright, he has the rules; he has the grid. He has the simple fireplace, and he plays themes and variations. The Usonian house is a type: it's like a Bach Fugue, and then he just keeps playing the notes. It's interesting. If you look back to the '50s or up to '50s, you could still get books on architectural composition. And unfortunately, you could probably only find them second hand anymore. When I think about it, they were really interesting. They had funny ideas about how you must have a vertical ascent.

Faculty And, you know, we probably know some of the techniques that Enric was able to develop and you mention some of Wright's and Corbusier's. So there was a set of techniques developed in order to systematize and in a way incorporate the issues that we have been talking about, because otherwise you just have to believe us, no? Without trying to set up a series of techniques or trying to transmit a series of techniques, it's very difficult to put those things in place. Otherwise, it's like somebody trying to compose music without having the techniques of composition. I mean, I tried, and I can't do it! I can't do it without knowing composition in music. Even though you have a great idea, or you want to incorporate storytelling—without the technique, it's impossible.

Student Eva—when you worked with Enric and you started to pick up his kind of drawing, how did you transition from that type of drawing to keeping your own voice in your own practice?

Eva Prats For me, it was through drawing. And after so many years in the office, how do you start your own work after this strong personality? In the end, it was a great experience. It was a great place to be, but also you take a lot of the everyday discipline from it: how you take the work, how you start the work, how you design your studio. Many books from our library are advice from Enric from when we were studying with him. Because I had Enric as a teacher, there was an affinity for the same ideas. If I went to his office, I felt very comfortable. So there are things that I probably embraced: there are ideas that stay. But every person is different, and what he did was a very personal architecture. But now with distance from that time, there are things that I am not as interested in—like much more formal solutions—because the way he organized buildings related to what was existing. There are ideas that we continue, but they are not only his ideas. I can find these ideas in previous architects, in other ones.

Faculty But you learned the technique from Miralles; many of us here today learned his techniques. We learned in school; we learned in the office. You learn the technique, and that's what you carry. Then there are ideas that come from before that go further, that you evolve from other architects. But we all learn the technique, a very serious and disciplined technique, and that is what makes a huge difference—that from one way or another, the technique was passed, and that's what we are not doing, in general.

It takes a while. It's more than six years of education to arrive at a place where you have the skill to really work with the technique—the techniques that you've learned and are aware of. It takes really being on a job site and seeing the construction of something and seeing the order of construction and understanding the way of making through actually making it and not just through designing. We didn't learn all of that in school.

Peter Buchanan It takes a long time to learn architecture, and the university is just the beginning. People ask me which university to attend, and I have no idea. The key thing is to know which office you want to work in. That's where you really start to learn. That's the graduate school—to get from a really good office and think about what kind of skills can get you into that good architecture office. If you look at the career of architects, Le Corbusier and Frank Lloyd Wright, they were building in their late teens, early 20s, and they were really good. However, when you look at their work, their true work starts in their late 60s because that's how long it takes to become a really good architect. Le Corbusier built Ronchamp in his late 60s; Fallingwater was built in Wright's late 60s. Architects are notoriously long lived because it takes so damn long to get good. And they are just getting good by the time they're 70. Look at the architects that die in their late 90s and around 100: they have been working right through their lives because it is the key thing in architecture, in the end, is not technique, but it's judgment. To know to do this much or that much, what influences are in this person's life—it just takes time. There's pressure in Europe to shorten architecture education because of this—judgment just takes time. The basic key to architecture education—I don't know about the U.S. exactly—but in Europe, you learn for two or three years, then go to work, and then you come back for more schooling. The leap from the third to fifth year is a completely different animal. In that expanding world, students are expanding their judgment. It is this nuance of judgment and all the things that influence judgment—philosophical position, understanding people's psychology, depth of empathy—that takes a long time to cultivate. The great thing about architecture is that you have let yourself into a whole life of development and something that impinges on everything you're thinking about—aesthetics and technique and psychology—that's the magic of it. And yes, in about 50 years you'll be getting there—that's a bit exciting I think!

Faculty I was fascinated, Eva, with your discussion of the apartments that you designed and how much that overlapped with what you were saying about Herman Hertzberger: there was a tremendous amount of commonality of values, I suspect. I don't know Miralles as much as many people in this room, but I suspect there wasn't that same focus in Miralles' work. But the sheer humanity of your work and Hertzberger's, someone who I've always admired, is because of this commitment to the ownership of the place you've created for the people who live there, which too many architects resent. They have no empathy for regular people—in so many of those houses published in the fancy magazines today, you have no idea how people are going to live in them. No idea at all. They've got the standard set of Mies and Le Corbusier furniture stuck in the middle of these great big yawning spaces. The notion that people are going to live full lives in there, which is what you are all about, is just not there.

Peter Buchanan Well, Hertzberger is one of the architects that you can learn the most from. I chose very simple things because I was trying to cover a lot of ground. He did an elderly home, and boy can you learn a lot from that. It would take an hour or two to discuss. Hertzberger is the most selfless person—I know him very well—he's the most self-critical, and he's constantly observing—he'll stand in the shadows of his buildings and watch what the people are doing. I remember once I was with him and nobody knew who he was. We were just sitting there in a corner of the cafeteria, watching people come and go, making comments about it. Suddenly one of the elderly people realized that he must be the architect. All these people came up and said, "You have transformed our lives." Some of them did not actually live in the building but just came and spent their day there. They said, "This building has done so much." The old people were grabbing him and kissing him. That's the highest praise for an architect.

Eva Prats When we did the social housing, it was not so common to have the kitchen open to the bedroom and all these areas open. So when the building was finished, we opened it to the public. On one day of the open house, Ricardo and I went to see people's reaction. People were asking questions: How do we organize this? Where is the dining room? What are all these angles? And we said, "The angles can help you put in some piece of furniture." After people left, we went to the owner in panic, and said, "We should put some furniture into one of these apartments, and it will help a lot." And they were like "Aaah!" because they didn't do this much. So they convinced the construction company to spend 3,000 Euros at IKEA, and we furnished one of the apartments. On our second visit, it worked much better. When people went into the living room, and instead of saying, "How do I put in the furniture," they said, "Look at this living room! Much bigger than the one we have, huh?" They were comparing already. So, this is one thing that we insist on a lot. The last time we visited, people wanted to show us their apartment. Some people are super proud of what they have done. Others were like, "I'll show you, but I'm ashamed because with the kids and everything…" So it was nice. And they were okay. A lot of the apartments were very okay.

Peter Buchanan I learned in Cape Town how to make buildings that were really enjoyable to live in, which makes for the kind of things that Eva was talking about, an enjoyable community life. So, it was a great place to learn architecture. The other thing I learned in architecture school is that it was really important to have some really good tutors. The school's attitude is, "Look, we don't care who you are or where you are from, we're going to get you a first class education." And everybody in the school really had to step up to the mark. Everybody benefits from the incredible improvements that this provoked within the school as students moved through.

Iteration

1. Utrecht City Hall, 1997, iteration #62.

2. Utrecht City Hall, iteration #63.

3. Utrecht City Hall, iteration #64.

4. Utrecht City Hall, iteration #68.

5. Utrecht City Hall, iteration #69.

6. Utrecht City Hall, iteration #67.

7. Utrecht City Hall, iteration #70.

8. Utrecht City Hall, iteration #71.

9. Utrecht City Hall, iteration #73.

10. Utrecht City Hall, iteration #74.

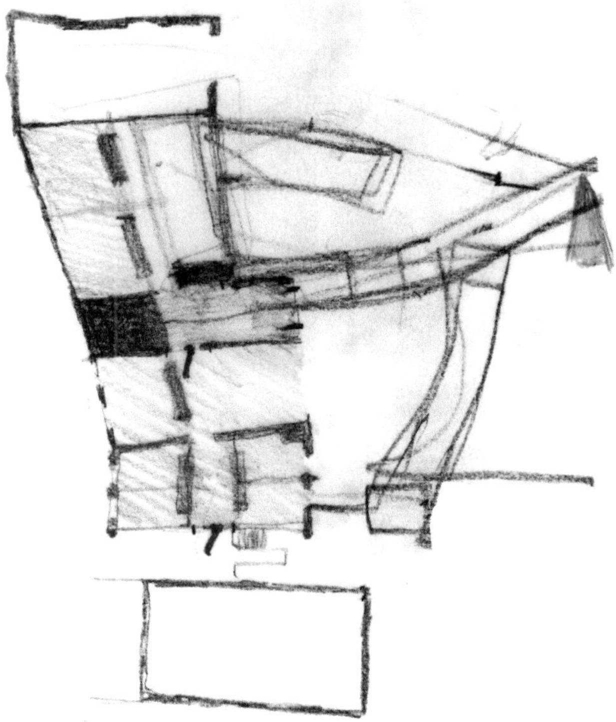

11. Utrecht City Hall, iteration #75.

12. Utrecht City Hall, iteration #77.

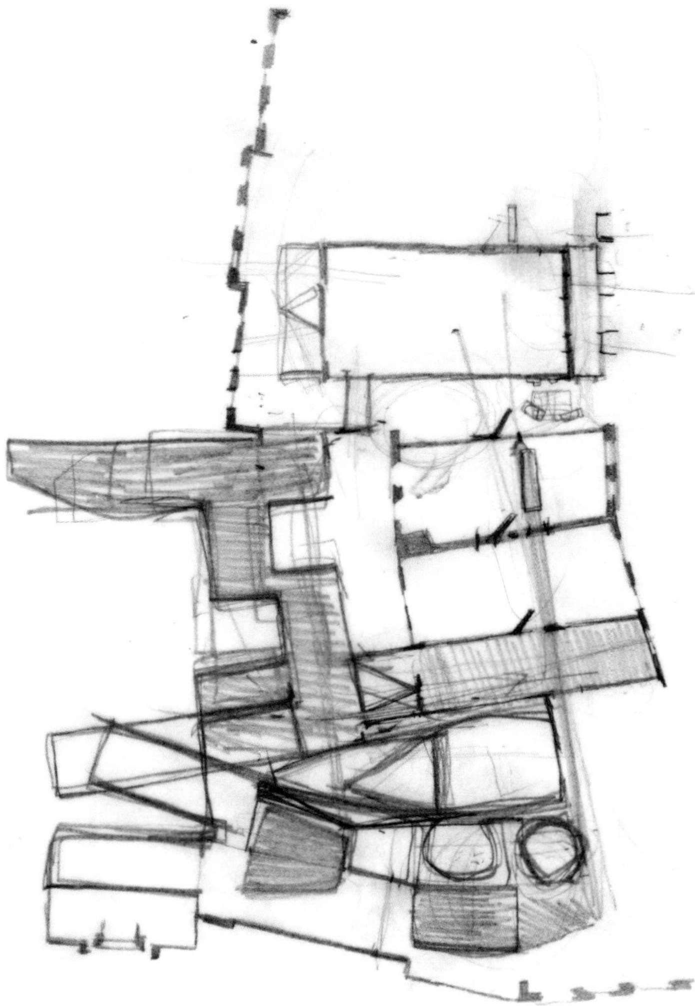

13. Utrecht City Hall, iteration #82.

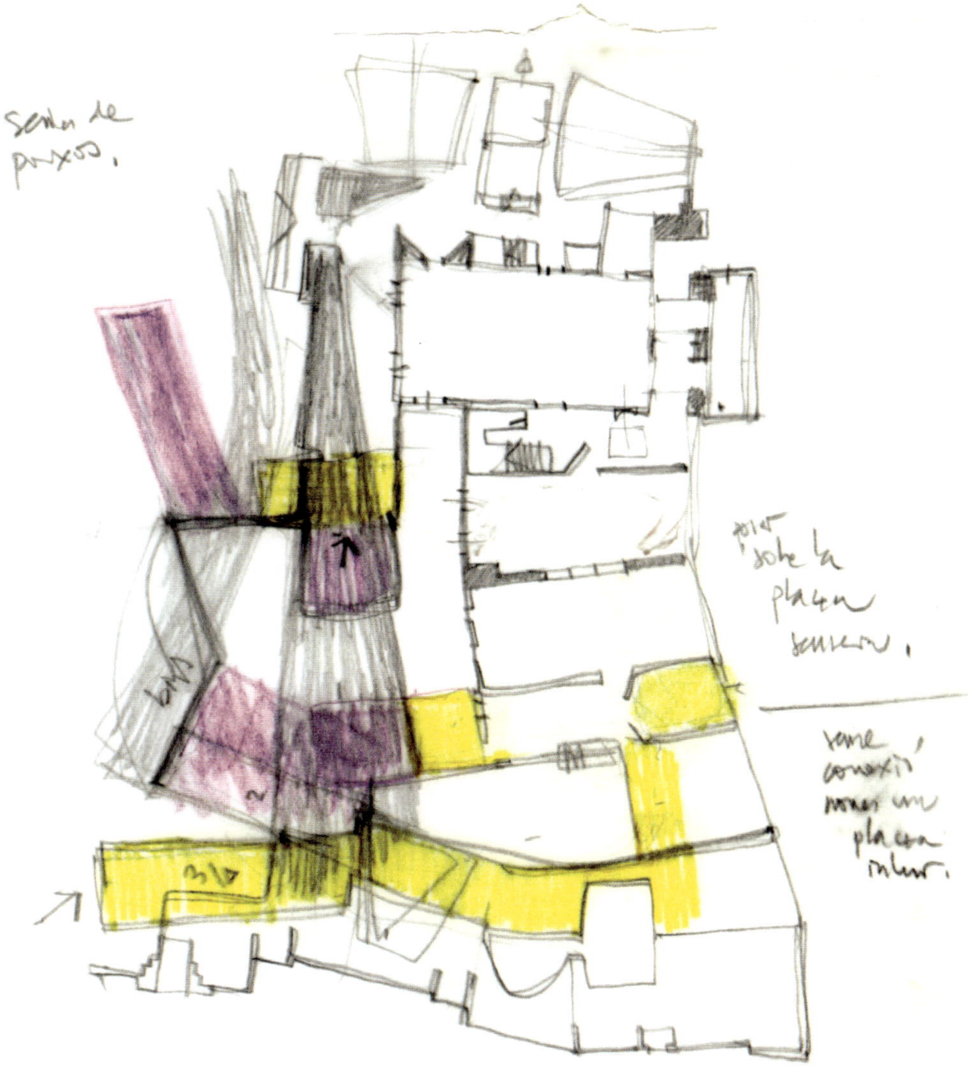

14. Utrecht City Hall, iteration #88.

Divine Collectors

Ana Valderrama

1. *Portrait of a Collector,* Il Parmigianino, ca. 1523.

In 2001, Claudio Vekstein gave a lecture in a Latin American architecture symposium called "From the Matter to the Project" organized by Matéricos Periféricos, a cultural movement at the School of Architecture of Rosario, Argentina. His memorable three-hour, 900-analog-slide lecture took place in a hall with over 500 hundred people listening in absolute silence. This was considered one of the most important pedagogical contributions to Matéricos Periféricos in the past 13 years. Vekstein's lecture included the story of the Rosenmuseum extension in Steinfurth, Germany, which was done in collaboration with Enric Miralles and Karl Unglaub in 1995. Vekstein's tale showed a sequence of creeper roses taking over a building, rose perfume, a rose garden in a backyard, a rose in a vase with a blurred man wearing a hat in the background, rose petals spread on a table, threaded rose petals, and everything tangible or intangible related to a rose. That obsessive accumulation of classified information, little by little, informed the configuration of collages, models, and drawings that were used to design the Rosenmuseum. Claudio named that moment of suspense in the design process—which also means a conscious restriction of form anticipation or prefiguration—as a collection.

By the word "collection," I refer to the action of accumulating and classifying the thing and related things to the original, including the latency of a process of displaced archaeology and metaphysical transformation—sometimes also called transmutation.[1] The collection in the Rosenmuseum seemed an operation of capturing the essence of the rose—through accumulation of data and geometry—displacing the presence of the rose to another place, time, and dimension and extending the life of the rose through its transmutation into architecture's consistency. In other words, collection was the very process of design generation in this collaborative work—which put on the table not only his particular way of making but also essential questions of any humanistic creative activity ever.

Seeds of collections with the particularities described above—actual collection with latency of a process of displaced archaeology and metaphysical transformation or transmutation—could be tracked in Western civilization in "cabinets of curiosities," also know as Kunstkammer.[2] Between the sixteenth and eighteenth centuries, cabinets of curiosities flourished in Europe as private collections and exhibits of works of art and natural and technological artifacts. Collector-artists not only gather objects for exhibit purposes, but they also

2. Salvaging of ancient architectural relics. Illustration in: Jacques Besson, *Theatrum Instrumentorum et Machinarum*, 1578.

used their cabinets as laboratories for studying the raw material and testing their human divine power of transformation of nature—or their sacred place as medium for nature's transformation.[3] The creative human power was placed at the same level as Nature (or God?) and Nature was considered as powerful as humans as to create works of art. In fact, the products of humans, and the rest of nature, were considered part of the same chain of natural history and genealogy: natural formations—ancient sculptures—works of art—machines.[4] In a broader sense, the creative process was considered a progressive chain of transformations—sometimes also transmutations.[5]

It seems to be that at the beginning of Kunstkammer[6]—when classification of things was consciously or unconsciously blurred, and the notion of evolution of nature was incipient—objects were sometimes grouped according to formal attributes[7] in spite of their genetic or historical origins. That is, the forms seemed to have their own life, traveling without distinction across artifacts created by nature and the ones made by human counterparts (Fig. 2). In *The Lure of Antiquity and the Cult of the Machine: The Kunstkammer and the Evolution of Nature, Art, and Technology*, Horst Bredekamp points out that "Statues of antiquity were categorized as fossils because they, too, derived from the earth."[8] In the same text, Bredekamp asserts that Bolognese scholar Ulisse Aldrovandi assumed that nature was capable of producing works of art.[9] At the end of 1770s—the appearance of the first automaton—the writer Pierre Jaquet-Droz introduced a more bizarre concept of evolution of nature: the ability of humans to give soul to sculptures by giving them independence of movement.

Since the creative process was considered a progressive chain of transformations —sometimes also transmutations—there was a requirement for collector-artists to study, mimic, and produce their work of art as an evolution of nature, taking antiquity as part of nature. Bredekamp asserts that Prince Karl Eusebius of Liechtenstein (1611–1684) evaluated the quality of works of art for his collection according to their similar appearance with natural products, and Robert W. Gaston explains the weight of historical accuracy related to ancient Rome required for painters and architects of that time.[10] In order to prove that level of co-related accuracy between the raw material and the work of art, and at the same time preserve their creative capacity, artists had developed different techniques of documentation and transformation. Pirro Ligorio (1510–1583), architect, antiquarian, engineer, archaeologist, and painter, had drawn ancient Rome based upon his data taken from archaeological studies—some of them from ancient coins (sometimes minted by himself).[11] Ligorio's drawings had a high degree of speculative displacement. That is, he didn't necessarily invent inexistent elements, but he reproduced accurate findings arbitrarily. Drawing ancient Rome in that way implied that there was no linear cause-effect relationship with the raw material; instead, there was always subjectivity, a translation of the original data. Bernard Palissy (1510–1590), antiquarian, collector, cartographer, natural philosopher, and surveyor, had his own cabinet that functioned as a kind of laboratory that included stones, raw metals, shells, fossils, and all the necessities to prove his written and drawn documents of scientific studies (Fig. 3). Palissy chose to become a ceramist. His work as ceramist included life-like pieces of art and utilitarian artifacts with incorporation of animals, plants, and human parts, all cast directly from life. Palissy took molds to steal a creature's formal qualities without mediation of abstraction.[12] He also invented the translucent glaze to create the illusion of life on his ceramics.[13] However, Palissy did something more curious: he used the form of plants and animals to create casting shape-related things. The images illustrate the "Stylized Leaf-shaped Dish with Jasper Glazing" (1556–1590), a product of an illusory metaphysical transmutation—or genetic modification—from the original material—a fish?—to another creature—a leaf.[14]

Sources of this passion for transformation—related to humans' obsession for testing their divine creative power in a broader sense and scale—could also be found in poetry, alchemy, and geometry. At the beginning of the current era, poet Ovid (43 BCE–CE 17–18) had speculated through poetry about everything that could become other things in his book *Metamorphoses* (ca. 1–8 CE). In *Metamorphoses*, the history of gods, humans, animals, and natural elements

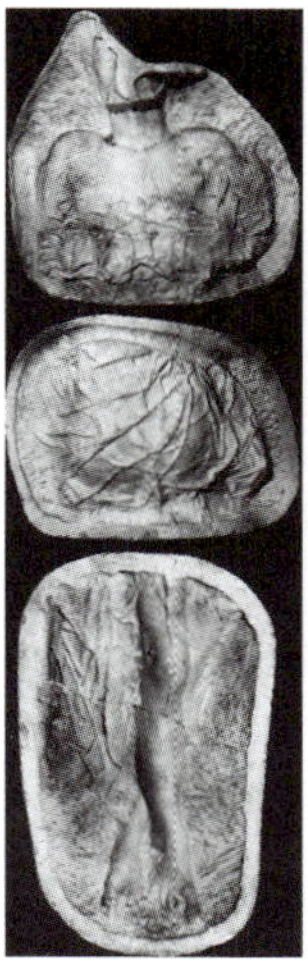

3. Bernard Palissy and Atelier, "Life Casts of Human Bust, Torso, and Legs for Term Figures," nineteenth century casts from lost molds of 1556–1567.

disguise themselves, shift their shape, or become other creature.[15] In 1618, in the book *Atalanta Fugiens, hoc est, Emblemata Nova de Secretis Naturae Chymica* (1964; 1st ed. 1618), the physician, composer, and alchemist Michael Maier (1568–1622) proposed progressive transformation of the same concept—across different formats or states: drawing, followed by text (with a motto, an epigram, and a discourse), followed by musical score. Michael Maier reproduced—50 times—Atlanta's mythical escape as a metaphor for the larger context of transmutation of things, assuming that people who transited the path provided by the book would achieve a spiritual transformation towards illumination.[16] Later, in 1917 in the book *On Growth and Form* (1952; 1st ed. 1917), the biologist and mathematician D'Arcy Wentworth Thompson speculated with geometry about the way species evolve in form and structure over time, creating new genealogies of species related by formal transformations.[17] He also established links between the form of living creatures and the form of physical phenomena, such as the form of a Medusa and the form of the drop crashing on a viscous liquid. In the last chapter, "The theory of transformation," he expresses the disappointment that any artist with divine sensitivity would feel: he laments the limitations of his theory, in that mathematic representation seemed to be far from understanding nature because the methods of the former were oversimplified relative to the dynamic processes and forces that appeared in the development of living things. After completing 1,000 pages of geometrical drawings of living creatures' transformations, Thompson wrote: "Here, since a change of material form is only affected by the movement of matter, we have once again the support of the schoolman's and the philosopher's axiom: *ignorato motu, ignoratur natura*[18] or if we ignore the motion, consequently we ignore the nature."

Enric Miralles would make transformations through geometry at the scale, in space and time, of a particular project—as in Rosenmuseum, from rose to architectural consistency—as well as at the scale of his work as a whole—from one project to another. That is, the life of the rose would be extended towards the museum's consistency and then propagated to future projects. In *El Croquis,* "Conversation with Enric Miralles," Enric says, "My work also includes this translation of information from one project to another, as if the search was taking place in several territories at the same time. [...] I think it has to do with a very deep conviction that projects are never completed. They rather enter successive stages in which, maybe, we no longer have direct control over them, or perhaps they are reincarnated in other projects we design."[19] Geometry was a tool for capturing the formal essence of things—their complex specificity as in the croissant, not the reduction to perfect Euclidean shapes—and all the forces and resistances that took place on them, as in the multiple-feet columns. Geometry was also a strategy of forgetting[20] and liberating the original towards progressive transformations and adjustment to new conditions: the original could even become the void of the next adjustment. In "Concept for a Car Showroom," Miralles noted: "Step 1. The very surface of the car is able to capture the reflected image of the city. Register this material. Step 2. Transform these registers into material to close a precinct. Step 3. Seek a client. Note. The one you had to start with has probably disappeared."[21] Curiously, Enric Miralles had the same feeling of disappointment related to the lack of transmutation capacity of geometry as Thompson had (Fig. 4). In "How to Lay out a Croissant: Horizontal Equilibrium," Miralles said, "We recognize this form in the roof of the mouth...(a mystery comparable to that of the knife which breaks when introduced into a glass of water). When measuring it, numbers return transparency to the form, with all its negative qualities: the lack of color, smell, and taste. Because a croissant, or half moon in Argentina, is meant to be eaten."[22]

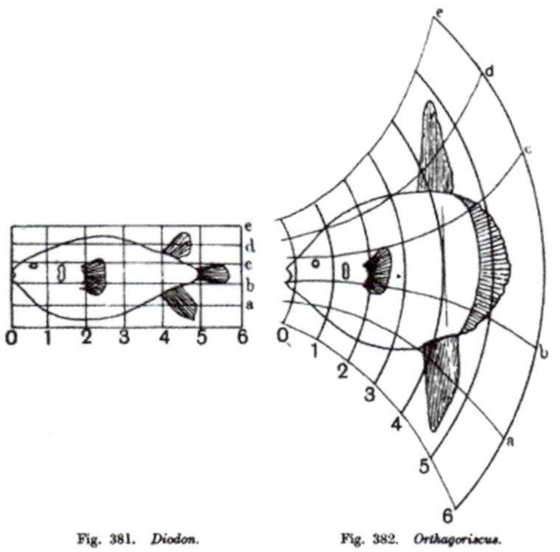

4. D'Arcy Wentworth Thompson, *On Growth and Form.*

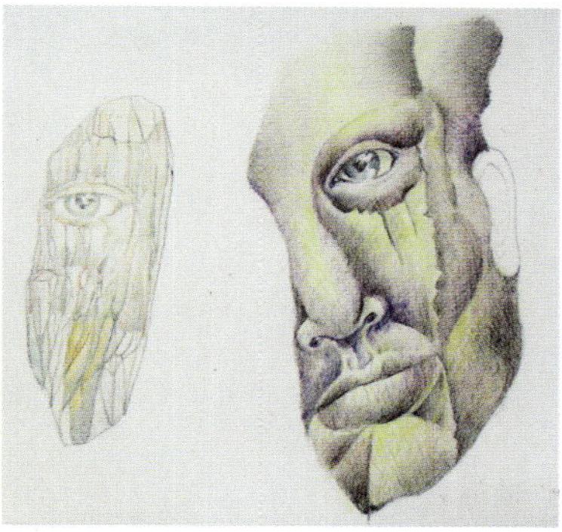

5. Progression of transformations by student Eugenia Castellini.

Notes

1. Etymology of transmutation: Late fourteenth century from O.Fr. transmutation (12c.), from the Latin, transmutationem (nom. transmutatio) "a change, shift," noun of action from the Latin, transmutare "change from one condition to another," from trans- "thoroughly" + mutare "to change." "A word from alchemy." Online Etymology Dictionary http://www.etymonline.com.
2. According to Bredekamp, collectors deserved the category of Prometheus. Horst Bredekamp, *The Lure of Antiquity and the Cult of the Machine: The Kunstkammer and the Evolution of Nature, Art and Technology*, trans. Allison Brown (Princeton: Markus Wiener Publishers, 1995; 1st ed. 1947), 19.
3. Horst Bredekamp, *The Lure of Antiquity and the Cult of the Machine: The Kunstkammer and the Evolution of Nature, Art and Technology,* trans. Allison Brown (Princeton: Markus Wiener Publishers, 1995; 1st ed., 1947), 27.
4. Online Etymology Dictionary, http://www.etymonline.com: transformation: mid-fourteenth century from the Latin, transformare "change the shape or form of," from trans- "across" + formare "to form."
5. According to Bredekamp, in 1607, Emperor Rudolf would introduce a form of classification: naturalia, artificialia, scientifica, and exotica. However, in 1647, Rene Decartes still declared that there was "no difference between machines built by artisans and objects created by nature alone." Horst Bredekamp, *The Lure of Antiquity and the Cult of the Machine: The Kunstkammer and the Evolution of Nature, Art and Technology*, trans. Allison Brown (Princeton: Markus Wiener Publishers, 1995; 1st ed. 1947), 33, 34, 39.
6. Mary Ann Kluth, *The Berkeley Kunstkammer*. Printed exhibition handout. Berkeley, CA: April 17 through October 14, 2007. http://www.stretcher.org/features/the_berkeley_kunstkammer/ Berkeley Art Museum. "Works in the Kunstkamme."
7. Bredekamp, op. cit., 11. See image 2.
8. Bredekamp, op. cit., 13.
9. Robert W.Gaston, *Pirro Ligorio: Artist and Antiquarian*, ed. Robert W. Gaston (Milan, Italy: Silvana, 1988), 11–18.
10. Gaston, op. cit.
11. According to Leonard Amico, Pallisy was the inventor of translucent glaze. Leonard N. Amico, *Bernard Palissy: In Search of Earthly Paradise* (Paris: Flammarion, 1996).
12. Image 3.
13. Ovid, *Ovid Metamorphoses*, trans. Stanley Lombardo (Indiana: Hackett Publishing Company Inc., 2010), 7. H. M. E. de Jong, *Michael Maier's Atalanta Fugiens: Sources of an Alchemical Book of Emblems* (Leiden: E. J. Brill, 1969).
14. D'Arcy Wentworth Thompson, *On Growth and Form* (London: Cambridge University Press, 1952; 1st ed. 1917), 1027.
15. Enric Miralles, in "A Conversation with Enric Miralles," *El Croquis 72*, 1995, 6–23, 12.
16. Ibid., 14.
17. Enric Miralles, in "Concept for a car showroom," *El Croquis 72,* 1995, 122–127.

18–21. Enric Miralles and Carme Pinós, "How to lay out a Croissant. Horizontal equilibrium," *El Croquis 49/50,* 1991, 190–191.

Intricacy and the Scottish Parliament Building

John Meunier

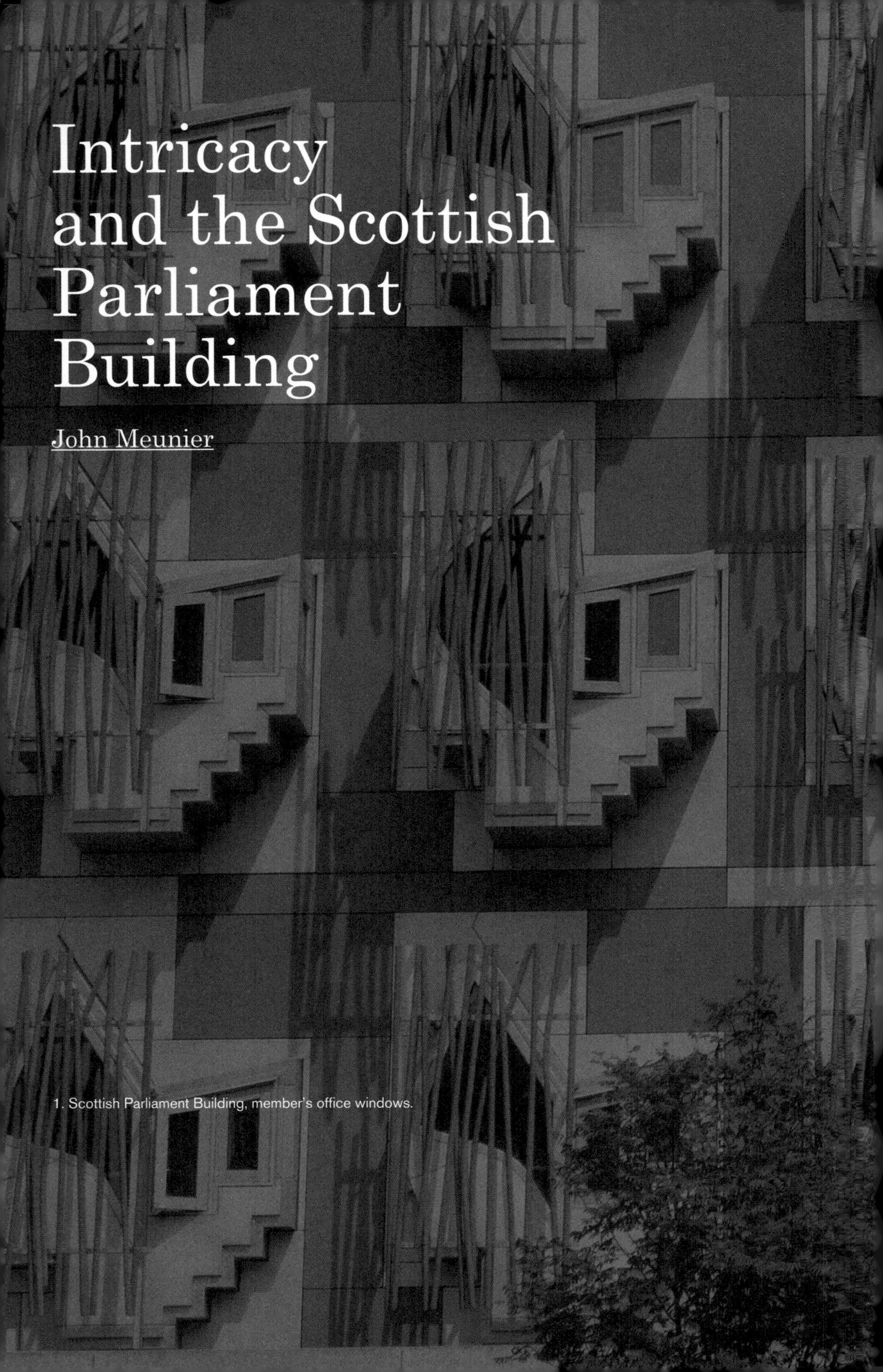

1. Scottish Parliament Building, member's office windows.

Preface

This essay came about because I was looking for a couple of relatively new buildings that I could use as case studies to test my ideas on INTRICACY, (more about those ideas later). I was looking for buildings that were clearly complex, and challenging to the understanding, and where there was some question as to whether they met the need for aesthetic coherence and ultimate understanding after prolonged contemplation, (one of my working definitions of architecture is 'buildings that reward contemplation'). For me it was important that I should be able not only to gain access to the literature about these buildings but also that I should be able to visit them and experience them, preferably in the company of those who occupy and use them. The two buildings that I chose were the Musee Branly by Jean Nouvel, and, the subject of this essay, the Scottish Parliament Building by Enric Miralles.

Enric Miralles was already familiar to me, first and foremost through my admired colleague Professor Catherine Spellman, the editor of this volume, who brought Enric to our academic home, Arizona State University. She brought him not only physically as a visitor on the occasion when she mounted an exhibition about his work, but as a part of the architectural cultural atmosphere of our school, a process in which she has been assisted by another colleague, Professor Claudio Vekstein. Both of them were dramatically shaped architecturally and as educators by working and teaching with Enric Miralles. The extended symposium that Catherine organized, extensively referred to elsewhere in this volume, brought many of those who worked closely with Enric , including his wife Benedetta Tagliabue, as well as another new colleague Elena Rocchi, to discuss his work, and I benefited from extended conversations with them about the Scottish Parliament Building, notably with Karl Unglaub.

Although I came to Arizona in 1987 as Dean of what was then the College of Architecture and Environmental Design, and still live in Arizona most of the year, I have a second home just outside Cambridge in England where we spend most of the summer months. Having been born in England my own family lives and works in the UK, and a nephew, James Loxley, is Professor of Early Modern Literature in the department of English Literature at Edinburgh University. It was through him that we spent a good many hours on July 4th, 2011, visiting the Scottish Parliament building accompanied by one of the Members of the Scottish Parliament.

Introduction to the idea of INTRICACY

For this author Intricacy is the missing ingredient in much of the architecture and urbanism of the modern world, and its lack is the cause of the banality and superficiality that results in our feelings of dissatisfaction with that world. This essay reflects the author's belief that environments possessing this quality of intricacy will be elevating to the spirits, the mind, and our sensibilities; that when we live amidst such buildings, streets and places, our lives will be enriched instead of, as so often is now the case, being diminished.

The word, and the idea, are of course not unique. Others have pursued them. In particular this author was interested to learn of an exhibit at the Institute of Contemporary Art at the University of Pennsylvania in 2003 organized by Greg Lynn whose title was *INTRICACY*. The exhibit focused primarily on recent developments in art, and to a certain extent in architecture, influenced largely by recent digital and genetic engineering developments. This work is not irrelevant to our interests, but it is not central. A comparison between Lynn's definition and ours might be informative:

"Among artists, designers, and architects there is an emerging sensibility of intricacy. Partially heralded by the digital and genetic engineering revolutions, the term intricacy connotes a new model of connectionism composed of extremely small scale and incredibly diverse elements. Intricacy is the fusion of disparate elements into continuity, the becoming whole of components that retain their status as pieces of a larger composition. Unlike simple hierarchy, subdivision, compartmentalization or modularity, intricacy involves a variation of the parts that is not reducible to the structure of the whole."[1]

The definition of Intricacy that informs this piece is somewhat different; but shares the commitment to an ultimate "continuity" linking "disparate elements":

"Intricacy is an intellectual construct that interprets a challenging set of perceived phenomena within a rich structure of relationships that link each member of the set consequentially to the rest. An object of our attention is perceived as intricate when its comprehension requires and rewards such intellectual engagement. Such an object may have complex form, but it can also be intricate because of its ambiguity of form or significance. Multiple readings of simple form may also imply intricacy.

"Art, Music, Architecture, and Literature must necessarily be "intricate" to qualify as substantial works of long-term cultural significance. Their formal structure and their multiple layers of meaning may separately, or together, achieve the quality of intricacy. It is this quality that lends major works the ability to reward those who revisit them many times."

Intricacy and Cities

The intricacy of towns and cities is inevitably different from that of intricate works of architecture. Whereas in the latter case the enquiring intellect might ultimately be able to comprehend a subtle logic or argument that informs and disciplines both the parts and the whole, a logic or argument that was developed by a single creative mind. In the former case the disparity of parts is likely to be greater, the whole less fully resolved but still recognizable, and it is clearly not the product of a single creative mind even when its matrix might have a single author, as is the case in so many colonial cities throughout history. However the danger of many planned cities is that the simplicity and lack of articulation of their structure can reduce or destroy any chance of them achieving urban intricacy.

So what is the intricacy that we can find in towns and cities? It is the intricacy that attracts engagement, that rewards the encounter, that yields delightful surprise, that stimulates through the spatial contrast that moves from constrained to open, from dark to light, from close to far, from small to large. It is the intricacy that invites and frames human occupancy by the individual and the group. It is the intricacy that celebrates and brings together the rich variety of human institutions, from the private home, the school, the place of government, the market, and the places of worship and assembly. It is the intricacy that connects the human made to the natural world. It is the intricacy that does all these things but does them in a way that they relate to each other, that they do not ignore each other, that they do not deny each other. It is the intricacy that enjoys transition and connection, particularly between the private and the communal, where the concept of threshold is valued.

Intricacy and Architectural Stories

All buildings contain stories. There are the human stories about who built them and why, what challenges had to be overcome in the building of them, how they were occupied and used, how did they respond to changes in both use and context. And then there are the technical stories about how they were built and what with....and so on.

What we are discussing here, however, are the carefully contrived, intricate, uniquely architectural stories that a building can tell in the hands of a good designer; we are talking about the architectural equivalent of a play, a piece of classical music, or a well contrived work of literature.

An architectural story uses the elements of a building—columns, beams, arches, rough and smooth stones, flat and curved walls, doors and windows, and the spaces between them—as the equivalent of the protagonists, instruments, intervals and sounds, characters, and their relationships in works of drama, music, and literature.

Intricacy and The Scottish Parliament Building

There is no question that this building is complex, but is it intricate? The complexity is immediately apparent. There is nothing simple here. More than fifty percent of its area is in landscape rather than building. Like a city It incorporates old buildings, Queensbury House. It has a rich palette of materials: wood, concrete, stones both light and dark, painted steel, gleaming metal sheet roofing, clear glass or glass with a thin layer of wood veneer. It has a wide array of forms: straight and curved, vertical and angled, repeated and varied, shallow and deep, smooth and textured, rounded and sharply pointed. The facades are multi-layered. Joints and window mullions and muntins are often discontinuous. Potentially large elements are nearly always elaborated so that their scale is reduced. Natural light is introduced both directly and indirectly. Artificial lights are clustered and dispersed, hung at many different levels or emerging out of recesses, holes and slots. Similar spaces are never exactly the same. The circulation is oblique and indirect. The largest space, the Debating Chamber, is hard to identify from outside and not easy to find inside.

So what are the characteristics that would qualify it as intricate architecture? Does it have a convincing architectural story to tell? Is it coherent in the sense that there are convincing relationships between the rich array of parts and the whole? Does it welcome human engagement and occupation at all scales and textures? Does it respond to its program and its technology in a way that not only accommodates but also celebrates its purposes?

So let us start with the issue of an architectural story. There are, of course, many stories to be told about this building: the history of Scottish Parliaments, the decision to build a new building after the decision was made to devolve many powers from Westminster to Edinburgh in the late 1990's, the selection of a site among several options including the highly visible neo-classical Royal High School on Calton Hill, the winning by Enric Miralles of the competition to select the architect with a handful of hand-drawn sketches, the development of the design in the face of growing public anger about the escalating cost estimates from the initial 40 million pounds to an ultimate cost of ten times as much, the premature deaths of not only Enric Miralles on July 3, 2000 but also, only a few months later, of Donald Dewar, the leader of the client team, the former Scottish Secretary and then the First Minister of Scotland, the subsequent realization of the building by the firm now led by Miralles' wife Benedetta Tagliabue in partnership with the Scottish architectural firm RMJM. But these are not the architectural stories told by the building.

2. Debate chamber and committee rooms.

3. Garden lobby and members dining room.

And then there are the metaphorical stories told by Miralles as he secured the commission and developed the design. Stories about twigs and leaves, about upturned boats and fishes. Stories about the influence of paintings such as Sir Henry Raeburn's painting of the Reverend Robert Walker Skating on Duddington Loch that was supposed to have helped shape important elements of the facades. These have all become part of the mythology of the building as the public has attempted to come to terms with it and understand it. However these are not stories told by the building, they are stories told about the building.

So what are the stories that we could learn from our experience of the building? First and foremost it is a building of curves; walls curve, and roofs and ceilings curve. But the curves are neither segmental nor parabolic; at their center they are segmental but before they could close they extend in straight-line tangents. The curves in plan are nearly always in opposition to each other, around a central space, but meeting often at an acute angle. That this can also be a description of the edges of a leaf or a boat may be of interest iconographically but that is not a sufficient reason for their existence. Far more important architecturally is the role of the curve as it embraces and signals a space of gathering. This is a building devoted to bringing groups of individuals together, sub-groups in the Committee Rooms and the entire Parliament in the Debating Chamber (Fig. 2), but also in smaller informal gatherings in the highly articulated Garden Lobby (Fig. 3). The particular nature of these curves, that they do not close as in a circle or oval,

4. Garden lobby interlocks with the garden and entrance plaza with an acute angle.

5. Exhibition area in the vaulted lobby.

6. Scottish Parliament building, member's office windows.

7. Offices of the members of the Scottish Parliament showing their window seats.

has a more subtle implication. The circle, particularly, is finite. These gathering spaces are intended to be more open-ended and flexible. As Jencks has suggested, "Miralles evolved a gentle, more convivial curve. It opens up to the sides, so that conversation and consensus come before disagreement, at least architecturally. And Miralles provided each party with seats in the front row, and movable seating, to follow changes in political fortune."[2]

Architecturally the sharp acute angles that result from the meeting of these curves in plan are the contrasting antitheses to the smooth shallow convex curves. Their presence accentuates the other, but spatially they carry incisive exclamatory power. They also act like saw teeth when acting in concert with others as in the relationship between the Garden and the Garden Lobby (Fig. 4).

Even many of the linear spaces, such as those in the Main Lobby (Fig. 5) and the individual offices of the Members of the Scottish Parliament, have curved vaults to help define them. The basic curve is used in elevation to help identify the individual Members of the Scottish Parliament through their differentially projecting window seats or bays, each of which is a variation on a generic model. Even the blast wall, introduced late in the design to combat terrorist attacks, adopts the curve.

The Members' window seats are a typically idiosyncratic creation by Enric Miralles, (Figs. 6, 7) as are several of the components of this design, but their raison d'etre is not flippant. Their purpose is to avoid the appearance of an office

8. Stepped gables.

block. It is to 'convey the sense of the building as a series of individuals. The Parliament should not have the appearance of an office building'.[3] Almost like separate sedan chairs protruding differentially from the main building they indicate the significance and individuality of their intended occupant. The seat is indicated in the larger step. The smaller steps suggest different placements for the feet. They also, as has been pointed out by others, echo the stepped gables of older Edinburgh buildings at the entrance to Holyrood Palace nearby (Fig. 8).

The screen of wooden posts that cover most of the major windows are a part of a theme of veiling, fencing, screening, filtering that is to be found in many different places throughout the building.

Urban Intricacy and the Scottish Parliament Building

Others have written eloquently about the almost urban quality of the building. In the book *Creating a Scottish Parliament* by Alan Balfour[4] there is a forward by George Reid Presiding Officer of the Scottish Parliament

"Miralles' parliament is therefore neither grand nor patrician. But for those of us who work there, it feels more like a village – a natural continuation of the Royal Mile, with its marketplace in the Garden Lobby, and its nooks and crannies reflecting the vennels and closes of the Old Town of Edinburgh and the barrios of Barcelona."[5]

And Balfour himself writes:

"The Parliament exists in the fusion between the topography of the Park and the structure of the City, embedded in the geological and social history of the place. Its form neither a preconceived portrait nor representation but drawn out of the physical residue of the place and the multiple performances of Parliament."[6]

Summary; does the Scottish Parliament building meet the criteria for Intricacy?

The answer is yes. For all its almost bewildering complexity the building has a coherent formal language that operates at a huge variety of scales, and that formal language is built around the theme of an architectural story that embraces, defines, and identifies the individuals, informal gatherings, small formal gatherings, and ultimately a coming together of the entire membership of the Scottish Parliament.

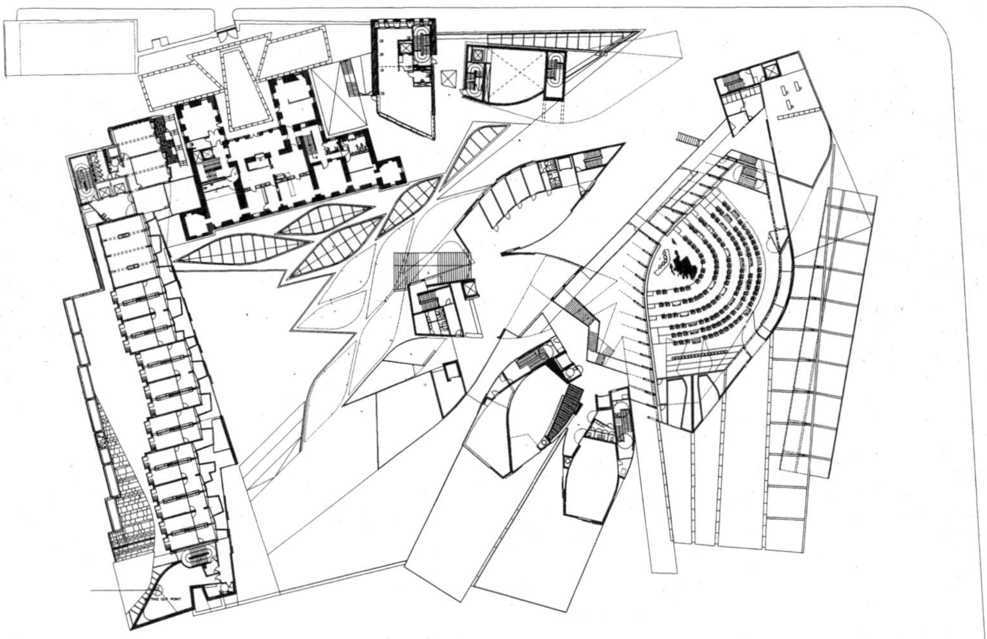

9. First level plan.

Notes

1. Greg Lynn's definition from his Essay in the catalogue for his exhibition: *INTRICACY: A Project By Greg Lynn FORM*
2. *The Scottish Parliament,* Charles Jencks, Scala Publishers Ltd 2005, pg. 13.
3. Miralles quoted by Alan Balfour in *Creating a Scottish Parliament*, (Finlay Brown 2005), pg. 52.
4. *Creating a Scottish Parliament*, Alan Balfour, (Finlay Brown 2005).
5. Ibid. Balfour, pg. 2.
6. Ibid. Ibid. Balfour, pg. 59.

Connection and Transmission, Translating the Potential of Site

Teresa Galí-Izard

1. Catalan farmers circa 1900.

When I was a child, I wanted to be an architect. I started drawing houses when I was 10 or 11 years old. When I was 15, I had teacher that was an architect and learned about Alvar Aalto. I was totally affected by the dream that through architecture, life can change–and in Barcelona, architecture is extraordinary. But one day I started drawing landscapes. Because the landscape architecture profession didn't exist when I was 20 years old, my father told me that I had to study something, so instead of starting architecture, I studied agronomy.

As a landscape architect and an agronomist, I have a very close relationship with the land. I was trained as an engineer, so in school I learned how to design irrigation systems, how to look at soils, how to improve soils, and how to have production with the objective of growing something. But, I have the mentality of an engineer. In school, I was very pragmatic, always working with reality, with jurisdiction. I am very serious when I design. I don't want to waste time.

At one point because I was an engineer, I actually had a reaction against design, but I worked with architects, a lot of architects. I thought sometimes that architects were too much and that there was no room for other's opinions–they want to control everything to the end! Though some say its "ego," architects do have the attitude of changing the world.

However, then I started working with architects who have a different way of working. Enric Miralles and other twentieth-century designers in Spain, and specifically in the region of Spain that runs through the country that is Catalonia, were thinking creatively; they used culture and the world of culture and the arts in their thought process. Inspired by them, I started to have my own way of designing and discovering a methodology of designing.

There is something universal in Mediterranean landscapes. If you go to Italy, Greece, or Spain, there are similar rules or logic in the landscape through the people who lived there and created it, though they don't know each other. It is like a homogeneous landscape with universal roots. As landscape architects, we are a filter. We try to transcribe the universality of a place. Each project is different, but we translate it for the best use of the place. It becomes an important part of the design process to be able to read the place (Fig. 2).

Generations of average people in Catalonia built the landscape and had to work very hard to have moments of leisure and to build the human environment, the human

2. Catalan agricultural landscape.

ecosystem in this area of Spain. But despite all their hard work, they are happy and proud workers. We have a difficult landscape to work with and don't have much money, so we have to be very smart and adapt if want to enjoy life. There is a Catalan expression "diversity and rationality": it means that we work in a very rational manner with a lot of constraints, but we have these moments of creativity. It comes from a lack of materials and a lack of richness. We are poor, and we have a poor landscape. Geography and culture affect the way we are. We are from a Mediterranean place.

This tradition of landscape culture across generations is about connections and transmissions. It is a common point for some designers in Catalonia, like Miralles, of context, place, and the same transmission of knowledge between generations, something that generally doesn't happen in design. As designers, we cannot avoid our past and our history. It is important to keep the transmission of this link between the past and the future.

Park Güell

Park Güell in Barcelona by Antoni Gaudí is well known for its explosion of colors and amazing shapes–truly a masterpiece. But, Park Güell is, in fact, a machine for harvesting water. Gaudí had a plan, a very hard-to-find plan, for the hydrology to follow the topography of the park. Water flowing from the mountain above moves to a central plaza area and is harvested. In the main upper plaza is a flat area, supported by columns. This plaza harvests water, and the water flows to the columns into a water tank. There is a system of reservoirs or tanks, so the whole butte system of the mountain is harvesting water, trying it to keep it on site (Figs. 3, 4).

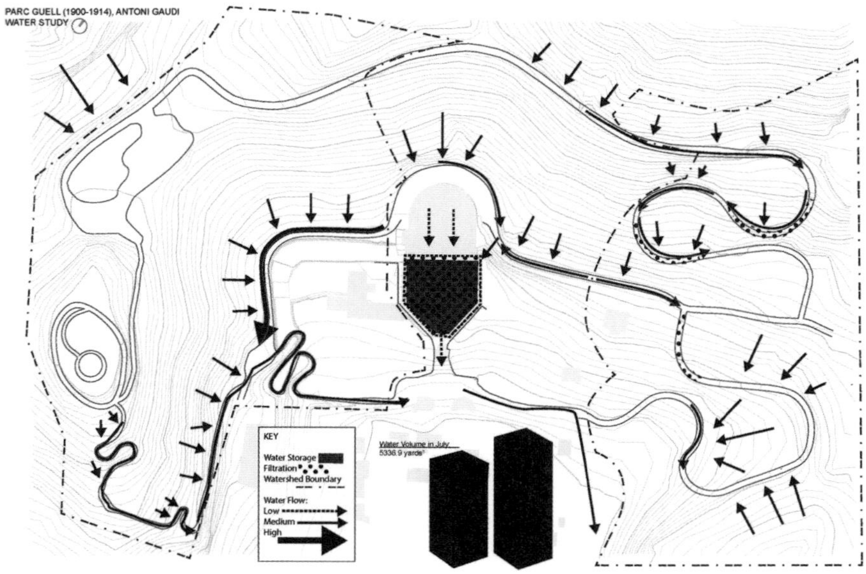

3. Drawing of water flow in Park Güell.

It is not only this central area that is harvesting water, but all the paths and sidewalks are a system of harvesting water as a system of viaducts. The slope of the mountain is very steep. Gaudí designed a system of paths to have a gentle slope and to use these paths as viaducts. These viaducts, built in a dry landscape, act like a sponge. The ground of the viaduct is permeable, which means water flows inside the viaduct and under the viaduct, and all the water is harvested through the land. Each piece of the park, each architecture of the land, has a relationship with water, and the final objective of this architecture was to harvest and to keep water inside the park.

At Park Güell, there are also walls made of dry stones, like Igualada Cemetery. Water flows through the wall and the lower part is compacted for strength–harvesting water and holding the land in place. It is clear that Gaudí understood that this would happen. He understood that the winds that bring moisture in the air from the sea and from the rain would accumulate into the structures of stones to be able to harvest the majority of the water in a very smart and a very simple way.

4. Park Güell main entrance by Antoni Gaudí.

A large part of the park is paths dividing the park into plots. The big idea of the park was a development: Gaudí built a system of plots to build housing. Between each plot are steps that channel water. If there is a summer storm, which usually happens in Barcelona, the steps and path and two walls on either side transform into a water channel. It is interesting to see how Gaudí was designing a path but thinking about water at the same time.

In September 2013, there was a discussion about how to maintain the park. Because the park was built with columns and paths to harvest water, there is a lot of vegetation growing around the columns, and vegetation is hiding the columns. The park manager was cutting the vegetation down, but what Gaudí intended was just the opposite. His intention was to have vegetation retain water, to harvest water, and to transform this very dry mountain into paradise of vegetation. So there is this contradiction between the intended function of the park and the outcome of its management.

Barcelona is a very local place where we resolve the problems we're facing very locally. I learned a lot about how to read place and how to translate place because I trained to do that there. In Barcelona, we are now in a moment where the urbanists and the architects have created an amazing city, but now it is time to think about natural living systems and how this is going to inform the city. Because people are interested in having healthy parks with trees along the streets and fountains and more biodiversity and natural spaces inside and outside the city.

5, 6. Igualada Cemetery by Miralles Pinós.

Igualada

The Igualada Cemetery was designed by Miralles and Carmen Pinós in a dry area of Spain. As a landscape project, it shows an attitude, a powerful way of understanding place–and it is a masterpiece. In a very smart, clear, intelligent way, it supports the conditions of and connection with the landscape (Figs. 5, 6).

At the end of the cemetery, there is a circle plaza where walls, landscape, and geology create the site. In Catalonia, there are simple and common structures called a "terra" made of stacked stone where farmers split the grain from the straw. The cemetery is in this same geological landscape, and Miralles and Pinós used basic stone and wood materials, reflecting who the Catalan people are.

The project resides in the landscape in a way that you don't know where the project ends or where the landscape begins or where the geology is man-made or natural. There is a translation of the relationship between natural dry stone hills in the landscape and the dry stone walls of the cemetery that mix the color and size of the stones to improve and to integrate the landscape. Stones are used to stop erosion and to harvest water, which encourages native plants to grow in between the stones and makes better conditions for plants. Miralles and Pinós designed that place using the power of architecture and the power of materials to respond to the landscape.

Sant Joan Landfill Restoration

In Spain, the landscape is beautiful. There is a mountain top in Barcelona– Montjuïc –a place that has inspired me a lot. From the mountaintop, you can see the hills and valleys spread out below and a series of flat terraces on the sides of the hills to grow fruit, like olives or apples. These interventions in the landscape cause patterns and paths that run from each other. You look horizontally and see a pattern of terraces or look vertically and see another pattern of terraces, which are very similar and open to an intellectual way of reading the landscape related to the direct experience of the land and of walking through and trying to discover the potential of the mountain. Because we live in a dry area and have little rain throughout the year, farmers build these terraces to keep the water on the land. There are different traditional strategies to stop erosion from the terraces, including stone walls on the edge of the fields for water retention (Fig. 7).

7. Aerial photographs, plan and section drawings of the Vall d'en Joan Landfill –inside the El Garraf Natural Park.

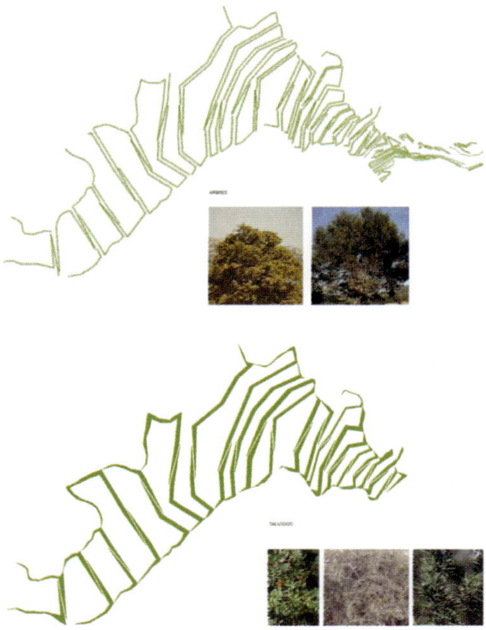

8. Plan drawings of Vall d'en Joan Landfill, El Garraf Natural Park.

I was the agricultural engineer on a landfill restoration project–a project that I care deeply about. In 1974, Barcelona built a landfill in a valley south of the city–the Vall d'en Joan Landfill–inside the El Garraf Natural Park, an interesting area in a classic Catalan landscape, meaning that the composition of the geology is classic–water flows through stones, but there is no clear drainage system. It was the worst place to have landfill, but in 1974, there were no other options for trash repository. There is no forest, only small shrubs, because there is not enough soil to grow a forest. Because the valley faces south, conditions are hard for agricultural production (Fig. 8).

In 2002, Spain received money from the European Union to be able to finish and restore the landfill and to change the way of managing it. The project was formidable. We were working together as a team with the municipality of Barcelona and different architects and engineers that were closer to the project than we were. But no one really understood what needed to be done, so we all learned a lot though the process. We had to start the restoration from the bottom instead of starting from the top, and it was very difficult to work from the bottom of the landfill, but that was the decision by the government.

The geology of the landfill was a valley of trash on top of some caves underneath, which were now full of contamination. The contamination is going to be there for many, many years, which I think is very important to say. Our job was to restore the condition of the landscape in the best way that we could, but the contamination is there and will be there for many years.

The landfill is a mix of organic and inorganic material. The reactions of the organic materials was producing gas, and the land was settling–a very important piece of the restoration to understand. We had to establish a system that could be applied over time. We built a system of 11 terraces in the first phase. The system we devised was simple—it would be a system of terraces and a system of flat areas where there would be revegetation. Since it was a landfill, we were not able to dig into the trash, so we had to add soil on top of the trash—over 90 meters of soil, which meant that the earthworks was an important piece of the project.

In the first phase, we were compacting soil and building the terraces. We spent nine months adding layers of soil. The landfill continued to settle, however, and would not maintain the elevation that we had in our plans, so we realized that we were not even working with stable land. When we finally arrived at the required elevation for making a terrace, we added a layer of gravel and a layer of geo-textile plastic that was insulating the trash from the new layer of soil. So it was quite complicated.

We also had to build a system of wells to extract the landfill gas and a system of drains for water—both important parts of the restoration. We worked with the engineers to build a network of wells that were extracting the gas and a network of drainages to control water, while trying to find a solution for the future water management and extraction of the gas. We were mixing the logic of architecture, the logic of engineers, and the logic of technology (Fig. 9).

As we were building the system of terraces, the terraces were draining into flat areas of the land. There was an existing channel for clean water, coming from the mountain. So our idea was to add one channel on each edge of the restoration. This was a problem because the highest point of the terraces was supposed to be in the center of the terrace and had to slope to the edges. But we were adding soil and the soil was settling. We constructed a system of stones to filter the water that was coming from the mountain and directed the water through the stones, like a sponge, using traditional materials to work in the land, like Miralles, like Gaudí, like traditional dry-land farmers.

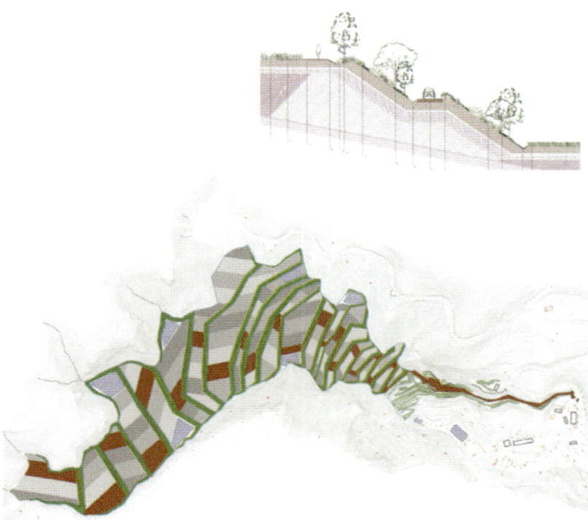

9. Plan and section drawing of Vall d'en Joan Landfill, El Garraf Natural Park.

At the bottom part of the landfill water system, we built two water tanks or reservoirs to retain water to irrigate the fields and flood the terraces. We used gravity as way of irrigating. The extraction of the gases and the irrigation system followed the same pattern.

We were also using traditional techniques in the remediation of the land. We were restoring a large area, so it was impossible to have high-quality organic soil. We planted legume herbs in the flat areas to improve the quality of the soil. We were planting a high density of shrubs and seeding herbs in the terraces. It is cheap to seed a flat area, but it is expensive to plant a high density of shrubs in front of dams. We decided to invest a lot of money in planting white pine trees in front of the terrace dams to have a fast improvement in soil stabilization. We used cows to help us with the weeds, because in between the new shrubs, we had a lot of invasive species that were not helping the shrubs that we wanted to grow.

Management of the project was to be an important part of this very interesting work. After finishing the construction, I spent three years going there and working with the manager. The project changes a lot depending on summer, spring, or winter. Over that time, we were able to deduce different ways of managing the landscape to help all the vegetation to grow in better conditions. I am quite happy about the results, because we connected the two slopes of the mountain and made this new landscape that is responding to the conditions of the landfill. We are building a new landscape and a new typology of landscape.

I was there last year and everything is getting wilder. The restoration is adding a new biology inside this park. But it is the context that we have learned so much from. We need to be able to change our management techniques due to new technologies and draw on old techniques to inform new projects to keep the link between the past and the future.

10, 11. Photographs of Vall d'en Joan Landfill, El Garraf Natural Park.

To arrive at sustainable world, there is an in-between step where we, as designers, must communicate what is

going on in the landscape to the rest of the community. We have to show how we are living, to show the metabolism of the city to the people who live there. When I was doing the landfill, the landfill was hidden from the city.

So nobody in Barcelona knows where the trash goes. It would be a nice exercise for everyone to visit a landfill to realize where the trash is going. When I was doing the restoration of the landfill, I thought, okay, I should have known this before! It changed the way I make decisions, how and why I buy things, and made me realize, "Okay, I don't have to produce so much trash."

As designers, we have the responsibility of doing projects that are beautiful and well designed, but we have to show how we live and how our ecosystem works. Now is the time to stop hiding how the water system works, how the drainage system works, or where the trash goes: then people will understand what our ecosystem is about. For me that is the step in-between. This amazing word "sustainability" comes from the top, but I think the only way of changing society and people is from the bottom, with the people. And for me the only way that society will change is for people to become aware of what's going on.

Design needs a new language. So, I am going to work for living systems—I am going to be the living systems woman in a world of architects. After working and trying to change what I can in the world, I have realized that the way of making change is through architecture. Because architecture is communicating. It is direct. It is something that you can see and you can understand and you can remember. It is one moment. It is something fixed, but it can play the role of starting the process of having life change with dynamic landscapes. So finally…I am an architect.

Exercises in Style

Carles Muro

1. Raymond Queneau, *One Hundred Million Million Poems*, 1961.

Enric Miralles understood both the history of architecture and the design process itself as a form of conversation –a conversation whose start had already taken place and in which we simply had to engage. In this presentation I would like to continue a conversation that started between Enric and myself many years ago or, rather, continue a conversation that he and I both happily joined.

I would like to share some thoughts about the mechanisms for the production of art in general, and architecture in particular, which I believe are relevant to contemporary practice. Over the past few years, I have been exploring the notion of a "Potential Architecture" that works with systems of self-imposed constraints in the production of architecture. The work of the architect is conditioned by a number of parameters and variables that delimit and demarcate the designer's field of action. These parameters may relate to site, climate, budget, regulations, material availability, construction technique, etc. Architects often refer to them in order to justify unsuccessful aspects of their designs but the steepest of sites, the most extreme of climates, the skimpiest of budgets, the strictest of regulations and the most severe material and technical limitations could instead be transformed into springboards for unique design opportunities. It is my contention that architects can achieve greater freedom in their work through an apparent limitation of that very same freedom.

The title of this talk, Exercises in Style, was also the title of a seminar that some colleagues and I taught in Barcelona, under the direction of Enric Miralles, in 1995. The title was borrowed from a book by Raymond Queneau, published in 1947, in which an event of the utmost banality is told in 99 different ways. The idea for the book came to Queneau in the 1930s after attending a concert together with his friend Michel Leiris at the Salle Pleyel in Paris, where Bach's The Art of Fugue had been played. He entertained the idea of exploring the notion of the variation on a theme in the territory of literature. The event described in the book consists of only two short paragraphs and is about a young man on a crowded bus at peak time who gets into an argument with another man. Two hours later, the writer sees the same man in another part of Paris speaking to a friend who suggests he should have an additional button put on his overcoat. The story is then told in 99 different ways. The inconsequentiality of the event is key to the exercises and allowed Queneau to concentrate on the literary investigation. The large number of variations chosen by Queneau forced him to explore new and unexpected approaches to the production of text.

2. Ray and Charles Eames, advertisement for the Eames chairs.

Enric had just come across a recent Catalan translation of the book and, strongly fascinated by it and with his usual intuition, immediately decided to use it as a pedagogical tool in architecture. This led to the Exercises in Style seminar at the Barcelona School of Architecture, where we playfully organized a series of lectures under constraint and students developed a number of variations on the idea of the column. This was my introduction to the work of Queneau and the Oulipo and, eventually, this also led to my initial explorations of the territory of Potential Architecture.

I would like to start the talk with an image showing two characters who were also very dear to Enric Miralles: Ray and Charles Eames (Fig. 2). It is a self-portrait intended to be part of the promotional material for the DCM chair (1946). A number of metal chair structures seem to be holding them in place, like giant staples preventing or limiting their movements: a visual allusion to the notion of constraint. Probably the work of no other designer summons up the feeling of freedom and optimism of Postwar America more clearly and powerfully than that of the Eames'. However, their playful and spirited work and their very understanding of the design process is heavily governed by the notion of constraint. In the interview conducted by Madame Amic as the basis of their contribution to the exhibition What is Design? (Paris,1969) and later in the film Design Q&A (1972), Charles Eames makes the following statement:

Mme. L. Amic: Does the creation of design admit constraint?

Charles Eames: Design depends largely on constraints.

Mme. L. Amic: What constraints?

Charles Eames: The sum of all constraints. Here is one of the few effective keys to the design problem: the ability of the designer to recognize as many of the constraints as possible, his willingness and enthusiasm for working within these constraints. The constraints of price, of size, of strength, of balance, of time, etc.; each problem has its own peculiar list.

The notion of Potential Architecture directly alludes to that of Potential Literature and the work of the Oulipo, an acronym for Ouvroir de littérature potentielle (Workshop for Potential Literature). The group deals not so much with specific works of literature but with the mechanisms for their production. It seeks to find not so much what literature is –nor what it should be– but rather what it could be. The group was founded by Raymond Queneau –a writer with a passion for mathematics– and François Le Lionnais –a mathematician with a passion for literature– in 1960, when Queneau was working on One Hundred Thousand Billion Poems and often discussed the progress of his work with Le Lionnais and, more widely, the use of mathematical structures and models in the production of literature. Queneau's book consists of only ten pages, each containing one sonnet. Each of the fourteen lines of each sonnet is then cut into individual strips. As the sonnets follow the same structure and rhyme scheme, by flipping the strips a potential reader can freely recombine the lines and temporarily capture one of the 100,000,000,000,000 (1014) fleeting poems contained in this extremely thin book. To give a quick idea of the enormity of the task, at a pace of one poem per minute, eight hours a day, seven days a week, it would take more than 570 million years for someone to read all the poems carefully packed in this book.
It should be clear by now that the aim of this book was not necessarily to be read in its entirety.

In addition to Queneau and Le Lionnais the group would eventually include Noël Arnaud, Marcel Bénabou, Italo Calvino, Marcel Duchamp, Jean Lescure, Harry Mathews, Georges Perec and Jacques Roubaud, among others. The members of the group have been passionately investigating new forms and structures which may be used by writers. The notion of constraint is central to their investigations. The work of the writer is limited or constrained by the nature of language, by literary genres, etc. In addition to these, Oulipians centered their investigations on the use of self-imposed constraints in an attempt to gain a different kind of freedom and explore new paths for literature.

3. Saul Steinberg drawing *The Art of Living,* 1976, inspired by the Georges Perec book *Life A User's Manual,* 1978.

No one explored the potential of the use of self-imposed constraints in literature simultaneously more playfully and more radically than Georges Perec (Fig. 3). In A Void (La Disparition, 1969) he wrote a 300-page novel without using the letter "e". The story is centered around a group of people searching for a missing companion. Given that the letter "e" is the most used in French, the writing of this piece forced him to make very unique choices of vocabulary, structures and constructions which allowed him to rediscover his own language through a process of defamiliarization or estrangement. The fact that some of the first reviewers of the novel failed to notice such a harsh constraint speaks of his incredible mastery of language. This lipogram was followed by The Exeter Text: Jewels, Secrets, Sex (Les Revenentes, 1972), a work in which, almost as a form of retribution, "e" was the only vowel used. The translation of these works, by the way, constitutes a very sophisticated rewriting project in itself as the translations should be written through analogous constraints: that is, for instance, without using the most frequent vowel in the target language.

Georges Perec died in Paris in March 1982 at the age of forty-five. He was probably not able to complete his life's project but he definitely left a piece that bears witness to his talent and the uniqueness of his endeavors. Extraordinary from many points of view Life: A User's Manual has rightfully been described as "a tapestry of interwoven stories and ideas." All the events described in the book refer to a certain place and a particular time. The place is an apartment building at 11 Rue Simon-Crubellier in Paris and the time, June 23, 1975, just before 8pm: the exact location and time of the main character's death. One of the visual inspirations for the project was a drawing by Saul Steinberg whose facade had been removed so that one could see inside like in

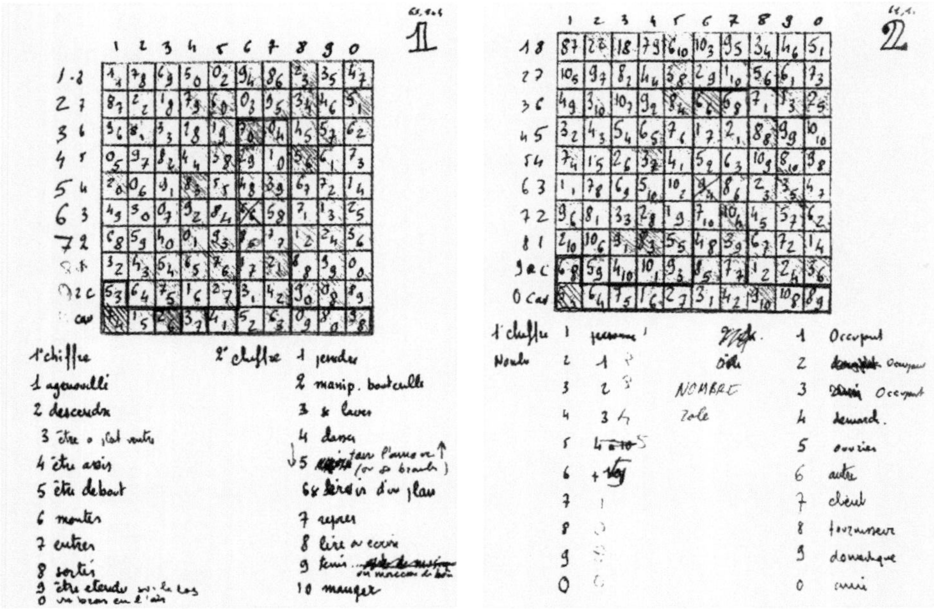

4. Raymond Queneau, drawings for "The Story as You Like," 1959.

a dollhouse. Perec devised a section of the building based on a 10x10 square grid: 10 squares high (including basements, eight storeys and attics) and 10 squares wide (allowing for different combinations of rooms, apartments and the stairwell). The book was written in accordance with a series of extremely sophisticated formal procedures and constraints. Each square is assigned a chapter and the order of the chapters is determined by a Knight's Tour: that is, following the movements of a knight on this expanded chessboard in such a way that the knight visits each square once and only once. However, one of the basements is bypassed, resulting in a book with 99 chapters (like the 99 variations of Queneau's Exercises). Perec also devised a complex system that would provide him, through the use of another mathematical device, with a long list of objects, conditions or references that each chapter had to include, comply or allude to. These came from other sets of lists containing animals, colors, furniture, style, quotations by writers, the very length of the chapter in pages, etc. As he wrote, he would check that he complied with all these conditions. Perec kept many notebooks full of lists and squares and he rightfully called them "specifications", like the detailed descriptions that accompany construction documents. The work of Perec has often been referred to as "linguistic acrobatics". However, he always understood constraints as a form of literary scaffolding. As in building, they are meant to be temporary structures that, once removed, leave no traces on the constructions they have assisted and supported. This brief description gives an idea of the ambition of Perec's work and the complexity of his task, but it is important to note that the innumerable constraints that aided him in the production of the book do not get in the way of a conventional and extremely enjoyable reading. Life: A User's Manual can be seen as one of the most fascinating literary experiments in French literature but also remains one of the most important works of literature, in its own right, of the late twentieth century.

Before moving to other fields of artistic creation, it should be noted that many Oulipian authors and most of the visual artists I will be referring to often used sketches and diagrams to support their thinking and present their ideas. This is the case of A Story as You Like It (1967) (Fig. 4), in which Raymond Queneau uses a graph that allows the reader to combine 21 different story lines to produce a number of different stories, by continuously making choices while walking in a garden of forking paths.

This diagram is not that dissimilar to the blueprint that Wile E. Coyote holds in his hands in Beep, Beep (1952) (Fig. 5). Few territories would be less suspicious of being governed by rules and constraints than that of animated cartoons. However, the series' creator Chuck Jones disclosed in his autobiography that all the episodes were based on constraints. This is quite fantastic, but on the other hand, quite natural. If you think about what we like about cartoons is that they are based on rules, and this is precisely what makes them funny. The Wile E. Coyote and the Road Runner cartoons are subject to constraints of language, of environment, of tool and gadget origin, etc. Here are some of the rules: no dialogue ever, except "beep-beep"!; the Road Runner must stay on the road –otherwise, logically,

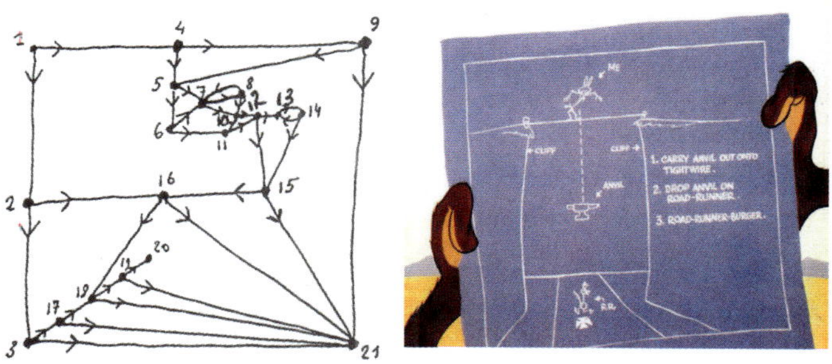

5. Chuck Jones, drawing and cartoon for Wile E. Coyote.

he would not be called Road Runner; all action must be confined to the natural environment of the two characters –the Southwest American Desert; and all materials, tools, weapons, or mechanical conveniences must be obtained from the ACME Corporation. The Coyote and Road Runner cartoons –arguably the best animated series of all time– relied heavily on constraints and can be seen as a very special form of the variations on a theme.

I have been particularly interested in artists that have obsessively worked through series and variations exploring and expanding the limits of their disciplines with the conscious introduction of self-imposed constraints. It has helped them define precise and productive territories for research. This is the case of Jasper Johns and his series of American flags (Fig. 6). Johns said that he had chosen the American flag because it already provided a specific geometric structure that needed no justification and allowed him to concentrate strictly on a pure painterly investigation. His first Flag, painted in 1954-55, opened up 40 years of work on this theme, which would include variations based on different drawing, painting and printing techniques as well as on the manipulation of color or pattern –including monochromes, nestings, duplications, inversions, etc.

Sol LeWitt presents one of the most consistent trajectories in American art of the late twentieth century. His work, be it drawings, photographs, structures, wall drawings or books is always informed by the notion of seriality. LeWitt started an extraordinary investigation on the cube in the mid-1960s. Works such as Incomplete Open Cubes (1974) –where he explores the 122 variations which could be created by systematically subtracting edges from a cube following a precise set of rules– or Cube (1988) –where he explores, through Carol Huebner's photographs, the "511 permutations of 9 light sources directed from different angles on a single white cube"– bear witness to the rigorous and obsessive nature of his work (Fig. 7). Le Witt, similarly to Jasper Johns when commenting on his choice of the American flag as a subject, once said: "the most interesting characteristic of the cube is

6. Jasper Johns, one of over forty paintings of the American Flag.

7. Sol LeWitt, 122 permutations of a single white cube.

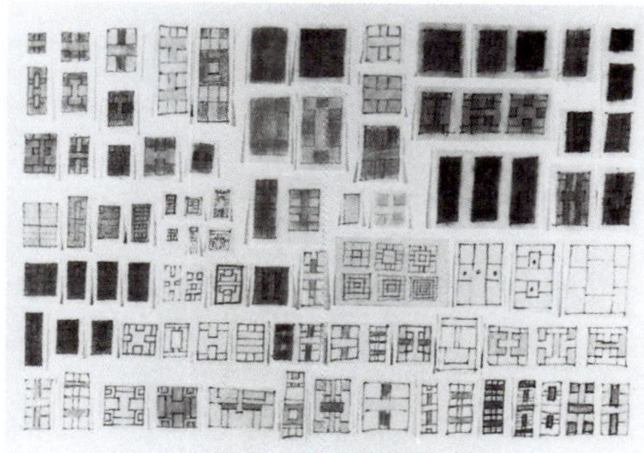

8. Ad Reinhardt, drawing for 120 black square paintings, 1956.

that it is relatively uninteresting." It is precisely (once again) the neutrality of the subject that allows the artist to concentrate on very specific issues of his choice. But, contrary to Johns' use of the variation as an endless mechanism for the production of work, LeWitt's variations tend to completely exhaust all the possibilities of the chosen theme.

Probably one of the more radical artists of the 1960s was Ad Reinhardt (Fig. 8), who progressively narrowed his field of research to monochrome paintings –mostly red or blue–, and eventually concentrated, from 1953 until his death in 1967, exclusively on black paintings. A visitor walking into the retrospective exhibition held at The Jewish Museum in 1966, would find rooms with a large number of apparently identical black square paintings, all the same size: "five feet wide, five feet high [...] (not large, not small, sizeless)." The paintings are divided into nine squares, and the difference of the shine on the finish and the direction of the brush stroke created, on closer examination and sustained observation, a number of variations that clearly resist reproduction. He had radically narrowed his field with the ambition to produce "the last paintings anyone can paint."

Max Bill's Fifteen Variations on a Single Theme (1935-38) develop from a very interesting spiraling construction of partially open equilateral regular polygons, starting with an equilateral triangle and leaving the progression with a regular octagon. Then Bill produces fifteen variations on the same figure by applying a number of rules to sides, vertices, etc. Bill's proposition aimed at showing how such a rigorous geometry contained a huge artistic potential and allowed for "individual inclination and

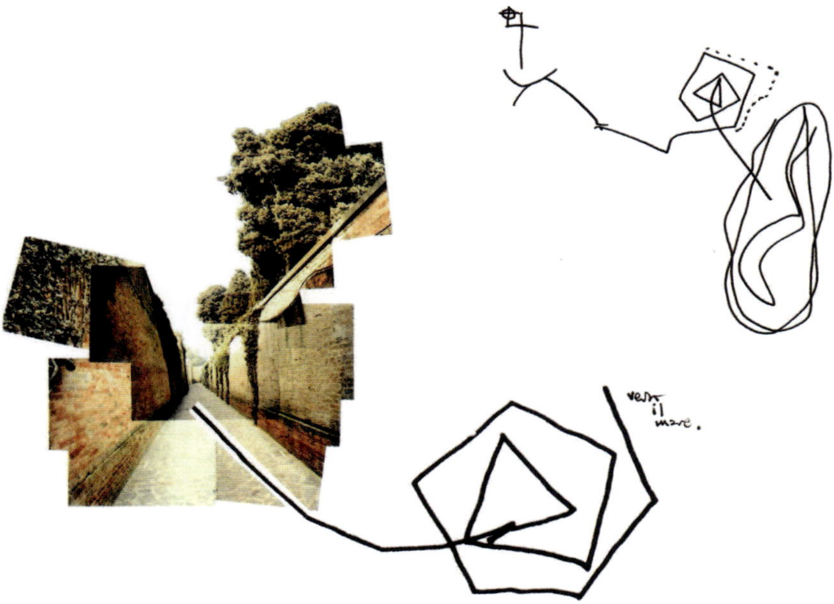

9. Enric Miralles, collage for Isola San Michele, Venice, 1998.

temperament" to manifest itself. Enric Miralles borrowed Max Bill's geometry and used it in his competition entry for the extension of the Cemetery of San Michele in Venice (1998) (Fig. 9).

We could trace the use of self-imposed constraints in the work of many more artists –from Paul Klee to Ed Ruscha or Sophie Calle–, filmmakers –from Alfred Hitchcock to Lars von Trier–, musicians –from Johann Sebastian Bach to Arnold Schönberg, Igor Stravinsky (Fig. 10), John Cage or Brian Eno–, writers, etc. It could be said that the use of self-imposed constraints is a necessary precondition for a relevant contemporary practice.

Even in the work of such a gigantic figure as Picasso (Fig. 11), moments of intense work under constraint can be found. Picasso produced a large number of drawings where he did not raise his pencil from the paper until the drawing was finished. These single line drawings –which include a collection of animals, circus scenes or dancers– forced him to draw in a different way and allowed him to explore new potentials for

10. Igor Stravinsky, musical composition, ca.1950.

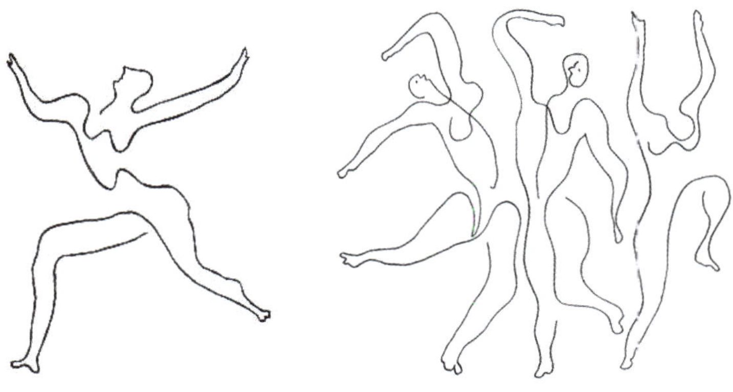

11. Pablo Picasso , drawings of dancing figures, 1924.

drawing in his continuous reinvention of the artist's practice. In his own words: "Forcing yourself to use restricted means is the sort of restraint that liberates invention. It obliges you to make a kind of progress that you can't even imagine in advance."

12. Philippe Petit, tightrope walk between Twin Towers, New York, 1974.

Before we walk back into architecture, I will show an image that beautifully condenses the notion of constraint. This is an image of Philippe Petit during his famous high-wire walk between the Twin Towers in New York City, on August 7, 1974 (Fig. 12). He stayed on the tightrope for some 45 minutes, during which he walked, danced and even lay down, feeling safe and comfortable on the wire. That was for him the easy part, the difficult being the planning of the feat. He had to learn everything about the buildings, their construction and their structural performance, as well as their security systems, etc. in order to be able to get to the top and rig the cable across the 42m gap between the towers. He described this complex process in a fascinating book, On the High Wire, which Paul Auster translated into English. Auster had met Petit in Paris, when he was working there as a translator and Petit was walking between the towers of Notre Dame. Paul Auster later described Petit's venture in the most precise and beautiful of ways: "Working under the greatest possible constraints on a stage no more than an inch across., the high-walker's job is to create a sensation of limitless freedom."

In the winter of 1928, Ludwig Mies van der Rohe was working on the German Pavilion for the International Exposition in Barcelona to be held the following year (Fig. 13). At some point, he decided that a freestanding wall would be central to his design and started looking for a block of stone to build the wall. He wanted it to be very unique but did not have a preconceived idea of the type of stone to be used for the wall. Mies trained as a stonemason and knew that marble cannot be moved from the quarry in

13. Mies van der Rohe, German Pavilion for the 1929 International Exposition in Barcelona.

winter because the moisture contained within it could freeze and cause it to break. Mies visited a great many warehouses in Berlin, looking for a dry block of marble, but could not find anything satisfactory. Eventually in Hamburg, he came across an extraordinary block of onyx, 240 x 160 x 60 centimetres in size. This block was to determine one of the Pavilion's most important dimensions: its interior height. Many years later, Mies recalled this decision: "This block had a certain size and, since I only had the possibility of taking this block, I made the Pavilion twice that height." The time constraints and the desire to make optimum use of such an expensive material led Mies to fix the interior height of the Pavilion at 310 centimetres.

Immediately after the Exposition, the structure was dismantled, but was later reconstructed on its original site in the 1980s. The architects that rebuilt it went around the world looking for a new stone for the wall. They eventually found a block of onyx doré in Algeria and brought it back to Barcelona. They actually cut it to fit the height of the original pavilion, discarding some of the stone. They reproduced the dimensions, but did not reproduce the criteria for deciding them. I always thought that if Mies van der Rohe would have rebuilt the pavilion, he would have allowed himself to reproduce the decision making process. and not only its outcome Thus, a new block would have informed the new construction's height and it would have been either a little bit higher or a little bit lower.

As almost anywhere in the world, Japanese regulations require a certain safety distance to be left, a space one cannot build in, around high-tension wires. When Kazuo Shinohara received the commission to design a house on a small plot situated in a dense area of Tokyo (Fig. 14), he realised that to leave the orthogonal projection of the two cables that cross the plot free would excessively condition the project and would make it impossible to respond to the programme his client requested from him. Free from prejudice, Shinohara was to make an intelligent and literal reading of the regulations and push them to their limit. By transforming the safety distance from a planimetric projection into a radius, two virtual overlapping cylinders –one around each

14. Katsuyoshi Ohara, residential house in Tokyo, Japan.

15. Hugh Ferriss, drawing from The Metropolis of Tomorrow, 1929.

cable– were generated. The intersection of the virtual cylinders with the projection of the buildable area defines the building's envelope. That twin groove, which like a double blow defines the roof, is undoubtedly the design's most characteristic formal feature and, as a side effect, produced a number of unique interior spaces that would have been unimaginable under a more conventional design process. This project clearly shows an ability to recognize a given constraint, to push it to its limits, and to explore all of its spatial implications.

The very same year in which Mies built the Barcelona pavilion, Hugh Ferriss published The Metropolis of Tomorrow. The book includes a series of drawings that illustrate the maximum envelope that the 1916 Zoning Law would allow for a typical Manhattan block (Fig. 15). Some of his drawings present, without formal preconceptions and with extreme beauty, the image of a new and surprising potential city. Manhattan could be seen as a series of variations on that theme, informed by additional variables and constraints. In Delirious New York, Rem Koolhaas synthesized the nature and potential of the New York Zoning Law: "it isn't just a legal document; it's also a project."

In 1998 MVRDV published FARMAX, which explores the possibilities of extremes within a larger project that tries to go beyond "artistic" intuition or known geometries in the production of architectural form. One of the pieces contained in the book is "Gothics: study for the densification of the centre of Amsterdam, the Netherlands." This exercise tries to investigate and visualize the maximum density of an 18th century block in the centre of Amsterdam without changing its image from street level. To do so, they make an extrusion of all the unbuilt area at the centre of the block, and then, they trim this mass according to sightlines from each of the streets surrounding the block. In this process, the original FAR of 0.8 is increased to 7.8. From a bird's-eye view, the new constructions inhabiting the old Amsterdam blocks bear an incredible resemblance to Ferris' Manhattan blocks (Fig. 16).

So far, we have been looking at projects informed by either self-imposed or given constraints. To conclude our tour, we will examine a building informed by both types. If we were to write the history of Modern Architecture under constraint, we would probably have to start (or impose on ourselves to start), like some other histories have, with a visit to the Great Exhibition of the Works of Industry of All Nations, which took place in London in 1851. The Crystal Palace is framed by two numbers –49 and 1851. The former stands for a given constraint while the latter stands for a

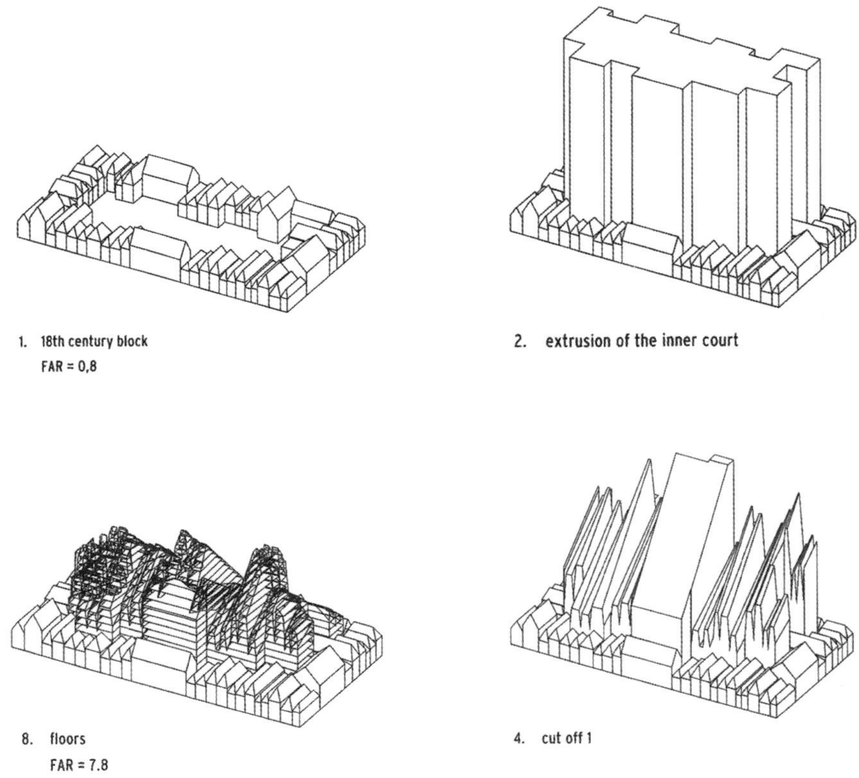

16. MVRDV Architects, "Aztec" studies for Amsterdam, 1997.

self-imposed one. 49 was the maximum size, in inches, that the British industry could produce flat glass. 1851 was the total length, in feet, of the building. The construction had to be very big, as it was meant to contain, as a sort of physical encyclopedia, the whole world. However, it was very difficult to decide on its exact dimensions. The year of the Exhibition offered an arbitrary and very welcome solution to this problem. Finally, Paxton modified the design shortly before construction began in order to respond to what could be seen as an additional given constraint: the high, barrel-vaulted transept was designed to accommodate some elm trees existing in the site, so that no trees had to be felled in Hyde Park because of the Exhibition (Fig. 17).

In our walk through the woods of constraints, we could pay a visit to many other works of art and architecture. I believe that the diversity of the examples examined will allow for a reevaluation of the role of the constraint in contemporary practice. The understanding of the potential of given and self-imposed constraints erases the deep-rooted opposition between necessity and arbitrariness, and gives us a better understanding of how artists and architects make decisions in their practices.

17. Joseph Paxton, Crystal Palace from the Great Exhibition of 1851.

Conversation

Teresa Galí-Izard
+
Carles Muro
+
Students

Conversation with Teresa Galí-Izard

Student I thought the description of the farmers and explorers was great. In your design work, do you think of yourself as an engineer, farmer, or architect?

Teresa Galí-Izard In my work, I pretend not to be an author but to try to transcribe the universality of the place. That's what I try to teach to my students. As landscape architects, we are a filter. I have this attitude of, "Teresa, don't be so strict with yourself. You can play a little. You can have this moment of creativity." But I think it is because of my education. I always want to be very humorous, but I am very serious. People say that in my work, there is some part of this creativity. Each project is different because I translate it for the best of the place. It becomes important to be able to read the place. So this is one important part of the process.

You talk about reading place. Can you describe what types of things you are reading?

Reading the place comes from this rural tour idea of giving the world to the natural elements of the place. For example when we were studying the river, I ask the students to be the river—"you are the river"—when we were studying the river crossing in Charlottesville. So I said, don't think about the river as a problem, don't think about flooding, don't think about erosion: you are the river, you are free; as the river, you tell the inhabitants of Charlottesville what the relationship has to be, to do this you have to be the river.

That means that they had to draw. And, for example, a student was drawing the banks of the river and, instead of talking about erosion, she was drawing the shapes of the erosion. She was drawing the different ways that water cuts the bank when water from the watershed arrives to the river, but in a very free way, and so, suddenly, we were discovering new languages.

I tell my students that our message has to be optimistic, which means that we are not going to save the world, but we have to try. We can do very nice things with contaminated water, for example, or we can work with erosion in a different way. We can include this input into our designs in a more free way of looking differently.

To arrive at a sustainable world in-between, there is a step, which is being able to communicate what is going on to everyone else. As designers, I think that in this in-between, we have to show how we are living, to show the metabolism of the city to the people who live in the city.

There is a lot of recycling that's happening here in the U.S., and it is much more in the public eye, but we are a long way from being what you would call sustainable.

If we have, right in front of us, how we live and how our ecosystem works, we are being responsible as designers. It is the end of hiding the processes; we need to show people how the systems work: water system, the drainage system, the trash system—everything! People have to understand what the food ecosystem is in order to change the way that they eat. As designers, we have the responsibility of doing projects that are beautiful and well designed. But for me, it's a step in-between, because this amazing word "sustainability" comes from the top, and we, as architects, talk about it; but no, the only way of changing is that society changes. And for me, the only way that society changes is that society has to be aware of what's going on if we design a city where the drainage system is clear and presentable.

There is a second part of this: how do we redistribute resources in the larger context of the world? This is a key question. The world is not global, because people don't have the same basic rights in all of the countries in the world. So if you don't have basic rights, like a health system and food, that means it is not global. As intellectuals, we have to go against this idea that the world is global. It is global for economics, for business, for financial things, but it is not global for people.

Faculty This idea that we live in a global world is interesting. We live locally. We're not responding to the rainforest problem; we're responding to whether or not it rains in our backyard. We are aware of what's happening globally more than we ever have before, but we have the same problems that are local when you talk about design.

Barcelona is a very local place where we resolve the problems we're facing very locally. I can be here because I was local. I learned a lot in Barcelona about how to read place and how to translate place, and I have the training to do that here. I think that the U.S. is totally different, but I understand that because I spent a lot of time and energy looking at the local things.

About this idea of globalization—I have information about everywhere, and I am here. For example, I don't have the same health system that I have when I am in Spain. I am the same person. But it is totally different and makes me feel totally different if I am there or here. I have a health system in Spain that is amazing, but it costs a lot, and I don't know who is paying, and Spain has this big debt. However, I feel that I am protected in my country, but here I am not covered. This feeling makes me react differently to everything in my life. We are not global when we have to work locally.

Student There are many architects that are practicing globally and certainly many of Miralles' projects were not local. Many of the major design studios, and I'm sure a number of the ones in Spain, now are practicing in an international way. What do you think about that?

I am working in Caracas, Venezuela. Because I learned how to read place, I am using the same ideas there as a landscape architect. In Caracas, the city is growing against the landscape. Now, in a lot of cities, it is the landscapes that are informing the city. So what I am doing is understanding the mountain, understanding the geology, understanding earth movements that have occurred in the mountain, in a very free way. The way that I work is that the language is very important, so I translate all of the information into drawings from the beginning. I don't say that I am doing an analysis; I say that I am doing a translation. And everything has to be a drawing. I put all of my drawings in front of me, and it is like, obsessive; all of the information has to be translated. What is amazing, for example, is that I am reading the drainage system, the topography, how the topography has changed. I am reading the system of paths, of roads, the flat areas, the slopes, and I am drawing all that. At the end, when I have all of these drawings, with all of the logic, is that suddenly I have to ask, what is the next step?

Are you drawing exactly what's there?

Yes, exactly what it is. I have long discussions with one of my mentors, the French landscape architect Jacques Simon. He is not very well known, and he is now 80. He is always using diagrams. I say, how do you know that this is going to work? It is like I am checking, like in any situation. But, this is a system that works very well for me. So I say to myself, wait, you have to let the place talk. And my way of doing that is by drawing. It is very important. It can be hand drawings or AutoCAD, but you have to understand what you are doing. For example, I do AutoCAD all in black and white, because when you start adding color, it is too refined.

Drawing is a language. This means, for example, in Caracas I waited and one day the design appeared. And it is not me; it is the place that is creating the result. Or it is telling me where the potential is. For example, the project in Caracas has the mountain as the background. They have done a lot of earth movement. I say, okay, it's always the city against the mountain, and we have to finish the mountain, and we have to shape the mountain. It is a place to harvest water, but this knowledge comes from a study of what has happened in the past.

Isn't it that the drawing intuitively appears? I am missing how it can be read by others, that I may read your information in a different way.

I am sure it is intuitive, but when you are drawing, you are choosing the hatch, the weight of the line; you are making a lot of decisions, and all of these decisions come from your intuition. It is like you are choosing the language, because you are making choices. Sometimes you don't know why you are drawing the section like that, but through drawing, you are making a lot of decisions.

Faculty When you draw, you are making a direct translation of what you are thinking. That's the difference between drawing and photographing. I completely learned this process from working with Enric—this process of drawing the place very carefully with the same 0.18mm repediograph pen—everything drawn independently, separately, to be able to put it back together.

The other thing I found was that drawing that way gives you a lot of confidence. The more you know the place, the more problems are going to be solved because you understand what's going on there, and the more confident you are about the decisions you make. When you know, for example, how the water is flowing, then when you decide to put the road in, you know if the road will interrupt the direction of the water. You really understand how the place is working, then it is much easier to make decisions on how to construct something there.

I just say to my students, you have to enjoy, you have to love, these places; you have to be a tree, be a forest.

Student The more time spent with the place, the better relationship you'll have with it.

But, don't be apathetic. Don't be anxious about having a quick idea. Usually it is just another understanding of the place. I have had this discussion with Jacques Simon, who says, wait, wait, let the place tell us. We can do this exercise, and I think it is time to do this exercise. Because then you can be very global; if you know how to read the place in Barcelona or in Caracas, you can read anywhere.

Architects can get obsessive with the idea of how much is enough. How do you deal with this?

It is that architects want to have control of everything. In landscape, you can't control everything, because you are working with something that is changing over time and uncertainty. You don't know if you're going to have a drought and how it will react with the place. What's important and what's less important? And you want to have a feedback between this variable and the project. The key point is, what do you want to change? What is going to start a new process that you can't control? It is much more open, and you have to imagine many more alternatives. Like the Miralles cemetery, it is a masterpiece; it is an attitude; for me, it is a way of understanding place that makes the project pretty powerful.

And that I think you need to make your own beliefs. That is what I'm gathering from you—that you listen to the project, to the site, but you also converse with the site—like a person having a chat.

Sometimes I am much too rigorous with myself. Jacques Simon was always engaging new things, new languages, from the site. Like I said, I think that I am too serious, and he was always playing with topography, making sculptures with earth and planting trees, but not vertically. He started a new process in a very careful way using few materials and not a lot of money. I would like to be him, sometimes, to be much more playful. I am trying to play a little.

We have this obsession of looking for excellence. Maybe it's the same as I was talking about yesterday, that people from Catalonia have this expression that says diversity and rationality and the heck with you! I don't know why, but I think it comes from this idea of lack of materials, lack of richness. The geography affects us a lot and we have to work very hard to have food in this context. Yes, finally, culture affects the way we are—our past and our history—you cannot avoid that.

I am the coauthor of a book, written with Jacques Simon, called *The Same Landscapes: Ideas and Interpretations* that shows my youthful anxiousness. It is a compilation of my ideas when I was 25 and had a lot of ideas in my mind. I started working with architects and seeing things I was not comfortable with. I thought I had to write about these ideas, and after working a lot, I was self-imposing certain restrictions. I was looking at living and dynamic systems, because this was what the landscape was about. I was learning how to design, how to think on different moments in a projects, how to play with living systems and natural systems in my work. Also, I was teaching, and when you are teaching, you have to rethink what you are doing—how to explain it, how to make it, and how people can learn from you and your experience.

When I was in Spain teaching landscape at university, one day I decided to stop teaching inside a building and told my students to come to my country house for a workshop. I organized two workshops with the Architectural Association School of Architecture in London. The assignment was reading place using a string. The first day, we strung a line crossing the ridge of the mountain to the foot of the mountain using five parallel lines. We spent eight hours doing that! The students had to read the landscape using the line and had to draw one element. The Mediterranean forest is very dense with a lot of shrubs, and it wasn't easy to cross the forest with a straight line, so we had to spend a lot of time making this line.

I learned that this process opened a lot of potential for learning—and I learned a lot! Training in architecture is amazing because you learn to have a very open mind in an abstract way. There was a student making notes about branches that were crossing the line. He was reading the branches in a very strict way. By drawing the branches inside the forest, he was drawing the forest. By drawing the density of branches crossing the line, he was talking about the forest. Where the line was crossing a field, there were no lines. The line crossed the edge between the field and the forest, and again there were a lot of branches crossing. He was drawing the landscape in an abstract but very vigorous way. Each student was drawing in a different way. After that, we did the same exercise in the forest trying to draw a circle. It was very difficult, because they had to figure out how to draw a circle through the forest. It is easy when you are in an open space, but when you are in a forest, you have to worry about density and the structure of the forest. So it was a way of reading place like an overlapping of abstract geometric forms. We spent eight hours looking at the same place and discovered a lot. There was a student only drawing the shadows, and again, the shadows were explaining the forest, the canopy. You have a lot of different ways of reading. It was very systematic and rigorous, but free. And finally, the interesting thing is that we had different layers of information about the place. All of this information can inform a project.

Student We talked a lot about the suburban area. But what about designing a landscape in the city?
I worked on a project with my students on trees in Barcelona. As a landscape architect, again, I am just trying to work on one layer and the layer of the system—the physiology of the layer in this urban condition. I know how this system works quite well. I hate to say "green" because I think it means nothing. So as far as a tree in the city, what I am interested in now is just knowing how the living systems or the forest can inform the city. In the case of Barcelona, I was doing a studio that was about introducing a forest to the city but investigating what the forest can be in an urban condition—the ground and the typology of the city. It would be wonderful to have a forest in the city, but how does the city have to change? The city is the human ecosystem, and we have choices. We don't have to have nature in cities if we don't want it. If we want nature, we have to build the city that allows nature to live in good conditions. It's a compromise. If we want

nature, we have to change the city. The majority of the trees in Barcelona are in a very bad condition, and we have data about that. In the case of Barcelona, we are changing the trees in the streets, because the trees are 100 years old. They came from the Cerdá urban plan. They are not healthy anymore, but the conditions of the street have changed, so we have to rethink the street. If you want to share nature in the city, you have to change the city. Managing it means introducing living cycles.

Faculty It means changing traffic patterns too, in Phoenix for example, there is discussion about creating a green city. But the reality is that the streets authorities are completely unwilling to change the condition of the street. Therefore planting trees seems like a waste of time. They aren't okay with changing the configuration of the street so that trees can flourish. If you go to downtown Phoenix, every tree they plant dies. The reason is all about the most efficient traffic patterns that you possibly can have. But you can't have both.

I think that we are in a moment that we have enough information to begin to start playing with that. We have information about how trees grow. In France, they are studying trees, and how trees change in their context. We know that we need trees, but if we want trees in cities, they have to be in better conditions. My students were designing an urban forest and thinking about generations of trees, about density, about phasing, and about how to inform a new streetscape in certain areas of the city—not everywhere. I look at the city from that lens. I don't know if we will ever be able to say that trees need a certain situation to live. But if we want shade, we need a healthy environment for the tree.

Natural systems should be available in cities and, for me, the park is where everything needs to be, like a living museum or a place where you should be able to understand the cycles of nature—short cycles, long-term cycles, and natural events. So what we were proposing to the city was natural environments and to make elements interact in a different way. What does it mean for a tree to have this shape? What does a field of flowers need to be like so you could interact with it? Because of the management of the park and because I am from an engineering background, I have this idea of production—instead of producing fruit, the park would produce a natural event. It would be universal but only with nature. In certain areas like Barcelona, because we have good weather, we were looking at what kind of natural events we could have together—a mix of ecology and of natural production. This could be an explosion of everything—biodiversity, short- and long-term changes, and productivity of events.

And to make all of those events happen, all of the systems need tc work together. It is not going to happen if you don't have a good water system.

What we were doing was like hardware and software. What we were proposing was a system, a set of rules that are set on the management of the project. A system of paths are crossing the park like the skeleton of the park. We are planting the forest near the plants by an empty area around the fence. It was like the software was the program, and this program was also where people had information about the events.

For example, one event was going to be sitting in a field of flowers because we wanted people to have this experience. The event was only going to happen during three months, because after that, the field of flowers was going to be dry. Then, because people are going to be there, the field of flowers will be affected, and the flowers will disappear more quickly. Also, everything was related to the path of the machines that are used to take care of the park. The park was used densely and managed extensively. So the idea was to have this basic structure that was the path and the trees, and the area where the flower event was taking place.

At the beginning of the project, the managers of the park would be introduced to the team—the team of people who were managing the machines. For me, it's a totally different way of using the park. It is like productivity but also the idea was to collect data about water and climate to explain how the system works and how it is a very complex living system. If you want a tree, you need to water the tree according to that condition and determine how much water you need. So, if you don't use water for this thing, then you can use it for another purpose. And not just using this opportunity within the park but always explaining what's going on to the people who are using it.

I am worried about how we are losing this connection with nature. We talk about sustainability, but we don't know how it works. A dry field can be exciting if you are creative. How can you harvest water and how much water can you harvest to use in the dry season? If you only have this much water, can you be creative and do amazing things with the water that you have? I measured the water so that I know how much it has rained. I am very obsessed with communicating these basic things to people.

Student What you are saying about having a dry-scapes and how it can be beautiful is interesting because I didn't know that desert landscape could be beautiful till I moved to Arizona. But many people here want a very green landscape.

I understand that people in Arizona want the green. The green is the garden in the desert. It is about how to play with the rain and how to manage the water you can harvest. It is being optimistic about responding to interventions. It is being very smart with fewer options. In an urban context, that it is normal, but you have an urge to have vegetation.

When I did my job talk lecture in Virginia during the application process, I wasn't talking about people. I was talking about the mountain and the river and that we have to care about natural processes. People were asking, what about the people? I said, I don't work for people. I teach my students to produce studio presentations in black and white and not to care about people till the end. The last things I give them are the people that they have to put in to their project. It is the idea of not imposing anything onto nature, but to let the place talk. At the end, it is for people, but what I am teaching my students is that there has to be a gap between. We have to play with nature and with living systems and with process in order to improve the quality of life for people. But people are at the end of the project. People are so worried about social justice, but for me, it's about how to put that into the process of design. So, I am just figuring out how to do that. I am always working for people. So in Spain, I ask people to make an effort to give a place to the living systems. Here in the U.S., it is different because maybe here it is about social justice. Lots of people believe social justice should be before nature, because you have this amazing nature, but you also have problems with contamination.

I was wondering, how do you work with such a harsh landscape and not contaminate it, but actually be part of such a harsh landscape? I feel like we're going to have to change the environment just to make it liveable, but not even liveable, but inhabitable. It seems like it's really difficult to do that without literally contaminating the site.

What I recommend is to think about it like an exercise. Think, so what happens if you contaminate the place? Try to dissect every world that you have before you in your mind. Or try to be the salt, try to be the lake, try to be very open, very free, and not to have this idea that we have to do the woods always as the landscape. Don't be afraid of people touching what you have created. Why not allow for that? All of these landscapes built in Spain are totally artificial. So, what I'm saying is, why not, why not be totally artificial? Try to understand how the salt works: have a sample, play with water, mix materials, look at the edges, just play, try to make connections—but in a very important way. My recommendation is enjoy—enjoy the idea with a very free attitude because it is an exercise. Maybe at the end, you decide that maybe the commission is not a good commission. This could be the final conclusion. But at the beginning, be very open.

Faculty I was also thinking back to what you were talking about earlier—that you draw every question or every piece of information you gather about the place. So that drawing all of these things is part of the exercise and will give you an enormous amount of work—things to do while you figure out the project.

Yes and try to think of different scales. Think about what this area in context means—if you just move 10 or 15 meters—what that means; it is about playing, trying to discover. For discovery, you have to provoke a different point of view. My father was the director of a Montessori school. Every year he introduced experimental exercises with no intended results. So I think that this idea of not starting with a result in mind is very important. For example, in my family we take walks. We just walk, and we don't know why we are walking. We just walk. We don't want to go anywhere; we just randomly go for a walk. For me, this part of my culture. One day I was talking with somebody, who asked why, what's that about? And I don't know. I just walk. It is like by walking you discover things; you meet people, you find a new place, and you discover a fountain. Sometimes, I think we need this space with no mission—a place without stress or wanting, and very free. I learned that from Jacque Simon's landscape architecture. He didn't care about things; he was just trying to explain and explore. And I always say, you have to explore your curiosity. It is this idea of curiosity about things, not objectivity. We do not always have to have a result. It's not a failure. It is just that you are playing, which is just a good exercise to do as a designers.

Conversation with Carles Muro

Student Please expand on your discussion about Italo Calvino, Raymond Queneau, and their literary group.

Carles Muro The group was called "Workshop for Potential Literature," with the French acronym "OuLiPo." It was founded in 1960 by Queneau and François Le Lionnais. Other members included Georges Perec, Italo Calvino, Marcel Duchamp, Marcel Bénabou or Jacques Roubaud. It still exists today. Most of the members that I talked about are now dead, but others are still alive, and they keep meeting. They continue to explore issues of language and have a publication that comes out regularly. Apart from their own works, they also did very rigorous analysis on great works from literature, trying to theorize the notion of constraint and the exception to constraint in the history of literature.

Faculty The literary movements from the 1940s, '50s, and '60s have been very influential and inspiring to architects of different periods from the '70s, '80s, and '90s following that group. It was a real shift politically and functionally from the late-modern period. Can you elaborate on the influence of literature on architecture?

Well literature is not really my field of expertise, but one has an interest in many fields. It is true—it was very influential. The ultimate question that Oulipo posed was, "Why write?" Of course, it is the essential question, and it was being asked across the globe. Obviously, different cultures had different responses. But the question was a call to both reinvent the discipline and reinvent society. This was influential to many architects who were also asking themselves similar questions. After World War II, when thinking of Auschwitz and Hiroshima, many people asked themselves: "How could this happen?" The war changed the way people thought about themselves and their relationship to society. That was a very powerful movement that started in a very particular time with questioning "why write," but also "why live," why do anything after this?

Student Why design?

Yes. During the war, there was a veil of silence that covered Europe. After the war people could start to talk again, they were able to express what they were thinking and feeling. They could take a position again. Oulipo was a second moment of that reaction. For instance, Georges Perec, one of the most brilliant figures in the group, was Jewish, and that is very present in his work. His father died in a concentration camp. The presence of everything around the war and the Nazi occupation produced fear that had to be dealt with in order to move forward. His work contains a great del of humor and irony, which is also a good way to recover from trauma.

I was fascinated with your whole discussion about constraints and how it actually opens up opportunity. I think we can all agree that's true in architecture. I understand constraints in the urban environment, but natural areas are a different thing. Can you address constraints in non-urban environments?

An interesting question. It depends very much on the layers you would like to address. In cities, you have much more complex codes. The issue of money is more pressing there in terms of additional constraints due to the economies of dense and powerful cities. These are external constraints imposed by the realities of the place. However, there are also internal constraints that we impose on ourselves out of a particular interest or point of view. That said, I think architects need to realize that natural environments are very fragile and have enormous constraints if they are to be protected and preserved.

Alvaro Siza wrote a beautiful text in which he provocatively states that he would like to build in the Sahara desert. For those of us who don't have the culture of a desert, the desert symbolizes emptiness. But for you who live here, I am certain that the desert means lots of things. Siza suggested that, when the foundations were dug, something would probably appear. It is about being able to see more and to identify the most productive constraints. In this sense, many seemingly barren environments are actually full of richness and constraints, as many as you can find in Manhattan for sure.

I recently studied Le Corbusier's Venice Hospital and his use of the bed as a building unit. What do you think about this as a type of design constraint?

Well you have to be careful about the interpretation of projects. It is true what you say about the bed as a unit, but this is combined with many other ideas and constraints. The Venice Hospital is a very interesting project—it was one of Enric's favorite projects. When I started teaching with Enric, he proposed a series of studios where we would be working each year in a different city and we would choose a building that would represent and contain that city. The first year in the series we worked in Venice, and the project that represented the city was the Le Corbusier's Hospital. That year, we learned, amongst many other things, not to distinguish between built and unbuilt pieces of architecture. Everything that has been though for a specific place is already part of that place. It was a playful constraint to see Venice through the lens of the Venice Hospital.

Relative to the hospital, you could say that the bed was the starting point for the project, but I actually would go further—that it was not so much the bed as a modular unit, but the experience of someone lying on the bed, which is very different. The exact height of the person lying in bed and what he or she can see is a completely different experience than that of walking or standing. So the position of the patient was key to the design.

It was a piece of information for Le Corbusier, but he transformed it into a very powerful design tool based on rules and constraints: the whole building was based on a rigorous additive process which engages in conversation with the notion of the mat-building. You can also say that what is appealing about the building is that it is rich in many readings. For example, the repetitive dimension and interconnectivity of the project is also part of the scale and pattern of the city.

Faculty So on one hand, you can explain the project in terms of the scale of a person in the bed, and on the other hand, you can explain the projects in the terms of the continuity or the growth of the scale of urbanism that exists really only in the way that it does in Venice because of the interconnectivity of the water, the paths, the buildings, the courtyard, and the street. Unless you connect into that pattern of urbanism, you're not really doing a Venice project. What was fascinating about the Venice Hospital was that it really was a Venice project because it connected to the scale of the canal, the scale of the sidewalk, the scale of the buildings, the scale of the courtyards. It was a different geometry: it was an orthogonal geometry opposed to this kind of much more organically constructed geometry of the older city, but it continued that standard, which is a whole different scale of constraints.

It's part of this smart choice of Le Corbusier's—in his set of chosen constraints. There are constraints that are external, which are mostly about dealing with, recognizing, and transforming given data into actual working tools, design tools. Other constraints are, in a sense, arbitrary. Some might be devised for a specific project, but there are also constraints that have to do with your own long-term interests. And here, as part of what you were explaining in terms of the analogy of the building and the city, there is a smart set of constraints that actually reproduce the campi, the little squares of Venice, in terms of the meeting points of the paths in the structure of the Hospital. So, that structure transforms the design into a logical system, which aims at having the same richness. So, there is a notion of form that is deeper than the way things look in terms of the actual shapes or their materiality, but which is stronger. It could be said that the Venice Hospital represents Venice and reproduces Venice in its own way.

Student Do you teach this way of rigorous exploration? How do you deal with the time constraints within the structure of a school project?

In terms of what we should do in School, I do not want to be prescriptive. I come from the School of Architecture in Barcelona, which was good school but pretty conventional in its teaching. There was a continuity between practice and teaching that was very natural. But it is impossible to bring the complexity of real professional life to school, so trying to do that is always destined to fail. We shouldn't waste time trying to do that; in architecture schools we should try to explore everything else and, in doing so, we can also train people to respond to complex situations. There are many ways of doing that. You used the word "rigor," but rigor also needs to be clarified. Irrational thoughts should be also explored rigorously. We should learn to explore architecture rigorously in such a way that will allow us to respond to difficult situations. We should be exploring, incorporating the culture and nature of architecture and the social responsibility of architecture.

Faculty I agree completely. I believe the responsibility of education is to help students develop a way of dealing with complexity and develop a confidence in thinking through complex situations—really thinking in a rigorous way about the complexity of what they are doing.

Student How do we become experts at outlining our own constraints?

At some point, you are ready, but it is wise to start with one idea at a time. A possible constraint could be: "I am going to build a project with one single material." One single material introduces an incredible discipline to the design process. It is not just that it might make sense in terms of sustainability—think about a time when materials were all very close to the building sites. I just met an amazing architect from Paraguay, Solano Benitez, who was teaching at the GSD in the Fall. Standard construction materials, such as steel and concrete, are extremely expensive in Paraguay, while there is an abundance of clay. All his works are built with clay and only clay, with a bit of wood and glass. Solano has transformed this given constraint into an opportunity for investigation of new forms of brick and clay architecture and has produced an amazing collection of structures with such a humble material.

Available construction materials are seen here as a design opportunity. What is more valuable in terms of materials? It could be said that all materials hold exactly the same architectural value. Material constraints depend on location and climatic conditions, while price fluctuates according to availability, so price is not necessarily an indicator of higher quality. You need to know exactly when and why to choose a certain material—when to choose brick, when to choose glass, when to choose steel. While the most recent new or last generation materials are fascinating and hold an incredible design potential yet to be explored, traditional materials, like brick and stone, still have an amazing potential also yet to be fully unfolded.

The discussion of the architectural value of materials brings to my mind some ideas by the world renowned Catalan chef Ferran Adrià about ingredients and their value. When asked to synthesize his ideas in a number of principles, he stated: "All products have the same gastronomic value, regardless of their price." So which what has a higher economic value—a potato or a lobster? Perhaps the potato would actually have a much higher potential than a lobster. It is amazing what you can do with a potato... and it is normally cheaper –except, perhaps, in Maine!

You explained in your lecture that Enric often set up a game of constraints for himself while he designed, but he rarely shared the game with others. Why was that?

There are many issues that your question brings up. There are lots of people who try to be very private about their creative process, sometimes even shy. But it is not that Enric was shy. There are just some things that need to remain pretty intimate about the way you take a position. I mentioned in the lecture that Perec was a very talented writer, but he didn't always unveil his constraints either. He also died very young—he must have died near the same age as Enric, around 45. What Perec was saying was that a literary scaffold helps you build a work of literature. But as an architect, our buildings must be more than the scaffolding; the architecture has to be assessed in its own terms, and the scaffolding does not come into consideration. Therefore, keeping the game to yourself is often better. And Enric sometimes kept all these things very private...

So when we have a critique, and the critics ask why we did something, we could tell them that it was private?

(Laughter) No, not at all. Catherine [Spellman] said something that is very beautiful and true. She talked about the importance of explaining a project with one set of slides, but with each presentation, you could explain the project entirely differently. When you present the same project to your grandmother, to your contractor or to the architect that you respect the most in the world, you highlight different aspects of the project, but always present rigorously the coherence between the processes and how you think without questioning whether the initial positions are right or wrong, better or worse, but that there is the coherence in the development of an idea. You should be able to explain, at least in five different ways, how your project developed.

Faculty Could you say that the constraints do not necessarily make great work, but they guide the work, they help develop the work to be consistent?

That's a beautiful way of relating rationality and response in design. There is an issue that we're coming to here, which is more about freedom in design. An excess of freedom is not very productive and may lead to a lack of intensity in the work. The use of constraints helps to narrow down to something to have a real freedom. In a sense, it is more a recognition of the external or given constraints. I do think also that part of the pedagogical approach could be seen as a series of warming up exercises. You need to practice, to exercise, which is also a beautiful way of trying to reproduce the conditions of real life, of practice. In school, it is more about warming up and preparing with exercises that will allow you to work. To play basketball, you are not only shooting at the basket, but you need to train your body and your mind, running, lifting, whatever—you are preparing to have the best possible performance at each match.

Faculty I think in the contemporary practice of architecture, of literature, of art, or whatever, that the awareness of the producer is absolutely essential. We cannot be naïve or wild savage artists. To do good work we have to have a goal, a plan. For example, to write, one does not just sit down and put words on paper; this is not writing. To write, you need ideas and a plan, and you cannot be naïve about that. You need to know the context of your discipline, its techniques and constraints, and your own goals.

Frank Lloyd Wright worked with constraints and variations in geometry, variations in construction systems, variations from history, and so on. He probably wouldn't agree—he was always claiming that he was reinventing the world and that he had no architectural references, but this is an absolute lie. However, this does not matter; as architects, we can read the constraints, variations, and references in his work, and these things make his work much richer and fascinating.

Peter Buchanan has spoken about the techniques of making architecture and was the first to make this discussion relative to Enric's work. He talks about the craft of designing a building, the crafting of the plan. He said the craftsman manages techniques and the relationship to life. The craftsman is able to produce an object that is useful for everyday life and uses techniques to produce his objects—a pottery wheel, chisel, weaving, etc. Peter claims that in the best-case scenario, an architect should be a craftsman, to use a set of techniques to create the project that is useful, which makes a relationship to everyday life. To me, what is most unique about Enric's work is that the relationship to life was always combined with techniques: the movement of the user, the light, the graffiti, whatever. It's coming from the everyday life. It is always bringing life back into the technical work or the technical development of the project. The relationship between technique and life is very crucial. The constraints alone can make a work, but when it is not combined with a relationship to life, then the work is not very strong.

I agree. Le Corbusier stated it something like this: techniques are the very support of poetry. This is something obvious in Enric's architecture. Like all great architecture, it has many different supports—one being techniques along with history and context, among others, and life.

Method

1. Collage drawing for Diagonal Mar Park, 1997.

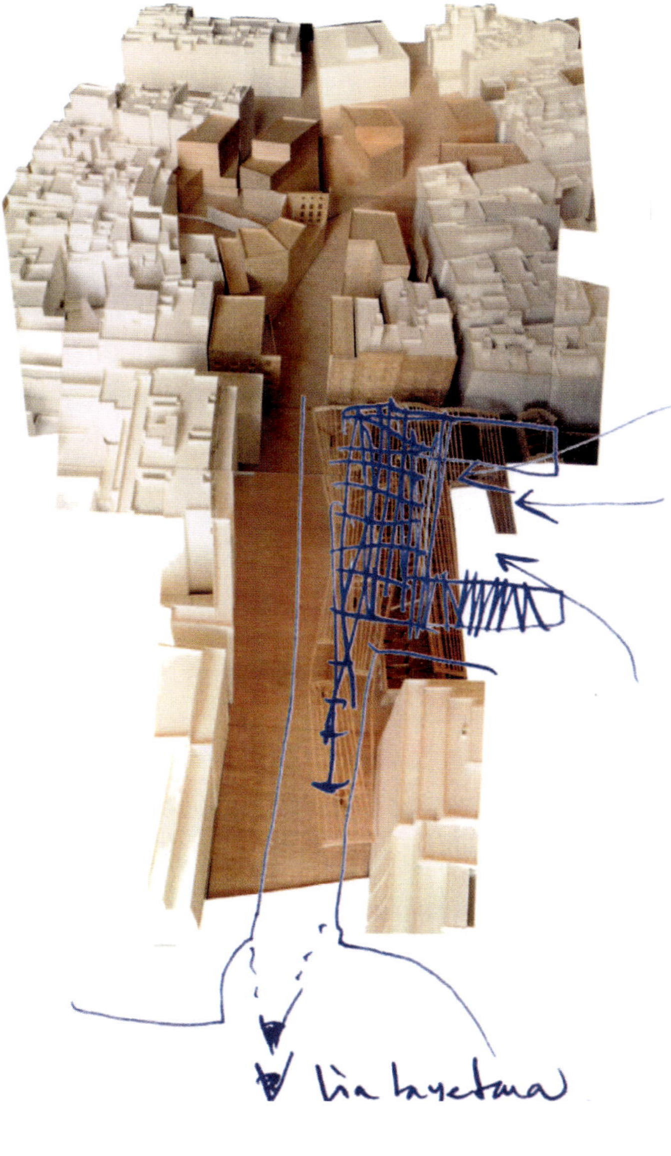

2. Collage with model for Santa Catarina Market, 1998.

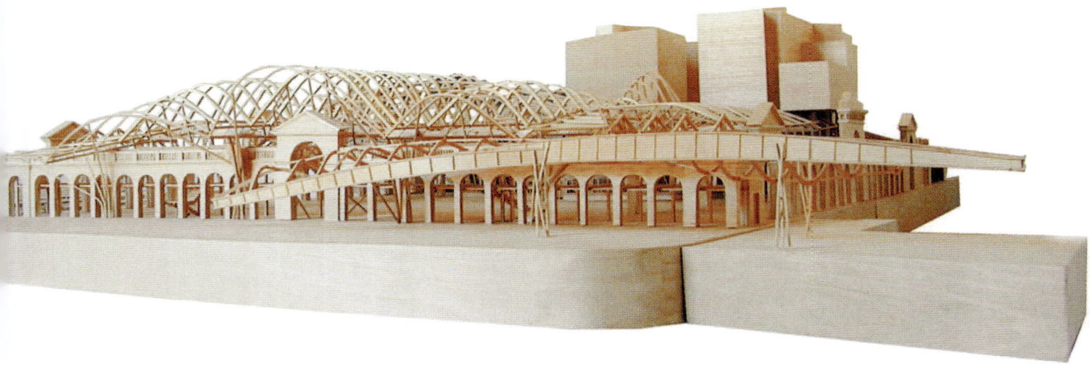

3. Model for Santa Catarina Market, 1998.

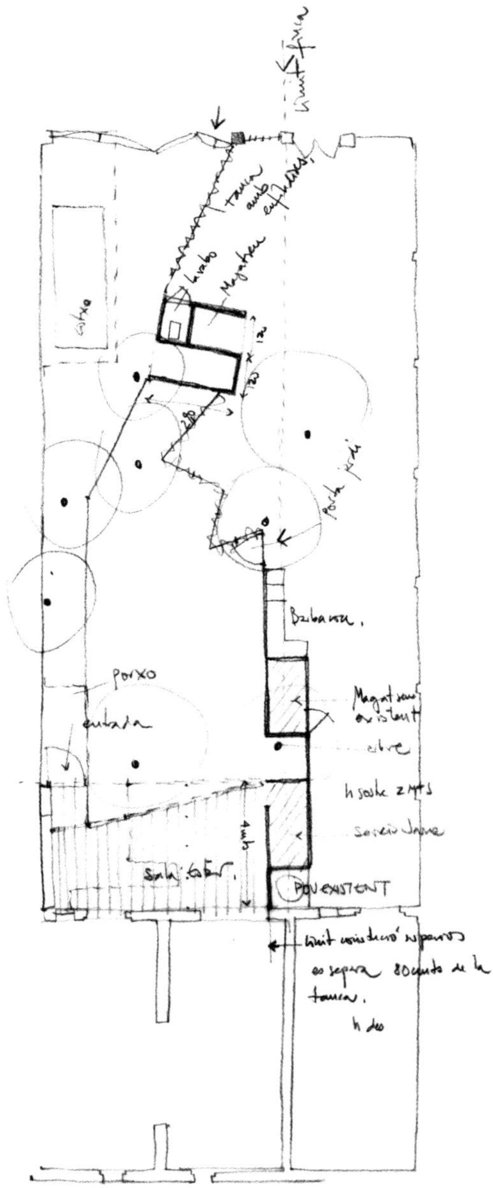

4. Plan sketch for La Clota House, 1999.

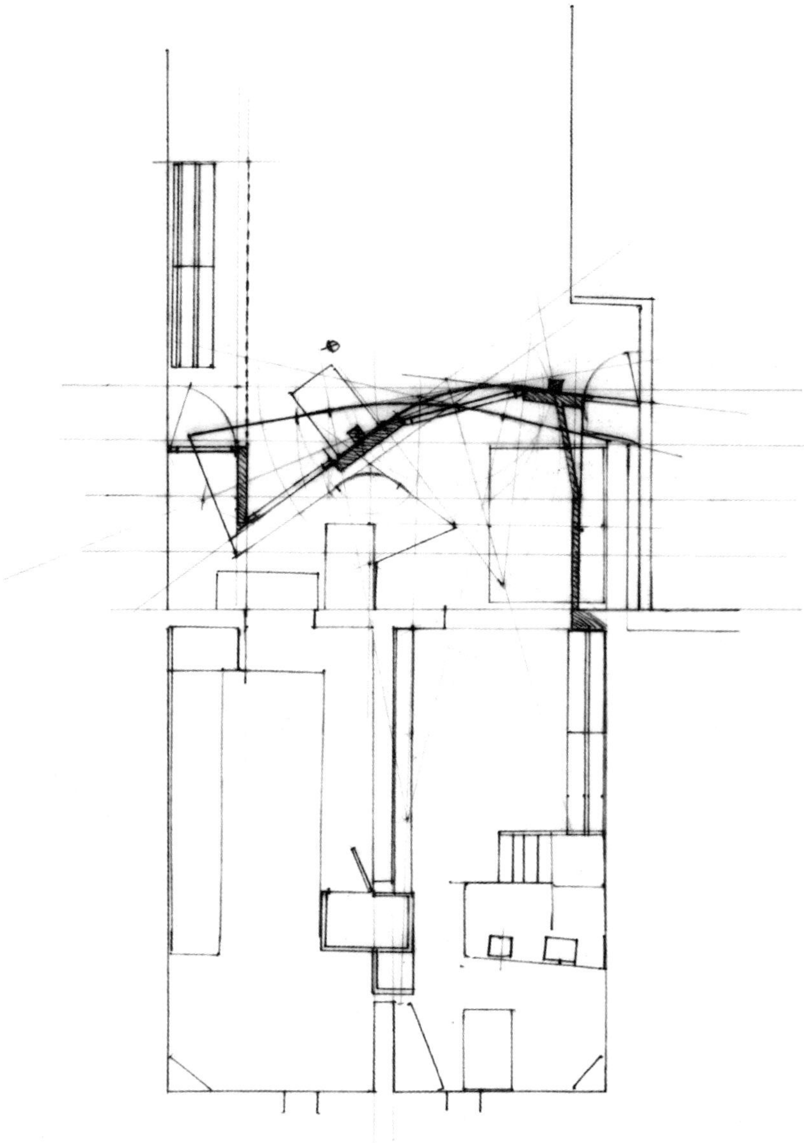

5. Plan iteration for La Clota House, 1999.

6. Model for Mollet Park, 1992-97.

7. Letters for Mollet Park, 1992-97.

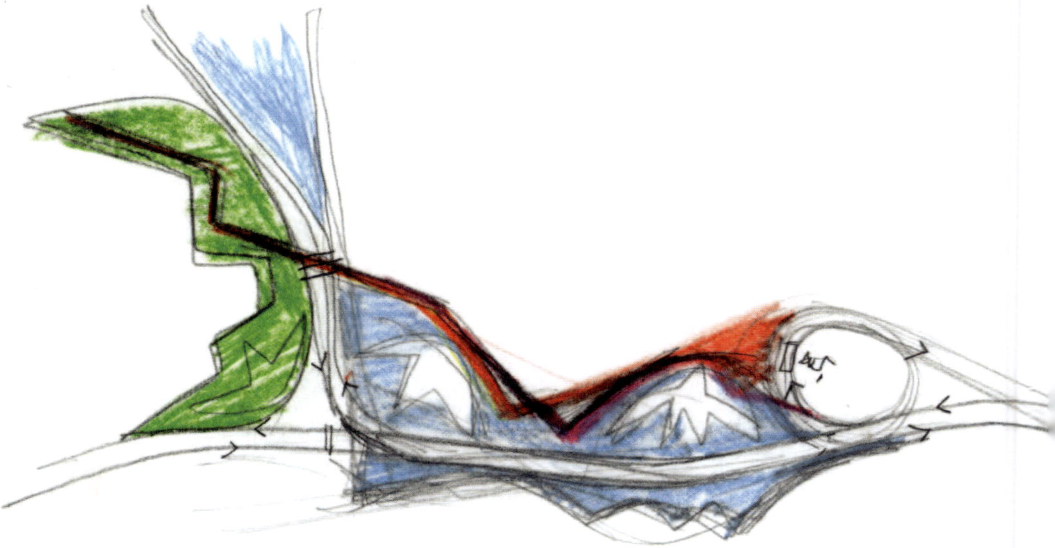

8. Sketch plan iterations for Diagonal Mar park, 1997-98.

9. Sketch plan iterations for Diagonal Mar park, 1997-98.

10. Photo collage for Santa Catarina Market, 1997-2000.

11. Photo collage for Santa Catarina Market, 1997-2000.

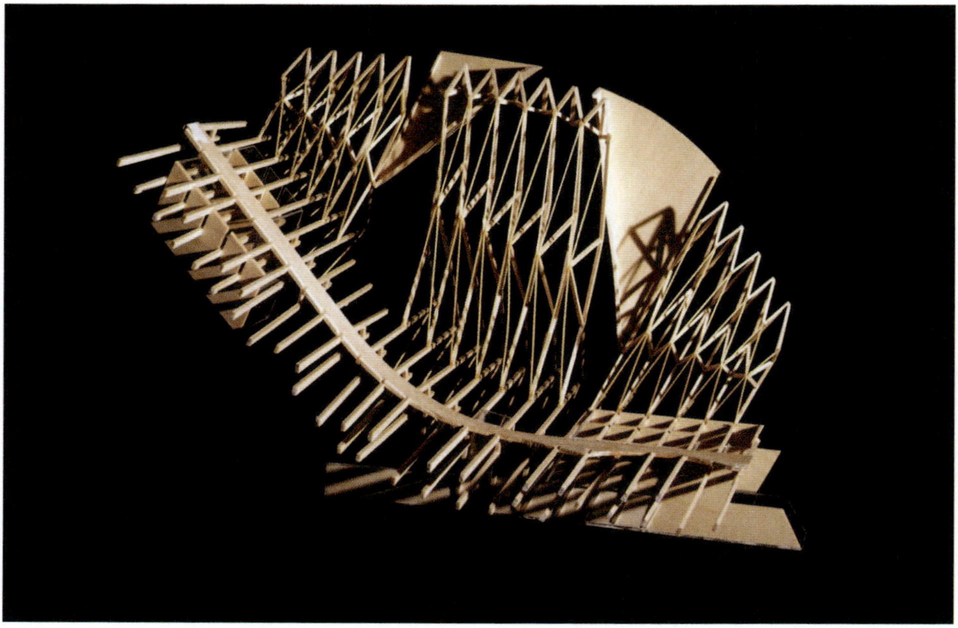

12. Model for Scottish Parliament Meeting Hall roof structure, 1998-2000.

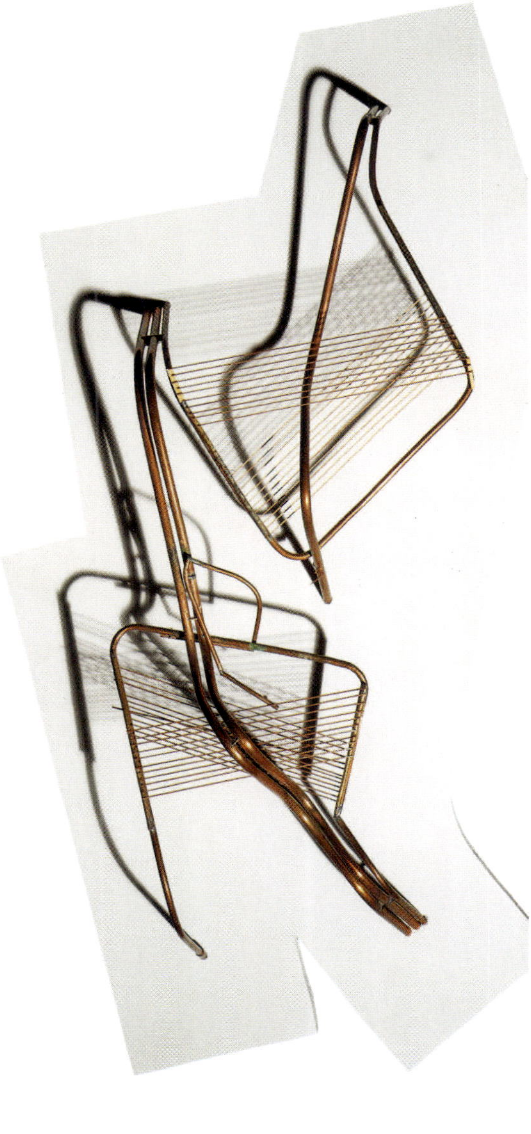

13. Study model for Diagonal Mar park, 1997-98.

14. Photo collage for Frankfurt Rose Museum, 1994.

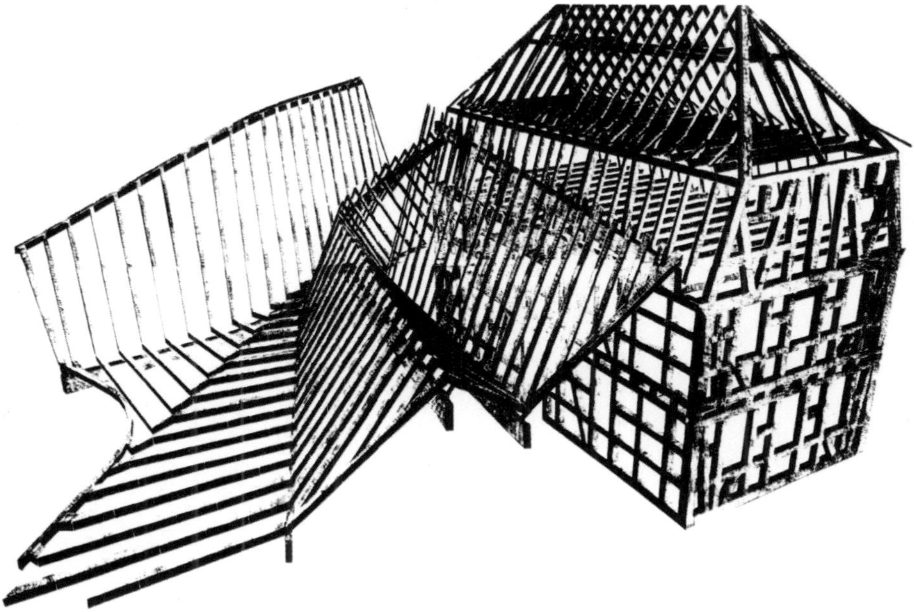

15. Collage and model for Frankfurt Rose Museum, 1994.

Walking to Begin

Catherine Spellman

1. Miralles Pinós detail at Igualada Cemetery.

Enric Miralles talked a lot about the beginning of a project. How to begin, where to begin, and what to begin with? These are complex and important questions to discuss, because a project's beginning will determine its direction. There are many productive ways to begin a project and each implies a certain process of working. Miralles also said that an architectural project could begin with anything. How is one to decide on a particular beginning? When asked, Miralles suggested a book by the literary theorist Edward Said titled *Beginnings: Intention and Method.* It is a volume on beginnings in literature with many themes overlapping with architecture. Substitute the word "architect" for "writer" and you will find that the book speaks directly to our discipline. Said writes, "Every writer knows that the choice of beginnings is crucial because it determines much of what follows but also because a work's beginning is, practically speaking, the main entrance into what it offers...A beginning immediately establishes relationships with works already existing, relationships of either continuity or antagonism...The beginning is the first step in the intentional production of meaning."[1] On finishing this book, I too was convinced, architecture and all creative work can begin with anything; later, it is a question of how the work is developed.

My first class at the Städelschule with Miralles began in October 1992 with an informal lecture about his recent walk to the Acropolis in Athens, Greece. He talked about architecture and walking as parallel activities that informed and influenced the reconstruction of the path from the city to the Acropolis. The project by Dimitri Pikionis happened over two decades with the architect continuously present on the site. Miralles proposed that the project began with Pikionis simply walking. Many architects do begin a project by walking the site either literally or in their mind. It is a common way of experiencing the place, learning the dimensions, gathering knowledge. However, Miralles suggested something quite different, the physical experience of walking was turned into an idea for the project to relate the past to the present. This really intrigued me, probably because I walk a lot, which embeds in my memory details of the places walked.

Consequently, I have strong memories of conversations with Miralles while walking. During the time I taught with Miralles at the Städelschule and later as a friend, we would walk: with students, family, friends, collaborators; to see architecture projects, to go eat or shop, to meet sponsors or visit sites for projects, to catch the train or plane. Conversations were mundane, extraordinary, and fragmented by the circumstance of time and place. This essay develops segments of these conversations with Miralles around the topic of "Walking to Begin." Each segment begins with some historical background to establish a common context around the topic.

Walking with Pikionis

The landscape renovation and path to the Acropolis was awarded to Pikionis in 1951 (Fig. 2). The route that traverses the mountain had not been maintained for centuries and was greatly damaged during the Second World War when it was paved over with a black tarmac that erased almost all traces of its history. In classical times, the path connected a series of resting places for people participating in celebrations, memorials, and devotional rituals. Throughout history, walking the route to the Acropolis was a way to renew and remember the political and social ideals of a classical period that established the first form of democracy.

Miralles was fascinated by "this powerful sense of social justice" one feels walking this path. He liked to tell students that when you start a project with a great site the first goal is "not to make an awful mistake." This is why he found the simplicity of the line/path that became Pikionis' project so strong. This line/path grows from the existing context: physical, historical, and social, in the most natural way. It is almost like Pikionis gave water to the path, and it grew from the ancient seeds latent beneath the dust. This would not have been Miralles' manner of intervening, but he did appreciate the sensitivity of Pikionis' design.

2. Dimitri Pikionis, Acropolis path, ca.1970.

Miralles was certain that Pikionis had probably walked the path daily since he was young. It seemed obvious to Miralles that Pikionis knew the path by the way it felt below his feet. This way of understanding a place is

3. Miralles Pinós, Igualada path, ca. 1996.

relatively rare but remarkably beneficial. Pikionis shows great restraint and respect in developing this path and toward the ancient buildings by not referring to them directly, rather, Pikionis extends the time spent relating to the Acropolis by making the path a longer and pleasurable experience that encourages daily use.

Developed step-by-step the surface of the path is constantly changing and filled with ambiguity between what is material of the past and what is of the present, which continuously engages the walker. Each pace reveals a fragment of recycled stone (some ancient some not), combinations of matured trees and indigenous plants, and urban furniture derived from vernacular Greek structures. These elements, combined with carefully orchestrated views, blend into a rich composition of phenomenal and physical experiences that can only be understood by walking the distance of the project, over and over again. Miralles wrote a short essay titled "Walking" that can be read with multiple meanings: as movement in time and space, a description of the Igualada project (Fig. 3), or a metaphor for how to design. It could also serve as a description of Pikionis' path:

Tracks as writing on the surface we move or ponder on…That trace which corresponds to the movement we believe we discover in the place. That elementary sign accompanying the shift from one place to another…fragments of these movements describe a geometry linked to reality; they envelope real shapes…. working from the foregoing lines; halting movement. Halting to think of something else, multiplying the forking paths, the intermediate spaces, the escape points…[2]

Repetitive walking is related to repetitive drawing, and both are a way to memorize and understand the particularities of a place. Each architect has a distinctive and innate way of walking/drawing, which is an expression of his or her sensibilities. Some prefer long distances and a slow pace. Others move fast and are able to process a great deal of information in a short amount of time. Pikionis' drawings show a thick palimpsest of lines in pencil, tracing the realities

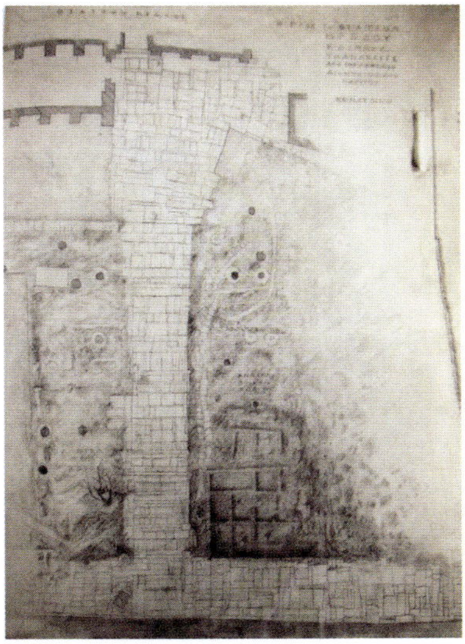

4. Dimitri Pikionis, plan drawing of the Acropolis, 1951.

of the existing situation, overlapping his ideas and desire to clarify and improve the existing context and search for the best position of each element (Fig. 4). These drawings are slow and intentional. They evoke the actual materiality of the path. Reading one of these drawings creates an experience very near to standing in a specific location on the path.

Miralles' drawings likewise emerge from the repetitive tracing of the site; however, they are a very different expression. Miralles moved fast and with an abounding amount of energy and ability to make complex connections. He could very quickly trace the same drawing 50 or 60 times to discover a working solution to a spatial problem—with each iteration walking through the space in his head and adjusting the placement of the elements. His drawings often began with a series of sketches and descriptive images that capture the intentions and ideas about the project. These sketch/images are overlapped with the site, generating a series of new site plans. This process is repeated over and over again at multiple scales of the plan and section. At moments in the development of the project, new sketches/images representing other ideas are added to the layers of drawings. The selection of the lines to draw is guided by a straightforward knowledge of the project parameters, technical possibilities, and developed talent to determine which lines best express the idea. It takes practice to acquire fluidity with this method and, similar to the avid walker, the right way home eventually becomes intuitive (Fig. 5).

Shortly after Miralles gave his lecture on the Acropolis path, the Städelschule architecture class, Miralles, and several of his friends were on a bus from Delhi to Chandigarh, India. Miralles asked to see an essay that I was reading, which was "Walking," by Henry David Thoreau. Conversations about walking inevitably led to the great American author. On returning the essay, Miralles commented "Thoreau was a very good architect, no?" We both laughed. Thinking back on that

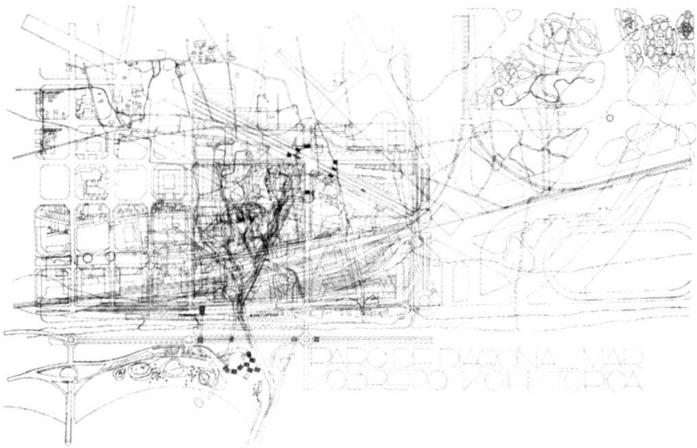

5. Enric Miralles, plan drawing of Park Diagonal Mar, 1998.

exchange, I am certain Miralles meant that a very good architect involves a commitment to individual thought and expression.

In his essay, Thoreau speaks for "absolute freedom and wildness, as contrasted with a freedom and culture merely civil—to regard man as an inhabitant, or a part and parcel of Nature, rather than a member of society." The essay continues with expanded thoughts on man's need to "walk" in order to understand his place in the world, relationship to nature, and clarity of thought. Thoreau speculates on the difficulty of finding the best way to walk. He posits that the walk we should take "is perfectly symbolical of the path which we love to travel in the interior and ideal world—a path difficult to determine because it does not yet exist distinctly in our idea."[3] In the essay, the word "walking" is analogous to writing or any creative occupation. Thoreau describes many of the commonalities between walking and writing, such as intuitive directions, physical engagement, and the search for self-awareness and iteration as the process of all creative activity. Thoreau talks about his practice of walking each day: "I think that I cannot preserve my health and spirits unless I spend four hours a day at least—and it is commonly more than that—sauntering through the woods and over the hills and fields absolutely free from all worldly engagements."[4]

The capacity for introspection and the ability to recognize oneself as an individual, separate from the environment and other individuals, is crucial to creating brilliant original work. Thoreau writes, "I have met with but one or two persons in the course of my life who understood the art of walking, that is, of taking walks—who had a genius, so to speak, for sauntering: which word is beautifully derived from 'idle people who roved about the country in the Middle Ages, and asked charity, under pretense of going à la Sainte Terre (to the Holy Land)'...Some, however, would derive the word form sans terre, without land or a home, which, therefore, in the good sense, will mean, having no particular home, but equally at home everywhere."[5] In my opinion, Miralles was the "sans terre" type of walker, at home wherever he went, finding inspiration and understanding with each step and turning this into his particular architecture.

To walk in the sense that Thoreau describes is to be physically engaged and aware of ones' surroundings. During his walking adventures, all senses are acutely aware of the specifics of the environment. That awareness of the materiality of place is likewise a common element in Miralles' work. The projects can be thought of as instruments to measure the tactile qualities of the place. Projects cast stark shadows—patterns that describe the position and strength of the sun. Many projects have entry conditions that funnel the wind through the building much like ancient wind tunnels. Screen and window exterior materials are often rich in texture inviting touch. Fragrant landscapes fill the park and urban plazas with a memorable scent and recall the richness of the rural landscapes near to the urban centers. The projects' carefully considered pavement patterns that cover walkways, plazas, and internal circulation are often distinct and memorable to the feeling of your foot. Miralles' projects convey a very strongly physical gesture often experienced through the movement through the project.

Creative work tends to move in a direction particular to the natural instincts of the author (*modus operandi*). Thoreau talks of his tendency "to head west, where the earth is more un-exhausted and richer."[6] He explains that west is a movement away from the history and ties to the Old World; west is in the direction of the future, adventure, and individual expression. He recalls the myth about the original founders of Rome, Romulus and Remus, who were suckled by a wild wolf, demonstrating that civilization has drawn strength from the wild and that nature is beyond the reach of civilized societies. Likewise Miralles' *modus operandi* is in the direction of the west and the wild. Miralles' work separates from the direction of international modernism focusing on the specific of qualities of the local situation. In Miralles' case, we find an instinct tendency toward bold structures, complex sequences of movement, raw material, dramatic light, strong juxtapositions, and dualities and opposing forces expressed through a medium of abstraction.

This exchange on walking continued back in Frankfurt where Miralles suggested I study Eadweard Muybridge's photographs of movement, Alberto Giacometti's *Walking Men* sculptures, and Joan Miró's prints titled the *Barcelona Series*. In the modern period of the visual arts, walking aimlessly or wandering is often an expression of physical or conceptual displacement brought on in part by the industrial revolution and disruption of the two world wars. Miralles, born in 1955, studied architecture during the transition from the Franco dictatorship to the democratic form of government Spain holds today. The condition of displacement and its expression in the visual arts interested Miralles and myself as well.

Muybridge started photographing the English and American landscape and went on to conduct some of the earliest visual studies of movement, producing over 100,000 images of animals and people in movement. By breaking motion into split-second frames, Muybridge revealed the complexities of movement and the relationship between muscle and bone, balance and gravity, and mass and acceleration. Although these studies greatly influenced scientific fields and later led to the development of motion pictures, this was not what interested Muybridge or inspired him to follow this subject matter so intently for so many years. His interest was to capture on film the invisible moments that could not be seen by the human eye. His first invisible moment shows the gait of a horse in the flash of a second when all four legs of the horse were off the ground. To do this, Muybridge carefully calibrated movements in abstracted spaces across fractions of a second. He set up dark backgrounds with a white grid of string and numerous cameras, in front of which his subjects would move. This setup allowed Muybridge to measure and track the movement from multiple angles at once and simultaneously to exhibit movement from numerous vantage points, something previously unseen.

These photographs expose both the invisible beauty and extreme awkwardness of everyday movements. This aspect of the photographs was of interest to Miralles. I think it is fair to say that Miralles considered the user to be the most important element in the architectural composition of a project. How and why a user might move through the project was a careful consideration, providing a complex and layered experience of movements that are mostly invisible but appear when an unwitting user moves in a surprising way relative to the project. In such moments, because the Miralles' projects have many layers of complexity and many ways of being experienced, the projects are exceptionally well prepared to engage the user both perceptually and intellectually.

The Cemetery at Igualada is a good example of this. Designed by Miralles and Pinós in 1986, the cemetery has been under different phases of construction since 1990 (Fig. 6). They describe the cemetery as creating (for the visitor) "a relationship with the landscape and with forgetting."[7] In other words, as the visitor moves through the cemetery while they are paying respect to the dead, they are simultaneously made aware of the presence of life/nature in the site. The duality of life and death are present everywhere as one moves through the cemetery. Take for example the stepped ramps that connect the lower to upper sections of tombs. Passing through this space, one is overwhelmingly aware that he/she is moving between the buried bodies in a volume of the same proportion. As well, the "river" of wooden tie bars, embedded in the passage way that takes you down into the main gathering space at the bottom of the culvert, mark the visitor's movement and suggest earlier times when water would rush through the wash.

Miralles wrote, "Developing the project has meant distancing ourselves from the narrative aspects that accompany garden paths, which in a cemetery are unbearable. It has meant working inside the foregoing lines: halting in movement. Halting to think of something else."[8] The natural phenomena of the site—sunlight, wind, rain—are each engaged in a way that heightens the experience: the depth of relief in the tombstones cast distinctive shadows that follow the movement of the sun; the trees rustle loudly when the breeze passes through; and the constructed

6. Miralles Pinós, Igualada Cemetery, 1992.

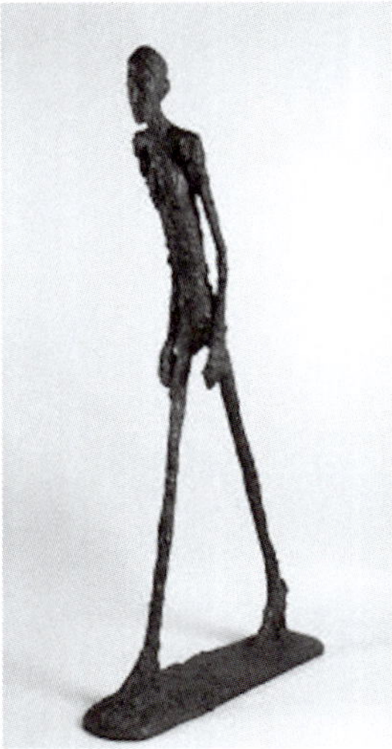

7. Alberto Giacometti "Walking Man," ca.1950.

water system gathers the limited rainfall and delivers it to the trees in the center of the project. In each instance, the architects are capturing the various movements of the site and program "exposing" them to the visitor in a manner as straightforward and powerful as the photographs of Muybridge.

The sculptor and painter Alberto Giacometti is known for his work with themes of the accidental and circumstantial that arise with processes of variation. As part of the Surrealist movement started in Paris in the 1920s, Giacometti's work focused on the heighten awareness of the complexity of everyday life. Miralles wrote about Giacometti's drawings of James Lord.[9] He was very interested in the element of surprise and unexpected juxtapositions found in Giacometti's work with walking figures. In 1947, Giacometti began producing images of walking figures (which he worked on through the early 1960s), and soon "Walking Man" (Fig. 7). was everywhere in his sculptures, paintings, and drawings. The first figures are thought to be triggered by the artist's observation of refugees from the death camps walking on the streets of Paris. These figures depict the sense of loss and isolation felt by many in the years following the war.[10] The later walking figures developed confidence in their stride and could be found out in the different weather, in the sun and in the rain, in company with other men and women. His early and later walking figures speak to the individuality of every person while part of the common kinship between all human beings.[11]

A similar sense of variation of a common theme can be found across the body of Miralles' work. Like Giacometti, Miralles sometimes would begin a new project with a particular moment (topic/subject) from a previous project. Variation leads to new and unexpected possibilities. Miralles wrote, "I tend to operate by variations...when one thinks about the construction of a wall, to use an example of a very elementary object, I am interested in thinking about all the possibilities that this element can or could contain. It is hard to think of a wall without thinking of the possibility of a niche, which reveals the depth of the wall space. It is difficult to ignore the structure that makes the wall possible, the counter-

8. Miralles Pinós, entry gate at Igualada Cemetery and columns at the Archery Pavilion, 1992.

forts, columns, or the multiple layers of the wall which open up the concept of the wall to a multiplicity of readings… (Fig. 8). These are material qualities, they are independent of subjective interpretations or generalizations. When I assert the idea of variation, it is because I want the elements to be able to incorporate the variety of material conditions. I never work by reduction; I try to reveal the multiplicities."[12]

Catalan artist Joan Miró, a contemporary of Giacometti and affiliated with the Surrealists, was born in the Barri Gòtic neighborhood of Barcelona. Miralles had a strong affinity for Miró, who intended his work to be an instigator of social change. Miró's work was a beautiful banner of protest and call for change to the suppression Catalonia experienced as a result of the Spanish Civil War. Miró intentionally severed any connection to conventional painting and bourgeois society that supported it. He was interested in activating his canvases with startling juxtapositions of abstracted figures and complex themes. The work is simultaneously joyful (in its use of color, shape, line movement, composition) and disturbing in its commentary on the social and political injustices of the time. Along with others (Picasso, Tapias, Gaudí), Miró shifted the culture of Catalonia from the regional to the international by accepting and developing abstraction. In a similar way, Miralles (with Pinós early in his career) makes a conscious break from the late modern architecture of generation before them. William Curtis adeptly explains this in his essay, "Mental Maps and Social Landscapes," that while Miralles and Pinós draw from "local lineage" (Coderch, Gaudí, Jujol,

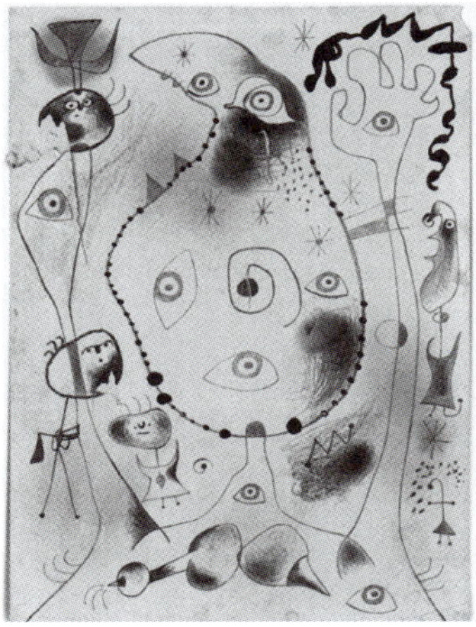

9. Joan Miró, "Barcelona VII" from *Barelona Series* (Mourlot 12), 1944.

Viaplana/Piñon) and "wider ranging influences" (Le Corbusier, Utzon, Aalto), they were also interested in random patterns of nature. Curtis writes, "After all, artists tend to invent their own pedigree to fit their own preoccupations."[13]

Miró is interesting to consider at this point. (Fig. 9). Unlike the previous examples, Miró does not directly address the subject of walking. That said, his work is everywhere in Barcelona: sculptures in public plazas, building murals, and sidewalk pavements in addition to a large museum that holds a large collection of his work, and he holds a strong position in the collective consciousness of the citizens. The sense of walking found in Miró's work comes through his use of line and visual movement. The complexity within the drawings and paintings can best be deciphered by visually following the line(s) that swirl around and map out multiple routes or paths connecting the many figures and pieces within the frame. Ultimately, the line moves on the surface of the paper/canvas and moves the viewer through the work. The line also creates a sense of time passing. Like a musical score or dimensions in architecture, Miró's lines carry with them a record of the passing of time. Each linear segment records the movement of a distance across time. This particular way of using line is also very present in Miralles' work. Miralles wrote, "For me, time has to do with the journey, and the journey to do with movement. Once, while presenting us in Japan, Arata Isozaki called us 'marevitos.' Marevitos translates as 'actor.' These were old-time puppeteers who, as well as taking a theater show from village to village, also carried the news, the latest, from one place to another. What interests me about itinerant artists is such movement. They arrived in villages, left a few things, took other things away. That idea of movement and time is what interests me about ephemeral architecture."[14]

The presence of time and movement depicted by line is apparent in both Miralles' and Miró's drawings and is part of the magic that makes both so visually captivating. The time it takes to read the drawings is in itself a movement, the eye across the page, the body across the site, the mind back and forth across different historical periods. All this results in a high level of visual and spatial

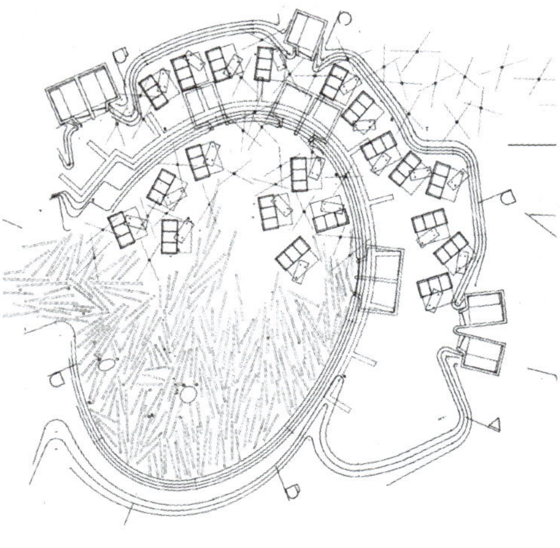

10. Miralles Pinós, plan detail Igualada Cemetery, 1986.

tension that is reinforced with the constant combining of interior and exterior space. The incomplete and open figures in Miró's drawings create an ambiguity between in and out, edge and center, boundary and bound. Similarly, it is difficult to understand what is interior and exterior in a Miralles drawing. The constant line weight and superimposition of all spatial information in a singular plan drawing has the effect of erasing the boundary between interior and exterior. This appreciation of ambiguity is a magical quality common to both the work of Miralles and Miró. One of the best bits of advice that Miralles told to students was that projects needed the support of good friends. He meant this both literally—in terms of collaborators—and figuratively—in terms of the great works by other architects. Any project in the studio was accompanied by a stack of books opened to projects relating (in terms of typology and ideas) to the project on the table. More often than not, Le Corbusier was at the table and frequently sat alongside Peter and Alison Smithson.

Common to all Miralles projects is a highly developed pattern of circulation (Fig. 10). Miralles was an astute student of the modernist architects from the generations before him. He was particularly interested in the work of Le Corbusier and Alison and Peter Smithson, each of whom directly address the element of circulation in their projects and writings. The work of Le Corbusier focuses on the development of the "architectural promenade" at the scale of the city, site, and building. The term suggests a richer spatial experience than the element of a building circulation.[15] At the urban scale, Le Corbusier thought merging nature and the city along pedestrian pathways connecting zones of living, work, and recreation would resolve the social problems created by overcrowding and rapid industrialization. Most of Corbusier's idealized urban plans contain very strong linear parkways that provide open space, natural

11. Le Corbusier, entry ramp at the Mill Owners Association, Ahmedabad, 1951.

elements, and a way for urban dwellers to cross the city uninterrupted by traffic and congestion.

Visit a Le Corbusier project and you will be convinced that he was a master at developing circulation and walking the visitor through the site and building. With constant awareness of the position of the horizon relative to the project, Le Corbusier offers his visitors an almost endless variety of visual and spatial experiences as they move through a project. Staring at the ground of the site, Le Corbusier often folds the plane to create oblique views of the building and foretell the eventual connection to a set of stairs or ramp. Many entry conditions begin this way. Once within the project, there are often multiple levels of spaces—a juxtaposition of forms that make the interior reconnect to the site with interrupted views. Le Corbusier's ramped projects often conclude on a roof top garden that brings the visitor back to the landscape where they started in the entry to the project. These spaces also provide a new idealized landscape for fantastic recreational activities and creative thought (Fig. 11).

In a similar, but perhaps more open-ended way, Miralles was also extremely adept at connecting a site to its larger situation and the building to the site through the circulation. With almost all of Miralles' projects, there are multiple approaches to the site and building. Often located at the edge of city in an area of transition from defined urban fabric to something less developed, these projects are considered a place of transition from one pattern of movement to another. The community center at Hostalets, for example, is located at the boundary between the city and its periphery (Fig. 12). The series of wedge-shaped forms invite the visitor to enter from several directions. Approaching from the city center, the four-level height of the project is placed on the street corner creating a type of ancient wall that clearly marks the boundary between inside and outside of the

12. Miralles Pinós, entry ramp at Hostalets Civic Center, 1992.

city. This wall slopes down to a gate at the southwest corner that provides entrance to an outdoor gathering space on the west side of the building. The auditorium/recreation space is placed on this corner just behind the wall. A large pivoting entry door on the street is directly below a three-level plane of glass that provides the city with a constant glimpse through the building to the less-developed neighborhood beyond the site. Along the north side of the site, a jagged ramp follows the exterior walls of the building providing access to the three terraces adjacent to the classrooms and offices on the west side of the project. These terraces overlook the plaza, which also provides parking. Below this ramp is the secondary entrance to the auditorium space and direct connection to the street.

Miralles was fortunate to become friends with the English architects Peter and Alison Smithson. They met while Miralles was a student participating in a workshop about Palladian architecture in Italy. The Smithsons wrote numerous books on their ideas about architecture and urbanism covering a wide variety of topics, including walking, which they referred to as "Ways." They wrote: "From the beginning, we had followed the ways of the exiting interconnected buildings, discovering the perceived pathways within...We seem to have used Ways as an ordering device almost from the very beginning...Ways have played a crucial role in the emergent notion of Conglomerate Ordering."[16] They continue, "The idea of an ordering system has taken differing forms in our work. Sometimes 'ways' are employed in a manner that is latent and discreet; in other instances they are the most public part of a project, a spine providing a variety of spatial experiences, couples with the means by which circulation is distributed."[17]

The Robin Hood Gardens social housing project in London depicts the Smithson's interest and skill at organizing a building around the circulation (Fig. 13). Here,

13. Peter and Alison Smithson, Robin Hood Gardens social housing, 1972.

the public garden becomes the center of the project creating multiple circulation patterns between the two housing blocks and surrounding neighborhood. The garden establishes a line of view to the shipyard in the distance, reconnecting it to the region while offering a natural safe zone in an industrial setting. The garden, with its large play mound, mitigates the size of the housing blocks by breaking up the view line between the two building and giving the children who climb the mound a privileged position at five levels above the garden.[18]

The circulation that serves the units are considered elevated streets that run parallel to the common area. These exterior hallways are twice the common hall dimension so children can play "out on the street in front of their flat" and others can easily walk by. This generosity of space was afforded by staggering the location of the circulation on every third level. This is made to work with one- and two-level flats that are accessed from above and below. The common area consists of a large green surrounded by a wide walkway that connects to four circular playgrounds that are compressed into the ground. These areas provide protected and controlled area for small children whereas the open green provides ample space for older children to run and play. In the center of the green are two big mounds built from the remains of the construction. The larger mound reaches almost four levels, which is about one-third the height of the taller building. These grand earth constructions create a landscape that puts the green in the foreground and the building in the background. As one walks around the mounds, the view of the buildings is constantly changing.

Park Diagonal Mar in Barcelona is the centerpiece to a large housing project developed in an abandoned industrial area where Avenue Diagonal was cut off from meeting the Mediterranean Sea by various transportation systems. Not unlike the public garden of Robin Hood Gardens, Park Diagonal Mar intends to reconnect the edge of the city to the sea. The park takes on the grand scale of other Barcelona city parks, stretching from Avinguada Diagonal to the sea. The design drawings show sinuous movement connecting each surrounding urban movement to the other through the park. The shaping of the park landscape results in a space created by this web of movement. With its many entrances and pathways, the park is both a popular and beautiful destination for biking, skating, sliding, walking, and watching and an easy short cut between previously disconnected parts of the city (Fig. 14).

Diagonal Mar Park also makes a direct reference to Robin Hood Gardens with the use of large hills that both obstruct the view of the housing projects and create a new scale within the park. The result is a landscape that pushes the buildings away from the park making it seem more connected to nature and removed from the dense urban setting. As well, these hills provide a viewing platform from which one can see beyond the immediate urban fabric out to the sea in the distance. This connection to the sea is further established by the series of ponds that start at the highest park elevation and step down toward the lowest park elevation and closest distance to the sea. The primary park pathway criss-crosses the ponds with an arched bridge that brings you up high enough to see out of the park and eye level with the landscape hills. This walkway gives the pedestrian a very privileged view of the park, the urban context, and the sea.

Miralles and I often joked about the different cultural traditions between the Unites States and Spain. For example, he enjoyed going on about how many decisions needed to be made to have a sandwich in the United States: type of bread, meat, cheese, lettuce, tomato...on a plate, in a bag, etc...He would say this was good practice for designing a small building.

14. Miralles Tagliabue, play mound at Diagonal Mar Park, 2002.

In Spain, there is a cultural tradition of walking. From approximately 44 CE, pilgrims in search of the tomb of Santiago the Greater crossed the peninsula on foot in order to give homage to the first apostle martyred because of his faith, Saint James. The following is an example of one of the

15. Giant figures dancing in Placita de la Seu.

many beatitudes from the period that get to the true value of a pilgrimage: "Blessed are you, pilgrim, if you find that the road opens your eyes to the unseen... because you have discovered that the true road begins at its end...if what concerns you most is not arriving, but arriving with the others...etc."[19] There is no doubt that a pilgrimage was a very long journey to a destination, but it was also a process of intense social interaction and personal discoveries along the way. As with any journey of a great adventurer, the pilgrimage was about finding the unknown and determining how to make the most of it.

Another strong walking tradition includes the daily paseo and the celebratory parades. The paseo has been a daily tradition across Spain for centuries. This tradition is particularly strong in Barcelona where after work, people take a leisurely walk, meeting friends and family and sharing the news of the day. Generally, the paseo happens along streets that are connectors between one part of the city and another. The Ramblas, for example, connects the sea to the Plaça Cataluña, originally the main marketplace of the city. Streets that are the most common gathering places are designed specifically for this activity. Pedestrian ways are wider, trees are planted, places to sit are provided, and the pavement is decorative. In other words, all aspects of the activity are considered. This level of urban design not only accommodates the activity but also encourages it.

Walking also revolves around the many local festivals that are celebrated with parades through the streets. With the establishment of democracy after the time of Franco, La Mercè, the patron saint of Barcelona, became the most popular festival thanks to the cooperation of organizations from all parts of the city (Fig. 15). Today, several hundred events take place across the city with the general topic of Mediterranean culture. The festivals highlight giant figures of queens and kings, nobles and saints, who march the streets of Barcelona. The giants dance on the streets and march around in circles, accompanied by the play of flutes and drums. Their scale and circular groupings create small urban spaces within the streets. This idea of creating smaller scale urban spaces by using giants directly influenced the design of the pergolas of Icaria for the 1992 Olympics.

16. Enric Miralles, Icaria Pergolas, 1992.

About the pergolas, Miralles wrote, "The pergolas express the festive character of the moment of their construction. They resemble the form of the traditional procession of giants in the 'Parada de la Mercè,' especially during those first moments when the outsized participants cluster together, defining a kind of small-scale urban space in the center of the avenue. Perhaps the best means of approaching this work—without forgetting that the procession is animated only because of the people who are hidden beneath its elements—would be to concentrate on how the shadows fall on the ground so far away from the structures, from the point of origination, while the structures themselves grow tall from the point of contact with the ground."[20] (Fig. 16).

To Miralles, and to many of us fortunate to have known him, a project can begin with any type of material and ideas if one accepts that the material sets you on a path of discovery that has its own logic embedded within it. This path is your walkway through the development of the project. The key is to keep walking in the direction of the logic of the project, to follow the flow of the idea and allow it to become your map and guide. Every designer must find his or her manner of walking with the path of their project, and each designer must be prepared to walk a long distance remembering that the process of the walk is the project. Happy journeys.

Notes

1. Edward W. Said, *Beginnings, Intentions and Methods* (New York: Columbia University Press, 1985), 3.
2. Enric Miralles, essay "Walking," Enric Miralles 1990–1994, *El Croquis 30+49/50,* 1995, 40.
3. Henry Thoreau, "Walking," republished with copyright (Red Wing, MN: Cricket House Books, LLC, 2010), 7.
4. Ibid, Thoreau, 7.
5. Ibid, Thoreau, 5.
6. Ibid, Thoreau, 17.
7. Enric Miralles, *El Croquis 49/50*, 1991, 70.
8. Ibid, Miralles, 70.
9. Enric Miralles, "A Portrait by Giacometti," *El Croquis 72*, 1995, 128.
10. Laurie Wilson, *Alberto Giacometti: Myth, Magic and the Man* (New Haven, CT: Yale University Press, 2005), 237.
11. Ibid, Wilson, 235–243.
12. Alejandro Zaera, "A Conversation with Enric Miralles," *El Croquis 72,* 1995, 17–18.
13. William Curtis, "Mental Maps and Social Landscapes," *El Croquis 49/50,* 1991, 8.
14. Enric Miralles and Benedetta Tagliabue, *Time Architecture* (Barcelona: Gustavo Gili, 1999).
15. Flora Samuel, *Le Corbusier and the Architectural Promenade*, (Switzerland: Birkhäuser, 2010).
16. Alison and Peter Smithson, "14. Roofs and Ways," *Charged Void: Architecture* (New York: The Monacelli Press, 2001), 544–552.
17. Max Risselada, editor. *Peter and Alison Smithson, A Critical Anthology* (Barcelona: Ediciones Poligrafa, 2011).
18. Ibid, Risselada, 404.
19. Credited to Santiago el Mayor, sixteenth century.
20. Enric Miralles, "Paseo Icaria Roofing," Enric Miralles 1990-1994, *El Croquis 30+49/50,* 1995, 176.

Mystery and Mastery: Colloquy at a Courtyard

Claudio Vekstein and Enric Miralles

1. Jantar Mantar Observatories, New Delhi, India.

Ahmedabad, India, March 1992

During the second semester of my graduate studies at the Architecture Class, Academy of Arts Städelschule in Frankfurt, Germany, with Professor Enric Miralles, the class (including my classmate Catherine Spellman) took a field trip to India to visit the traditional and modern Indian architecture in Delhi, Agra, Jaipur, Chandigarh, Ahmedabad, and Bombay (now Mumbai), including the study of works by Le Corbusier and Louis Kahn.

At the time, after I lived in Germany for a year, I was fervidly reading the literary works of modern Argentinean writers such as Jorge Luis Borges, Julio Cortazar, and others, which were pleasingly available at the city's public libraries in Frankfurt. Paradoxically, I did not have the same access to some of these books in my native Buenos Aires. I was deeply impacted by one tiny book of only 80 pages—the *Prosa del Observatorio* by Julio Cortazar.[1] It was a well-cared-for 1972 first edition, with the text mostly in prose and certain sections in verse. It was dated by Cortazar in Paris and Saignon in 1971.[2]

The book was recommended to me a couple of years earlier by my mentor at Buenos Aires University, architect Jorge Goldemberg, because it contained original photographs taken by Cortazar during his visit to the eighteenth-century observatories built by the Indian Maharajah Jai Singh in Jaipur and Delhi.[3] The book was not in the National Library in Buenos Aires, although later I was able to find a 1986 reprinted copy in a used bookstore on Corrientes Ave; the book is still in my library today.

During a desk critique before the trip, Miralles recognized the book on my desk, and it stimulated a lively conversation about the great Latin American literature of the 1960s and 1970s, and in particular, Cortazar's influence on Miralles' formative years of university education. He had not read this specific book, which I took as an opportunity to continue our exchange during travel. Enric read the book on the long plane ride to India. Once he quickly finished the book, he jumped from his seat and only said, "Fantastic, fantastic! No?" After which, we were both eager to visit the observatories as soon as we arrived Delhi and Jaipur.

Because of the tight travel schedule, there was very little opportunity for further discussions until one evening when we sat down with a drink at the hotel courtyard in Ahmedabad. We had just arrived in the city and taken a first look outside of the Villa Shodhan (1951–1956) by Le Corbusier. I carried a small tape recorder and suggested we record a conversation in Spanish on the subject of the Cortazar prose and topics introduced by our travels. I intended to later edit the discussion into a colloquy for possible publication. The topics ranged from previous interests I had explored before reading *Prose,* which openly resonated with the visited works, to the observatories and Miralles' own works that I was just discovering.

In the discussion, I referenced the German philosopher Theodor Adorno, a leading member of the Frankfurt School of Critical Theory whom I studied intensely for over three years before moving to Frankfurt, especially his posthumously compiled and published Aesthetic Theory.[4] Even though the book is a philosophical study of the artwork—with comments relative to architecture—it incorporates elements of political philosophy, sociology, and metaphysics, which also interested me before going to Frankfurt. Jürgen Habermas, Adorno's student, assistant, and Germany's foremost social philosopher after 1970, was still lecturing at the Institute for Social Research in 1991 when Miralles started his tenure as professor of the Architecture Class at the Städelschule and I arrived in Frankfurt.

In early February 1992, when the journey and the brief dialogue took place, Enric had just turned 37 years old and I turned 27. This close span between professor and student was appreciated by Enric as the ideal master-apprentice relationship, allowing a level of sharing and discussion of common aspects of our training, noted during the interview. At the same time, our attained knowledge, experience, and crafts were not an impossible distance to overcome. When colleague Catherine Spellman asked me to write a piece on Miralles for this book, instead, though only having heard this tape once in 24 years, I decided to rescue the cassette of this conversation. I delicately and laboriously transcribed it from Spanish and translated it to English from a digital version. It is fascinating to be immersed in this early lesson again...while in the midst of my current architectural and teaching career.

I started with an extensive first inquiry, which is followed by a sequence of continuous responses by Miralles where he carefully unravels matters and thoughts as he proceeds within his own projects. With successive attempts, reiterated beginnings, proliferating bifurcations, and turns, Miralles wisely dismantles abstract formulations, building for it new tools and techniques, accumulating and intensifying subtle traces, diffuse secrets, constantly displacing, replacing, transfiguring, deformalizing them. Thus he draws "a whole mess" as he makes turns around the real and the particular imperfections of things with the ideas that surround them. Meanwhile, time goes by to describe the invisible though tangibly lush room of the "Colloquy at an Indian Courtyard"; once embarked in this intricate parallax, here some of the tilts and postures I discerned from it.

Concrete (hyper) Element

Claudio Vekstein Regarding the Jantar Mantar Observatory, which I will use here as a first guide, there was something that particularly surprised me when I first saw your work, and I am surprised again when we were talking about the works of Le Corbusier in Ahmedabad (Villa Shodhan, Sanskar Kendra City Museum, and the Mill Owners' Association). It is in connection with what I would call "the concrete element," or a certain "concreteness" that is not premature, nor abstract, but it has to do with or is actually generated by the same object. This also has to do with our project at school where we are trying to engender in the object all this data and information that is not given or obvious to move it forward; I would not say invent but to generate...

Enric Miralles To find them.

Claudio Vekstein To find them in the object. On the one hand, I thought we could agree that an object is composed of given elements such as pillars, etc. And on the other hand, this new "concrete" element appears with these observatories, which is an element of invention, something not given and do not have an explicit function. Theodor Adorno would say that these elements represent themselves as the enigmatic character of the artwork, making it so that one can not recognize exactly what it is, which is to say, doing things we do not know what they are, but still contain information which is objective but not given, right?

Enric Miralles Right.

Claudio Vekstein This is the issue I thought could connect some of what we're seeing here in India and relate it to the roof drain spouts in your Archery Pavilion project. This inverted water spout (since the roofs are not actually draining their waters on it) is also the only place where light enters the building, so it is a hyper-element. Another example is the high-roof element in Amancio Williams' Bunge and Born Pavilion. The over-roofing concrete shells that Le Corbusier mentions in The Modulor as an object of the invention—I thought of the Archery drains when I tried to discover the meaning of the section of Le Corbusier's Ahmedabad City Museum.

2. Le Corbusier, Ahmedabad City Museum, India, 1956.

3. Le Corbusier, Ahmedabad City Museum, detail of planter, referred to here as a (hyper) object.

Enric Miralles Yes.

Claudio Vekstein This is a kind of lower lip, which has to make the joint between the brick wall and the ceiling. It seems like it is the ceiling continuing beyond the wall and turning to conceal the articulation that should happen between the wall and the horizontal slab. We see this type of thing in the Bank of London and South America in Buenos Aires by Clorindo Testa, where the brise-soleil does not remain as such; it exceeds its function as brise-soleil and becomes something very interesting as a concrete (hyper) object in the section, where it comes to grow more complex and be spatially structural to support the big roof from which the building hangs and the glass comes behind it.

Enric Miralles Yes.

Claudio Vekstein This brise-soleil develops extra plates that alternate sides. The interesting thing is that there are holes in the plates. In elevation, you'd see the holes here in the front, and the ones behind these sidewalls put them in shade, so you can see inward and through the other side; you see from the inside out by the same effect. Someone said that this object we saw today—the lower lip—is out of scale, and so I've said, well, isn't it that all of these concrete (hyper) elements, objects of the invention, exceed the scale of the building, exceeding its level of function. Then does this not exceed the function for which it is given? Then I propose...

Enric Miralles To continue from there...

Claudio Vekstein Right.

Technic and Craft

Enric Miralles The first thing I would say is that I find it quite fine how you have been interpreting these things—even things that I asked about in class, you speak very well about, for instance "to do things we do not know what they are". Perhaps for our class, it is a kind of collective suicide (laughter). But I think it is important, especially at a time when you are starting the work, that we take this risk. I do not know if this was so before or not, but I think with my generation and yours also because there is not much difference—one develops the critical capacity before the capacity to make things.

Claudio Vekstein Yes.

Enric Miralles Look how clearly you can quote Adorno. I believe from the time of Baudelaire to now (but I really do not know because perhaps in prior periods was like this as well), we've had these very lucid critics. They have been able to tell us the problem of form, the formal creation, and then they put it to a very high level and make it accessible through writing. Then we would say that we can approach them intellectually and get closer and recognize things, right?

So especially when you are learning, or when more than learning, you've not yet found the need to have to develop what you know, which is not that you are learning but only that no one is asking you to submit a project the day after tomorrow to be built. It is that you are or we are in a different moment. Then it continues looking like your critical capacity is much higher and, at school, far superior. For example, you are able to discover these pieces, right? Then we talk about them, but you are able to discover these pieces without your being convinced that you have the fabric to make them or place them. Note that instead, everything is weaker when you talk about objects or pillars or things like that.

Claudio Vekstein True. (Laughter)

Enric Miralles You do not know what to say. Your voice trembles. You're embarrassed. Instead, with these concrete things, you know how to go like a bullet, right? More or less...

Claudio Vekstein (Laughter) All right.

Enric Miralles And it is all right. What happens next, I would say, is something that is very important; there are no known things. Everything, even the most elemental thing, or what is known, must be done through the project, meaning you have to know how to do it. For example, as during this trip, I thought that (and it is something that I'm very conscious of) in the end, we've made a lot of projects that are not more than just developing this kind of almost aesthetic understanding of things that are along a path, right? That is to say, if you noted what we saw along a path, and then you translated it in an elementary way on to a construction, it will be many of the projects that I have done especially at the beginning, right?

Claudio Vekstein Yes.

Enric Miralles For example, in one of my projects, there may be the intersection of two streets, a place to sit at a table, a covering, and three cows looking at each other. (Laughter) The formal side of things has never concerned me. I've been much more interested in the possibilities of these things. But regarding readings, I would say on the texts by Wittkower and the Renaissance proportions—this kind of input and not the one that knows about the quality of the materials or the distinction between a cornice, etc.—I am just now learning how to interpret a cornice, and it is a work that will still take me a long time.

When I was beginning, it took me a long time to design a pillar in a project. It is just now that I am starting to really try something with the pillars. Before, there were always limits—made from the limitations of the distances between things (usually walls and ceilings) and always as a support or a prosthesis. You put it there so that something does not fall down (i.e., from here to there are fourteen meters, put one in 7 but not 7, so leave 3 and 4, and that's it!). To do a thing carries a very important technical knowledge to understand before seeing an over interpretation of the pillar; we should see it very directly.

For example, you know there is something mysterious about a spiral shell. But to go with it, you need to know how to draw it and realize how you get from here to here, and then delete it to know that the dimensional relationships have something to do with it. At this point I feel a little more secure to start working in this intermediate distance above the head that you mentioned before in the museum or the Archery. I think it's still a very difficult distance because between the floor and ceiling works much easier than the kind of things which are up there, at the height of the cornices.

Drawing as Knowing

Enric Miralles The point is that there is significant technical knowledge to be constantly woven into the design process. For example, I remember one of the few trace drawings I did (I have never done this task to redraw projects seriously; I've done it with two, well with three, actually more, but seriously) with some of the Adolf Loos houses. It was about trying to repeat the way they were drawn in order to understand them.[5] I also did the Falling Water Residence by Frank Lloyd Wright before going to see it. I wanted to draw it well and big, in order to really understand the cantilever piece and how it worked.

Then the one that really surprised me (I did it when I was quite young, in the second course) was the Chandigarh Capitol building by Le Corbusier, the Assembly Hall, which seems a very easy building. You think it is a grid of pillars, right? Well then, you sit down and do not know where to start tracing, because it is very difficult to orient yourself in that grid. Although the measuring relationships are fairly easy, the central bays are equal one to another, etc. There is no clear place to start, but then you realize the disposition of the swastika in the plan. I am saying this because at this moment I remembered the plan of the Sanskar Kendra City Museum: if you make an outline of this plan, it is identical! Right?

Claudio Vekstein Yes.

Enric Miralles You realize that there is a repeated technical knowledge that is

4. Le Corbusier, Assembly building, Chandgarh, India, 1955.
5. Le Corbusier, Chandgarh Museum and Art Gallery, India, 1947.

not the project itself but constitutes it. Whether it is above or below, this technical knowledge is in the projects. It is a mysterious thing. It is not that you have to learn how to write: it has nothing to do with writing and nothing that can be learned and fits all. You cannot learn the alphabet and then tell the story you want. How to constitute is part of your architecture, but it is not the only thing, right? Note how Le Corbusier works with a plan (take the museum or the plan of Chandigarh) and a set of transformations: put this panel in here, move the other one in between this and the void in the middle, and all of a sudden you have the Assembly building, done! Even the layout of the building blocks is the swastika shape; the expansion joints are in the same location, and apparently, there is no difference, right?

Claudio Vekstein Now, for example in the Assembly, it appears then that concrete elements start exceeding the configuration?

Enric Miralles Yes sure I would also say this, but let's look at the portico of the Assembly Building. It is absolutely fantastic and very difficult to draw. When you cannot draw a building element very well, it means that you do not know what it is about. It is even difficult to redraw Le Corbusier's original hand drawing of the portico. It is even harder to make a sketch of it; everything goes wrong, wrong, wrong. It may seem that this kind of thing depends a lot on the hand, but it is not true. The proportions of the columns and the drain spouts are super excessive as you've said, and they don't seem to work in anyway. Felix Candela has spent his life criticizing this portico saying that it is the wrong understanding of a concrete shell of minimum thickness and a support point that could normally be held with a finger. But what you have to realize is that the drawing of the portico is the same as the drawing of the lamp that we will see at the Villa Shodhan or the handrail that we have seen at the Mill Owners' building. There is not a scale to these drawings, but each one has a size. Then the size of the thing is fixed; it cannot be larger or smaller, and this makes them very real, you know?

Claudio Vekstein Sure thing.

Form, Measure, and Transposition

Enric Miralles It is a problem of the fabric, or not. As we just saw, it is the problem of the transformation of things. I cannot move from the lamp to the portico, from the portico to the railing, without a transformation, even if it is almost exactly the same drawing. These things have a dimension, but this really has nothing to do with something utilitarian; it is something I am not sure how to define, something older. Then note that these things must be drawn technically in order for them to work; you need to use a compass and measure, find tangents and seek the other piece, make another test and look for this turn. Its intensity is in what happens here, in the continuity of this piece. In how there is a rib and that surely the rib is excessive. Then surely there is a relationship between the rib and the mere fact that it has to be

6. Le Corbusier, Villa Shodhan, Ahmedabad, India, 1951.

supported by the pillar, which finds a relationship with the rib. Things like this just have nothing to do with the perception.

Claudio Vekstein Ha.

Enric Miralles Let's consider Ahmedabad now from the more intellectual point of view that you were talking about before and not from the one that has to do with the logic of things. Even finding it a worse solution, we would be more in favor of the small molding/planter in the Ahmedabad Museum than the portico in Chandigarh, right? Of course. But instead, you see that it works much worse and on top of that it is almost ridiculous. Here, this thing! People here have dared to poorly copy the portico's form with dismal results, with 40,000 buildings that start like this…yueee!

Claudio Vekstein Right, right.

Enric Miralles Then clearly what happens—surely these things we have seen, to these things I put little faith, you know—you understand it as a very selfish act by the architect. Of course, it is interesting from an intellectual point of view: the displacement of the form that he makes from the Chandigarh Museum, where it pulls the water, then comes to Ahmedabad as the molding/planter. It is incredibly sybaritic to make the same building again…since I guess Le Corbusier was doing at least 10 buildings at the same time in India alone.

But you know what, this displacement of the drain spout from there to here carries an entire project. In the Villa de Madame Sarabhai, the building had no overhead light; it has roof garden plants climbing through here, and this is a forest. Then what happens? One of these little moves for him makes the project. In this regard, it is very clear. What I've said before about the ability to make a building with things that can be drawn—like the side beneath, the ticket booth, the bar, the I don't know what, right? You then suddenly could say the project...

Claudio Vekstein It is that.

Enric Miralles Well look, that which is there is here and has nothing to do with the other. The result is an airy building, with water, and I don't know what. Here with the Mill Owners' building, if the trail had worked, then it would be exactly the Villa Sarabhai: here, there are precious art objects. It would be a great building but as an office building? To me it is disastrous (laughter), right? Interpreted like this, for example, the workplace we have seen under the roof is surprising, right? Which is to say that you'd have this piece as a perfect roof, with the trees. Here, there is vegetation that you almost die, a ventilation of noses, the works, and some pieces coming up here—and here, the artworks. This is clear, once you accept it as your own architecture, then you can do this in this way; this piece from right here goes over there. That is, of course, provided that the project totally changes, and it demonstrates that it is not just the use of a repertoire.

Claudio Vekstein Right.

Enric Miralles Instead, when you talk to an experienced architect, he will tell you, "In this case, the project was to split the program into two parts," and that's it! (Laughter) Of course, the key is this: there are people like Le Corbusier that can make these things happen. There is a willingness to leave formal marks of this clarity, right? Also, I think it's a little bit linked to what we are talking about. He also learned from these kinds of texts an almost iconographic interpretation of things.

When you look at the books in his library, they are also clues he leaves, right? So from what we saw this morning, we think this piece is this and that one is that. But in the case of Le Corbusier, he did not develop these things himself. For example, very few times he has truly integrated one of these pieces into the building to become part of it. Now that I have several projects going at once, and even though the drawings are still mine (because we are very few people in my studio and I continue to draw), I know that he could not have developed everything.

For example, earlier in my studio I was all the time on the project; now with many more projects, I am not. The end result surprises you, because it is still the result of your drawings, but these drawings have passed through the hands of five engineers, three for the air-conditioning, it is redrawn three times, and then you give it to, I don't know who, to change a thing because something happened. Then from 100 percent of the time on a project—as far as the number of plans once it is to be built—I would say without exaggeration that it is only a 10 or 20 percent time in your hands.

Claudio Vekstein Right.

Enric Miralles Right! But this does not mean that you have not done the project! So here with Le Corbusier, you understand that these projects really were not very much in his hands. As the architect, you have to search for strategies to keep the project as you intend it and allow the project to remain the project, not to give up important things.

Claudio Vekstein So you prepare and intensely manipulate a certain material that becomes available and then a few transpositions and adaptations.

Rooster Reloaded

Enric Miralles For example, I've noticed a very clear tactic that is used in the Assembly building—when I saw where these famous reliefs were placed. You know, the one with the roosters—it all looks like something of obscure symbolism (and it is that too!), but it is also something as basic if you think of how this is done. There's a little sketch, which is made to 1:1 scale, that Le Corbusier makes or he asks someone to make, like the famous cook, some are from Pierre Jeanneret's cook.

Claudio Vekstein Ah, yes?

Enric Miralles Well, he was remarkably difficult. In the notes, he said: "Ah, your chef draws great, look at this rooster!" He was an intractable character! And then what happens? Look, to do that, what does one need to do? It is really very difficult that the roosters would be marked where they were in a plan. It could be a cross. In some drawings of the complete works, there are some reliefs drawn on the elevations, but I doubt they are real plans. For example, in the Garland[6] archives, they are not there. So, if you see where they were, it was in unlikely places, such as in the straps of the pillars in one series, at points in the ceiling, on the first level of the basement on the walls as well.

So when a wall is going to be built, someone has to phone you and tell you, Monsieur Le Corbusier, and so on…then you have to send a drawing for the wall. You know that this wall is being built immediately, and you have the building very clear in your head. That's very difficult. You know one month prior to when the building is going to be capped, and if they haven't asked for it, you are calm because you also know they are not making mistakes, don't you? It is all right, and they will warn me.

Sometimes, I think that you can leave the project to a point where your intervention is absolutely necessary, right? Yet you are very easy and you go and say, "It is already ok. Have you laid it towards here? It was towards there, but anyway, it is the same. What drawing do you want? Well look, I sent you one by letter." The advantage is knowing that this piece is there, right? And for example, this was always a guarantee to a good start of a brick building.

Claudio Vekstein Right.

Enric Miralles These things would be, for example, for other people that the marble joint is perfectly fitted and no joints will break between this wall and that one, like in any classic unfolded elevation from Adolf Loos or another of his time. In this case, the architect has to be there on that day with those cuts drawn in the plans. If the stones are not right, then it needs to be repeated. And then of course, there are people, like in the case of Louis Kahn, which is a bit extreme, right? And there are other people that dissolve this issue in the project. For example, for Le Corbusier, it is another world; it is the contrary. At a certain moment in his profession, he decides to expose these problems. I believe he does it because of certain generosity but also to demonstrate, so many times, the limitations that architecture has when it wants to exceed itself and be or express other things.

So we come back to the question of the Observatories in Delhi that are so magnificent that one is almost afraid to touch them. Well, but I'm going to try to dare with this! (Laughter) It is really amazing, because it depends on so many things—the material qualities as well. I don't know—it's really impressive.

Mystery and Mastery

Claudio Vekstein I was thinking about what we do for the project at school where I believe we craft a relationship between ideas and concrete elements. Which reminds me of William Curtis[7] in reference to your work, quoting William Carlos Williams' "no ideas but in things."[8] Then the other day when you said, "The idea is not important": the idea is not there, or it no longer exists. We are discussing, I guess, the same issue here, right? This brise-soleil of Le Corbusier's is an object that ultimately is what it is, or it is the consequence of, or it is rather an anticipation of... (an idea).

Enric Miralles Ha.

Claudio Vekstein This is to say that the brise-soleil is something, as Catherine [Spellman] said today, about perception: "You walk around here and see how this is changing. Then you have the light passing, the passage of people, or the air, and this is the transparency of the building." Or if it is not that consequence, but that which anticipates it, meaning the material thing. Then this is a brise-soleil, and this is a hole, and this is a frame on a door that needs to be in a hole, then all it needs is a frame, etc. Therefore, the passage from the idea, which is not an idea in the building until it is not concrete, until it is not a thing. Or if there is an idea at all, if there is an early, anticipatory idea of the object...then...

Enric Miralles I don't know. Notice for example, that the Mill Owners' building has never been closely interpreted. I want for us to analyze it seriously. For sure, Mogens Krustrup[9] would have found a self-portrait of Le Corbusier in the work. Because you know what happens: there is also a figure that inadvertently repeats itself, right?

Claudio Vekstein Yes.

Enric Miralles You know this saying, "If I know the painting, I can do your portrait?" Well almost always there is a mystery of human forms with which we draw. I don't know why, but maybe because they come from our education. I believe that the abstraction of our culture is much more linked to the human figure than to other things. I am not sure if the textiles from the Aborigines apply here or if it is something else. But even the Bauhaus and the De Stijl walls, before Piet Mondrian started painting, it was people moving; the same is true of Wassily Kandinsky, all of them. It is amazing to see how *cherchez la femme* (look for the woman) has always been around. Even Auguste Rodin, before buying a stone with a hole, saw a woman crouching. Isn't it really impressive?

Apart from the human figure present in the abstraction, Le Corbusier pushes the Mill Owner's building in an absolutely amazing way. Although he always cheated the dates—because it says 1954. In this issue of the dates, Le Corbusier is so tricky, really a disaster...it cannot be 1954, because if Chandigarh is going on—perhaps

7. Le Corbusier, Mill Owners' Association, Ahmedabad, India, 1954.

they've commissioned him in 1954. Look, it is very difficult because if you're looking at the various projects, the first projects are never so, and there are some very important changes. You take the package, and you say the Carpenter Center at Harvard (1961), then the Dr. Curutchet House (1949), then Villa Shodhan (1951), and yes, you can catch others, but with these we would do it, right?

I think there are many lessons at the Curutchet House in La Plata, Argentina. It is curious that in the *Oeuvre Complete*[10] there are not photographs of the building. Perhaps there was some "bad blood"? I do not know why he would do it. However, in the paperback book,[11] there is a photo of the façade where you can see a little of the adjacent building, which was nice, right? I think this building caught Le Corbusier off guard. It is a very honest building; it is like something from the very honest Le Corbusier buildings. For example, the Villa Cook is one of his houses where you see the effort to accommodate the people in the best place. The Curutchet House has some of this quality; it is a very honest home.

Claudio Vekstein Sure.

Enric Miralles Well you told me that Dr. Curutchet never liked to live in it. I still haven't been there,[12] but I see no reason to believe it is not a good house.

Claudio Vekstein Absolutely, it is a perfectly livable house.

Enric Miralles It is a very honest house, that is, even the efforts of that tree growing there in the middle, as if you were to locate things in their right place, and all this ritual of movement in the house; it is not an abstract house.

Claudio Vekstein Like having displaced the doctor's office from the house to reveal this movement, right?

Enric Miralles Yes, look at this displacement, it almost induces him to go back outside, and then what the architect does is almost on the contrary actually, to inhabit it to the fullest.

Claudio Vekstein Right.

Enric Miralles Then appears the nice thing of breaking of the two brise-soleils between the doctor's office and the house, which when it is closed might be very beautiful. It is not so new. Le Corbusier has done this before, but here it has nothing to do with the Mill Owners' building. For me, there is one reason the Mill Owners' is more impressive than any other building that Le Corbusier has done—how he treats the horizontal plane, meaning the slab. It is made to be a ground, isn't it? This is a building that I like to interpret because it has a very long and changing project history; there are very beautiful drawings that we will see, and then suddenly, it's like demonstrating a mastery, right?

Look, the pieces are, without a doubt, resolved structurally. For example, the roof is reinforced at the top and is done with (as we may say) a mastery, as are the anchors to hold the railing. This is the building where Le Corbusier has most demonstrated that he is not so present. He knows how to be away from things (namely this, this, this, and this), being directly in the building where it is needed, and nothing more, right? I think here with the horizontal ground, Le Corbusier does it more subtly and beautifully than he has ever done in any project. Here, the horizontal plane is at very different heights, but everything on the ground is horizontal. It was really lovely to see how all the pieces were coming to it.

Ground, Nature, Start, and Continue

Enric Miralles Note that the ground is a somewhat curious concept. The ground there is now a little spoiled because it is so dirty, but floors and walls are all the same stone from Pakistan or maybe Delhi. I think it is very rare in a Le Corbusier project that the floor and walls are the same material. Then on the outside, he lines them with brick. The stone and brick are the two fundamental definitions. Then it closes with the brise-soleils, made out of wood or with this more textile thing, etc. Right? But it is a building, like no other one he has developed. Again, there is the idea of the ground—a ground that can support this room that has no dimensions. For example, there isn't much spatial interlocking work, as always happens, isn't it?

Claudio Vekstein Right.

Enric Miralles Today we have been able to take a look at the outside of the Villa Shodhan. When we can go in it tomorrow, I am sure it will be a great surprise. To me, the view of this house today has been the big surprise in all of the Le Corbusier tour. I did not expect this house because of the construction of those surfaces, right? This is something that seldom happens in Le Corbusier's projects. But of course, this condition remains quite in the margin. It is a building that I believe has some disadvantage due to the excessive presence of Le Corbusier's "mastery."

8. Le Corbusier, Villa Shodhan, Ahmedabad, India, 1951.

The brise-soleil respect to the river is a place entirely—from this door, which is a suspended door, you go out into the sky, which is well above. Thomas Bayrle[13] said something very nice today, and notice it is not coming from an architect. He said, "Look at all that is ugly in the building, the stairs, etc. He has brought them out." Right? He has taken them out to make that plane, because notice that there is a lot of architecture that seeks to find its expression with the stairs, which is the worst! It is that you can't do anything with it! Look, in this sense for example, the delicacy of the staircase in the Carpenter Center is so much better. Do you know it?

Claudio Vekstein Yes, sure.

Enric Miralles That staircase is a masterpiece—a staircase that is almost shy, hidden in a small nook of the building, because it goes up from the ramp. That is marvelous, right?

(Other classmates start gathering around the table at this point.)

I am going to ask Vittorio Lampugnani[14] about this German movement on earth and homeland and architects like Heinrich Tessenow[15] before Albert Speer—the ones who made the first national-socialist architecture, which is very much about cottage, hut, handcraft—this kind of going back to the earth. This movement may correspond with the change in Le Corbusier's projects, which is nice. Because later, it has became something else also with the GATEPAC[16] group in that period, where we have the interest in the craftsmanship, the rural pottery, the photographs of a piece of wood, right? This is the moment of reaching the abstraction of the natural, more rooted things.

And it is a moment when Le Corbusier starts making his first drawings of what is going to be later the Villa Sarabhai, for instance, the vaulted houses and this kind of thing. It must have been the '30s or '40s or something like that, right? We see the stones and this kind of materiality happening already in the Swiss Pavilion, where the back wall becomes stone, a little bit like this here. It is curious that they were taking photographs of pieces of nature, you remember, a bit of sand, the sea, the rock, the trees, and 12 years later, he comes back and makes these beautiful paintings, about the interpretation of the *Le Poeme de l'Angle Droit.*[17] So I think there is the moment when these things start, right?

Claudio Vekstein Let's continue tomorrow.

Notes

1. Julio Cortazar. *Prosa del Observatorio*. Colección Palabra Menor ed. (Barcelona: Lumen, 1972). English translation Anne McLean: Julio Cortazar. *From the Observatory* (Brooklyn, NY: Archipelago Books, 2011), 78.

2. Saignon is a commune in the Vaucluse department in the Provence-Alpes-Côte d'Azur region in southeastern France. The area was first occupied in the Middle Paleolithic age. The rock at Saignon, on a prominent location over the valley, was used as an ancient observatory and possibly a signal station. The name Saignon is believed to derive from the word "Sagnio," which comes from "signum." There is a bakery/cafe, two restaurants, and a general store. The school has about 100 students and is attached to the post office.

3. "Cortázar's text is a strangely beautiful prose poem in the guise of an essay, using the fabulous architecture of the astronomical observatory as the launching point for a text that twists and flows through time and space. Accompanying his text are nearly forty of his own photographs, disorienting images in which light and shadow sculpt the monumental astronomical structures into architectural and landscape fantasies that seem to emanate from the stories of Borges or the frames of Last Year at Marienbad. To my eye, From the Observatory bears the unmistakable birthmark of the year in which Cortázar visited Jaipur–1968. As student protest movements erupted in Paris and elsewhere, Cortázar wandered among the structures of an astronomical observatory built 250 years earlier, trying to imagine a new, pantheistical-infused philosophy that could derive its moral power from the same immeasurable forces that created and energize the universe. And his Möbius-like text invokes a continuum between the micro and the macro, between mortality and the infinite, between the night sky and its twin black galaxy beneath the surface of the oceans. To Cortázar, Jai Singh was 'a guerrilla of the absolute,' more explorer than scientist. He was a small-time Maharaja who stood up to more powerful figures, a man who turned to astronomy in order to avoid the 'astrological fatality that guided his lineage.' But instead of 'organizing the cold chaos,' as Cortázar put it, Jai Singh engaged 'in a slow, interminable copulation with a sky.'" Terry Pitts. "Julio in Jaipur," *Vertigo* February 7, 2012, web January 17, 2016.

4. Theodor W. Adorno. *Ästhetische Theorie*, ed. Gretel Adorno and Rolf Tiedemann. (Frankfurt am Main: Suhrkamp Verlag, 1970). *Aesthetic Theory* (1970), trans. R. Hullot-Kentor. (Minneapolis: University of Minnesota Press, 1997).

5. "Drawings reveal the process of their own making, their own looking, more clearly." John Berger, "Drawn to That Moment," published in *Berger on Drawing* (Cork, Ireland: Occasional Press, 2005), 67–72; (first appeared in New Society Magazine, 1976, and also published in the collection *The White Bird* (London: Hogarth Press, 1985).

6. Le Corbusier and Alexander Tzonis. Drawings from the Le Corbusier Archive: Fondation Le Corbusier in Paris. Published by Garland Architectural Archives (32 volumes) (New York, London, Paris: Architectural Design, 1983).

7. William J. R. Curtis. "Mental Maps and Social Landscapes, the Architecture of Miralles and Pinos" *El Croquis 49/50,* 1990–91, 6–21.

8. *William Carlos Williams*, ed. Christopher MacGowan. Paterson: Revised Edition (New York: New Directions, 1992).

9. Mogens Krustrup (1921–2011), Danish author, art historian, and archeology professor, was invited by EM to guide our group in India especially for Le Corbusier's works. Mogens studied art history at the University of Copenhagen and then received a classical archeology MA in 1949. Worked at the National Museum in the antiques collection; from 1955 was a lecturer in non-Nordic architectural history at the School of Architecture. He made several study trips to Italy, France, England, North Africa, Central Asia, Syria, and India and participated in P.V. Glob's Danish archaeological expedition to Bahrain. Krustrup specialized in the French architect and painter Le Corbusier. Lectured on this, both in Denmark and abroad, and wrote the book *L' Iliade Dessins by Le Corbusier* (Copenhagen: Borgen, 1986) and also *La Porte Emaillée, The Enamel Door: Le Corbusier, Palais de l 'Assemblée de Chandigarh* (Copenhagen: Arkitektens Forlag, 1991) with an analysis of the artist's masterpiece, the painting on the gate to the parliament building in the Indian City of Chandigarh. In 1992, he was awarded the Art Historian Niels Laurits Høyen's Medal and received the 2002 title of Honorary Professor.

10. Willy Boesiger. *Le Corbusier, Œuvre Complete/ Complete Works*, 8-volume set (Basel: Birkhauser, 1910–1970).

11. Willy Boesiger. *Le Corbusier, Studio Paperback* (Berlin: Birkhauser, 1998).

12. Miralles and Vekstein later together visited the House in the City of La Plata, Argentina in 1994, chronicled by Vekstein, Claudio. "Miralles De a Pie." *Summa +*, September 1994, 18–19.

13. Thomas Bayrle is a German visual artist born in 1937 in Berlin. He lives and works in Frankfurt, Germany, where he taught at the Städelschule between 1975–2007 and traveled with the group to India invited by Miralles. He is one of the pioneers of Pop Art, and serial and new media. Bayrle always cited his experience in a weaving factory as the detonator of its formal artistique practice. The yarn interlacing, the reason for the assembly line, resonated with mass communication, the industrialization of the Europe 1960, and the one currently in China. Bayrle has continued to observe and interpret the social, political, and biological between individuals; his gaze is that of an ethnologist.

14. In 1990–94, Vittorio Magnago Lampugnani was the Director of the German Architecture Museum (DAM) and professor at the Academy of Arts (Städelschule) in Frankfurt am Main, teaching a supporting history lecture course for Enric Miralles' Architecture Class. Since 1994, he has been professor of the History of Urban Design at the Swiss Federal Institute of Technology (ETH), and since 2010, head of the Institute for the History and Theory of Architecture (GTA) at ETH Zurich.

15. Heinrich Tessenow is considered one of the most important German architects during the Weimar Republic along Hans Poelzig, Bruno Taut, Peter Behrens, Fritz Höger, Ernst May, Erich Mendelsohn, Walter Gropius, and Mies van der Rohe. He taught at the Institute of Technology in Berlin-Charlottenburg from 1926 until 1934, when he was fired by the Nazis. Albert Speer, who later became a cabinet minister during the Third Reich, was his student in 1925 and one-time assistant in 1927.

16. GATEPAC (Grupo de Artistas y Técnicos Españoles para la Arquitectura Contemporánea) was a group of architects formed in the 1930s during the Second Spanish Republic as a Spanish branch of C.I.A.M, including among its most important members Josep Lluís Sert, Antoni Bonet Castellana, Josep Torres Clavé, José Manuel Aizpurúa, Fernando García Mercadal, and Sixte Illescas. The Catalan section (Eastern) founding of the group called GATCPAC (Grup d'Arquitectes i Tècnics Catalans per al Progrés de l'Arquitectura Contemporània) was more successful than the Central or Northern sections and carried out government contracts during the Second Republic and published the magazine *A.C. (Actividad Contemporánea),* which remains an important document of the Modern Movement in Spain.

17. *Le Poeme de l'Angle Droit (The Poem of the Right Angle)* was composed by Le Corbusier over a period of seven years between 1947 and 1953 as a series of 19 paintings and writings, one of the most lucid synthesis of his ideas about the artistic and architectural creativity and its role in the contemporary world. The paintings are arranged symmetrically in seven rows, or "zones," lettered A–G, assigned a title, corresponding color, and read across, in order, 5, 3, 5, 1, 3, 1, 1, such that the entire composition appears top-heavy and cross-like. Each piece, as well as the significance of its placement in the color-coded sets, draws from and illuminates the dialectic of opposites inherent in alchemical processes.

Drawing in the Edges

Elena Cánovas

1. Sagrada Familia ca.1900.

I was born in Barcelona. I took all my studies in architecture there, and after teaching and practicing for more than twenty years, I am living in the United States teaching at Washington University in St. Louis and leading their summer program in Barcelona. I'm in the U.S. because I want to be involved in architectural education, and I think the academic environment here is extremely powerful, dedicated, and alert.

However, I am far from everything that surrounded me, far from my beloved sea and city. Barcelona is an old, dense city by the Mediterranean Sea in southern Europe. It was founded by the Romans in the second century before Christ for Roman military retirement–a kind of summer resort. The city grew protected by several city walls during the Middle Ages, maintained as a protecting device from attacks, mainly from the sea. The city suffered a siege in 1714 by the King Filipe V and the French allied army as part of the War of the Spanish Succession. After the end of that 13-month war, in order to control the city, the Citadel was constructed. Throughout the next 100 years, the Citadel was alternately destroyed and reconstructed depending on politics and population sentiment.

In the eighteenth century, the city became so extremely dense that it challenged the health and security of the people living there. Using Ildefons Cerdà's l'Eixample master plan, they demolished the city walls and expanded throughout the predominant geography. Cerdà's plan was a powerful three-dimensional grid that provided the pattern, the information, and infrastructure to build and extend the city around a network. The pattern that Cerdà created allowed the streets to grow and the grid to grow, as well as to deploy a modernist architecture.

The city was quiet after the Spanish Civil War in 1939 until democracy was regained in 1975. From 1975 until now, the old town, the city, and the metropolitan area have been working together to expand connections and infrastructure over the metropolitan area and improve public spaces, facilities, schools, healthcare centers, and neighborhoods with a central idea of retaining historical character while creating new spaces.

In 1992 for the Olympics, the city made a strong effort to turn development towards the seafront and to finish the highway around the city to improve the inner traffic, as well as to build several facilities in urban spaces. Because of this effort and the worldwide attention, the city became internationally known and open.

For the 2004 Universal Forum of Cultures, development along the seafront for urban regeneration, begun for the Olympics, culminated in a new area of centrality anchored by the Herzog and de Meuron Forum building. It is at the end of Avinguda

Diagonal, connecting the seafront through the old town to the north. Barcelona today encompasses the old town, the Roman city, the diagonal boundaries, the Cerdà grid, the hills in the north protecting the city from the cold winds, the upper and lower river, and the seafront. It is a city of many layers, revealing a deep palimpsest of historical, social, political, and physical stories. The city of Barcelona is a model for architectural studies that has a strong relationship between urban design and architecture over the main periods of the city and today through modernism and contemporary architecture.

Since democracy, the school of architecture–Escola d'Arquitectura de Barcelona (ETSAB)–had a closed, narrow culture for many reasons: the lack of international contact for many years, the small community of architects, the tradition, the amount of public competition for the local community minimally open internationally, and a strong cultural and political leadership. Oriol Bohigas i Guardiola, among others, was the director of Barcelona city planning from 1980–84 and director of the architecture school.

It was at that time and in this context that Enric Miralles developed his work. Miralles was my first professor in design studio–a traditional coordinated studio with 300 students (all trembling) and six professors. It was my first year, but also Miralles' first year in the course. He was used to teaching upper levels, and it took me a while to understand his ideas. But I trusted him because of the deep respect that he showed while telling you, "You have no idea what you are doing!"

While I was designing a public space for his studio, he told me something that has remained in my mind: "When you are having a problem with a design, you are focusing too much in one point. You must get away from it to find a solution. You need to go somewhere else. Go and draw somewhere else, and it will come. Go to the edges. Go to the edges, not to the point."

In the following semesters, I kept learning from him. I learned that architecture was made by little approaches, by meandering with the trembling pencil around the edges, measuring, testing, sensing, referring, not by big points, not by big words, not yelling but whispering. I learned how to find my own way of drawing through Miralles and Pinós' published work, as they had little built at this time. I was trying to find how they would draw something similar to what I was working on. Since there was nothing built, we did not know how it would look. There were no renderings, just emotions coming from drawings, from deep drawings. There was not any gesture of their work in my work, but I found a deep learning and a great learning–it was magic!

So I learned drawing in the edges, but also drawing within the edges, and drawing in and out the edges. I was searching for some architecture in the transitional moments, drawing everything, leaving all traces of the drawings, drawing all the traces of a place, drawing the edges, searching for some architectures in between the drawings and the construction, in between inside and outside, and of course, drawing in and out to the edges to expand them, bring an outsider inside, in the thresholds, in the edges.

Miralles was a professor in his office and a colleague at school: his office–his work–was a school, an academy, alma mater. At that time, he was splitting his collaboration with his Estudi Viaplana Piñon, where he collaborated on two design in Barcelona–Plaça de Sants, one of the first public spaces he designed in democracy, and Plaça Barangé, the second iteration of their understanding of the contemporary urban space in the early 1980s (Fig. 2).

The beauty of drawing in the edges in Miralles' work can be found by looking at the Santa Caterina Market in Barcelona to see the understanding of needing to be generous with the neighbors–with the roofs and with the views as an essential interface, a boundary. In the little plaza in front of the market, the façade retires and the edge becomes thick in order to give some breath to the dense neighborhood (Fig. 3).

Miralles' Igualada Cemetery, to me, is a referential project for designing from the edges for many reasons (Fig. 4). The edge is a counter line, a hidden abstract trace on the landscape that becomes built. It becomes not only the physical generator of the project but also the poetical one: to build the line between life and death, the subtle boundary between the alive and the buried. The principal access boundary is defined by a cross, which is a basic trace to signal a point, a reference to art, and of course, a religious symbol.

2. Enric Miralles, drawing of Plaça de Sants, Estudi Viaplana Piñon, ca.1980.

There is an unfinished chapel, with little holes, cuttings, so that the light slides through and makes the space. These are again the symbols, the little messages, the whispers from Miralles. He was a great whisperer. I visit the project with students from Washington University every year. We go there and

3. Miralles Tagliabue, Santa Caterina Market aerial view, 2005.

4. Miralles Pinós, Igualada Cemetery, 1986–1996.

we draw. We go in the summer, in the afternoon when the sun is high and strong–it toasts the place. For me, the learning there is never-ending. It is a masterpiece.

How do I understand drawing in the edges in my own work? After several years of joint professional and academic experiences, Antonio Sanmartín and I founded aSZ Arquitectes in 1996. We decided to share and collaborate with multidisciplinary colleagues where we try to do what we teach and to teach what we do. When we are asked to explain our work–it is not linear. It is something that turns around, appears and disappears through the time and process of work. We look at our projects through their extension in time–some of them keep us busy for over a decade, others a year, a month, a week, a day, and some do not go beyond a conversation.

Our projects include the Badalona Central Library, the Santiago de Compostela Towers at the Cidade da Cultura, the Vidrà Housing, the Auditorium in Rianxo, the Capuchinas Building for Huesca University, and the Tramway system for Barcelona. Every project operates at diverse steps and speeds–time made of diverse simultaneities.

I selected the following projects to provide an understanding of our design processes that integrate landscape and urbanism, public and private, past and future, and man-made and natural systems.

There was a design competition in Barcelona called Portes de Collcerola. Two years ago, the city decided to regain its "face" back to the hills, as it had in redeveloping the seafront for the Olympics 20 years earlier, and to understand the connection between the city and the little hill that we call Collcerola. The city identified 16 areas

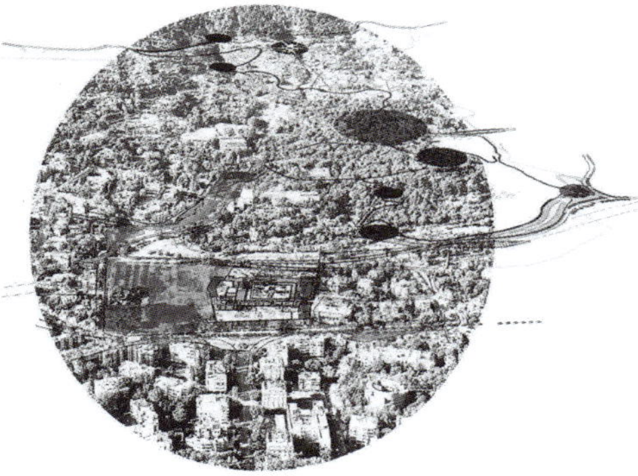

5. aSZ Arquitectes, collage drawing for Portes de Collcerola competition.

6. aSZ Arquitectes, collage drawing for Portes de Collcerola competition.

for green corridors to the Collcerola Mountains, which were called "gates" or "portes." We were selected to work on one of the gates called Ellerabis, from the neighborhood's name. The area has a monastery, a hill, and several other areas (Fig. 5).

We decided not to look at it as a gate or door but as a constellation of fields of action. We used dots as a lens to emphasize and focus on the topography and over time to transform the landscape into urban and the urban into landscape as islands in the same conglomerate. We envisioned each dot as a color, a material, a geometry, a section, to provide order and qualify each point to guarantee the transitions and economy of interventions. These are continuous surfaces of the same color and the same material as steps to accommodate the topography. The area of the intervention is a colorful one with the potential to transform and heal with a chromatic acupuncture. Working through these spots liberates the main area for us to understand where the green areas should be. In order to keep the forest as it is, we intervened only in these little dots (Fig. 6).

We created a system of paths that connected the dots so that every area was reinforcing some users. There is an area related to a monastery, which is the most urban part. We wanted to stop cars there and not allow cars to go up into the hill. It was also a way to reinforce the wall of the monastery.

There is an urban harvest zone in an area protected from noise, which protected other areas from the noises of the skaters in the young urban zone. There

7. aSZ Arquitectes, plan drawings for Portes de Collcerola competition.

was a treatment for a creek in another area that is reaching up to the hill, some areas up in the hill with a green labyrinth and a formal sand collector, and a place for playgrounds to have views and to understand the ruins of a nearby castle (Fig. 7).

The power points are designed to be adaptable to form, shape, and topography, but also to be responsive to a participative model of citizen intervention. Mainly, the power points preserve the site and generate the boundaries to protect the forest as it is. So, maybe they are not points but boundaries. They act as symbolic places, identified through a community participation process and, through looking at places of gathering, they provide color, form, and texture. They promote a shared management in urban and school agriculture and an intergenerational transmission of values.

Valdebebas was also an urban park competition in Madrid that is a new urban development project under construction with plans to develop 12,500 apartments for a population of 40,000 inhabitants (Fig. 8). The plans include a large urban park system. The development is near the Barajas Airport and is also the home of training facilities for the Real Madrid football club. Because it is a new development, when we were designing, we only knew what is planned to happen in the future. We proposed

8. aSZ Arquitectes, plan drawing for Valdebebas Park competition.

a grid or system, in which through time and interventions, we could understand different moments of the process. We drew our vision of the maturity of the park ten years after its completion, and then we drew the construction or the beginning of the intervention.

We envisioned a system of paths to provide open uses that could be developed and evaluated throughout time. The edges of the urban and the park would be modified and extended to have some urban areas before the access to the park. Reading the topography, reading the site, and drawing the site brought us to understand the water system where the topography was driving water from a specific point, the traditional agricultural lots and urban agricultural lots that could be rented and shared with the school of agriculture, and the seeding of a tree that is traditional in the area and would grow because they would be following the water system and naturally would just keep colonizing the area through an evolution of tree growth. Around a lagoon, we planned for birds that migrate through the area. This would all receive technical support from urban arbors and green houses. We took an existing canvas to figure how would it look throughout the years and what our desire was to make our plan happen.

A final example is a built project—a public library in a former industrial building in Badalona, north of Barcelona (Fig. 9). The building was originally an eighteenth-century factory that had an interesting system of trusses that traditionally was a double-tilted roof. It is an extension of an original library and has a space for exhibitions and a lecture room, all connected by a passage that goes from one street to the other.

Through the movement of the roof, we wanted to bring natural light into the library. To bring light through, a part of the roof was folded so light from two sides could come from the north and south. This is not the traditional way to have light in an industrial building, which uses northern light to have a constant light throughout the day. But we wanted some perception of a change of light during the day, so we mixed the cold northern light and the warm southern light. The original trusses are made from cast-iron with carved elements. We wrapped a perforated metal material around the trusses to bring the light in, which worked acoustically for the library as well.

Outside, we designed a modern wall mural on a blank street-facing wall to echo the outline of windows in bright colors so that the street would have an interaction with the building. For this project, we needed to draw all the time, all the lines, all the traces, all the things that could happen for the design.

Our studio's architecture results from translations: a fiction—what happens from one translation to another and measures the time of a project; a chronicle of proceeding from the present, backwards, reaching possible foundations. Sites and places, for us, are the result of architecture built or thought. Site happens when architecture pinches the surface of a place. Sites and places are not an unreachable jewel. They exist as the project action operates and extends for a certain time.

Architecture is an open site and an empty book to carry issues, matters, thoughts, and proceedings. Every project has a specific procedure, housing data, events, and incidents. There is not such a thing as the origin of a project, for us it is a myth. Each time a transfer between systems is built, we find a tangible outcome.

9. aSZ Arquitectes, photograph of Badalona Public Library.

From Body to Field

Manuel Bailo

1. Antoni Gaudí, Colònia Güell in Santa Coloma de Cervelló, a.1900.
Enric Miralles photographing one column of the site when the chapel was still in a state of ruin.

The Chapel Güell in Santa Coloma de Cervelló near Barcelona by Antoni Gaudí was abandoned in the late nineteenth century and later restored. It is a beautiful chapel that has a strong connection to the site that is established through a series of columns strewn across the site in a seemingly hapless manner. The columns are similar to the columns that support the chapel and are cut from stone in an irregular fashion.

The scale of the column is that of a large man thick in diameter. The column/man is resting in the landscape around the chapel. It is not supporting anything but suggests the potential to support quite a weight if it were needed to do so. It suggests the same type of latent potential that a chapel offers and therefore extends the spirituality of the chapel out into the landscape, connecting the two.

I came to understand the idea of connection between the body and site in a seminar "From Body to Field" that I took with Enric Miralles while studying at Escola Técnica Superior D'Arquitectura de Barcelona (ETSAB). To illustrate the idea of the scale of the body in relationship to the scale of the landscape, there is a beautiful drawing by Le Corbusier of the landscape in relationship to Barcelona on his first visit to the city. He clearly connects the two scales in this drawing and explains how the city evolved from the landscape (Fig. 2).

I can remember Miralles talking about the Venice Hospital project by Le Corbusier and how it was developed from the scale of the bed to the scale of the city with the idea to resolve the project at both scales simultaneously (Fig. 3). The scale of the bed is a unit that in combination makes up rooms, corridors, building wings, courtyards, and a complex that interconnects with the scale and fabric of the city of Venice. In the end, the building is a huge complex—the scale of a city. In a section drawing, the bed

2. Le Corbusier, sketch and photograph of traditional Indian bed.

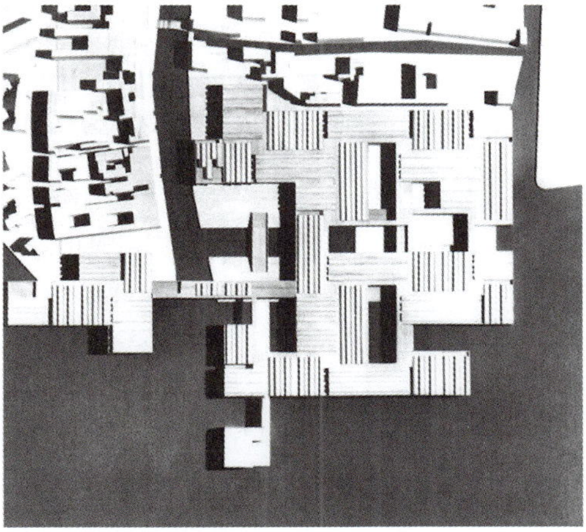

3. Le Corbusier, Venice Hospital project, 1964.

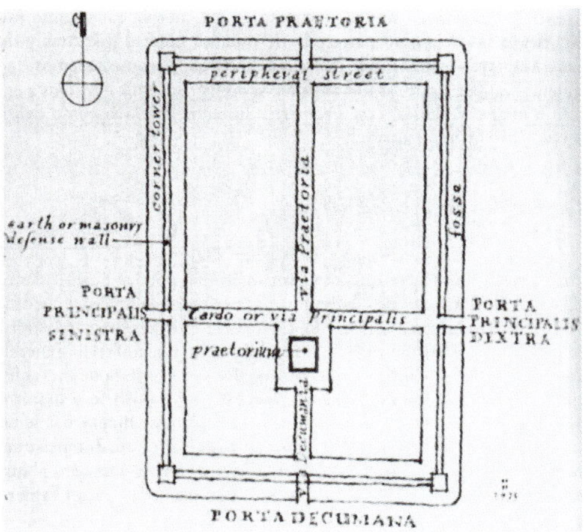

4. Roman basis for city plan.

and every person has direct natural light. There is a corridor with a cut to allow the light to enter. The bed is related to the room, which relates to the building, and then to the city. It is a beautiful building that has an amazing relationship to the people and at the same time with all the city around it.

A book given to me by Miralles early architectural partner, Carme Pinós, titled *Flesh and Stone* by Richard Sennett, is about how cities are related to the human body. In one chapter, Sennet explains how the ancient Romans decided where to locate a vertical axis near an intersection of a cardo (north-south oriented street) and a decumanus (east-west oriented street) in order to establish a relationship between the ground and the sun (Fig. 4). At this place, the Romans would leave gifts for the spirits of the ground, and for this reason, the point of connection was not at the center of the axis intersection but a strategic location near the center, providing the possibility to dig in the ground. Leonardo da Vinci also tried to understand a geometry that relates the world and the human body. He drew the bellybutton at the center of a drawing as the point of connection between the two elements of the drawing. In fact, every one of us has a “bellybutton” that ties us to a very specific place. The idea of relating the body to the universe to a specific site is a very ancient idea but one that still has meaning today.

5. Miralles Tagliabue, collage drawing for the Scottish Parliament.

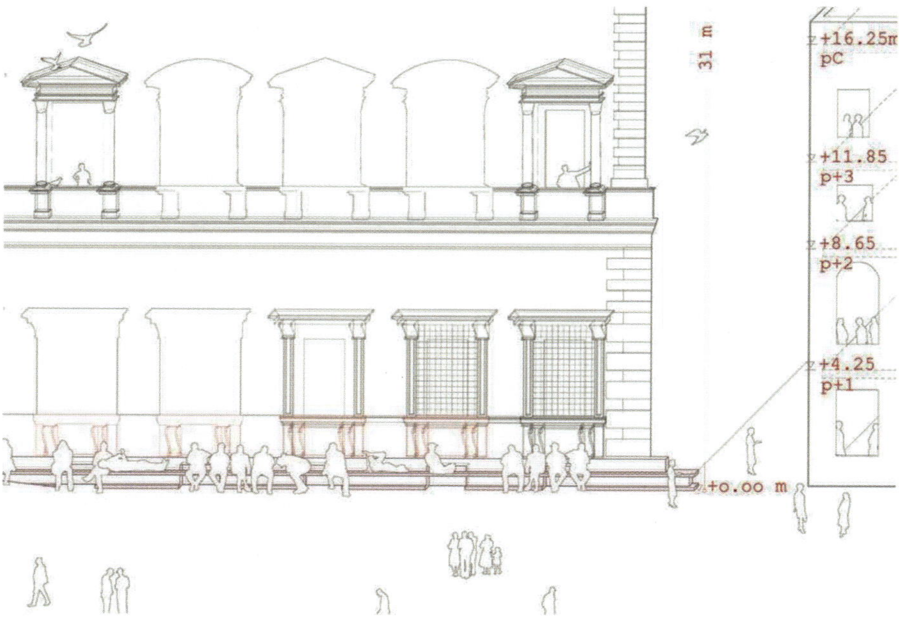

6. Manuel Bailo, drawing of Palazzo Farnese.

Collages by Miralles and Benedetta Tagliabue's studio, EMBT, show an initial sketch for the Scottish Parliament project, one of the last projects that Miralles designed, and the completed project (Fig. 5). The collage explains how the project is connected to the land. It is about locating the topographic lines that are altered to accept the project and connect it to the site like a "bellybutton." From the very first drawing, there is this relation with the building and the topography. These are amazing drawings that show a search to understand the urban condition, to find a place of connecting the project, and at the same time to look for how someone could sit in this place. The Scottish Parliament building is an example of two extremely different scales, the urban scale and the human scale, existing in one place.

The Palazzo Farnese in Rome by Michelangelo has a magnificent scale. The building has three levels like the others on the street, yet the Palazzo Farnese towers over the other buildings. It has a very strange proportion and is a huge building. There is a bench on the front façade of the palazzo that provides a place for the public to sit and mitigates the large scale of the building and the scale of the humans. The bench is a catalyst that creates life in a public space by providing place for people to interact. It makes the life of the site (Fig. 6).

A catalyst is a chemical, a person, or an event that quickly causes change or action. Elías Torres was asked to write about the Hostalets stair designed by Miralles and Pinós. Torres made a drawing that describes the sound as someone walks across the stair. It is nice because it talks about how architecture also has music and how, like music, it is an art that is constantly moving and changing. In the end, this drawing is a catalyst to discuss Miralles' work.

7. Manuel Bailo, drawing of Parets del Valles shade structure by Enric Miralles.

The Parets del Valles shade structure by Miralles again becomes a catalyst (Fig. 7). The stark contrast between the light and shadow, which are in constant, slow

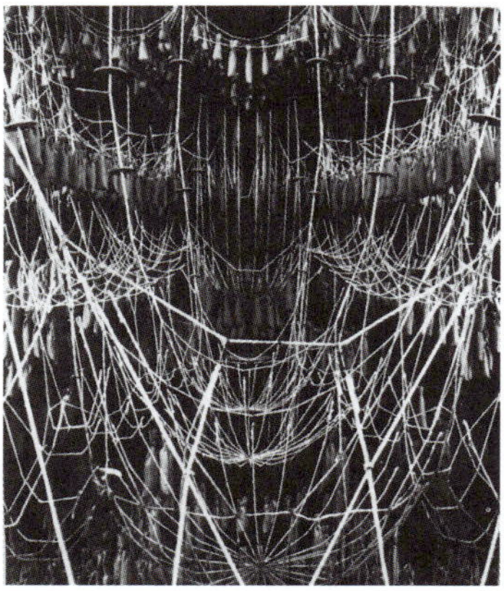

8. Antoni Gaudí, Sagrada Familia sand bag model, ca.1915.

movement across the plaza, creates a very powerful space. It appears that the placement of the structure is very chaotic, perhaps because it does not follow a grid and or visually clear ordering system. Its system is one of balance between the foundations, columns, and trellis. Each piece counterbalances another piece in such a way the whole of the parts is perfectly stable. It works much like a Calder sculpture. The organization of the structural pieces may look chaotic, but they are not. The column and beam pieces form a series of simple triangles that when connected can easily support the rectilinear trellis pieces. The project is about a system of balance and not one of visual order as you find in a grid.

Miralles was a master at working with geometry. All architects in Barcelona learn the relationship between geometry and beauty through the example of Antoni Gaudí (Fig. 8). The complexity of Gaudí's structures could only be achieved through geometry. His famed sand-bag structural models enabled him to visualize the structural forces as they would move through the building. For us, geometry is directly related to the structural system in a very natural way.

In my studio, Bailo Rull Arquitectura, we worked on a renovation project of a community center in the town of Igualada (Figs. 9, 12, 13). The commission was to restore the back façade, which was in ruin, and to reorganize the interior circulation. The building is sited in the old city on a plaza near the cathedral and river. The immediate context is very dense and immediately outside the center, the topography increases and you can see the mountain of Montserrat in the distance. The project was a competition, and we presented the idea of using the existing window frames to make a connection to the old city and the distant landscape. We

9. Bailo Rull, Mansara Community Center model.

10. Paintings of Monteserrat magistrates circa fifteenth century.

also proposed a new layer of construction that would be juxtaposed to the old building creating a dialogue between the two and to bring the space of the new construction through the existing façade, using it to reorganize the interior public space.

Additionally, we know that Montserrat is very important to Catalan culture. I found beautiful painted portraits inside the town hall of many former town mayors painted with Montserrat in the distance, showing their affiliation with the landscape and the culture (Fig. 10). In our project, we decided to create a relationship between the landscape and the building by pushing the new stairway out of the building and giving it a direct view to the landscape in the distance.

The common space and stair act as a new layer over the old building creating framed views of the landscape while connecting the different levels. The stair gives the public a new view of the path and the landscape. As you move on the stair, the landscape in the distance changes. The project gave us a chance to consider how architecture can deal with the history and culture of a place. We were looking for some type of relationship between the ruins of the old city, the landscape in the distance, and our new addition.

Catalan has a very old and dense history, but at the same time we are contemporary, so we chose to work with this shape in the addition and insert this modern shape into the structure of the old building. We wanted to respect the texture and materiality of the façade while creating a dialogue between what was old and what is new,

11. Bailo Rull, Mansara Community Center collage.

working with the plaster to build a space between the old façade and the new façade. We separated the elevators and stair and wanted each to create different interesting places. We created a new bridge that connected the elevator to the stair across the foyer. The bridge and stair hang from a thin suspension structure. I spent one year detailing the structure and refining the joints. The joints are very complicated with multiple angles coming together in one place. To develop a simplified system that could be adjusted for each joint condition, I drew the force vectors as arrows, and the in-between space became the connecting joint.

Performances are held in Catalonia for a celebration of any type and take place in the plazas and public spaces around the city. We wanted to create a new public space on the backside of the building adjacent to the new stair. The stair is also a type of performance activating the public space and creating a catalyst for performances. It has worked (Fig. 11).

I found a video of a dancer, which I think is perfect to explain this idea. In the video, there is a dancer, and he changes his t-shirt. He is visiting an apartment in a housing block–one of the last housing extensions made by Franco. The dancer takes the measurements of the space in the really small apartment–the body and the space and the relation between the body and the furniture–this is something that Enric explained many times. I remember Enric talking about Le Corbusier's bathrooms–they were always round–and he explained that when you take off your towel you make a sweeping movement. The dancer is moving like that, measuring like Leonardo Vinci, having a walk through the apartment and perfectly measuring body and space.

When Eva Prats worked in the Miralles studio, she made a drawing of a croissant that was published in *El Croquis.* It shows a series of section cuts through a croissant, which could also be thought of cuts through a landscape or site. The drawing is trying to find the rule that gives order to the croissant, and it is a bit of a joke, but it is also a very careful and serious measurement of that specific croissant. Every different croissant would produce a different series of cuts and drawings. This drawing is about the importance of precision, which is what Miralles was always looking for.

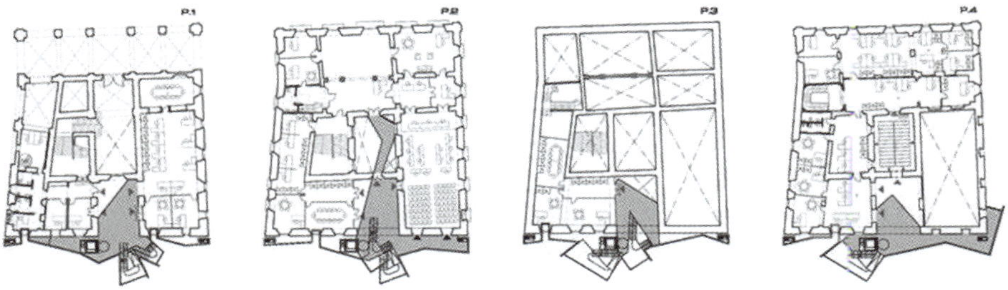

12. Bailo Rull, Mansara Community Center plans.

13. Bailo Rull, Mansara Community Center photos.

Conversation

Manuel Manuel Bailo
+
Elena Cánovas
+
Students

Student What is your design process?

Elena Cánovas I would say that every project is different, every question is different, and every timing is different. Each time, you are in a different moment, you are interested in different things; but over the years, you see that there are patterns that happen constantly or something that is repeated.

In the beginning, we try to start from a combination of things, not just from one thing, but the one important thing for us to draw and to know very well is the site. When we say draw, we mean to try to transfer everything we think is important into a document. Of course, using pictures is good, but then you manipulate them, and then you draw the site. You will never get a good site drawing unless you make it on your own, because you combine information that you are looking for every time. We work with models a lot, and these little models make you figure out what the thing is going to be about or what your response is about. They become very important. Of course at some point, how to transfer that into architecture is another moment, because you have something there, but you are trying to understand what it is—trying to understand how this can be transferred into something more formal, more positive, architecturally speaking.

Do you always start with site as a primary source of information, rather than starting out with what the client is after?

This is right. It may seems like we don't think about the client, but of course we do. We understand the client; they tell us what they do want, but also they tell you what they don't know, and they want you to figure it out. Sometimes a private developer says, "Help me figure out what kind of housing and how many I should organize," and then, of course, they will decide and tell you the program and the square footage for everything. But there is something else that they want, which is why we do competitions, because architects want an answer that also fits with the city and other things. We understand that this is our part.

First, my team—me, my office, my partner—we understand that the program has to work perfectly, but we usually don't think that the program is going to give you this park or design. It has to be there, and it has to work perfectly—it is a condition that has to happen—but only a very few times will the program bring you to an architectural design. That's our personal point of view.

Is the interpretation of the program the driver in any of your projects?

We really don't believe that the program is the originator of the architecture today, but, of course, for housing, it is. Housing has to be thought from the point of view of the house. We could explain all present housing is based on the program, but I wonder if it is useful for the students. We are used to managing programs, because in every competition you need to understand the program—you need to know how a hospital works, how a corporate building works—we need to know, of course, how a house works and how do we want them to work. I would say it is a way to make space. It's like the houses in Barcelona. They are great because they are meant to be houses specifically and then they are great for whatever purpose you want to have—so that's good architecture—one that can change the program and is still good.

Manuel Bailo But we have to cook, no? It is what the architect has to do. The program is one ingredient of the recipe. We can look at the health elements of architecture, right? For example, in the Scottish Parliament project, the stair is an element of architecture. It's amazing because the stair is something that you experience in space because you are changing your height. It's something unique. And it's something very simple. It's a stair. It's just that. But it's a space. It's the movement. So we can talk about elements that I love to design, for example. I always say that if I know something, which I don't remember, then I draw. Doors and handrails are my specialty—designing handrails is very difficult. It's not easy. But it is where you touch the architecture. It is when you touch and you feel secure with the architecture, so it's also a simple element to design a handrail or to design a door. For the cemetery in the Igualada project, the decision of designing the cemetery door was just an amazing one. It's kind of a cross. It's a perfect design of just a door. It is an element for how you trespass from the landscape of the outside with something that is not closed, but it is fixing this edge between what is in and what is out.

What is your process of teaching architecture?

Elena Cánovas Relative to teaching I like to remember Herman Hertzberger when he was celebrating 25 years of teaching at the Berlage Institute. He did a lecture and explained the main commitment in teaching was to continue learning. That's a nice thing: how to generate a context in which you don't feel like you teach by just giving instructions, but teaching by being there—to journey with someone who is trying to discover things. You provide the security and understanding of how to be there in the moment. I thought about this like a Chinese landscape. You want to go from here to there, but you cannot go straight; you have to meander. Through meandering, you have the structure, the program, and the client input, which makes you arrive to the point. This approach provides the confidence to the student for you to say, okay, keep in mind that our book for the year is going to be your work; we will not have an extra book. Your book will be the one that provides the knowledge. So you better start producing things. And then we, as teachers, better trust in the students and enjoy them, of course, and join them in a deep exertion, but in depth. It doesn't have to be a playground; it has to be about something that is enjoyed, of course, but it has been taken seriously.

Manuel Bailo But of course, you learn too, no? When I try to listen, but I don't know where the things are going to go, I become stressed. But then I try to learn how to enjoy learning from that, which is not easy, but to enjoy the confusion. When the students say, I'm confused, I say, that's great, you need to be confused, and then you will figure out how to get somewhere, and then you will learn and then be confused again. Confusion is part of the creation. When artists try to do art, what they try to do is to understand the work. That's why they are doing the art. The writers are writing because they are trying to understand the work too. So I think we are also trying to understand the work when we produce.

What kind of exercises do you give your students to help them work through a project? Or is it sort of self-discovery?

Elena Cánovas For a beginning student, in Barcelona where I was teaching the first year and many years, we created questions, but the question had very few variables. We didn't introduce all the ingredients of the recipe at the same time. We were just cooking fragments. Well, after cooking several fragments, you figure out that at the end, this was the story of the dish, of the meal, of a sample. But we don't put all the questions out there. Just like biology research: you try to understand the wing of a fly and to understand that very deeply and understand how it works. You understand the wing of a fly, then you try to understand something else. Or through the addition of new ingredients, you make the soup or the broth. In the first year, we think there are strategies to bring students through and allow the time to pass and to cook slowly. There are many different strategies. In the later years of learning, I think it should be more like Hertzberger: teach me without teaching. You shouldn't be teaching anymore; you should be there talking and trying to figure out when to jump from one moment to the other—maybe you're ready to jump into this question knowing your project, with this question and this question, until everything comes into the conversation. The structure has to come at some point—how to provide the materiality for things to happen so maybe we can provide some conversation on the issues.

When did you start to incorporate the computer into your work process?

Elena Cánovas I remember when we were starting that. At some point Enric came back from the States. He brought all these templates—rulers to draw curves. That is why he would start with the geometries, because he could use these big radial devices to draw better. These materials were coming to our country, so we could draw much more complex things. When you had these rulers, you could manage, control the angle. Then we started to be more playful. What I was thinking when you were talking is that, I wouldn't blame the programs that much. For instance, what I don't understand is why AutoCAD is taught by people with expertise in digital computers and not by people who know how to draw geometry and how to understand geometry. Because if you know these programs well and if you know geometry well, you could just go to the same place. And then because AutoCAD allows you to print, it allows you to physically feel the geometry. So the programs allow us to do this. When Elías Torres was teaching first year, one of the exercises was to draw the doors of our classroom one by one, to understand how a door works, deeply. So we had to dismantle the door and draw element by element how to understand it. Of course, even though this is not a total project, the next time you had to draw a door, you are more careful in the moment. You are not just cutting out a place to go from one side to the other side and maybe avoid to have a door, like Miralles, who did that cross door at Igualada. You will figure out more ways to understand a door than the more traditional standard one. Going to details back and forward can happen during the whole process of learning. You can have all kinds of knowledge—from learning how a book is made, learning how glass is made—there is a lot to architecture in just touching the glass. So I think to go back and forward is a very good exercise.

Manuel Bailo I suppose also, it's going to change how things are going to be built in the future. It's something that is happening right now. Ten years ago, it was absolutely impossible to think that you need to have a pattern and to repeat the pattern. The quality was going to be cheap because you are repeating. But today, how is it changing? It's absolutely amazing because you press the button on the computer and you can cut all the different measurements, because the computer is just cutting the parts. It's changed absolutely. So I agree with you. We would like to do the models like we are going to build the building. It forces you to think in other ways of how you can prove the project, because you are so disciplined. You are doing the model as a tool. It's not just a representation; it's also a way of creating the idea. But today, I think not only that. Not just changing how the models are done, which is with a laser cut, but also the industry—it's changing technology.

And that's a direct effect of the process of construction. In terms of the stair project, we had a discussion with the builder, and we said, yes, we are going to have these stairs with holes, and we are going to perforate them. Suddenly I imagine the building with the stair. I'm looking for the holes. The builder said, do you know how to side this magical stair? I said, no, let's think of another way.

Elena Cánovas I would say that even though you have more possibilities nowadays, and in Europe you are going to have more and more, you have better control over the process, but you might do better to know how the process works. For instance, to have all these different shapes: you can do it, but you need to know how many fit in a sheet in order to have this piece of sheet metal to be cheap. You are the one who is going to control how the design matches into a piece of metal and how they are going to cut it. You had better control that. If you leave your drawing to a contractor, you lose the control, the geometry, or the conceptual control of your project. In this kind of architecture, we can see that the lines are matching, that all the moments of the structure, and that all the rhythms of the structure are matching. In this new architecture, you can see which shapes and tectonics they are taking seriously and which are the ones they are just drawing and giving to someone else very fast with the scales.

How important was it to achieve complexity while still using simple means and making it cheap? Why is complexity so important?

Elena Cánovas That's why I think minimal architecture coming from the arts has been a bit confusing. To me, the minimal movement is very complex and sophisticated. Yet clients are still telling the office, simple and basic. At some point, I think architecture has confused the two things. I would say you get into the minimal after cleaning and cleaning and cleaning and purifying.

I don't think you will understand if you don't try. Several times, not only once. Going back to the idea of the cooking...you cook better when you try several times and you burn the fuel—sometimes it's warm, others times it's too salty, and the next time you figure out what to do, and after a few trials you know what to do.

Faculty The analogy for me would be the Greek temple—the Greek temple looks very simple, but in fact it's not. It's got incredible sophistication: the columns aren't even vertical; the horizontal isn't even flat. All of those things are true of the Greek temple. I see a kind of richness that I am used to seeing in the plan of Islamic North African cities, which is incredibly rich and not straight forward. Why is that important, is the question.

Manuel Bailo Well, we didn't want to build complexity just for building complexity. No, never. Complexity is rising up through the process, because we do not work with a finished idea. So we need to work with a finished image more than an idea. We don't go with this way of designing, which is this is the image that I want to reach, and ask, what do I have to do to arrive there—we never do that. I think it is more similar to what Elena was saying: it is a complex process and this complexity arises. Miralles knew how to simplify all of that. Which for me is better; if you know how to simplify all of this, you are not just a victim of this complex process. For example, Miralles knew more in the beginning than at the end from my point of view.

There is a beautiful book by an American art journalist—*A Giacometti Portrait by James Lord*. It is nice because it is useful for explaining this variation of repeating a drawing. In this book, there are, I think, 18 portraits of this journalist. The book includes the conversations that James Lord had with Alberto Giacometti during the portrait.

Lord visited Giacometti and asked for a portrait. He thought that he was just going to be there for one or two days, but he stayed for six months. Every day, Giacometti was drawing, and every day Giacometti started another drawing and another drawing and another drawing. When you look at the drawings, they are very similar, but they are also really different. The last day when James Lord said, well I have to leave because I just came for two days and I am now here for six months, Giacometti said, it's done. So the portrait was finished. The conversation was about his expression and how it was changing. All the time, he was doing the same drawing and repeating and repeating—not using time for creating this complexity.

Elena Cánovas Sometimes you are studying, and you say, okay well, I'll wait for the inspiration. I'm not going to do anything until I know what to do. What Enric explained in his sequence of 16 steps of a project is that you normally start from what you know, so to cook a project is about getting to 16. He was really explaining, like, number one: you do what you know; number two, fear; number three, you relax; number four, you say to your client, hey don't worry I know what I am doing. So, if you are lost in a project, you follow the sequence, which I normally explain to students. It's like beginning a project by repeating something you have already done and having fear, but at the end by repetition. Like putting one paper on top of the other—the first one you toss and by the translation, you understand the new project.

Manuel Bailo Also, what is interesting is that Giacometti never finishes the portrait until Lord says, "Hey I have to go." So that is the moment when it is finished.

That is the nature of design. You do iteration after iteration as long as time permits, but there comes a point when time doesn't last any longer, and you have to commit yourself.

Manuel Bailo And you need time for doing that. Or you are just going to repeat, which is what has happened to a lot of well-known architects. At the end, they are just repeating what they have discovered in the beginning, because they don't have time, so they just repeat. I suppose that is the reason why a lot of architects are more interesting in the first part of their career then the last, because they were trying to understand.

I remember one day that I arrived to my studio class with Enric, and I was carrying this book by Kenneth Frampton, *Modern Architecture: A Critical History.* Enric took the book and asked me, when was the Villa Savoye built? I say, I don't know. When was Mies' pavilion built in Barcelona? What is the plan? I don't know. So he says, architects need to learn history by tracing, so take one sheet of paper and trace and trace over the pictures of the plans and the façades—this is how we will learn history.

There is a phrase that I like by Albert Einstein. He said, "If I don't know how to draw it, it's because I didn't understand it." And this was said by Albert Einstein, so it's a way of understanding things. I like to draw to create knowledge.

<u>Student</u> How do you package a lot of things into one thing; how do you begin to start understanding how all those things are working together along with the structure and everything that has to do with the space?

<u>Manuel Bailo</u> You need to create an order with ideas—you need to think. But you need to establish a kind of hierarchy immediately. There was an interesting discussion between a planner and Miralles, who was closer to being a planner, but was more synthetic in some ways, more abstract. The planner did an interesting exhibition—it was just to explain one idea with every project, just one, to simplify the project with this idea and everything was organized around this main idea with the rest a kind of hierarchy, a clear organization. Well perhaps Enric was learning a lot from being a planner, but I think at the end, he did the absolute opposite—managing different ideas at the same time because he knew how to do it. I always used to say that this is my case: I have never resolved equations well—there is a different cognitive process in mathematics. So, you have this matrix and to resolve a matrix is very complicated—I always arrive at another resolution.

<u>Elena Cánovas</u> I understood that when I went to see Picasso's work, because you have the chance to see what Picasso went through—all the languages. When he was 12 or 13 years old, he knew how to draw orders and draw all the figurations that you need to know, so he went into the real deep abstraction through learning how to do everything—the still life, the figuration of whatever—then he started to clean.

Manuel Bailo This is what I am saying—he knew how to manage a lot of things at the same time. This is why a lot of dyslexics have this capacity of seeing things in another way. Enric was dyslexic, absolutely. He didn't know how to back a car up. He never did that. He knew if he was going back then he was going to crash.

Experience

2. Enric Miralles, Huesca Stadium, shadow letters created by the building, 1996.

3. Enric Miralles, Huesca Stadium, 1994.

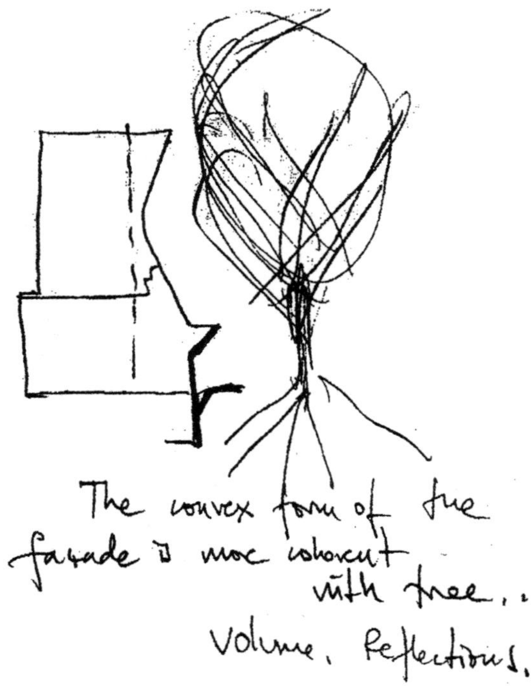

4. Enric Miralles, sketch for Hamburg Music School, 1996.

5. Enric Miralles, Hamburg Music School, 1998.

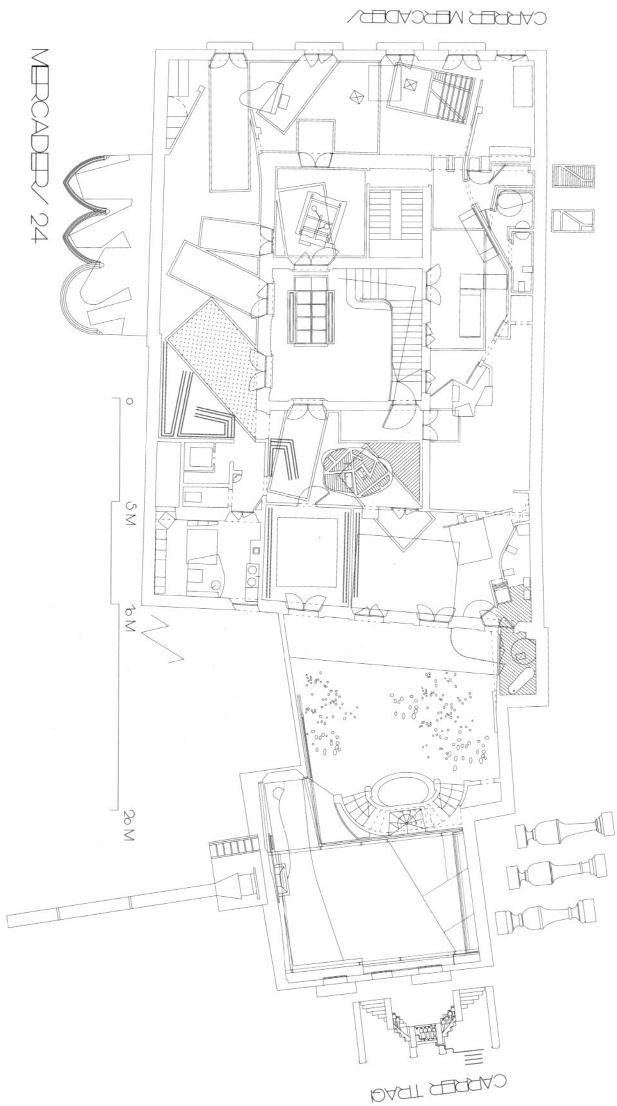

6. Miralles Tagliabue, Mercaders Residence plan and sections, 1994.

7 Miralles Tagliabue, Mercaders Residence.

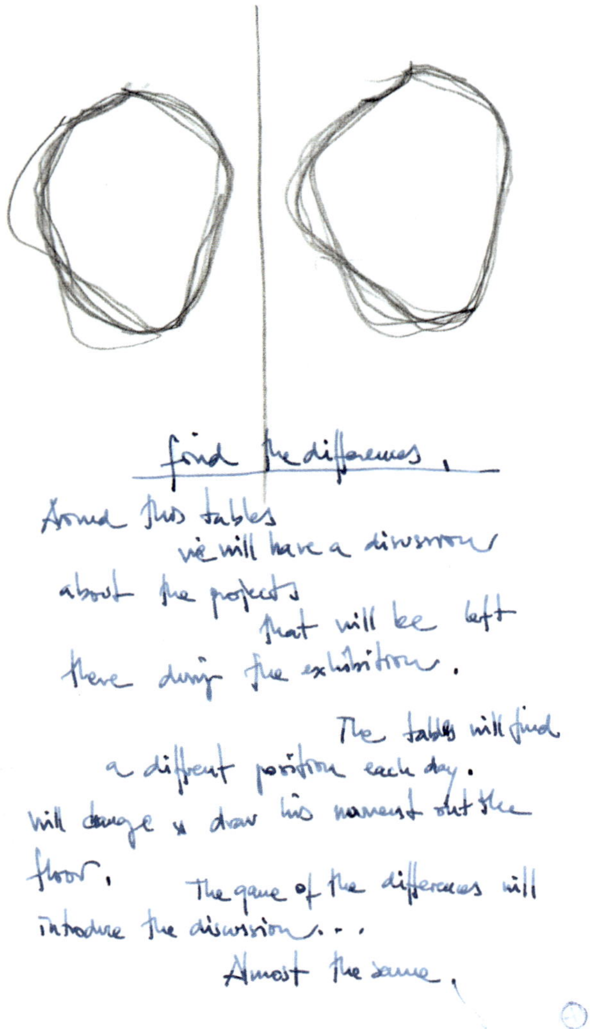

8. Enric Miralles, Innes Table, sketch and notes, 1993.

Photos: Giovanni Zanzi

9. Enric Miralles, Innes Table, 1993.

10. Enric Miralles, Kolonhaven Playhouse at the Barcelona Museum of Contemporary Art, 2002.

11. Enric Miralles, Kolonhaven Playhouse in Diagonal Mar Park, 2004.

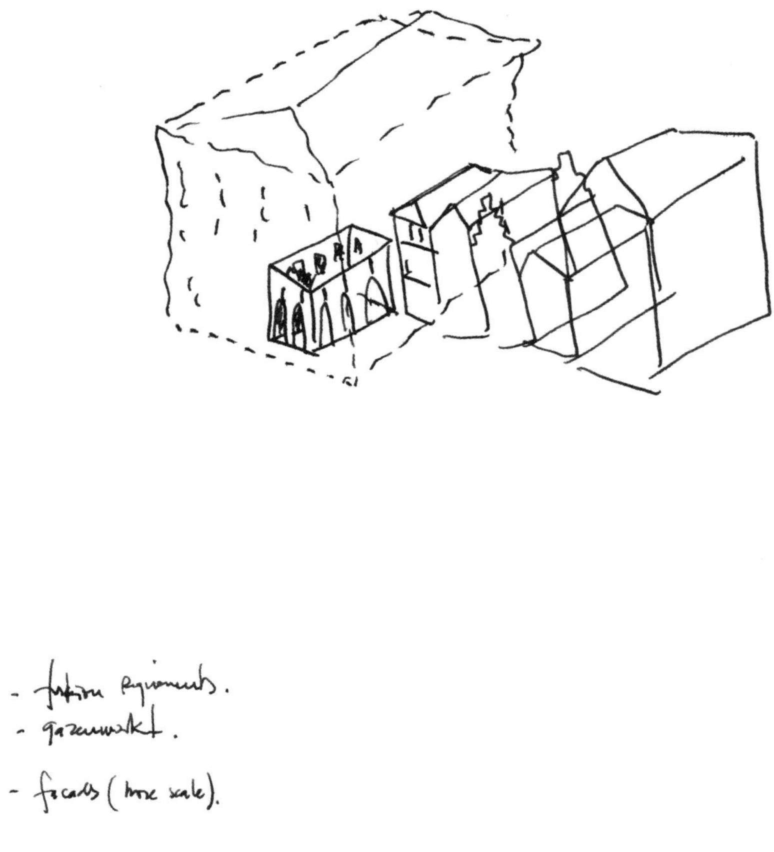

12. Miralles Tagliabue, Utrecht Town Hall sketch, 1997.

13. Miralles Tagliabue, Utrecht Town Hall, 2001.

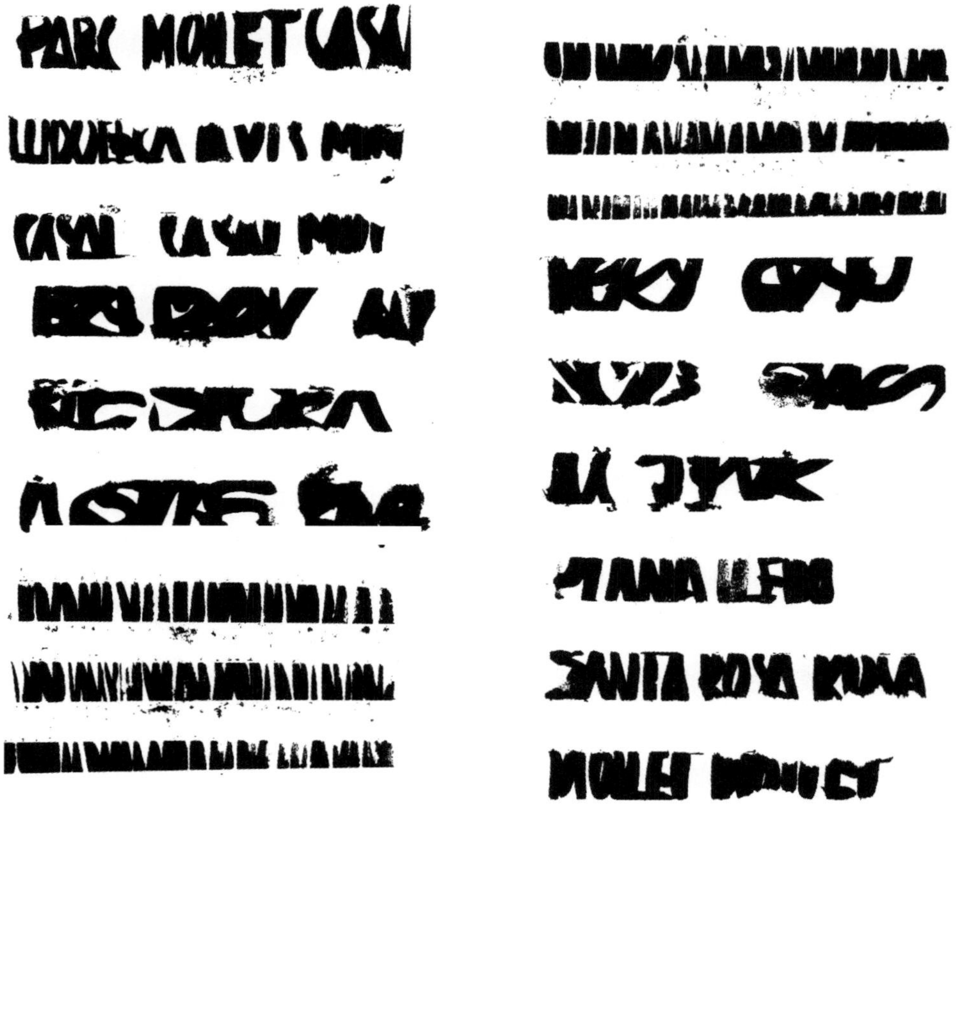

14. Miralles Tagliabue, Mollet Park, graffiti letters, 1998.

15. Miralles Tagliabue, Mollet Park, 2000.

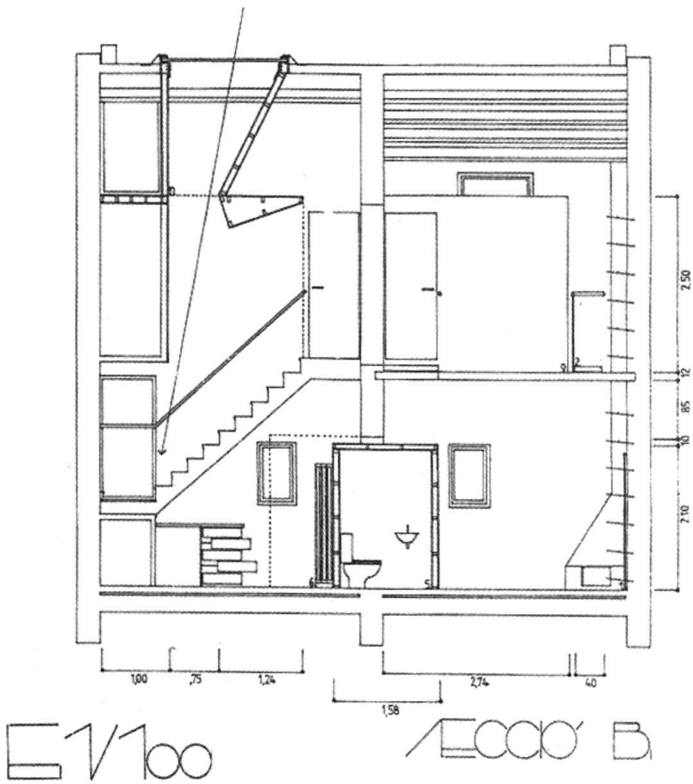

16. Miralles Tagliabue, Clota House section, 1999.

17. Miralles Tagliabue, Clota House, 1999.

Enric Miralles
The Sweep of a Hand

Josep Quetglas

1. Enric Miralles, 1992: Sketch, India landscape.

Flair and Duende[1]

I attended Enric Miralles' doctoral thesis defense in 1987. It was held in the large hall of the former Barcelona School of Architecture, a packed house with an expectant audience. The thesis, titled "Things Seen Left to Right (Without Glasses)"—a reference to one of Erik Satie's works—comprised four brief chapters, all of which alluded to movements of that piece: "Hypocritical Chorale," "Fumbling Fugue," "Muscular Fantasy," and "Strokes/Writings."[2] The jury members were Rafael Moneo, Juan Navarro Baldeweg, Félix de Azua, Josep Muntañola, and someone else whose name I've since forgotten.

I remember little about that confusing and tumultuous event, because from where I was sitting, I could only see some of the members of the audience, among them Carme Pinós, Enric's partner at the time. I've never had occasion to encounter a gorgon, but the way Carme glared at the jury may be the closest I've ever come to that.

Because they were all very negative. I listened as one said that Enric's thesis did not reflect work. The reviewer said that any work, be it chipping stone, kneading pastry dough, or writing a doctoral thesis, requires confronting resistant material and giving it form—struggling with it, changing it, shaping it. That writing is like Jacob wrestling with the angel, asking him to give a name to something that is no more than a presage. That writing is about achieving meaning, struggling with words that give names to things and with things named. That writing is not, as adolescents believe, about baring feelings, but rather about being readable, making things understood. In Enric's text, however, everything was free and easy; it was a series of words trotted out on the page without kicking up any dust, one after the other, with no point of reference and nothing to push against, in the hopes that the reader would be the one to find meaning in those words and value in the text; the one who, through the course of the reading, would finish writing it. It was up to the reader to do the work.

It seems that one of the members of the jury went so far as to write a report on the thesis, previous to the defense, stating: "There is no question that the work is unintelligible. It is indecipherable in the sense that the reader can't understand what it is about, nor can it be considered literature with its own intrinsic value... More precisely, it is not that the text is poorly written, it is simply unreadable, because it is not written. It is not created to be read. The reading of a work is not what gives it shape, just as hearing is not what calls up colors…I am not making a value judgment here, but simply trying to describe how this material is perceived."[3]

According to the jury, it was an irresponsible piece of work, unable to be measured or evaluated, and could only be considered an exclamation; thus, given its lack of academic value, it did not pass the test. A fail! Enric Miralles failed! The darts shooting from Carme's stunned and indignant eyes were venomous.

I left before it was over—it was summertime and the room was hot and stuffy—without knowing whether the members of the jury had been turned to stone, as happens to those who cross a Gorgon, or if they were stone before the event had even begun.

Only many years later did I understand what the jury couldn't see on that occasion: that Enric's "irresponsibility," the easiness, rooted neither in leisure nor work, was precisely one of his strong points, one of the profoundly important qualities of his architecture and his way of doing things.

Moneo, of course, understood that before the rest of us did, when he wrote: "And so, today I see the thesis as a declaration of principles regarding what Enric viewed as architecture at that time…Reading it helps greatly to clarify current interpretations of his work. Much of what he later did is implicit in what he wrote there. That thesis plays a part in how I now view Enric's work."[4]

Indeed, any analysis of Enric Miralles' work must first take into consideration its unexplainable and easy nature; because ease and flair go hand-in-hand and, together with the qualities that make something pleasing, is the agility and skill in carrying it out. Enric had a flair; he could turn any gesture—a sketch of a wall or the path of an electric cable—into an unpremeditated surprise, thrilling yet natural, obvious. Effortless.

In his architecture, sketches, and writing, the form "takes flight";[5] it is neither pursued, nor composed, nor constructed. The sweep of the hand and the project's form are reflected in the strokes in the sketch. The architecture happens: it is not the end result of a project; it is simply what it is. Everything appears to take place before our very eyes.

Miralles did everything with a flair. Moneo alludes to the young basketball player, Enric, when noting the elegant and unpredictable zig-zag of his gestures and strokes, and he cites a phrase from the thesis: "Everything becomes fleeting moments, glances. Never knowing how the sketches take shape."

But it is not just about flair alone, because that instinctive ability necessarily brings with it a degree of innocence, of lack of consciousness, of not knowing how the sketches appear. Heinrich von Kleist expounds on this idea of unaffected grace, associating it with the movements of a marionette: the moment a dancer becomes minimally aware of a move, dances before a mirror, the grace disappears.

There was more than just mastery in Enric Miralles' stroke of hand and work. When the applause and surprise subside, "a wind of the spirit enters... announcing the endless baptism of freshly created things."[6] This wind is the duende, which, as described in the Diccionario de la Real Academia, is something ineffable, indescribable.

Federico García Lorca literally plays with the theory of the duende in his lecture "Theory and Play of the Duende." He reviews three principles, three supports to artistic creation: help from the angel, assistance from the muse, and the appearance of the duende. The angel, says Lorca, guides and grants, defends, announces and warns, dazzles. The muse proclaims. Angel and muse come from the outside, always bringing with them answers to pre-established questions. In contrast, duende comes from within, "roused from the furthest habitation of the blood," and arrives to contest any question or answer. It's there. And Lorca gives a description of duende which, word for word, could describe Enric Miralles' architecture: "The arrival of the duende presupposes a radical change to all the old kinds of form, brings totally unknown and fresh sensations with the qualities of a newly created rose, miraculous, generating an almost religious enthusiasm."

It is the duende that distinguishes Enric Miralles' architecture from that of any other architect I can think of. Others gradually erect the building, step by separate step. They may have pictured the finished structure in their heads in the course of designing it, but the project is not the same thing as the architecture. First comes the project, the necessary blueprint from which to then construct the architecture. On a blueprint, a line is not simply a line: it is a wall, a floor, always something else that has not yet taken shape. In Enric's case, the project, the sketch, the process of drawing or just looking and imagining, was already architecture.

I imagine that something similar occurred in the case of a very special group of architects: those who had previously been painters and had never left that behind, because the result is evident in each and every stroke. The names Le Corbusier, Alvar Aalto, and Juan Navarro Baldeweg come to mind. But as far as I know, that is not Enric's case who, on his own, and successfully, "turned his artist's vision expressed on paper into architecture."[7]

The Monkey and the Snake

In February 1992, five years after the thesis episode, a group of friends took a trip together to India. The travelers included Enric Miralles and Benedetta Tagliabue, together with Elías Torres, Mogens Krustrup, and others. The main focus of the trip was to see Le Corbusier's architecture in Chandigarh and Ahmedabad and also visit works by Louis Kahn.

With his blue-ink fountain pen, Enric Miralles filled five hardcover 5.5 x 3.5–inch sketchbooks—his favorites at the time—purchased at the Glasgow School of Art, with notes and drawings. Each one was of a different color: green, yellow, red, black, and blue.

Elías Torres, with his simple ballpoint pen filled every page of an 8 x 6–inch hardbound sketchbook to the brim.

Often Enric and Elías drew the same subject, standing next to each other, shoulder to shoulder. In addition, Enric took slides by the hundreds, to later turn them into pieces of a photographic jigsaw puzzle.

Looking back at the pages of those sketchbooks, it is hard to say what's most surprising: Enric's and Elías' abilities to view an object or a particular scenario (trees, animals, people, etc.) and turn that into architecture or the very same object's ability to become Elías Torres' architecture or Enric Miralles' architecture, depending upon who is doing the looking and sketching.

The same occurs in drawings by the masters. Aalto, Kahn, and Le Corbusier, for example, have all done sketches of the same Greek ruin. In each case, something different appears on the paper; it is the very same ruin, but transformed into an architectural concept by Alvar Aalto, Louis Kahn, or Le Corbusier. There is something vampire-like in an architect's or an artist's eye, which inevitably owns what it sees.

Let me provide a specific example.

When Enric and Elías visited the Sarabhai house in Ahmedabad, they met the owner, Manorama Sarabhai. Both of them did sketches of her from the same perspective, as she sat motionless, and Enric also took a picture of her which serves as an invaluable record of what each of them was observing as they sketched and conversed with Madam Sarabhai (Figs. 2, 3).

Manorama Sarabhai is seated in an armchair, "her armchair," and no one else's. She is getting on in age, rather stout and, no doubt, not very agile. She is comfortably ensconced in her chair next to the window that she insisted Le Corbusier include in the plans. From there she probably spends the better part of her day overseeing what is happening inside and outside of the house, without budging. On a little table next to the chair are two telephones and surrounding her are a myriad of

2. Elías Torres, 1992: Manorama Sarabhai (above, one of the Ahmedabad wells).
3. Photograph of Manorama Sarabhai by Enric Miralles.

objects, photographs, equipment, and papers, waiting to be used and reflecting her authority. I imagine her as Meret Peben, the relentlessly strict mother in Dreyer's film *Day of Wrath* (1943), with her ring of keys that open every door and closet in the house always jangling from her waist. A kinder version of Meret Preben, of course: she must have been influenced by Le Corbusier's architecture, although he recalled that his client demanded things that even his own mother wouldn't have dared to request of him—creating that window, for example.

Elías and Enric sketched her, and their drawings could not be more different. If it weren't for the photograph, it would be hard to know that they are reflections of the same scene, done at the same time.

Elías' eyes seem to have leapt right towards Madam Sarabhai, to take in every single fold, wrinkle, corner, and object. Touching it all with his eyes, eager not to overlook one single detail, from her slippers to her hair, the cushion behind her, or the plants outside the window. Elías gradually turned the sketch strokes into Madam Sarabhai.

Enric, on the other hand, seems to have stepped back, providing enough distance to not make any physical, tactile, or practically visual contact with the setting and turn the confused and simultaneous perceptions into a single, ordered and uninterrupted stroke. Once the sketch was done, Enric turned the page and began again with yet more distance. This time the drawing was not of Madam Sarabhai, but rather of the previous sketch. Enric transformed Madam Sarabhai into a stroke of the previous drawing. (Figs. 4, 5).

Enric focused more on the stroke than the drawing. How is it that so many of his drawings—that of Madam Sarabhai included—can turn into floor plans or sections of one of his architectural projects? How is it that so many of his plans and sections to scale are difficult, if not impossible, to translate into spatial terms? It is because Enric Miralles' view of the sketch differed from that of other architects.

For others, it is a document that precedes the architecture. It can serve as a tool for studying and developing the project, making it understandable to others, or calculating the construction details. In any case, it is a previous step. It may be beautiful, but is not the actual architecture itself; rather, it is an announcement, a signal of what is to come.

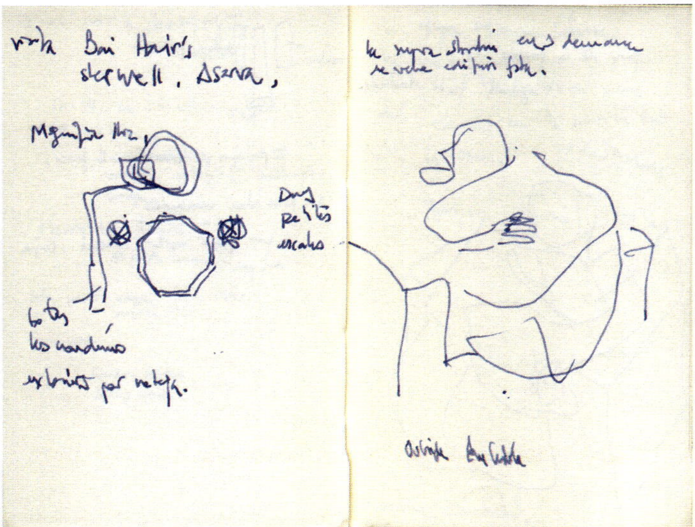

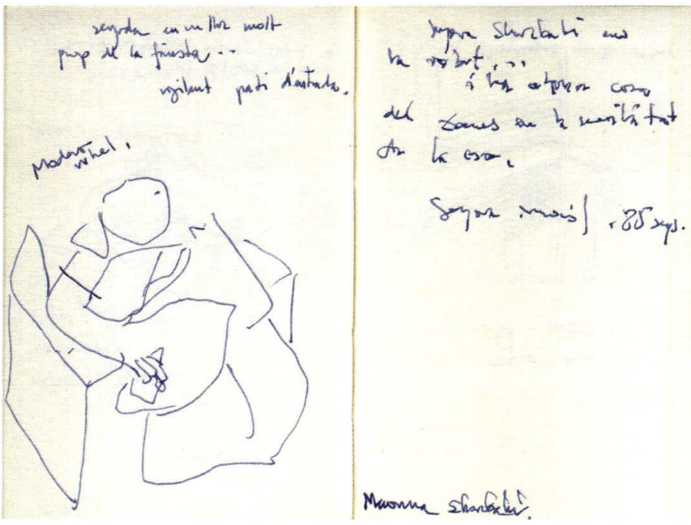

4, 5. Enric Miralles, 1992: Manorama Sarabhai "Madam Sarabhai wants us to visit buildings."

In Enric's case, drawing was creating architecture. Architecture begins with the faint scratch of the pen on the paper, as the still wet and glistening ink briefly reflects, like a convex mirror, everything it takes in. The stroke of ink on the paper is like a furrow plowed in the land, creating the space for the wall of a Roman city's foundation.

I refer specifically to drawing, but that can extend into every part of Enric's life, his every gesture and move. I recall how, at one point, Enric and Carme's kitchen turned into a work of architecture. Once the fresh pasta was cooked to a turn, they hung the damp strands of tagliatelle from one end of the kitchen to the other. The space suddenly turned into one of Enric's sharp-angled works of architecture. Perhaps only Alison and Peter Smithson could have managed, as did he, to spontaneously turn moments of everyday life into architecture.

Balkrishna Doshi, who worked with both Le Corbusier and Louis Kahn, titled his book that focused on both master architects, *The Acrobat and the Yogi*, two words that characterize each individual and his architecture. Were we to follow his example, the names we might apply to Elías Torres and Enric Miralles could be those of two sacred animals in the Indian culture: the monkey and the snake.

Elías, the monkey, leaping from here to there in an endless dance—onto the table, onto a shoulder, the windowsill, a head, all the while checking out every detail and playing with every shape. Enric, the serpent, motionless, hypnotic, letting the form slowly approach and stealthily wind its way towards him until it is trapped, internalized, and turned into the very snake that observes it with eyes that appear—only appear—to look inwards (without glasses).

Notes

1. In addition to the definitions of duende provided by the *Diccionario de la Real Academia Española,* referring to a goblin, sprite, leprechaun, or other like characters in folk stories, is that of "mysterious and ineffable charm."
2. Reference to Eric Satie's "Choses vues à droite et à gauche, sans lunettes, for violin and piano," 1914, although in the title of his thesis Enric Miralles reversed the order of wording: left to right.
3. Cited by Rafael Moneo in: "Things Seen Left to Right (Without Glasses)." Doctoral thesis by Enric Miralles Moya, 1987. See: http://upcommons.upc.edu/revistes/bitstream/2099/9303/1/05_moneo.pdf.
4. Rafael Moneo, Ibid.
5. Taken from a verse of "Cántico espiritual" by Juan de la Cruz.
6. Federico García Lorca, "Juego y teoría del duende," a lecture given on October 20, 1933, at the Sociedad de Amigos del Arte, Buenos Aires. Text cited from the publication edited and prefaced by José Lezama Lima: Federico García Lorca, Conferencias y Charlas. Havana, Cuba, National Council for Culture, 1961.Translator's note: Excerpts of text taken from "Theory and Play of the Duende," translated to English by A.S. Kline @2007.
7. Rafael Moneo, op. cit.

Paradox of Preference

Elena Rocchi

1. "La Ultima Cena" by Elena Rocchi, The NIROX Foundation, 2012.

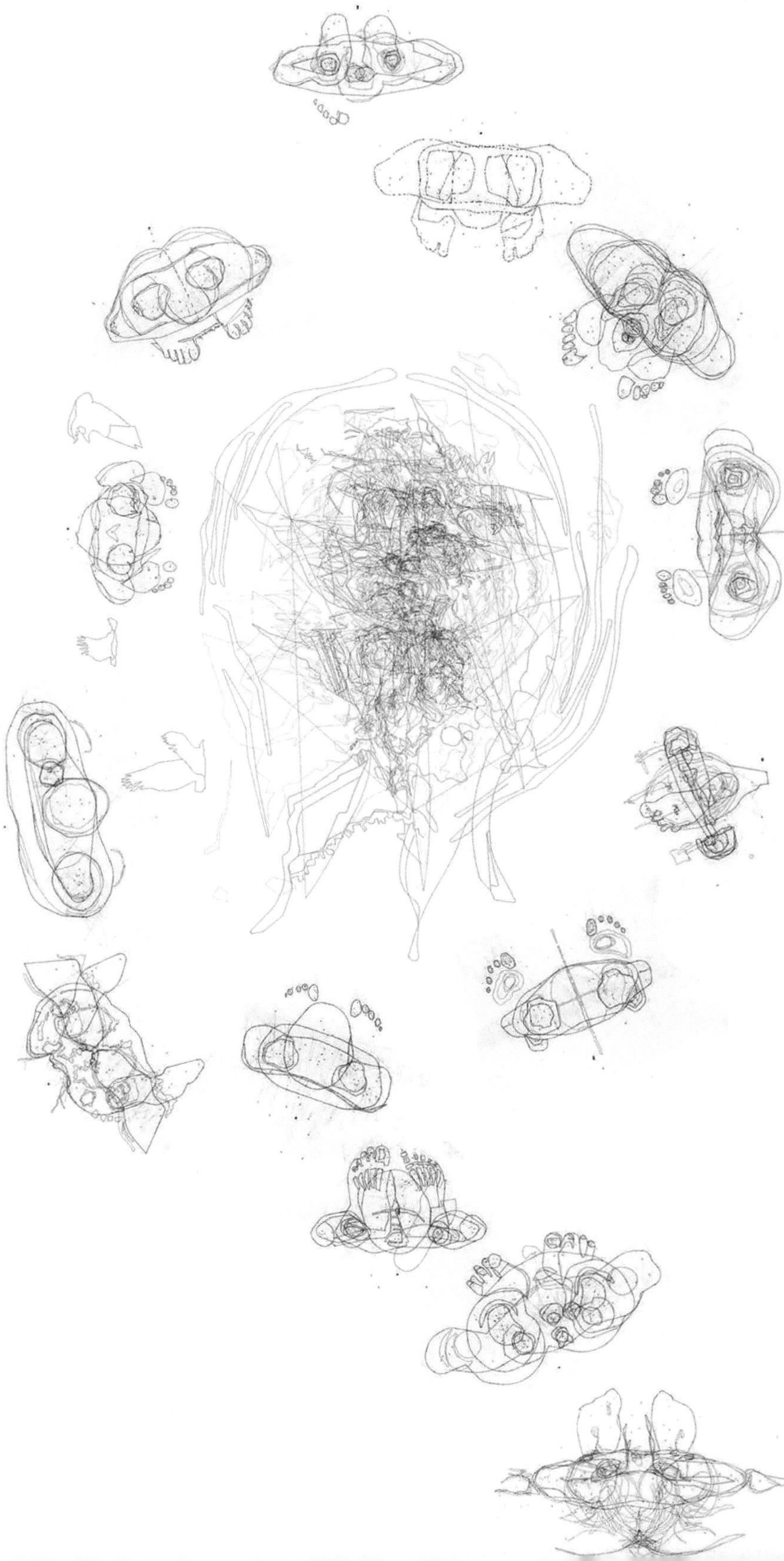

"I would prefer not to" was a something Enric Miralles often said in the studio. He said it relative to requirements in a competition brief, an invitation to write a critical essay for a journal, and the request to respond to student questions. It meant many things beyond the obvious statement of—"this is something I want, yet do not want to do." Much of the life of a designer is lived in a state of paradox. We do it because we love to do it, we want to do it, we believe in doing it, yet for one reason or another we often "would prefer not to."

In modern literature, there is a source to the statement "I would prefer not to" that Miralles knew well. It is "Bartleby, the Scrivener: A Story of Wall Street," a short story written by Herman Melville in 1853. It is thought that Melville wrote the story while he was frustrated with his progress on *Moby Dick* and that Bartleby's sentiment is a reflection of Melville's. The character Bartleby refuses to continue with the work of a scrivener, saying repeatedly "I would prefer not to," and the story proceeds from there to describe the consequences of his preference. The philosophical debate between free will and determinism is the central theme. This debate, started 100 years earlier by theologian Jonathan Edwards, argues that free will necessitates the ability to be completely isolated from the circumstances of the decision. Edwards believes that only with complete neutrality (complete objectivity, no attachment to anyone or anything) can we obtain free will.

It is very difficult, if not impossible, to be completely objective in the design process, in part because there are many things that we need to engage in order to design. Designers have preferences determined by the context they create for themselves. There is another story that Miralles referenced, *The Metamorphoses of the Circle*, written in 1966 by George Poulet. In his book on literary criticism, Poulet makes the argument that if a reader can identify the author's point of departure, he or she will have the key to author's perception, individuality, and way of interpreting the world.

Poulet writes: "The circle that Euclid describes and the one which modern mathematics traces not only resemble one another but also merge. The dial of the clock, the wheel of fortune, traverse time intact, without being modified by the variations they register or determine. Each time the mind wants to picture space, it sets in motion a selfsame curve around a selfsame center. No matter what the degree of angle may be, men of all epochs have used only one compass."

Poulet notes that to understand the circle of differing authors from different moments in time, the reader must go through all the available material of that particular author. The notes, letters, text, edits, etc., need to be studied to understand what the author is creating. In a manner of speaking, the reader gets into the mind of the author by recreating what Poulet called cogito, which is "each person's perception and creation of his own existence." Miralles understood this. Often when students or collaborators asked him to explain meaning, intentions, ideas behind the work, Miralles told them that everything they need to know about is in the studio, and indeed it is all there: books, sketches, drawings, maps, images, collected remnants, it is all there.

What follows here is a transcribed conversation between myself and an architecture student exploring ideas of preference relative to design.

Elena Rocchi Why did you choose "prefer not to," the topic of Bartleby?

Student I like the potential of the topic and the possibilities that can come from it.

Elena Rocchi "Bartleby, the Scrivener" is a very subtle story; it is a story about absurdity. It is in between the absurdity and the instability of situations described by Franz Kafka in his books. Everything can't be real, and in the end, it doesn't even matter. This is what makes it interesting to me. What is the process you are using to explore this topic?

Student I am asking classmates: "Relative to design, what do you prefer not to do?" There are many ways to interpret the question, but I am interested in the reasons why, as a student, you would choose not to do something, even though you are capable of doing it. One person's answer was: "I am actually writing my theory assignment right now… so these thoughts are not figured out yet. But yesterday when I was sitting in building development class, I found myself thinking, 'What the hell am I doing? I don't want to build buildings.' And maybe this is why I drag my feet through architectural solutions. I don't know. I am having a completely blunt rambling moment with you, and I have not said these thoughts to anyone. So if you could keep this anonymous that would be great. So yes, I would prefer not to do architecture."

Elena Rocchi Fantastic. You should try to get everyone you question to answer so directly as "I would prefer not to do architecture." Search for an essential answer: Bartleby answers/speaks to the narrator/lawyer of the story only 28 times in the entire story with his perpetual response, "I would prefer not to," his essential way to answer a question. According to this, it is important to get essential answers from the essential question that you ask.

For the first seven times that Bartleby speaks, he starts by only answering, "I would prefer not to." Most of the time he doesn't answer at all. It is in his sentence number eight when he starts to answer "I prefer." His answering mechanism, established by the system answer/no answer, is the one that starts to define his personality throughout the book. It is interesting to understand how, by asking the same question, answers start to change.

When Catherine (Spellman) asked me to participate in the seminar on Enric Miralles, she wrote an email with many questions. I didn't answer immediately because I did not know if I would like to do this. Then I remembered that many times Miralles would say, "No, preferiría no hacerlo" (I would prefer not to do it) in occasions when he didn't want to do things for reasons that were clear to him but maybe not to others. He even once used this phrase as a title for an introduction, "No, Preferiria No Hacerlo: On Three Houses by R.M. Schindler," to the publication *R.M. Schindler, 2G International Architecture Review* by Judith Sheine. Miralles was asked to write about Schindler as an architect who identified with place and explain how his architecture was rooted in place. Miralles acted like Bartleby by responding with the essay's title based on his difficulty of agreeing with the publisher's statement. He probably didn't want to write the article, but he did it. In the end, his disagreement was evident through imagining Schindler himself saying, I would prefer not to, as a way to insist on his personal strategy as an architect to postpone things—"to not say anything more than what we are asked for." He thought that as architects we should learn from Bartleby or Schindler and give, with our silence, more time to architecture.

At the end of the book, Bartleby dies of starvation in prison. His life, like the architect Miralles, is based on a series of preferences. To me, it is a fundamental statement of my profession and life to always prefer to do certain things and not others. My problem is that I prefer to do other things always. I prefer not to do this only because someone asks me. Being a young architect with Miralles, I started to understand that personal preferences are fundamental.

What is a preference? When you start to ask people what they would not prefer, I would suggest to start by understanding the real meaning of the word "prefer." Prefer is not "I want" or "I think": prefer is a Latin word composed by two words—*prae* (in front) and *ferre* (to bring). That is to say that someone needs to be aware of what he likes, but that he also needs to make an effort to understand by taking it from the back of his mind and bringing it to the front of his eyes. The word's meaning is not in the back but in the front, like "avant-garde" means to look in front of something that is physically in front of you, in the sense that it is clear and evident to you. What I like of the word "prefer" is its architectonic and physic condition, combined with one of the actions that it requires us, where *ferre* is the verb. The essence of this topic is to understand, by opposition, what you finally bring in front of you by understanding what you would not prefer to. We are in a time when we need to bring our things in front of us. We need time to constitute ourselves from ourselves. I really believe in the individual/local rather than the global. I teach at Instituto Europe di Design (IED) in Barcelona in a small neighborhood of Gracia, like a village inserted in a big city. A lot of the exercises I offer to my students are based in our neighborhood. I ask my students to start their projects from their own micro-utopia, asking them what they prefer and do not prefer. At a certain point of their studies, they need to be able to freely say, "I'm studying architecture, but I'm free to say I don't want to be an architect." This is amazing to me. So to "prefer" is an important word, for which etymology and structure should be studied.

What I like of the Melville story is that all of us would like to be the narrator, observing and discovering Bartleby through his perpetual response. As the narrator, we are all so fascinated by someone who is answering the truth over and over, like your friend telling you that he doesn't want to be an architect. To me, it is really revolutionary to ask students to critically question what they are doing. The essence of the book is not to understand Bartleby but to start to understand that you can say, "I would prefer not to." Bartleby begins to tell the narrator/lawyer that he is not going to work anymore because he doesn't want to copy anymore. Absurdly, the lawyer agrees and thinks that Bartleby is right. The insistence of his answer finally has convinced him. How do we start a project from preferences and not from a practice or theory?

What do you like about architecture? Why are you studying architecture? What do your projects have in common?

Student They're always different.

Elena Rocchi Are you sure? It is my experience that architects have one line that, for some reason, we have as an obsession and that we have to discover. Mine, I have found out after many years, is about representation. Whatever I do, I am interested in bringing into representation. It's the main reason why I am an architect. In analyzing architecture, I'm not interested in taking a picture or developing an idea, but investigating through representation. I started by drawing, and I became an architect.

If you have some money and you go to buy a book, you would spend this money on a preference. Which kinds of books are you reading now?

Student Guy Debord and *The Situationist International*, which I am reading for theory class.

Elena Rocchi That is your preference. What was the preference of Miralles? I would say, things. Ordinary things. Everyday things. Stories that come with things. Ideas that come with things. Many projects began with things.

Claudio Vekstein I came to the Bartleby book many years ago by reading Jorge Luis Borges, a reading preference of Miralles'. Borges was also somebody who liked things, everything. How do you select among things? Elena is quite right: it is a matter of preference. Borges mentioned many books: this is one by Melville and *Elective Affinities* by Johann Wolfgang von Goethe. You develop an affinity with things by preference. Once someone asked Enric, "To get to this drawing, to get to this very complex drawing, where do you start?" And he said, "Here, wherever," because it doesn't matter. You just take a preference. For example, if you were to start here, it would be a different project, and it doesn't matter. The most disarming thing was when I showed him something the first day, he would look at it and say, "Okay, go ahead." I had to continue with nothing more than my preference.

Borges was blind for most of his life, but he read a lot and wrote a lot. He was also a professor of English literature. He loved English literature. He would give lectures, exams, and the final exam where you needed to select a topic out of a list that was in a bowl. He gave the students a list of topics that could be on the exam to study. When the day of the exam would come, he simply asked: "Talk about whatever you want." And that was the exam. The preference was left up to you. It is absolutely essential that you know what path to take but also that you can take any one. There is no right or wrong. The third thing that Enric would always say was, "Don't decide, do both—try to do both." Not either/or, rather, this *and* that. Surpass the opposition of thinking. Because the opposition of thinking leaves something behind, always. And that is not the way. So I would prefer not to make a decision right now, and things will evolve from there. Maybe I start from here, but it could be somewhere else. At the end, for me, it is having everything in consideration, but you take preferences and elective affinities to things.

Elena Rocchi If we choose not to decide, then we must do other things. Let's think, as architects, not to do something anymore. I have preferred to have a conversation with you as a way to have a conversation about Enric, which we are doing. I like the idea of drawing the plan of the architecture of Melville's book, with thoughts and writings, remembering that a conversation with Enric must include drawings—with no drawing there is no conversation between architects.

Co-Incidental

Elías Torres

1. Elías Torres drawing of Igualada Cemetery at burial of Miralles, 2000.

I met Enric Miralles in 1978 and was his friend until he passed away in 2000. We were on parallel career tracks, except I am a bit older. Even though our work was close and sometimes related, we only worked on one project together. This talk is not about influence, but more about what happens sometimes in the air, in the dust that involves many people in different areas, in different countries, in different cities, or different schools. There are many matters of coincidence that happen in our careers, things that we have no control over, like the people we happen to meet, where we live, and what is going on in that place at the time we are practicing. These things just happen and they contribute to the forming of our careers.

When I first met Enric, I was part of jury that was evaluating his thesis project at the School of Architecture in Barcelona. Then, I was the youngest professor in the group with three others who were much older. We had been alerted that Enric was exceptional and difficult to ascertain. I found him and his ideas very strange and almost impossible to understand. In the end he passed his thesis–with a five out of ten–because we didn't know if he was making fun of us or if he was a genius. We didn't know at that time that he was a genius. Now I remember that Picasso said, "Genius steals, mediocre artists copy." Enric was always stealing.

In the early years of Enric's career, he worked on the Hostalets de Balenyà Civic Center near Barcelona with Carme Pinós (Fig. 2). At that time, there was a new magazine called ARXIU that was organized by very young architects who asked me to write comments about this project. Because it is hard for me to write but easy for me to draw, I decided to draw my comments. I looked at the plan of the stair design, an image of the built stair, and then I drew on a Mylar paper on top of the project image from the magazine page, covering the plan of the stairs with places where noise would be made as one stepped on the steel structure (Fig. 3). Because very thin steel makes very loud sounds as you step on it, there were sounds with every step and every corner. I am certain this was intentional and therefore made such a beautiful drawing that I like to refer to often.

2. Miralles Pinós, stair at Hostalets Civic Center, 1988–94.

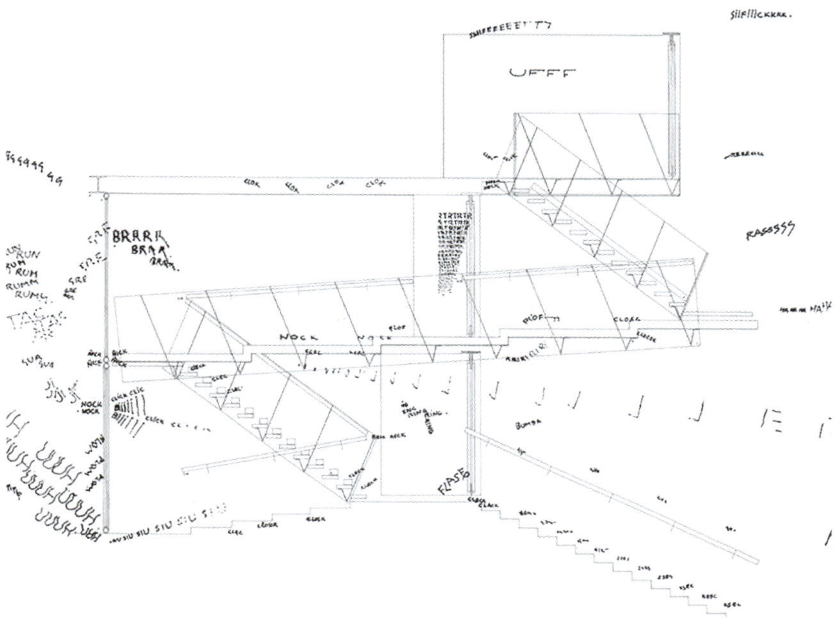

3. Elías Torres, drawing of stair at Hostalets Civic Center, ca.1988.

In my office, we have many books on Alvar Aalto. One of them, edited by Karl Fleig, is a kind of a bible in our office. Aalto was a sort of a god! And I think he still is–someone that you can continue to read and find ideas. Once Enric and I were flying together from Barcelona. I said, "Enric, you must like Alvar Aalto, because your work is similar to what Aalto does." And he said, "No! Come on!" But in reality, Enric and Aalto both work very much with layering: relating the ideas to the parts of the building through a series of seemingly coincidental layers. Therefore, the exterior and the interior, plan and section, often do not seem to fit together; this is also in part because many intersections in his projects happen by chance. Later to prove my point, I scanned the drawings and images of Vuoksenniska Church by Aalto and placed them adjacent to Enric's drawing of the 1992 Archery Pavilion (Figs. 4, 5). The similarities are obvious. Remember what I told you about Picasso and stealing? Enric was a genius.

Here is another example of Enric's abilities–this time in furniture. Both Alvar Aalto and Charles Eames liked to make bentwood furniture and both played with the reposition

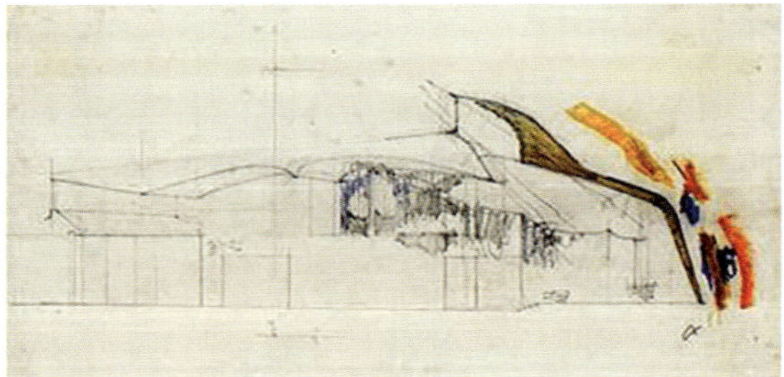

4. Alvar Aalto, Vuoksenniska Church, 1958.
5. Enric Miralles drawing for the Archery Pavilion 1992.

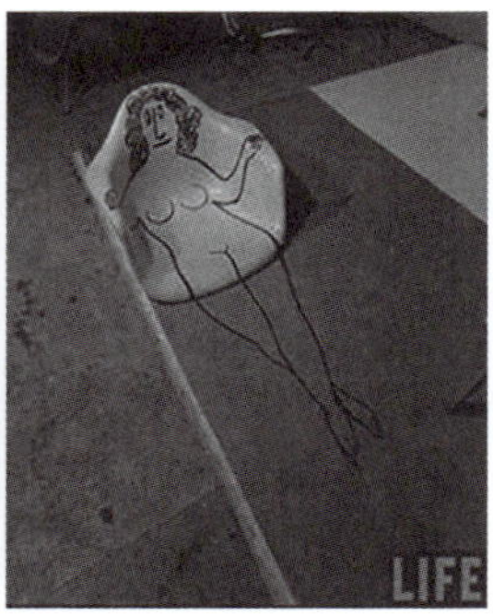

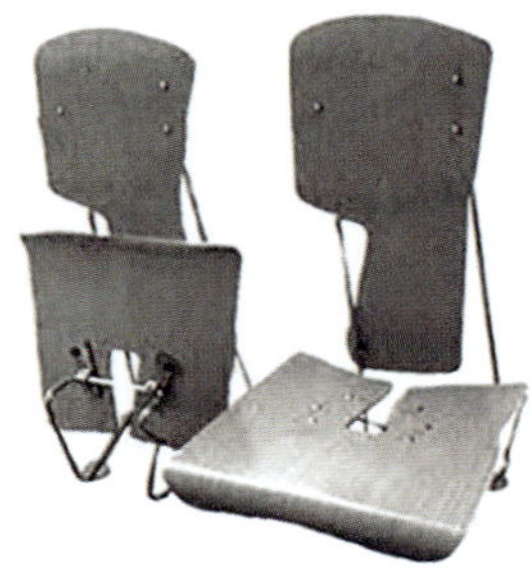

6. Charles and Ray Eames chair with Saul Steinberg cat drawing, ca.1950.
7. Enric Miralles, Circulo de Lectores chairs, 1992.

8. Miralles Tagliabue residence with Innes.
9. Torres LaPeña, church doors in Majorca.

of the forms from their ouvre of work to develop their furniture pieces. For example, you can see a relationship between Aalto's ceiling and the shape of a chair. Eames liked to reposition furniture parts for different purposes. Enric greatly enjoyed these games of repositioning. So when he began making furniture, Enric started by repositioning the ceiling shapes from the projects where the furniture was to be installed. For example, the chairs for the lecture hall in the Circulo de Lectores in Madrid take the shape of the ceiling and reshapes it into the chair. Also, look at the relationship between the Eames chairs with the drawn figures and Enric's landscape furniture. It is not a copy; these are fresh, brilliant. Yes, Enric steals (Figs. 6, 7).

In a palace in Majorca, there were tables 30 feet long that had weights on one side, and the table could move and fold. Enric was inspired and designed a table that is like magic: it folds up and has hidden drawers, but it's heavy and hard to move. The table is in the main entrance of Enric and Benedetta's house with a matching one in the EMBT architecture offices. At the house, it's full of flowers and everything that arrives to the house (Fig.8).

My office has done similar projects about folding. We did a renovation of a church in Ibiza, so that the front could be opened for a service or for the celebration of a religious act and closed for an exhibition or a concert. It is the same space but everything closes and opens (Fig. 9). For the renovation of a church doorway opening in Majorca, there are interior walls that stop the wind from coming in, but they also cut the view into the interior space. When you are at the main altar and you look at the street, there is protection. The entry is twisted, like the wind produced an effect on its formation.

10. Elías Torres, exhibition piece for Venice, 2012.

One last folding project was an idea of Todd Williams and Billy Tsien's. They sent 35 boxes of 1.2 meters to 35 different studios, architects, and artists. But they weren't boxes to be filled up with things, like a sarcophagus. The box arrived without any protection, and we needed to send it back to Venice, where it was to be displayed in an old building (Fig. 10). We started to fill up the box with objects, but it was very boring. So we decided to transform the box in the way that it could travel like a box. We decided that when it arrived in Venice, it would become a house, because we said, what do architects do? And always, the child says, houses. So we made a

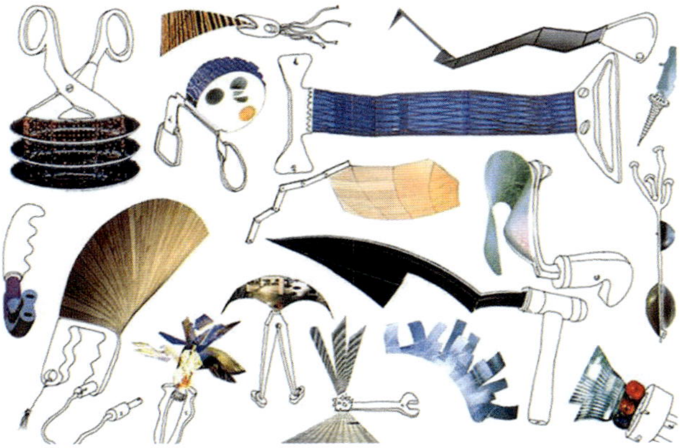

11. Elías Torres, collage drawings.

12. Elías Torres, collage drawing for Willis apartment.

house with an antenna, pencils for fingers, some eyes, some ears that were cut from a rubber face, and some lips and teeth with pearls. It is a copy of a Dalí jewel. In the box, there was a drawing of my grandson's. There was also the "Ecstasy of St. Teresa"–it was an ecstasy pill. People in the office had a lot of fun with it.

Enric and I often worked with the same company to construct ground pavements, benches, handrails, and lights for Barcelona. One day, I went to the factory and happened to see Enric's designs drawn in a kind of collage. I was surprised–we were working in a similar collage technique in our office, but with a different intent. I made a collage for a magazine about a book of Toyo Ito's–with pieces, fragments of his buildings. I used Mylar paper and added those fragments (Fig. 11).

In the Willis apartment project, my office created three-dimensional collages using fragments of real t-shirts, shirts, buttons, real things (Fig. 12). I also created a collage for a couple of dancers with real shoes. And my studio most recently created a collage just three months ago inside the Sir John Soane Museum–inside the tunnel for the Tube stop. The collage has telephones, televisions, and waterfalls–it is about the inhabitants.

13. Enric Miralles, collage plan drawing.

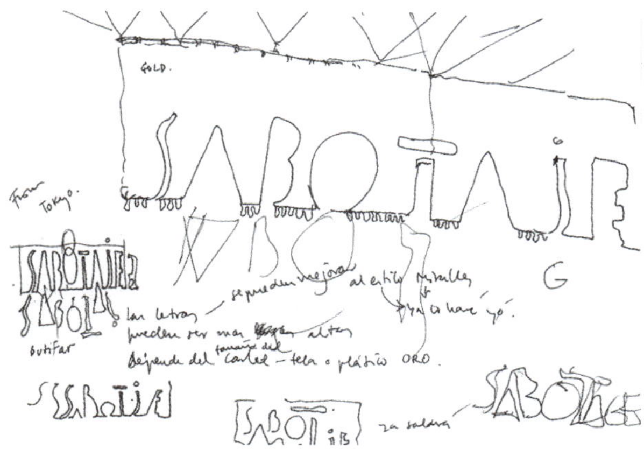

14. Torres and Miralles, sabotaier drawing and Situationists exhibition photograph.

Enric, on the other hand, was using collage to frame the way he was looking at the world. He was taking directly from the artist David Hockney who was doing this as well—both were taking from Picasso who was understanding the world in fragments and collaged pieces together to express an idea and create an image (Fig. 13).

Enric was superimposing images, like a building by Rafael Moneo or paintings by Joan Miró to create schematic plans and sections. It was again very direct. When you look at this work, it is very emotional and transfers very easily into the way things are made. You start with a piece of material that has a shape, texture, form. By changing the material, you create something immediately. If you start with very good material that you understand deeply, when you reposition it in a new context, the quality of the original goes along. This is the genius of stealing.

Enric and I taught in rooms next to each other for a number of years. I got a commission from the Museum of Modern Art in Barcelona to do an exhibition on the Situationist artists (Fig. 14). At the time, I didn't know anything about the Situationists, but Enric was next door teaching a class on it! So I said why don't we do it together?

15. Miralles Pinós, Olympic Archery Pavilion, 1992.

And that's what happened. The problem was that at that time, we were both preparing for the exam for promotion to full professor, and we found it difficult to work together. But I have my drawing of "Sabotaier"–proof that we had at least one hour of conversation. And it was quite fun, because we painted all the glass of the room; it was easy to scratch and write on top. So one painted with white, and the other painted with black. And everybody could write on top. It was very active and created participation. I had boxes of documents from the exhibition–I thought I had the plan, but it's gone! In the end, it was a great collaboration, but it is our only project together–we preferred to stay friends.

Enric's studio and my studio both worked on the Olympic Games. He had the commission for the Olympic Archery Range (which sadly has been very badly maintained), but it is something very unique (Fig. 15). It has a kind of vocabulary, completely different in the world of architecture–the way plans and sections were drawn. Sections are sometimes not exactly about how to construct the building but are the result of the plan produced; the sections grew out of the plans. The building has walls and a roof, but they are there without knowing that this building might need to be closed. The windows, or rather simple plates of glass, close the building from the elements. It was a condition of how you relate the plan to the roof and the structure. At the time, it was something very unique. You can like it or not, but it is

16. Torres and LaPeña, Olympic Athletes' Residence, 1992.

17. Enric Miralles, original roof structure Huesca Stadium, 1993.

really different. For the Olympic Village, Enric also designed a kind of a huge pergola, with a very thick structural element that were like branches, trussing around on top of the other.

Our firm worked on the Olympic Horse Jumping Arena, where people relax in their red hunting jackets and black caps. The committee wanted a replication of what would be found in the forest, but we did not find this interesting and decided to design with historical fragments from Barcelona, pieces of Roman mystery, Gaudí, Jujol. Our first presentation was a disaster! They didn't like it at all. We compromised and ended up with a design that was a little more fun but not exactly what we wanted. After that, the committee asked us to do one of the Olympic Housing Villages that was to become a permanent part of the city after the Olympics, so I guess our initial presentation was not a complete disaster (Fig. 16).

There is a story about Enric in the face of disaster that will give you a clue about the type of character he had. Enric designed a basketball stadium for Huesca (Fig. 17). The project was very innovative with a structurally intricate and complex suspended roof that pushes the limits of the strength of steel. It was beautiful under construction. When it was close to being complete, the roof collapsed. Nothing happened besides the collapse–nobody was hurt–it was just a miracle. As you can imagine, it was a tremendous scandal and absolute disaster. Benedetta tells us that Enric was certain he would have to leave architecture behind and find a new career...But to me, this did not seem to disrupt Enric. I ran into him at the airport in Frankfurt a few days after the

18. Enric Miralles, La Clota House, 1998.
19. Torres and LaPeña, residential project.

collapse. He was smiling and buying a new camera. He could have been absolutely sick because of the disaster, but he was calm. He had that kind of spirit without any barrier to stop him from moving ahead. For him, it was just an adventure to figure out how to produce a positive situation from the disaster. Ultimately at Huesca, he took advantage of the collapse: using the pieces of the collapsed structure to create a sculptural element next to the building with the new and less interesting roof. It was like nothing happened. He was able to transform a wrong thing into a virtue, showing that you could be very talented but at the same time you could have a very special spirit.

20. Miralles Tagliabue, playground at Diagonal Mar Park, 2002.

Enric designed only three residential projects, one house (Fig. 18). and two renovations of houses in Barcelona–a house for his cousin and his own house with Benedetta Tagliabue. This is unusual, because most architects design many renovations and houses while they slowly start to do larger public works. Our office has done many (Fig. 19), but not Enric. At any rate, you will find coincidental ideas between our residential works. We were both interested in breaking the limits of the house and trying to invade the outside and bring the exterior light deep into the interior. For instance, in a house I designed, I used the same principle of breaking the limits with walls, like fragments of

Alvar Aalto's home, to produce an effect of connections or to limit the views to avoid the presence of the neighbors. In a renovation in the Gothic section of Barcelona, we had the foundations of the ancient city, very heavy and beautiful in its own right. We contrast this with a very light stair that leads you to the apartment where we sculpt light into the interior of an otherwise dark and somber space.

Enric's plans for his cousin's house were complex and in many ways difficult to read. Yet the result is a very great renovation of a house that has won many awards. You can see that he too is breaking the limits of the house, sculpting the light, bringing the exterior to the interior and contrasting the heavy and lighter materials. His own house in Barcelona has three Gothic arches of an ancient façade. The drawn plans, sections, and elevations again are confusing sometimes but that confusion has produced an architecture that sometimes even Enric wasn't sure what would happen at the end–to me this is Enric's greatest project, maybe because I have been there so many times and keep finding places that surprise me. It is really a place to full of life.

In the mid-1990s, a developer from Houston, Texas, was given permission by the city of Barcelona to develop a 12-block area where Diagonal meets the sea. It was a huge project and many offices in Barcelona were asked by the developer to participate. This was unusual because these types of projects normally go to competitions in Spain. My office was one of five teams that ultimately worked on the project. Enric's studio was given the park design, which was built after Enric passed away (Fig. 20).

Following this development in the same area, the city decided to initiate the first Universal Forum of Culture to be opened in 2004 (Fig. 21). The idea was to build on the amazing urban development resulting from the 1992 Olympics with a new international gathering in Barcelona. The first sketches of the development were designed in 1999, and I have a few photographs of models and drawings of Enric's and of my firm's designs. The city organized 40 different

21. Torres LaPeña, Universal Forum of Cultures, 2004.

competitions. Carles Muro won one of the biggest in terms of surface; it was 25 acres in a huge square covered by plants. There were different ways that we were trying to solve connections from the city, which is away from the sea and coastal areas, by creating stairs and ramps to arrive at the harbor and marina. In the end, the area is huge, like Central Park. Probably 12 different design offices were chosen to develop the project and establish connections between their projects to avoid too many individual moments. The main "Forum" building was designed by Herzog and de Meuron. Our project is the last before the city meets the sea. It is 180 meters on each side and 25 meters in height, with a shade canopy tilted south, 35 degrees, covered with solar panels.

Members of four studios went to Le Bugue in France in 1992, including Enric, and my partner and his wife. We were walking across Cosant, a neighborhood designed by Le Corbusier, which has now been renovated. We were walking through the streets, and the houses were in very bad shape. Suddenly Enric said, "We are going to Chandigarh in 15 days." My ears, my brains said, what? I asked, is there a space available for me? He said, "Call me on Monday." It was Saturday. I called on Monday, and he said, "Yes you can come." Catherine Spellman, Benedetta Tagliabue, and Claudio Vekstein–the four of us were on that trip, and it was absolutely memorable. The trip was organized by Städelschule in Frankfurt. We went to Chandigarh, New Delhi, Agra, Ahmadabad, and ended up in Bangladesh. During the trip, Enric was always taking photos. He was designing at the same time that he was taking a picture, looking through his eye for the reality. I was taking normal pictures. He was taking something that was already in his mind and trying to legitimize what was in his brain at the same time that he was taking those pictures. He was stealing; he was not trying to remember things.

We were not allowed to take photographs in Chandigarh, so we were always drawing. A little booklet of some of these drawings was created by a friend, Josep Quetglas, who is a professor at a school in Barcelona. It was published three years ago. He wrote two pieces to go with the drawings–at least 100 pages. Each page shows one drawing by Enric with my drawing on the other side. When Enric and I were drawing, we were not sitting next to the other, but it became very interesting to compare the two perspectives. One set of drawings is of Mrs. Sarabhai at her house that was designed by Le Corbusier when we was also doing the Mill Owners' Association building. If you look at Enric's drawing of her, he has made her into a type of building; this was the type of nuance that our friend was interested in showing.

My office recently had a project under construction in the south of Spain to connect the old port to the city. The project is a gift from the port to the city, and the city will keep growing behind the port. We needed to extend the coastal basin area around 80 meters to adjust for some high and low tides and set up a group of facades. I was coming from Suso and had a piece of paper with little patches of black and white on it. We used it to design this project—sometimes we do silly things and sometimes they work! It is a late homage to Enric, with shapes and colors for the ground brickwork similar to the Santa Caterina market tile roof in Barcelona. It is not that we are copying the market. No, it is because we wanted something different for this area of Spain, Rio Tinto (Fig. 22). The inhabitants are a very poor people, but we took the colors for the different sections of the land. I used the market colors and shapes to say thank you to Enric; I'm not sure I realized it at the time, but there it is. The colors of the pavements are also like the fabric we bought in Chandigarh that men use to tie up their hair before wrapping on their turban.

For my 50th birthday on the beach in Ibiza, I had all my family, plus friends like Enric and Benedetta; today, many of whom are no longer with us. We were at a party in Girona, 100 km north of Barcelona, having dinner with friends. We were at least 20 people walking after dinner. We came up to the square, and it was packed with people setting off small fireworks. I had never taken a firework in my hand; it was the first time—when you drink sometimes you do things that are very weird. Enric was there with his cigar and was lighting the fireworks. We were trying to hit the clock on the church only three meters away, but we could not do it. We laughed and laughed. Our silly actions meant that we had a great time when we were together.

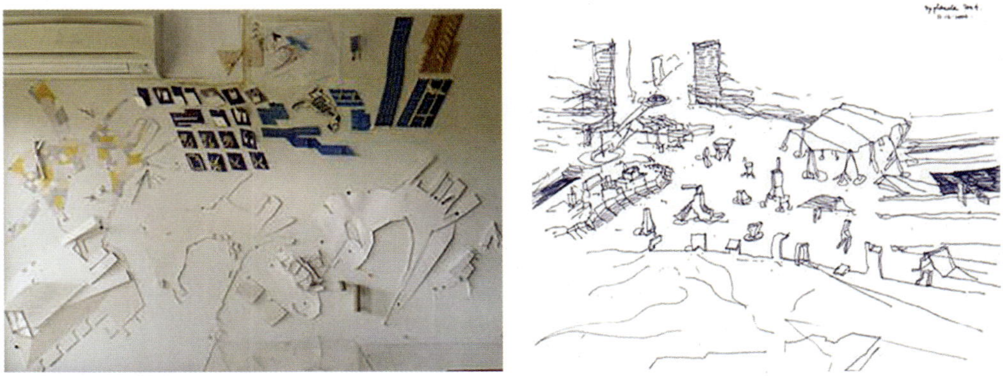

22. Torres LaPeña, collage and drawing for Rio Tinto.

Ephemeral Times

Benedetta Tagliabue

1. Opening of Fundació Enric Miralles, June 2014.

During the years that I was a partner to Enric and after he passed away in 2000, we received energy from Enric–myself and all the people in our community. After Enric was gone, we tried to go on with continuity, do architecture, and finish the projects that we started together and then do new ones following his inspiration. At a certain point, I thought maybe I really had to say goodbye to Enric. I always had a feeling that he was with us, but now we were taking the studio into a different direction. So we thought that this was the moment to start a foundation in his name–Fundació Enric Miralles. Through the foundation, we can do more things in the spirit of Enric, but with other people who may have never met him. We could take some fantastic ideas and try to do different, new things in a way that Enric would have liked. He liked to experiment, to always try something unexpected, this is what we would like to have in the foundation.

Starting the foundation was difficult for me. I was able to go on with the architectural office, but I didn't know how to lead a foundation or to manage a place that has different aim. However, I found that people were supporting me and showing me a lot of enthusiasm, as to say, start and you will see what will happen; we will be next to you, trying to make this experiment real. So now we are doing it with the support of people like Elías Torres, who is very important to us; Mosif Mustafavi, who is supportive and giving us strength; and Enric's mentors–Oriol Bohigas, who is really the father of this generation of architecture in Barcelona; Rafael Moneo, who is the father or the mentor of Spanish architecture of the last decade; and Arata Isozaki, as he was so important in promoting a kind of international exchange from Europe to Japan, from one place to the other.

The foundation is located just below the EMBT office; our office is on the primary floor of the building. We had the fantastic opportunity of using the space close to our office. There is exhibition space on the intermediate level of the building, and on the lower level is our storage where we keep all the boxes of our models, organized along the sides of the walls. In the middle of the space is a workshop where we invite local and international students to work together with us, and we have lectures there as well.

2. Exhibition "Enric Miralles in Time," Fundació Enric Miralles, 2014.

In the spirit of this place, we created an exhibition called "Enric Miralles in Time." (Fig. 2). The foundation began in 2014

3. Enric Miralles, exhibition "Heaven" Tenaki Kutu, Japan, 1995.

with an inaugural exhibition with projects that are ephemeral. We invited six architects from different places to collaborate with the city of Barcelona and the architecture school in Barcelona to produce something that will last only during summer in the old city of Barcelona.

The idea of an exhibition, the ephemeral, was something Enric would have liked very much. He loved small exhibitions, that could be created in a short time, more than building, that happen over an extend period and takes a lot of effort. With this kind of ephemeral architecture, or architecture in time, he could play a little more with raw ideas before developing something more complex.

An example of this was a commission from Arata Isozaki in Japan (Fig. 3). When Enric met Arata, he was designing a park. Arata asked Enric to do an installation inside a house in the park inspired by the theme of "Heaven"–someone else was doing Hell and Limbo. The house became a strange Heaven. When he was showing this to me or to other people in the office, he was always kind of amused. Enric's Heaven was a series of spaghetti-like sculptures. He sketched a series of fine ink lines, which were then created into rolled and bent metal tubes by a fantastic artist in Barcelona, who we like to collaborate with. Then all of this was sent to Japan where it was hung in the house. Maybe the most important part of the exhibition was the shadows created by the lines suspending the sculpture from the ceiling and illuminated by the light coming down from above. This exhibition was something that I was never actually able to see because the project was done during the time I was at home with young children. We reproduced a variation of it in a different space in Barcelona to let every visitor have the experience that you could only have had if you had been in Japan.

Another piece of the "Enric Miralles in Time" exhibition is from an opera that we did when we moved our studio from Calle Avinyó to Passatge de la Pau. Enric had the idea to produce an opera for the opening of the new studio. We called a friend who was writing texts for operas. We were supposed to produce something that was already written with music, but the friend said, no, we will do a special one, especially

4. Miralles working on the stage set for the opera, 1997.

for you. So we produced this opera, and another friend–a composer–composed the music. Some students from the theater school were the actors, and there was a very good vocalist. We found some old dresses and dressed up the actors. All the sets were done by hand with people from our office constructing the pieces to stage this complex history. There was a big structure in the opera that was supposed to be a stone, where someone falls and then doesn't come back. We made the stone out of wicker, which was moved up and down by hand with a very simple mechanism. We also made some very simple drawings, which were back-projected and became part of the cinematography that was constantly changing during the performance. The drawings created for this opera, in the end, remained as a facade for our office. So some of the opera remained as a fixed part of the studio itself.

It was a very special moment when the pianist and the composer were downstairs rehearsing, and music was filling the space of the office. Most of the people in our office were in the opera's chorus, so they were rehearsing and singing together with the composer (Fig. 4).

The opera was a difficult and expensive production. Even though it was homemade, it took a lot of time and so, it was expensive. Our friend who wrote the opera said, since this is expensive, I know of a small job for you to do so that you can pay for the opera. His father had a pharmaceutical company that needed a display for trade fairs. The display needed to be movable from one conference to the other to promote this pharmaceutical product: we were to provide the drawings and the construction of the display. Although our friend wanted to be an architect or an artist, he was committed to the family business, but in his spare time, he created operas.

So in exchange for the production of the opera, we designed the display for the trade fairs. We drew strange objects based on sifting colanders and mounted them on stands. The piece was an alphabet with 24 letters. It was very easy to set up and take down. It had an order to it but it could also be assembled in a more random way. There

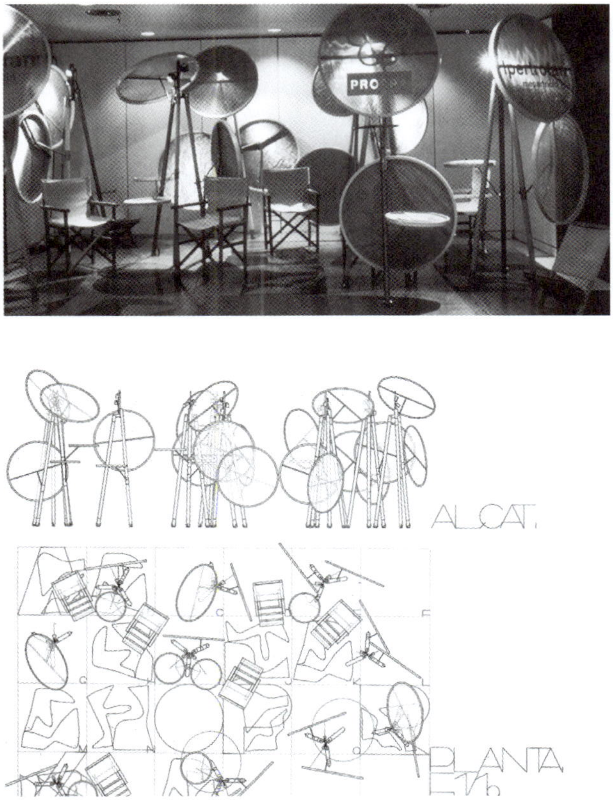

5. Miralles Tagliabue, drawings and final pieces for the pharmaceutical display, 1995.

were holes for poles that would become the stand and places where you could sit, chat, and sell the pharmaceutical product (Fig. 5).

For the foundation exhibition, we called the pharmaceutical company to check on the display and found that after more than 16 years they were still using the display pieces. They still had it very well conserved and agreed to send it to the exhibition on the condition that we send it back immediately afterwards. We are happy that they felt that this is an important piece that they had to keep.

For the Venice Bienalle in 1996, we organized an exhibition about the construction of the Huesca project. Enric's drawing of Huesca was not a building that you looked at from one point of view but from "eyes crossed" or many view points. It was also kind of an odd drawing because when this incredible building collapsed, that drawing became like a magical thing.

Huesca is a city with two sport halls–one built in the 1960s and the other built in the 1990s. In both buildings, the roof collapsed. The one in the 1990s was designed by Enric. It was incredibly lucky that when the first roof structure collapsed, no one died. It happened very early in the morning before the workers arrived. When the call came to inform us, a politician from Huesca told me, "It finally happened." And I said, "What?" "The second roof has collapsed." So I said, "Enric, the phone's for you."

It was terrible. It was really a shocking moment, and Enric was sure he would have to leave architecture and do something else. He was thinking maybe he would become a film director instead of an architect. Maybe that's why Elías Torres later said he saw Enric buying a Leika camera after that–I don't know. Then–this is the magical thing about Huesca–after the collapse, nobody talked about the building anymore, maybe because everybody thought it was a kind of a terrible shame for two roofs to collapse. They were able to resolve the crisis, construct a new roof, and open the building… and Enric continued to be an architect.

For the Venice Bienalle, we decided to present the Huesca building in a very different way than using the drawings and models. Remember, it was a building that you viewed with the "eye crossed," meaning Enric didn't want to look at the building from one point of view but with many different points of view. It was presented in three ways: as a round diorama, looking at parts of the building in a series of images like a film; as an alphabet made with found shadows; and through enlarged details of the building presented as oil paintings on canvas (Figs. 6, 7).

To make these pieces for the Venice Bienalle, Enric asked a photographer and friend to find different point of views to represent the project and to view the building as if seen by an ant. The photographer discovered a way to view the building like a book in a series of letters found in the building itself, mainly through its shadows and angles. Enric was absolutely enchanted by this alphabet because he disliked when people said that a buildings had a language. He would say, "Buildings don't talk." But in a

6. Miralles Tagliabue, exhibition for the Venice Bienalle, 1996.

7. Miralles Tagliabue, exhibition from the Venice Bienalle in the Barcelona Pavilion.

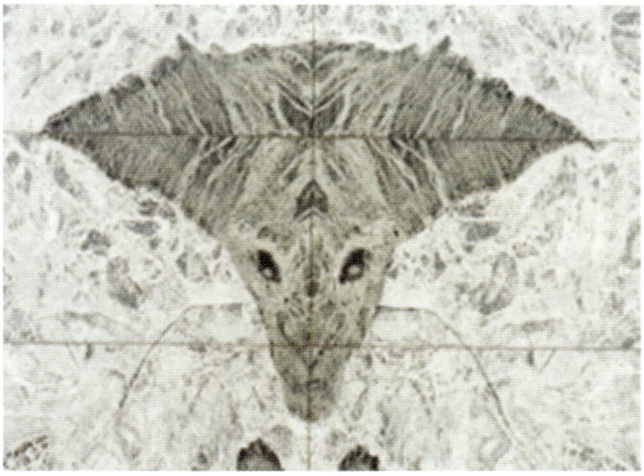

8. Miralles Tagliabue, exhibition detail from the Venice Bienalle in the Barcelona Pavilion, 1996.

way, this building had an alphabet. So this was one of the jokes he liked very much. We secretly thought that the Venice Bienalle exhibit was a kind of homage to the construction of Huesca–the fact that the building collapsed and was a great disaster, but at the same, nothing really terrible happened.

The exhibit won the Golden Lion Award from the Venice Bienalle–very prestigious. Because of the Golden Lion, the Mies van der Rohe Foundation asked us to bring the same installation into the Mies van der Rohe Pavilion in Barcelona. But Enric didn't like to do the same installation in a different space–every space is different. In the pavilion, Enric introduced another intervention, which were photographs in cylinders, done by the same photographer who did the letters in the Biennale exhibition.

Enric asked the photographer to do specific things, like to go to the Barcelona Pavilion and look at the marble for its primitiveness. Enric was conscious of the fact that the travertine has a cave-like quality; if you look closely, you can feel like you are in front of a cave wall. But the photographer, who was also an anthropologist, discovered other very surprising images–a kind of primitive world inside the marble of the pavilion. He found many figures, like insects, alien faces or heads, and animals like dogs and wolves (Fig. 8). This became a new part of the exhibition.

For the Fundació Miralles exhibition, instead of using the Huesca Sports Hall on the diorama, we used the Santa Caterina construction so when you step inside the diorama, you have the feeling of a film, of time passing in Santa Caterina during construction with layers of time, the archaeological excavation, the old market walls, and so on.

In the exhibition there is a table that Enric designed from an idea he found in a book by Aldo Rossi, who also designed a table as a symbol of life and death (Fig. 9). To Enric, this moving table was something deeply vital. The design is for two tables,

9. Innes Table in the Fundació Enric Miralles.
10. Enric Miralles, playing child, photomontage.

like a mirror but not a perfect mirror–one for our home and the other for the office. The form is a drawing of his own head, which becomes a table that can change into different positions and can host the life of the house and of everybody in he house.

We put a little wooden house on top of the table, which was from a project given to many different architects to design a little city in a garden. Enric always used these projects to create different drawings and different inspirations, but the inspiration for this design was very clearly our young daughter (Fig. 10).

A child in the house was a very new and different experience for him, and he was impressed by everything she was doing, as if it is something absolutely universal, which is true, like learning how to walk using a piece of furniture to become a standing human.

So in designing the pavilion, Enric was interpreting the house as a place where parents and children could meet. He was also thinking about and interpreting the cultivation of flowers, because the project was suppose to exist in the natural environment. We did many models, but because of budget and other difficulties, it was never built for the original garden.

11. Miralles Tagliabue, play house for Kolonihaven.
12. Enric Miralles, photomontage Igualada Cemetery.

When Enric died, we were able to build it, thanks to the Gerald Hines real estate development company that wanted to install it for their development at Diagonal Mar Park. Children who were playing on it knew nothing of Enric's story about the parents and the children. It was a very popular part of the park and did not last long. The City of Barcelona remade it in a more secluded location, so now if you want to see it, it's a real hidden Miralles piece in Barcelona–we also forget where it is (Fig. 11).

The curator of the "Miralles in Time" exhibition said, of course, we must include the cemetery in Igualada–a project that was very important to Enric. He worked on it for all his professional life (Fig. 12).

Two people worked there with Enric, who would go every two weeks or every month and tell them what to do. He worked with an artisan who made the door and was very clever. In the end, it is not very well maintained, but Enric was always finding a way to make something fantastic. It is an incredible place, and the exhibition had photographs cut out to underline pieces of the Igualada Cemetery, leaving you looking at the photographs in a different way, inventing the reality in another time.

In this same exhibition, we wanted to include a project that we did to celebrate Enric 10 years after his passing. I was conscious that it would be difficult to mark

10 years after Enric was gone, but we wanted to invent something joyous, something beautiful. The 3rd of July–10 years after his death–was a very hot day in Barcelona. We organized a picnic in the Diagonal Mar Park and invited artist Jorge Rodriguez-Gerada to create an intervention–a big painting of Enric's head on the basketball court of the park (Figs. 13, 14). The painting was to be drawn with colored sand during the day of the picnic. Jorge started at five in the morning and finished at nine in the night. Guests were coming and going, and at the end, when it was nearly finished, it was so large that we could only look at it from a camera positioned on a globe high above on a light post.

At the end of the celebration, all the guests were asked to come and take away some of the sand used to make this image of Enric. Children in the Diagonal Mar Park didn't really understand what was going on but thought that this is a fantastic game and were also collecting the sand and putting the sand into the little pots provided for this purpose.

13. Jorge Rodriquez Gerada, drawing and exhibition piece in Diagonal Mar Park, 2010.

Even if we had said, "Oh but it's so nice; we can leave it a couple of days more," the artist told us, "No, no, this is like a mandala. We draw it in one day, and at the end of the day it's gone." So, he took an instrument and made this beautiful drawing of Enric's face disappearing like a labyrinth where you could get lost again. There is a video of that day, which is kind of sad and beautiful at the same time.

The exhibitions are one of the fantastic possibilities of the Fundació Enric Miralles–to do new things and to produce knowledge altogether with many different people. This is my vision–to have people all around with a joyful time so that Enric can be a fantastic inspiration for new wonderful projects. to come.

14. Jorge Rodriquez Gerada, exhibition piece in Diagonal Mar Park, 2010.

Conversation

Elías Torres
+
Benedetta Tagliabue
+
Students

Student Elías, it is interesting what you said about most architects other than Miralles, have done many houses, can you expand on why you think this is?

Elías Torres Remember the houses of every architect that you respect; you will always find something unique that perfectly represents a moment of expression, which is like a relationship to a painting or poetry. As I was saying, it is about the atmosphere that puts people together who probably would not even talk to each other. It is the same for architecture students today—you have the same things around you—the same information that you receive, not just in school, but also in the world. And all those things together will produce an effect that will represent your generation as designers.

Houses are very important territory in the history of architecture. You can put single-family houses next to each other in terms of the years, which will give you exactly the figurative expression of different decades and artistic movements, because it represents the personality of the designers. The program is not significant; it's always the same—a couple, a single, kids, garage, kitchen, bathrooms, bedrooms. It can be tidy; it can be big; it can be a palace—it's always the same thing. There is no problem with the program. It can be an artist, a pianist, a blind person—doesn't matter, it's all the same. This produces the possibility of an expression that works very well or very badly—you don't know where the bathroom is, you need to cross the corridor to go to the other side—it is just chaos.

Another thing about the single-family house commission is that the architect does not just make his signature, you have relate to the age of the client and they have to relate to you. That is something that happens very often. Normally your first commission is your own house or you start from family commissions of relatives or people who are about the same age as you. I love the single-family houses; I think it's just something very unique.

I was really amazed about the very few houses that Enric designed: two reconstructions, but only one isolated new house.

Benedetta Tagliabue I think relative to houses, you are right. It is surprising that Enric designed so few houses, maybe this is because it was also a special moment in Spain. There was an incredible situation where young people, very young architects, could access public competitions. The public competitions were usually about public services and open spaces. It was also a kind of reflection of a social situation, political situation, where young architects could express themselves in Spain in that moment through the public works, through the public commission.

Elías Torres A fantastic book to read is *The Place of Houses* by Charles Moore. It is one of the two or three books I recommend, including, Aldo Rossi's *The Architecture of the City* and *Complexity and Contradiction in Architecture* by Robert Venturi. Charles Moore is a figure that is almost forgotten because he disappeared at the end of post-modernism. He includes the questions a client should ask an architect. Most examples use his houses. He designed many, many houses in a very easy way. His design relationship with context, including his five personal houses and the Sea Ranch house (designed with William Turnbull Jr., Donlyn Lyndon, and Richard Whitaker in 1965), established a connection in the world of buildings and minds in the U.S. Very few people have produced this result with their architecture. Even Venturi, though not exactly in the same way, was doing the same. He was a very cultivated person, well educated, and very conscience about what he was doing. I was teaching in UCLA when I was young and became acquainted with Venturi. He is one of those people who was around, and it was interesting to see his easiness.

Elías, how important is the context around your project to the development of the work?

Elías Torres In my opinion, I think working from the context is the only way to work. To know exactly where we are. It doesn't mean context in only physical terms—it's about culture, the acknowledgement of times, a place's history. It is about people who share this place, and a specific character that you need to extend. Context is very wide. The physical is very important, but what it means is very important.

Benedetta Tagliabue The context was so important to Enric. When I met Enric, he was drawing every site first thing. He was kind of strange [laughs]. He was very much in love with topography, and using this way of representing earth and its presentation was really important. He needed to make the lines of the project come out. He was also developing more with photographs, for example, strange photographs of Huesca as an alphabet. Many of his photographs are unpublished or unknown. He was trying to understand how other people are influenced by a building. Like when someone is walking on the opposite sidewalk from a building, you see the shadow of the building, or if you are even farther away, you have a view. So if you design some massive plan, it implies that you understand how your own building will be perceived and will influence its surroundings by extension.

How do you discover the meaning of the context?

Elías Torres If you want to have a more established conversation about designing and building, you can use a drawing to understand the soul of a place and then be able to establish the context. You can experiment in the beginning and use the drawing to bring something that used to be there before your intervention. Argentinian writer, César Aira, said something very beautiful about art: "One of the functions of art is to produce an effect of surprise that changes the habits of perception and to transform the old into new." This is not a definition of art, because I think this is almost impossible, but a possible understanding of art. This can also be a way of seeing a plan view or perspective. It was Pablo Picasso who said he was someone who was stealing and copying. Stealing is how you take one thing and transform it into something else. Copying is just reprinting the same thing in your work, but stealing implies transformation.

Benedetta Tagliabue I gather that there is intuition in that. Enric was very special, but sometimes you really couldn't understand what he meant! A friend of mine from Italy came to meet my new love (Enric) at one of his lectures, and after fifteen minutes, she looked at me and said, "I understood nothing" [laughs]. Elías was trying to explain the difference between copying and stealing. Enric would say: You know what? We have to be very fast. If you have an idea, you have to produce something, do it, and publish it, and make everybody know that we had this idea, because ideas are in the air. And maybe, if you are very good, and you have a very good intuition, you could get this from the air without much effort. Enric knew he had this capacity, but he also knew how to calculate how much time in advance he needed. He'd say, "We are maybe one or two years in advance, but we have to be fast" [Laughs]. I thought this was a very good to have these fantastic ideas, which are in the air and maybe belong to the moment or belong to the situation. This was something that everyone can grasp, and maybe, with someone explaining it to you in advance, you can understand faster. So this is the thing that real artists get that someone who copies does not.

Elías Torres I didn't mean to say that Eric was an artistic genius or not. He had something very special, I know of only two other people with a similar ability and attitude. A very well-known painter, Miquel Barceló, is probably the best paid painter in Spain and had something very special. He was able to understand the world around him and could sell anything. It is a kind of special perception surrounding him. Enric had this too. They could look at the world and say: I know something; I don't know what you want, but I am going to give you something that you don't expect, and you're going to buy it. It could be good or not, but it's going to transform into something that people need. At the same time, there is no very easy way of evaluating these things.

Benedetta Tagliabue Exactly, I did not understand what he was doing! [Laughs]

Elías Torres Here's another thing about being involved with a figure like Enric Miralles: I believe it could be said that heroes die young. There is something about the age, and the myth grows. Young people, like you, in Spain, don't know anything about Enric. He died in 2000, but they don't know anything about him. He was someone who was so close and had a presence. People want to know more now—there's a love, a desire today.

Faculty It is interesting to hear Benedetta talk about Enric's understanding that he had to work very fast to develop an idea that is out there. One of the things that was fascinating was how fast he worked, how many things he did simultaneously, and how he'd combine them to work back and forth between all of them. Just the quantity of work that he was producing by himself and, of course, with other people, was astounding. He was unbelievably quick.

Elías Torres It's true! He didn't suffer!

Benedetta Tagliabue No, no. He was really suffering. He was a terrible perfectionist, and he was truly suffering. For example, when he was doing the Diagonal Mar project, he was truly suffering.

Elías Torres Because that was a huge commission.[Laughing]

Benedetta Tagliabue It was not just because of that. It was because there was no real respect by our collaborators on the project for the lines he had been drawing on paper. He would bring it into the studio in Barcelona, and someone else had redrawn it. It was like someone stabbing a knife into his side.

Elías Torres I was talking about his sense of easiness in the way, for instance, competitions and activities related to the office appeared, and the way he was producing.

Student Benedetta how did your work evolve after Enric?

Benedetta Tagliabue I really feel the strength of a fantastic archive that I can go and find thousands of ideas that can be developed. This is a life-long possibility. But we also like to try new things, because you cannot repeat things that were done in the past. You can get ideas from the past, but you have to adapt. It is a kind of continuity of having someone there who is constantly helping you, which is why I always have this feeling that even though Enric died, he is in the office. He is still our main designer. But little by little, we are evolving. When Enric died, people came to visit and would say, "Oh, Bene, what do we do now?" And I answered, "I don't know, we just go on…" [Laughs].

Elías Torres I remember Rafael Moneo arrived late to Enric's funeral. And he was walking with you, and said, "Benedetta, you should finish all of Enric's projects." You were having doubts about finishing or even closing the office possibly. I understand that it was really a moment of difficulty. What you did was very brave, which was to finish five or six projects.

Benedetta Tagliabue Ten or twelve.

Elías Torres Twelve? More? Afterwards, she used the seeds of all the history of the office, as she was saying, to find her personal way. It is impossible to break away completely. Take, for instance, the pavilion in Shanghai—the Spanish pavilion for the World Expo—there is a remote memory of the beginning of Enric's idea, but it became something completely different. Benedetta was involved in all the relationships with the movie directors, painter, designers—everyone. That changed everything because she didn't want to try to be Enric; she wanted to be herself. It is impossible to erase the connection to Enric, because it's there. It would also be a sort of betrayal to Enric to erase everything, because underneath the office, in the basement, are all the seeds of his work enlightening or helping to grow the activities just a floor above.

Benedetta Tagliabue There is another consideration in this evolution process that every architect has to do, even when they are by themselves. It is so easy to arrive at a point where you are recognized for some type of work, for some way of doing architecture, and then you don't know the limits of how much you can repeat or how you can evolve from that. This is difficult.

Elías Torres Yes, but, it depends on the way you work. I hate to think about what I have done a month earlier—I forget everything we have done! You can't avoid being yourself by just forgetting. What's important is what you do that day, with influences that you don't know where they come from—maybe from friends, from the dust, from what you read, what you see, what your emotions are about. And this is important, just be yourself. Respond with the highest responsibility to the work you have in front of you. You have to answer to someone who is giving you the opportunity of being able to express yourself with sometimes very strict conditions.

Benedetta Tagliabue There is this kind of difficulty of continuity in our transformation as architects. At one time, we were doing so many projects and so many competitions that sometimes we needed to repeat ourselves a little bit. Something I really liked about Enric when we were doing a project, is that he would say: we do a little like this, and a little like this, and then we will introduce some recipes of the house. So it is very lovely to have some recipes, and sometimes you can't repeat them, but you need to understand how much to add. This is a kind of thinking in the world of art—artists repeat themselves or make a reference, much more than architects. It is incredible because art is a market, and you are totally recognizable. But for architects, we have a difficulty with repetition.

Elías Torres Very important architects, for instance, in the United States, go with their suitcases of the same portfolio, the same buildings, repeating buildings all over the world, with no shame.

Benedetta Tagliabue But they have no names.

Elías Torres Well that's the thing. It's the corporate name. Frank Gehry, for instance, started with a very beautiful, very small project in Los Angeles with a renovation for an art gallery. He ended up, just after Bilbao, saying that every single city wanted the same building. He could not avoid these requests because they want this thing again and again. You might hate it; however, you continue to do it because you have an office and that's the way you continue.

Faculty I am fascinated by Miralles' architectural language—that wonderful line that is straight and curved, which is such a constant presence in his work. It comes out again and again. It works so beautifully in the Parliament building because of its inclusive lines, its forms, and yet it goes to a sharp edge. The curve and sharp corner play off against each other in a really wonderful way. There is a consistency through that. I wonder, the language must be a challenge—is it a very personal language or is it the language of the office?

Benedetta Tagliabue It is a very personal language, which became the language that most of us have learned. We have it in our hands, or in the first sketches, or in the first approach to a site. But Enric himself was trying to escape his hand. He was very much concerned about that. He knew that he had a very strong hand in the sense that certain shapes came out and he liked them. I understood this and that it was increasing through people in the studio, so we began making more models, and making collages—other things that are not just lines drawn on the paper—as a way for Enric to escape himself or to evolve the office without a lot of pain. That's why I say he wasn't looking like he enjoyed it or being inclusive. He was doing this as a big effort against himself, because he was really a perfectionist.

Elías Torres The calligraphy, which he invented, has been used for many years in the office. In the end, it, too, is protective. It really became a trademark. How much do you want to escape from what you have produced and how much do you want to risk in a new territory? This is the thing.

Student Elías, you talked about geniuses dying young, what did you mean by this?

Elías Torres Even if you want to escape from yourself, you keep being the same. And this is always something very difficult to realize. But at least there is the intention of facing yourself.

Benedetta Tagliabue This is the reality when you face the fact of being able to respond to things that are very complex and sometimes very contradictory. You need to put equations with questions. It's not like engineers—sometimes they have one equation, and the answer is equal to this. Architects can't do that. This is exactly the most attractive virtue of our work—the unexpected things. Even if you copy work, the conditions will change and so the copy changes to something else. And if you copy only just the surface thing, immediately you see the fakeness of it.

Who did Enric study with and work for before going off on his own?

Benedetta Tagliabue From the first moment you enter a school, you have very clear influence on what is acceptable and what is not acceptable, and you immediately adopt the acceptable way. So, in a way we are all totally influenced and totally transformed by the same fact that we are here. When Enric was first drawing and first working on projects in school, he was very good at drawing. He did some beautiful drawings when he was 15 or 16 that were at his parent's house, very skillful. So he had this skill before even knowing the environment of school. But then I think he was very influenced by Rafael Moneo.

Elías Torres No...

Benedetta Tagliabue No? Okay...then who?

Elías Torres This is where these things start...I was teaching Enric with Rafael Moneo, who I think is ten or twelve years older than myself. Enric was trying to be completely different from everyone else—trying to be an artist. It was about principles—ethical principles—I am not going to say morals, because it is not that complex. But ethical principles are the thing to learn from your professors. An attitude, this is something else—aesthetic or otherwise. No, Enric was very smart, and he knew he needed to find a very personal way. That's why the calligraphy and the language of drawing became a trademark.

Benedetta Tagliabue I think that there is an influence, which maybe Elías can help me with. There is a very strange, strong influence between Spanish or Spanish-type of architecture and Nordic architecture. For example, this way of drawing with one fine line and letterings, which comes directly from Alvar Aalto.

Moneo worked with them?

Benedetta Tagliabue Exactly, but he was bringing things from the north.

Elías Torres Yes, but I think northern architects have taken from the Mediterranean languages. A lot of what they did was between the two world wars. And then, we took a version of the Mediterranean culture from the north back to the Mediterranean.

In our third-year studio we are working on a renovation project and some of us are studying Santa Caterina Market. Can you talk a little bit about its history and how to correlate it with the new program?

Benedetta Tagliabue When I met Enric, he was working on a project, which became the Picasso Museum on an old street of Barcelona. Enric was transforming this historical architecture into something very abstract. When we started to later work together, we had a fantastic adventure. We went into the old city, which during that time in Barcelona was like a rejected city. But we thought it was very special. I had been living in Venice for a long time, and I really needed an old city. The new part of Barcelona is very structured—a squared city that was too rigid for me. So we went together into the old city, which was at a beautiful moment because the old city was abandoned and nobody wanted it. We found incredible buildings with incredible histories. We understood how the buildings were carrying the history of the people that had been there before. We were finding hidden layers on the walls; we were scratching a door, and a golden column was being revealed. History was present. We had this experience in our house as well, which was even more fantastic because we had the possibility of transforming the space with the materials that we were finding. So our lesson, and mainly for Enric, was learning about the relationship between the historical house and inhabiting an historical place. When we did the Utrecht City Hall and the Santa Caterina building, we were telling the clients—no problem, we will do it like an extension of our house.

Elías Torres It is difficult to teach how to deal with this problem of old and new in any school of architecture, because no one project, no one building—even if you work on an empty lot—is nothing; it is a something because it's surrounded by something, by context. And with all building remains—historical remains and monuments—sometimes you need to bring life to them again. There is a resurrection of the building that you need to bring back to life again. It is a transfusion—not forgetting the idea of what it used to be and what to introduce to avoid this. You need to establish this relationship between old and new, not to mummify the old thing, but how to bring the old to the new and how the new will bring life to the old. The Italians were the first to consider this in the modern era—Franco Albini, a great architect—was probably the first one to do this in the 1950s. After that it was Carlo Scarpa. Offices in the 1950s and '60s were showing examples of what was the best way of touching, using, transforming old buildings into a new one. Spain learned from them, and we were able to do designs that we were not trained to do because we were trained on a wider context. We didn't want to become specialists on these things. I said a similar thing to an aesthetics professor in the university in Barcelona. I said, "I am a specialist in generalities." We architects need to learn so many things—you can become a specialist on structures, or construction, or being a professor of the drawing class, but you need context of why you can do something. Then you can choose. But you need to learn from experiences. I don't care if it's new, if it's old, if it's a monument or not—it's the attitude you have towards the project. You need to be respectful, but at the same time to be irreverent.

The word that I think I need to introduce is irony. The process of design is a continuous rational process. There is a moment, probably, when the project is right. You need to know how to arrive there. Picasso used to say that the most important thing about inspiration is that it finds you working. The irony is the festivity; people trying to see what works. There is a feast of producing, drawing, and proposing one thing upon the other, and if that idea works, then great, and if it doesn't, then that's okay. That's what I liked about Enric's attitude—it was very easy going in the way that if it isn't acceptable, it's still okay, and you will do it again. This is how we were used to working when he transformed difficulties into virtues.

I was eleven years older than Enric and was able to go with him to many different places—drinking, eating, and talking—not very often, but enough to produce a mutual respect. We had been drawing together many years. We were working on our PhD thesis projects together during the same year. We would call each other and say, "Would you like to come over or would you like to have lunch," and then we would show each other some point from our thesis, and say, "What do you think about this?" It was usually the same response, "Are you sure?" The same thing happens with my partner, but it is a little different. However, it is important to have someone that you can battle with for months and have something to say to each other, like "Why are you doing this?" It's so difficult to find, but you should cultivate those with friendships with people you can trust so that your work can stay fresh. My partner has been asked, "How have you been able to work for forty-seven years together?" He replies, "Just being patient." I have no idea how we worked so well together.

Is there a difference in the design process that you teach in school versus the process you use in your practice?

Elías Torres Both things are very complementary, very deep; it is different, but you are the same person. The only thing that changes is the age of the professor because students always stay the same age. When I started, students were almost my age, and now they are almost my grandchildren.

Benedetta Tagliabue One special thing in Spain is that there is this tradition of architects being very serious in their profession and education. So they go to the universities, and they have relationships with the people teaching them, which produces this fantastic exchange that does not happen everywhere. We need to thank people like Moneo, who exposed or showed everybody his way of teaching and his way of being very serious, but keeping relationships normal and real.

Elías Torres When Moneo came to speak in Barcelona in 1971, he introduced a completely different way of teaching. The school was the laboratory of the city and the opposite way too. In the 1960s, life was changing. People left because of the civil war, and many who remained were really old guys, mentally. Ideas of building and designing had been the same for many years. People like Moneo began breaking what you learned in new ways. Rafael brought a more intellectual vision, more theoretical.

Is the thing that is killing architecture now the idea of "sustainable-lite"?

Elías Torres We haven't talked about sustainability. Don't you think it is about attitude, as well as codes and rules, that you have to respond to? Someone was saying the other day that we must go from ego architecture to eco architecture. I said you are right, we should be very considerate about those things. It is about respect. How many of the buildings that we know are respectful? Very few, two percent of them. We try to teach people to be part of this two percent. The reality of projects and design drops people in very strange situations, but we cannot stop teaching that way.

Benedetta Tagliabue How can you use water in different ways and how is the richness of the climate? There are other groups, who are not architects, who can be helpful to what we do—people who have an interest in architecture and in landscape. It is really about the resources of the earth and respect for the resources of the world and how to transform them and how to provide life. There are many people who are supporting environmental concerns.

Elías Torres Yes and you cannot avoid sustainable ideas, like energy sources. Resources are becoming less, and we are already fighting over our resources. The important thing is to feel independent in a community or society and to know what it means to respect, to share resources. You have responsibilities to the others, and others have responsibilities to you. The rules to weave this together are very important.

Biographies

Manuel Bailo Esteve studied with Enric Miralles at Escola Técnica d'Arquitectura de Barcelona (ETSAB). Bailo is currently the Director of Urban Design at the University of Virginia. He previously taught architecture and urbanism at ETSAB. In 2010, he completed a PhD in Architectural Design at ETSAB with a dissertation titled "Urban Catalyst." In 1995, Bailo, in partnership with Rosa Rull, established BAILORULL ADD+ in Barcelona. Their work has been widely recognized, published, and exhibited.

Peter Buchanan is a freelance writer and architect known for his critical essays "The Big Rethink," published by *The Architecture Review,* and for his many books on architecture including *Renzo Piano Building Workshop* and *Ten Shades of Green: Architecture and the Natural World* coauthored with Kenneth Frampton. Buchanan was the first to publish on Miralles and Pinós' work with his essay "Dialogue and Distillation: The Architecture of Enric Miralles and Carme Pinós." Buchanan has curated numerous exhibitions, taught master classes, and lectured in a wide range of international locations, universities, and professional organizations.

Sir Peter Cook was a founder of Archigram, former Dean of the Bartlett School of Architecture and University College London, and head of the architecture class at the Städelschule in Frankfurt, Germany. Sir Cook has published over 20 books on architecture and numerous journal articles. In 2007, he was knighted by the Queen of England for his services to architecture and teaching. He is also a Royal Academician and a Commandeur de l'Ordre des Arts et des Lettres of the French Republic. His achievements with Archigram were recognized by the Royal Institute of British Architects with the Royal Gold Metal.

Elena Cánovas was a student of Miralles' at the Escola Técnica Superior d'Arquitectura de Barcelona (ETSAB) where she is currently a professor of architecture and a principal with Antonio Sanmartín of aSZ Arquitectes, Barcelona, started in 1996. Their work has been widely published and awarded. She has lectured and conducted workshops at several international schools, and she is currently a visiting professor of architecture at Washington University in St. Louis.

Teresa Galí-Izard was a student when Miralles taught at the Escola Técnica Superior d'Arquitectura de Barcelona. Galí-Izard is chair of the Landscape

Architecture Department at University of Virginia and principal of Arquitectura Agronomia, a landscape architecture firm located in Barcelona. With her partner Jordi Nebot, she has a large number of built projects in Spain including the Sant Joan Landfill restoration, which won the European Urban Public Space award in 2004. She is the author of *The Same Landscapes, Ideas and Interpretations.*

Jaun José Lahuerta was a classmate studying with Miralles at Escola Técnica Superior d'Arquitectura de Barcelona (ETSAB). Lahuerta is professor of the History of Art and Architecture at ETSAB and the Director of Collections at the National Museum of Art of Catalonia. He is a member of the Collegio Docenti della Scuola Dottorati del Istituto Universitario di Architettura of Venice and also holder of the King Juan Carlos I Chair of Spanish Culture and Civilization at New York University. He has authored of numerous books on contemporary art and architecture.

John Meunier is an architect and former Dean of the College of Architecture and Environmental Design at Arizona State University. Professor Meunier has many articles published on architectural education, is the editor of a monograph, *Language in Architecture*, was the founding editor of the journal, *CENTRAL Papers on Architecture*, and produced a television series for KAET and National Public Television called 'Desert Cities: Surviving the 21st Century'.

Carles Muro is an architect and educator. He studied at the Escola Tècnica Superior d'Arquitectura de Barcelona (ETSAB) and worked with Torres/Lapeña in Barcelona and Alvaro Siza in Oporto before setting up in private practice. The work of his practice has been widely published and awarded. He was a student of Miralles' and later taught with him at the ETSAB. He is currently an Associate Professor of Architecture at Harvard Graduate School of Design.

Maurici Pla Serra is a professor of architectural theory and criticism at Escola Técnica Superior d'Arquitectura de Barcelona, where he was a fellow student and colleague of Miralles'. Included amongst his publications are *Chicago and New York: Theory, Art and Architecture from the Nineteenth and Twentieth Centuries*, *Catalan Guide to Modern Architecture 1880–2007*, and *The Architectures of Language, Writings 1989–2002.*

Eva Prats is a professor of architecture at Escola Técnica Superior d'Arquitectura de Barcelona (ETSAB) and cofounder and partner of the Barcelona-based architecture firm Flores & Prats Arquitectura. Their work has been widely recognized, published, and exhibited. The recent publication, *Pensado a Mano,* catalogs the studios work to date. Prats is a former student of Miralles' and worked in his studio between 1990 and 1996. Together, Prats and Flores have coauthored *Through the Canvas: Architecture Inside Dutch Paintings.*

Joseph Quetglas is a professor at the Polytechnic University of Catalonia where he has taught in the areas of planning, aesthetics, and history of art and architecture. He is the author of numerous books including *Fear of Glass: Mies van der Rohe's Pavilion in Barcelona* and *Project and Architecture of the Villa Savoye Le Corbusier.* He organized the magazines *Street of the City, Technical Journal,* and *Web Architecture Magazine.* Quetglas was a professor of Miralles' at Escola Técnica Superior d'Arquitectura de Barcelona (ETSAB).

Elena Rocchi is an architect, artist, and currently PhD candidate in theory and history of architecture at Escola Técnica Superior d'Arquitectura de Barcelona. She was a senior architect in the Miralles Tagliabue studio from 1994 to 2010. She has lectured and taught in Europe, Mexico, South Africa, Argentina, and the United States. Her artwork has been exhibited at the Biennale of Venice and in Turin and Madrid in 2012. She is currently a visiting professor of architecture at Arizona State University.

Catherine Spellman is a professor of architecture at Arizona State University. She participated as research fellow in the architecture class of Professor Enric Miralles at the Staatliche Hochschule für Bildende Kunst, Frankfurt, Germany in 1991. There she continued as Miralles' teaching assistant to 1995. Simultaneously, she taught with Professor Peter Cook at the Bartlett School of Architecture, University College London. She is the editor of the anthology *Re-Envisioning Landscape/Architecture* and coeditor with Karl Unglaub of *A Space for our Generation, Conversations with Students, Peter Smithson.*

Benedetta Tagliabue and Enric Miralles founded the studio Enric Miralles Benedetta Tagliabue (EMBT) in 1991. Together, their work includes iconic buildings and public spaces in Barcelona such as the Gas Natural Tower, Santa Caterina Market, and Diagonal Mar Park. Buildings in other European cities include the Scottish Parliament in Edinburgh, Utrecht's Town Council, and Hamburg School of Music. Under Tagliabue's direction, the studio currently works not only within the scope of architecture but also within that of landscape, public space, building restoration, temporary installations, and design. She lectures in architectural forums all over the world and received the RIBA's International Fellowship and an Honorary Doctor of Arts degree from Napier University.

Elías Torres is a former professor of architecture at Escola Técnica Superior d'Arquitectura de Barcelona where he received a doctorate degree. He was a professor and later close friend of Miralles. Torres established an architectural practice in 1968 with José Antonio Martínez Lapeña. Their work is widely published and acclaimed including multiple years of the prestigious Spanish National FAD awards, the Belca Tokyo Prize, and the International Architecture Biennale in Venice. The recent publication, *José Antonio Martínez Lapeña and Elías Torres,* catalogs the work of their studio.

Ana Valderrama is Dean of the School of Architecture, Planning, and Design of Rosario National University. She is a Fulbright Scholar in Landscape Architecture and recipient of numerous awards for her academic and professional work. She has taught at several universities in Argentina and abroad. She is the director of Matericos Perifericos, a nonprofit organization that combines academic work and social service. Her work with the organization was recently published in a book of the same title.

Claudio Vekstein is a professor of architecture at Arizona State University and has an architecture practice [eCV] Opera Publica in Buenos Aires, Argentina and Phoenix Arizona, USA. His work has been widely published and has received several awards including the Baukunst Architecture Award by the Stiftung Städelschule für Baukunst, Germany and represented Argentina at the 2016 Venice Biennale in Italy. He studied with Enric Miralles at the Staatliche Hochschule für Bildende Kunst, Frankfurt, Germany, collaborated with Miralles and Karl Unglaub on the Rosenmuseum Steinfurt Project in Germany, and taught with Miralles in Latin America.

Acknowledgements

Special thanks to Benedetta Tagliabue who supported the book from the beginning, Karl Unglaub whose conversations about the book were invaluable, Ramon Prats at ACTAR, Director Craig Barton, my colleagues and many students at ASU who contributed to the discussions (identified in the book Introduction notes).

Thanks to the book essay contributors, Peter Cook, Jaun José Lahuerta, John Meunier, Maurici Pla Serra, Josep Quetglas, Elena Rocchi, Catherine Spellman, Ana Valderrama, Claudio Vekstein; and to the lecture contributors, Manuel Bailo Esteve, Peter Buchanan, Elena Cánovas, Teresa Galí-Izard, Carles Muro, Eva Prats, Benedetta Tagliabue, and Elías Torres, whose lectures were transcribe and edited. I was not able to use the complete richness of their spoken words and images, I have reduced and paraphrased as I thought necessary for clarity, so any mistakes are mine.

Enormous thanks to Julie Russ for her encouragement and tireless work on the transcribed texts and copy editing.

Endless gratitude to my life long friend Kathyrn Basil and to my patient and supportive family, Ana Zeta, Benjamin and Michael Groves.

Of course, in memory of Enric Miralles.

Image credits

Pages 10-25

1. Miralles Tagliabue, Diagonal Mar Park, Photograph from Fundació Enric Miralles, Barcelona.

Pages 26-35

1–8. Images from Fundació Enric Miralles, Barcelona.

Pages 36-55

1. Miralles Pinós, Igualada Cemetery, plan drawing, 1985–1996. Drawing from Fundació Enric Miralles, Barcelona.
2. Francesco di Giorgio Martini, measure of man in relationship to column capitals, 1439–1501.*Reconstructing Francesco di Giorgio Architect*, Frankfurt am Main, Berlin, Bern, Bruxelles, New York, 2011.
3. Diego de Sagredo, *Medidas del Romano,* 1526. Toledo: Remón de Petras. (Albatros Ediciones facsimile, 1976). (http://journal.eahn.org/articles/10.5334/ah.cu/).
4. Francesco di Giorgio, cornice profile superimposed over a man's head and shoulders, detail. Biblioteca Nazionale Centrale di Firenze, Florence, Italy, ms. II.I.141, Fig. 37.
5. Francesco di Giorgio, *Trattato di architettura civile e militare*, 1482. (http://lapisblog.epfl.ch/gallery3/var/albums/20140709-01/di_giorgio_martini_francesco_trattato_architettura_1482.jpg).
6. Michelangelo, drawings of base profiles, 1523. Casa Buonarroti, Florence, A10r, c. 1523. (http://journal.eahn.org/articles/10.5334/ah.cu/).
7. Bruno Taut, *The World Builder*, 1920. *Der Weltbaumeister (El constructor del món)* Hagen: Folkwang-Verlag, 1920. (https://elisavafreb.wordpress.com/2015/03/06/llibres-il%C2%B7lustrats-de-lexpressionisme-alemany-1907-1931/).
8. Ibid, Taut.
9. Francesco de Hollanda, *De Aetatibus Mundi Imagines*, 1565. (http://www.bne.es/es/Micrositios/Exposiciones/BNE300/Exposicion/Seccion1/sub2/Obra38.html?origen=galeria).
10. Claude-Nicolas Ledoux, Progetto per la Maison du Plaisir, ca.1775. (https://www.pinterest.com/qingwen/nicolas-ledoux/).
11. Ibid, Ledoux.
12. Antoni Gaudí, human skeleton, ca.1900.
13. Antoni Gaudí, human skeleton clothed as angel, ca.1900.
14. Andreas Vasalius, "De Humani Corpis Fabrica," ca.1534. "De Humani Corpis Fabrica" (On the Fabric of the Human Body). (http://www.bl.uk/learning/cult/bodies/vesalius/renaissance.html).
15. Nicolaus Beatrizet, *Juan de Valverde*, "La anatomía del cuerpo humano," 1556. (https://www.flickr.com/photos/maneraymodo/5193066239).
16. Francesco di Giorgio Martini, *Trattati di Archittecttura,* 1492. (http://www.jstor.org/stable/20166656?seq=1#page_scan_tab_contents).
17. Francesco di Giorgio Martini, *Trattati di Archittecttura,* 1492. (http://dame-licorne.pagesperso-orange.fr/IMAGES/codex2.jpg).
18. Ibid, di Giorgio.
19. Francesco di Giorgio Martini, *Trattati di Archittecttura,* 1492. (https://s-media-cache-ak0.pinimg.com/236x/83/7a/f/837adffeeb03d6760c3d577c3136cc3a.jpg).
20. Andre Masson, ca 1955. The painting, oil, behind the wooden sliding door is Gustave Courbet's L'Origine du Monde, from 1866. The carved picture on the wooden door is André Masson's draft of the painting behind the actual sliding door. It used to hang at Jacques Lacan's country house–in Guitrancourt, France. Silvia Macklès, Lacan's wife, charged her brother in law, André Mason, with the task of hiding such a potentially troublesome work-of-art.
21. Andre Masson, "La terre," 1939. (http://www.wikiart.org/en/andre-masson/earth).
22. Miralles Pinós, Igualada Cemetery, plan detail. Drawing from Fundacio Enric Miralles, Barcelona.
23. Medieval picture in the National Art Museum of Catalonia.
24. Günther Förg, photograph of himself fallen at bottom of stairs, ca. 1985.
25. Miralles Pinós, drawing detail Igualada Cemetery, 1987.
26. Charles Lebrun, leonine face, ca.1806. (http://madamepickwickartblog.com/2010/07/at-the-zoo/).
27. Cesare Cesariano. Cesariano drawing from *Vitruvius Pollio's De Architectura*, ca.1520. (https://s-media-cache-ak0.pinimg.com/236x/19/b8/c3/19b8c3ac2b2e72f859f731a80941d28d.jpg).
28. Giovanni Antonio Rusconi, Ideal proportions based on the human body, from "Della Architettura," ca.1590. (https://www.google.com/search?q=giovanni+antonio+rusconi&tbm).
29. Treatise writer of the sixteenth century.
30. Francesco di Giorgio Martini, *Trattato di architettura,* ca.1482. (https://upload.wikimedia.org/wikipedia/commons/2/24/FGMartini1.jpg).
31. Benito Arias Montano, *Antiquitatum Iudaicarum libri IX*, Leiden, 1593. (https://www.mhs.ox.ac.uk/gatt/catalog.).
32. Miralles Pinós, Igualada Cemetery, detail drawing of the chapel. Drawing from Fundacio Enric Miralles, Barcelona.
33. Antoni Gaudí, human skeleton on wooden planks, ca.1900.
34. Pablo Picasso, figure drawings.

35. Miralles Pinós, Igualada Cemetery, plan detail. Drawing from Fundacio Enric Miralles, Barcelona.

Pages 56-69

1. Helio Piñón, Albert Viaplana, Enric Miralles (contributor): Competition for the headquarters of the Council of Huesca, 1974. Second Prize. Perspective made from the carbon copy of a photograph.
2. Helio Piñón, Albert Viaplana, Enric Miralles (contributor): Competition for the headquarters in Seville, College of Architects of Western Andalusia, 1975. Third Prize. Perspective made from the carbon copy of a photograph. Source: *Janus Architecture no. 48*, June 1977, 32.
3. Helio Piñón, Albert Viaplana, Enric Miralles (contributor): Competition for the headquarters in Valencia, Official College of Architects of Valencia and Murcia, 1977. First Prize. Building perspective in their environment, through the pavement closed. Source: *Janus Architecture no.48*, June 1977, 46.
4. Helio Piñón, Albert Viaplana, Enric Miralles (contributor): Competiton drawing 1976.
5. Helio Piñón, Albert Viaplana, Enric Miralles (contributor): Competition for the expansion of the Barcelona headquarters of the College of Architects of Catalonia and the Balearic Islands, 1976. Building prospect conical object of competition, isolated. Source: *Janus Architecture no.48*, June 1977, 38.
6. Helio Piñón, Albert Viaplana, Enric Miralles (contributor): National Competition Teaching Institutions, 1978. Section leaked to the point of slight list view. Perspective view of a vacuum. Source: *AAVV: Viaplana/Piñón. Work*, Col.legi d'Arquitectes de Catalunya, Barcelona, 1996, 105.
7. Helio Piñón, Albert Viaplana, Enric Miralles (contributor): Competition for an Islamic Center, Madrid, 1980. Perspective with the view below the base, and the building represented by pictorial resources. Source: *AAVV: Viaplana/Piñón. Work*, Col.legi d'Arquitectes de Catalunya, Barcelona, 1996, 105.
8. Helio Piñón, Albert Viaplana, Enric Miralles (contributor): Competition for the development of the Polygon San Esteban, Murcia, 1977. Aerial perspective isolated enclosure with solid preexisting and newly created. Source: *AAVV: Viaplana/Piñón. Work*, Col.legi d'Arquitectes de Catalunya, Barcelona, 1996, 104.
9. Helio Piñón, Albert Viaplana, Enric Miralles (contributor): Competition for the rehabilitation of the College of Architects of Murcia, 1978. Central perspective with the main solid on the left flank and a reflective screen background. Source: *Quaderns d'Architecture and Urbanism no. 156*, January-February-March 1983, 11.
10. Helio Piñón, Albert Viaplana, Enric Miralles (contributor): Competition for the Parc del Besòs, Sant Adrià de Besòs, Barcelona, 1982. Freehand drawing respecting the laws of the conical perspective. The drawing is open in the foreground. Source: *Quaderns d'Architecture and Urbanism no. 156*, January-February-March 1983, 13.
11. Helio Piñón, Albert Viaplana, Enric Miralles (contributor): Competition for the Plaza de la Constitution, Girona, 1982. Freehand drawing of conical structure with a row of trees on the left flank of the line of sight. Source: *Quaderns d'Architecture and Urbanism no. 156*, January-February-March 1983, 13.
12. Helio Piñón, Albert Viaplana, Enric Miralles (contributor): Competition for the new headquarters of the Regional Government of La Rioja, Logroño, 1984. Central perspective proposed representation of a pure vacuum. Source: *Quaderns d'Architecture and Urbanism no. 163*, October-November-December 1984, 81.
13. Helio Piñón, Albert Viaplana, Enric Miralles (contributor): Square Project Barangé, Granollers, 1982–1997. The square is represented as an isolated object. Source: *Quaderns d'Architecture and Urbanism no. 163*, October-November-December 1984, 93.
14. Helio Piñón, Albert Viaplana, Enric Miralles (contributor): Draft Primary Health Care Centre, Sant Hipòlit of Voltregà, Barcelona, 1984–1986. A closed perspective of the building on the right flank of the viewing axis. Source: *Quaderns d'Architecture and Urbanism no. 163*, October-November-December 1984, 67.
15. Helio Piñón, Albert Viaplana, Enric Miralles (contributor): Draft Plaça Catalan Countries, Barcelona, 1981–1983. Closed perspective that includes a portion of the square and some isolated outside elements. Source: Benedetta Tagliabue: *Enric Miralles. Operate e progetti* (Milano: Electa, 1996), 29.
16. Helio Piñón, Albert Viaplana, Enric Miralles (contributor): Draft Plaça Catalan Countries, Barcelona, 1981–1983. The whole square, isolated and superimposed on pre-existing background in burnt photograph. Source: Benedetta Tagliabue: *Enric Miralles. Operate e progetti* (Milano: Electa, 1996), 33.

Pages 70-93

1. Miralles Pinós, plan drawing Archery Pavilion, 1992 Olympics, Barcelona. Fundació Enric Miralles, Barcelona.
2. Typical Renaissance urban plan and modernist urban plan. (https://www.google.com/search?q=Typical+Re-

naissance+urban+plan&tbm), (https://www.google.com/search?q=Typical+modern+urban+plan+nolli&tbm).
3. Traditional community laundry in rural France.
4. State capitol, Sacramento, California, 1874. (https://www.google.com/search?q=State+capitol+in+Sacramento,++California,+1874.&source)
5. Charles Eduard Jeanneret, Villa Fallet, La Chaux-de-Fonds, Switzerland, 1906–07. (https://www.google.com/search?q=Charles+Eduard+Jeanneret,+Villa+Fallet,++1906).
6. Le Corbusier, Villa Savoye, Poissy, France, 1928-31. (https://www.google.com/search?q=Le+Corbusier,+Villa+Savoye,+Poissy,+France,+1928-31).
7. Ken Wilber, "The Great Nest in Various Traditions" in *A Theory of Everything,* 2001.
8. Ken Wilber, All Quadrant, All Level (AQAL) diagram of Integral theory in *A Theory of Everything,* 2001.
9. Ludwig Hilberseimer, "Vertical City," 1924. (https://www.google.com/search?q=Ludwig+Hilberseimer,+%E2%80%9CVertical+City).
10. Nineteenth-century Functionalist plan, forerunner of the free plan.
11. Le Corbusier, Mason Citrohan a mass reproducible machine for living, 1920. (https://www.google.com/search?q=Le+Corbusier,+Maison+Citrohan+a+mass+reproducible+machine+for+living,+1920.&source).
12. Frank Lloyd Wright, plan for the Hershey Jacobs house, Madison, Wisconsin, 1936. (https://www.google.com/search?q=Frank+Lloyd+Wright,+plan+for+the+Hershey+Jacobs+house,+Madison,+Wisconsin,+1936.&tbm).
13. Ancient dolmen, Neolithic (4000–3000 BCE).
14. Le Corbusier, Ronchamp Chapel, France, 1954. (https://www.google.com/search?q=Le+Corbusier,+Ronchamp+Chapel,+1954).
15. Oscar Niemeyer, project for a yacht club Rio de Janiero, Brazil, 1945. (https://www.google.com/search?q=Oscar+Niemeyer,+project+for+a+yacht+club+Rio+de+Janeiro,+Brazil,+1945).
16. Alvar Aalto, plan drawing Rovaniemi Library, Finnland, 1945. (https://www.google.com/search?q=Alvar+Aalto,+plan+drawing+Rovaniemi+Library,+Finland,+1945).
17. Alvar Aalto , Essen Opera House, Germany, 1959-88. (https://www.google.com/search?q=Alvar+Aalto+plan+Essen+Opera+House,+Germany,+1959-88).
18. Alvar Aalto, Essen Opera House main lobby, Germany, 1959–88.
19. Renzo Piano, section Kansai Airport, Osaka, Japan, 1988–94. (https://www.google.com/search?q=Renzo+Piano,+section+Kansai+Airport,+Osaka,+Japan,+1988–94).
20. Renzo Piano, Kansai Airport, Osaka, Japan, 1988–94. (https://www.google.com/search?q=Renzo+Piano,+section+Kansai+Airport,+Osaka,+Japan,+1988–94).

Pages 94-107

1. Flores Prats studio Barcelona. Image of Flores Prats.
2. Miralles Pinós, plan drawing for bridge competition, 1986. Drawing from Fundació Enric Miralles, Barcelona.
3. Miralles Pinós, plan and section details for Huesca Stadium, 1988. Drawing from Fundació Enric Miralles, Barcelona.
4. Eva Prats, plan and section drawings of a croissant, 1992. Drawing from Fundació Enric Miralles, Barcelona.
5. Joan Prats and Joan Miró. Joan Prats' apartment. Image of Flores Prats.
6. Drawing Joan Miró, ca.1944.
7. Antoni Gaudí, entrance to Casa Batlló,1904. Image of Flores Prats.
8. Josep Maria Jujol and Antoni Gaudí, light opening in Montserrat Cathedral. Image of Flores Prats.
9. Flores Prats, plan drawing Windmill Museum, Majorca, Spain, 2001.
10. Flores Prats, plan and section drawings Windmill Museum Majorca, 2001.
11. Manuel Soto Morales, master plan model for social housing in Terrassa, Barcelona, 2005.
12. Flores Prats, plan and model for social housing in Terrassa, Barcelona, 2007-10.
13. Flores Prats, plan and axonometric drawings comparing the courtyard for residential community to the courtyard of San Filipe Neri Square in Barcelona.
14. Flores Prats, axonometric drawing for social housing in Terrassa, Barcelona, 2007-10.
15. Flores Prats, plans for social housing in Terressa, Barcelona, 2007-10.
16. Flores Prats, social Housing in Terrassa, Barcelona, 2007-10.

Pages 122-137

1-14. Utrecht City Hall, 1997, plan drawings by Enric Miralles. All drawings from Fundació Enric Miralles, Barcelona.

Pages 138-145

1. Portrait of a Collector, Il Parmigianino, ca. 1523, London, National Gallery. Horst Bredekamp, *The Lure of Antiquity*

and the Cult of the Machine: The Kunstkammer and the Evolution of Nature, Art and Technology, trans. Allison Brown (Princeton: Markus Wiener Publishers, 1995; 1st ed. 1947), 12.
2. Salvaging of ancient architectural relics. Illustration in: Jacques Besson, *Theatrum Instrumentorum et Machinarum*, 1578. Horst Bredekamp, *The Lure of Antiquity and the Cult of the Machine: The Kunstkammer and the Evolution of Nature, Art and Technology,* trans. Allison Brown (Princeton: Markus Wiener Publishers, 1995; 1st ed. 1947), 20.
3. Bernard Palissy and Atelier, "Life Casts of Human Bust, Torso, and Legs for Term Figures," nineteenth century casts from lost molds of 1556–1567. Plaster. Paris, Musée Carnavalet. Leonard N. Amico, *Bernard Palissy: In Search of Earthly Paradise* (Paris: Flammarion, 1996), 61.
3. Bernard Palissy and Atelier, "Stylized Leaf-shaped Dish with Jasper Glazing," 1556–1590. Lead- and tin-glazed ceramics; 27.5 x 21.3cm. Écouen, Musée de la Renaissance (EP 2231). Leonard N. Amico, *Bernard Palissy: In Search of Earthly Paradise* (Paris: Flammarion, 1996), 27.
4. D'Arcy Wentworth Thompson, *On Growth and Form* (London: Cambridge University Press, 1952; 1st ed. 1917), 751.
5. Progression of transformations by student Eugenia Castellini. First year undergraduate. Architecture Program. Cátedra Arq. Ana Valderrama. 2013. Facultad de Arquitectura, Planeamiento y Diseño. Universidad Nacional de Rosario.

Pages 146-157

1.-8. All photographs of the Scottish Parliament, Edinburgh are credited to the author John Meunier.
9. Scottish Parliament Building first level plan drawing. Miralles Tagliabue, Fundació Enric Miralles.

Pages 158-169

1. Catalan farmers circa 1900.
2. Catalan agricultural landscape.
3. Drawing of water flow in Park Güell.
4. Park Güell main entrance by Antoni Gaudí.
5. Igualada Cemetery by Miralles Pinós. Photo by Izard-Galí.
6. Igualada Cemetery by Miralles Pinós.
7. Aerial photographs, plan and section drawings of the Vall d'en Joan Landfill–inside the El Garraf Natural Park.
8. Plan drawings of Vall d'en Joan Landfill, El Garraf Natural Park, Teresa Izard-Galí.
9. Plan drawing of Vall d'en Joan Landfill, El Garraf Natural Park, Teresa Izard-Galí.
10. Section drawing of Vall d'en Joan Landfill, El Garraf Natural Park, Teresa Izard-Galí.
11. Photographs of Vall d'en Joan Landfill, El Garraf Natural Park.

Pages 170-187

1. Raymond Queneau, *One Hundred Million Million Poems*, 1961. (https://www.google.com/search?q=Raymond+Queneau,+One+Hundred+Million+Million+Poems,+1961).
2. Ray and Charles Eames, advertisement for the Eames chairs, 1948. (https://www.google.com/search?q=Ray+and+Charles+Eames,+advertisement+-for+the+Eames+chairs,+1948).
3. Saul Steinberg drawing *The Art of Living,* 1976, inspired by the Georges Perec book *Life A User's Manual,* 1978. (https://www.google.com/search?q=Saul+Steinberg+drawing+The+Art+of+Living,+1976,+inspired+by+the+Georges+Perec+book+Life+A+User's+Manual,+1978).
4. Raymond Queneau, drawings for "The Story as You Like," 1959.
5. Chuck Jones, drawing and cartoon for Wile E. Coyote, 1949. (https://www.google.com/search?q=Chuck+-Jones,+drawing+and+cartoon+for+Wile+E.+Coyote,+1949).
6. Jasper Johns, one of over forty paintings of the American Flag. (https://www.google.com/search?q=Jasper+–Johns+american+flag&source).
7. Sol LeWitt, 122 permutations of a single white cube, ca.1968. (https://www.google.com/search?q=sol+lewitt+single+white+cube&sa).
8. Ad Reinhardt, drawing for 120 black square paintings, 1956. (https://www.google.com/search?q=Ad+Reinhardt,+drawing+for+120+black+square+paintings,+1956).
9. Enric Miralles, collage for Isola San Michele, Venice, 1998. Fundació Enric Miralles, Barcelona.
10. Igor Stravinsky, musical composition, ca.1950. (https://www.google.com/search?q=Igor+Stravinsky,+musical+-composition,+ca.1950).
11. Pablo Picasso , drawings of dancing figures, 1924. (https://www.google.com/search?q=Pablo+Picasso+,+drawings+of+dancing+figures,+1924).
12. Philippe Petit, tightrope walk between Twin Towers, New York, 1974.(https://www.google.com/search?q=Philippe+Petit,+tightrope+walk+between+Twin+Towers,+New+York,+1974).

13. Mies van der Rohe, German Pavilion for the 1929 International Exposition in Barcelona. (https://www.google.com/search?q=Mies+van+der+Rohe,+German+Pavilion+for+the+1929+International+Exposition+in+Barcelona.&source).
14. Katsuyoshi Ohara, residential house in Tokyo, Japan.
15. Hugh Ferriss, drawing from *The Metropolis of Tomorrow,* 1929. (https://www.google.com/search?q=Hugh+-Ferriss,+drawing+from+The+Metropolis+of+Tomorrow,+1929).
16. MVRDV Architects, "Aztec" studies for Amsterdam, 1997.
17. Joseph Paxton, Crystal Palace from the Great Exhibition of 1851. (https://www.google.com/search?q=Joseph+-Paxton,+Crystal+Palace+from+the+Great+Exhibition+of+1851).

Pages 208-223

1–15. Images from Fundació Enric Miralles, Barcelona.

Pages 224-243

1. Miralles Pinós detail at Igualada Cemetery. Photograph from Fundació Enric Miralles, Barcelona.
2. Dimitri Pikionis, Acropolis path, ca.1970. (https://www.google.com/search?q=pikionis+acropolis&tbm=isch&tbs=rimg).
3. Miralles Pinós, Igualada path, ca. 1996. Photograph from Fundació Enric Miralles, Barcelona.
4. Dimitri Pikionis, plan drawing of the Acropolis, 1951. (https://www.google.com/search?q=pikionis+acropolis&tbm=isch&tbs=rimg).
5. Enric Miralles, plan drawing of Park Diagonal Mar, 1998. Fundació Enric Miralles, Barcelona.
6. Miralles Pinós, Igualada Cemetery, 1992. Photograph from Fundació Enric Miralles, Barcelona.
7. Alberto Giacometti, "Walking Man," ca.1950. (https://www.google.com/search?q=giacometti+walking+man&-source=lnms&tbm).
8. Miralles Pinós, entry gate at Igualada Cemetery and columns at the Archery Pavilion, 1992. Photograph from Fundació Enric Miralles, Barcelona.
9. Joan Miró, "Barcelona VII" from *Barelona Series* (Mourlot 12), 1944. (https://www.google.com/search?q=-joan+miro+barcelona+series&source).
10. Miralles Pinós, plan detail Igualada Cemetery, 1986. Fundació Enric Miralles, Barcelona.
11. Le Corbusier, entry ramp at the Mill Owners Association, Ahmedabad, 1951. (https://www.google.com/search?q=le+corbusier+mill+owners+association+building+ahmedabad&source).
12. Miralles Pinós, entry ramp at Hostalets Civic Center, 1992. Fundació Enric Miralles, Barcelona.
13. Peter and Alison Smithson, Robin Hood Gardens social housing, 1972. (https://www.google.com/search?q=-peter+and+alison+smithson+robin+hood+gardens&-source).
14. Miralles Tagliabue, play mound at Diagonal Mar Park, 2002. Fundació Enric Miralles, Barcelona.
15. Giant figures dancing in Placita de la Seu. (https://www.google.com/search?q=barcelona+giant+festival+figures&source).
16. Enric Miralles, Icaria Pergolas, 1992. Fundació Enric Miralles, Barcelona.

Pages 244-265

1.-5. Photographs by Claudio Vekstein.
6. Le Corbusier, Villa Shodhan, Ahmedabad, India, 1951. (https://www.google.com/search?q=Le+Corbusier,+Villa+Shodhan,+Ahmedabad,+India,+1951).
7.-8. Photographs by Claudio Vekstein.

Pages 266-275

1. Sagrada Familia ca.1900. (https://www.google.com/search?q=la+sagrada+familia+ca+1900&tbm).
2. Enric Miralles, drawing of Plaça de Sants, Estudi Viaplana Piñon, ca.1980.
3. Miralles Tagliabue, Santa Caterina Market aerial view, 2005. Fundació Enric Miralles, Barcelona.
4. Miralles Pinós, Igualada Cemetery, 1986–1996. Fundació Enric Miralles, Barcelona.
5. aSZ Arquitectes, collage drawing for Portes de Collcerola competition.
6. aSZ Arquitectes, collage drawing for Portes de Collcerola competition.
7. aSZ Arquitectes, plan drawings for Portes de Collcerola competition.
8. aSZ Arquitectes, plan drawing for Valdebebas Park competition.
9. aSZ Arquitectes, photograph of Badalona Public Library.

Pages 276-285

1. Antoni Gaudí, Colònia Güell in Santa Coloma de Cervelló, a.1900. Enric Miralles photographing one column of the site when the chapel was still in a state of ruin. Fundació Enric Miralles, Barcelona.
2. Le Corbusier, sketch and photograph of traditional Indian bed. *Le Corbusier Oeuvre Complete, Volume 8,* Artemis Zurich, Suisse, pgs. 112-113.

3. Le Corbusier, Venice Hospital project, 1964. *Le Corbusier Oeuvre Complete, Volume 7,* Artemis Zurich, Suisse, 141.
4. Roman basis for city plan. (https://www.google.com/search?q=plan+of+ancient+roman+city&tbm).
5. Miralles Tagliabue, collage drawing for the Scottish Parliament. Fundació Enric Miralles, Barcelona.
6. Manuel Bailo, drawing of Palazzo Farnese.
7. Manuel Bailo, drawing of Parets del Valles shade structure by Enric Miralles.
8. Antoni Gaudí, Sagrada Familia sand bag model, ca.1915. (https://www.google.com/search?q=gaudi+sandbag+model&tbm).
9. Paintings of Monteserrat magistrates circa fifteenth century.
10. Bailo Rull, Mansara Community Center model.
11. Bailo Rull, Mansara Community Center collage.
12. Bailo Rull, Mansara Community Center plans.
13. Bailo Rull, Mansara Community Center photos.

Pages 296-313

1–17. Images from Fundació Enric Miralles, Barcelona, except:
13.–15. Duccio Malagamba.
17. Eugeni Pons.

Pages 314-323

1. Enric Miralles, 1992: Sketch India landscape. Fundació Enric Miralles, Barcelona.
2. Photograph of Manorama Sarabhai by Enric Miralles. Fundació Enric Miralles, Barcelona.
3. Elías Torres, 1992: Manorama Sarabhai (above, one of the Ahmedabad wells).
4. Enric Miralles, 1992: Manorama Sarabhai "Madam Sarabhai wants us to visit buildings." Fundació Enric Miralles, Barcelona.
5. Enric Miralles, 1992: Manorama Sarabhai. Fundació Enric Miralles, Barcelona.

Pages 324-331

1. "La Ultima Cena" by Elena Rocchi, The NIROX Foundation, 2012.

Pages 332-345

1. Elías Torres drawing of Igualada Cemetery at burial of Miralles, 2000.
2. Miralles Pinós, stair at Hostalets Civic Center, 1988–94. Fundació Enric Miralles, Barcelona.
3. Elías Torres, drawing of stair at Hostalets Civic Center, ca.1988.
4. Alvar Aalto, Vuoksenniska Church, 1958. (https://www.google.com/search?q=Alvar+Aalto,+Vuoksenniska+Church,+1958&tbm).
5. Enric Miralles drawing for the Archery Pavilion, 1992. Fundació Enric Miralles, Barcelona.
6. Charles and Ray Eames chair with Saul Steinberg cat drawing, ca.1950. (https://www.google.com/search?q=Charles+and+Ray+Eames+chair+with+Saul+Steinberg+cat+drawing,+ca.1950).
7. Enric Miralles, Circulo de Lectores chairs, 1992. Fundació Enric Miralles, Barcelona.
8. Miralles Tagliabue residence with Innes table. Fundació Enric Miralles, Barcelona.
9. Torres LaPeña, church doors in Majorca.
10. Elías Torres, exhibition piece for Venice, 2012.
11. Elías Torres, collage drawing.
12. Elías Torres, collage drawing for Willis apartment.
13. Enric Miralles, collage plan drawing. Fundació Enric Miralles, Barcelona.
14. Torres and Miralles, Sabotaier drawing and Situationists exhibition photograph.
15. Miralles Pinós, Olympic Archery Pavilion, 1992. Fundació Enric Miralles, Barcelona.
16. Torres and LaPeña, Olympic Athletes' Residence 1992.
17. Enric Miralles, original roof structure Huesca Stadium, 1993. Fundació Enric Miralles, Barcelona.
18. Enric Miralles, La Clota House, 1998. Fundació Enric Miralles, Barcelona.
19. Torres and LaPeña, residential project.
20. Miralles Tagliabue, playground at Diagonal Mar Park, 2002. Fundació Enric Miralles, Barcelona.
21. Torres LaPeña, Universal Forum of Cultures, 2004.
22. Torres LaPeña, collage and drawing for Rio Tinto.

Pages 346-371

1. Opening of Fundació Enric Miralles, June 2012. Fundació Enric Miralles, Barcelona.
2. Exhibition "Enric Miralles in Time," Fundació Enric Miralles, 2014. Fundació Enric Miralles, Barcelona.
3. Enric Miralles, exhibition "Heaven" Tenaki Kutu, Japan, 1995. Fundació Enric Miralles, Barcelona.
4. Miralles working on the stage set for the opera, 1995. Fundació Enric Miralles, Barcelona.
5. Miralles Tagliabue, drawings and final pieces for the pharmaceutical display, 1995. Fundació Enric Miralles, Barcelona.
6. Miralles Tagliabue, exhibition for the 1996 Venice Bienal-

le. Fundació Enric Miralles, Barcelona.

7. Miralles Tagliabue, exhibition from the Venice Bienalle in the Barcelona Pavilion, 1996. Fundació Enric Miralles, Barcelona.
8. Miralles Tagliabue, exhibition detail from the Venice Bienalle in the Barcelona Pavilion, 1996. Fundació Enric Miralles, Barcelona.
9. Innes Table in the Fundació Enric Miralles. Fundació Enric Miralles, Barcelona.
10. Enric Miralles, playing child, photomontage. Fundació Enric Miralles, Barcelona.
11. Miralles Tagliabue, play house for Kolonihaven. Fundació Enric Miralles, Barcelona.
12. Enric Miralles, photomontage Igualada Cemetery. Fundació Enric Miralles, Barcelona.
13. Jorge Rodriquez Gerada, drawing and exhibition piece in Diagonal Mar Park, 2010. Fundació Enric Miralles, Barcelona.
14. Jorge Rodriquez Gerada, exhibition piece in Diagonal Mar Park, 2010. Fundació Enric Miralles, Barcelona.

Conversations and Allusions:
Enric Miralles

Author
Catherine Spellman

Graphic Design
Ramon Prat

Copyeditor
Julie Russ

Published by
Actar Publishers, New York, Barcelona
www.actar.com

Distributed by
Actar D Inc.

New York
440 Park Avenue South
17th Floor, 10016 New York, NY
T +1 212 966 2207
F +1 212 966 2214
salesnewyork@actar-d.com

Barcelona
Roca i Batlle 2
08023 Barcelona
T +34 933 282 183
eurosales@actar-d.com

Printed and Bound in China

ISBN 978-1-94029198-7
PCN 2017941961

A CIP catalogue record for this book is available from the Library of Congress, Washington D.C., USA.